1981

To Brenda

Being of questionable
mind and round body
I do hereby appoint you
executor of my fantasies.
May your Hanuka candles forever
be alight and may your New year
be fulfilled with your every wish.

With lust

[signature]

THE NYMPHO AND OTHER MANIACS

IRVING WALLACE

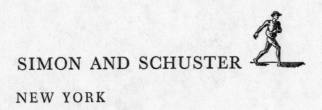

SIMON AND SCHUSTER

NEW YORK

Dedicated to

Amy Wallace
and
David Wallace
and
A Different Drummer

Contents

The great question that has never been answered
and which I have not yet been able to answer,
despite my thirty years of research into the feminine
soul, is: What does a woman want?

—DR. SIGMUND FREUD

Before Beginning

"DEAD SCANDALS," wrote Lord Byron in *Don Juan,* "form good subjects for dissection."

Indeed, they do. But what his lordship did not specify was which party made the "good subject" for dissection—the person whose behavior was scandalous, or the person who was scandalized. Perhaps, by reading the lurid but factual case histories that follow, the reader will be able to clarify this point for himself.

I, for one, am quite frankly captivated by the outrageous, rebellious, obsessed people in our past, especially by those feminine in gender who have behaved scandalously.

Scandal, we know, is brought to life by gossiping. And I fully agree with Oscar Wilde's remarks, in *Lady Windermere's Fan,* that gossip is charming, and that history is merely gossip. Where I part company with Wilde is when he adds, "But scandal is gossip made tedious by morality." Quite the opposite is true, I would suggest. Scandal is gossip made alive and exciting by the very fact that it threatens and conflicts with prevailing morality. Webster's Dictionary tells us that a scandalous act is behavior "offensive to public or individual sense of propriety or morality, exciting reprobation." Exactly. Exciting reprobation—or possibly secret admiration and envy—and certainly wonder and curiosity.

I have always wanted to bring together, in one book, a gallery of women, of varied ages, backgrounds, talents, whose lives and personalities have intrigued me—and who were well-known or infamous in past times or in times since, because they behaved scandalously and became controversial figures.

All of the ladies in this book, young and old, possess a common bond: Each and every one was involved in a scandal, or in many scandals, and each and every one gained fame or reaped infamy for conduct that affronted her family, friends, peers, and the public in general. Most of these women, perhaps all, by choice or accident, became scandalous figures because they were maniacs.

Now, a maniac is not necessarily a person who is mad, bereft of his senses. A maniac is also, by dictionary definition, a person with an intense or exaggerated or excessive enthusiasm or desire for someone or something. Thus, a nymphomaniac is "a woman suffering from abnormally strong and uncontrollable sexual desire," and a hedonomaniac is a woman "who feels intensely that pleasure is the chief good." Thus, also, a monomaniac is "a person with a pathological obsession with one idea."

Every woman in this book had a mania, became a maniac, because of her overenthusiasm either for a man—or many men—or for an idea. And because these women did not conceal their manias, they created scandals.

Their overenthusiasms were varied. Lady Jane Ellenborough was considered a nymphomaniac. Her behavior was scandalous because of her sexual excesses. Lady Emma Hamilton was very likely a hedonomaniac. And so, too, was Pauline Bonaparte. They caused scandals because they defied their societies' mores and sought pleasure according to their own standards. On the other hand, Anne Royall, Delia Bacon, and Victoria Woodhull were monomaniacs. They started scandals because each was obsessed with an idea—Anne Royall with fighting government institutions, Delia Bacon with proving that Shakespeare was a fake and a hoax, Victoria Woodhull with battling for female emancipation and women's rights.

They differed, one from the other, these women. Yet, they were alike in the fact that each one revolted against the ideas or morals of her time and each ran counter to conventional behavior—and each, to some degree, caused gossip and furor and anger among her contemporaries.

Because they were free people, free and unafraid, these women appealed to me. Now, I have brought them together—thirty of these women in sixteen chapters, fourteen of the chapters recounting individual stories at length. The lives of these women I have researched across many years in American cities, in London, in Paris, in Rome, in Madrid.

Nine of these biographies are new, written for this book, and they appear in print for the first time. Seven biographies have appeared in a considerably different form in two of my early books.

All of these women and their stories, I believe—the ones I have written for this volume and the ones I have brought forward from my earlier writings and have extensively revised with the addition of new researches for their inclusion here—belong together, combined at last in a single book. Few of my ladies modified the course of history. Few were movers or shakers in terms of changing the course of events, of fostering progress, of adding to our security or happiness or pleasure. Yet each one, in her way, contributed something to the cause of individual freedom—the right to do your thing, to find your way, to behave as you please if you do not harm society, or to object openly to old shibboleths and crusted moral yardsticks. And, perhaps, each in her way, unwittingly, did much to cast light on a society that was rutted and dulled, and therefore jolted and scandalized into giving second thoughts to its more hidebound ideas.

Some of these ladies were probably foolish, wrongheaded, exasperating, self-serving in their behavior, offering little and so achieving little of lasting value. Yet all of them are here, basically, because I found them unusual or entertaining or beautiful. With each, I had a literary love affair. Some proved too old for me, some too young, some too flawed, some too neurotic—and some were just right, indeed perfect, for me. Yet, perfect or imperfect, each won my heart, or else she would not have been invited into my life and onto these pages.

I have enjoyed my scandalous maniacs—and I can only hope that my reader will equally enjoy the stimulation of their sometimes pleasing and sometimes irritating—but always unorthodox —company.

Book One

THE MISTRESS
AS A SCANDAL

I

The Kept
Women

For me thou art repose from cares,
light even in a night of darkness,
a throng among the solitude.

—TIBULLUS

ON AN AFTERNOON in 1675, the tiny, red-haired Nell
Gwyn, who had served drinks in a brothel as a child, had portrayed a daughter of Montezuma on the stage, and had become
the royal favorite at the age of nineteen, stepped into the carriage that Charles II had presented to her, and rode through London town on her daily outing. Quickly, observers identified the
carriage—but not the occupant. The irate onlookers, crowding
about, thought the occupant was Louise de Kéroualle, the Duchess of Portsmouth, a Frenchwoman sent by Louis XIV to entertain
Charles. The mobs of people were incensed, because they knew
that Louise de Kéroualle was a Catholic, and it was a period when
anti-Catholic feeling was running high. As the carriage made its
laborious way through the crush, the people shouted curses at its
passenger. Nell Gwyn bore the insults as long as she could, and

then she bore them no longer. She ordered the coachman to stop, and put her head out the window.

"Pray, good people, be civil!" she shouted. "I am the Protestant whore!"

As one, the people screamed their delight. The Protestant whore—surely the brashest maid on the sceptered isle (did she not call her monarch Charles *III* because she had slept with two men named Charles before him?)—waved gaily to her public, and then sent her carriage proudly on its way. Among the hundreds watching, not one thought it improper that the king's mistress had so plainly and openly announced her station.

Just 231 years later, on an April day in 1906, another attractive actress—after a long journey with her lover across the Atlantic—arrived in New York to be enthusiastically hailed by throngs of welcomers including Mark Twain, Arthur Brisbane, Jane Addams, William Dean Howells, and H. G. Wells. Her name was Maria Andreyeva, and she was a highly literate Russian artist of some renown. Her lover, for whom the enthusiasm and excitement were really generated, was the great Russian novelist and playwright, the thirty-eight-year-old Maxim Gorky.

Gorky had come to the United States to obtain financial support for the Russian revolutionary movement. His prestige was high—President Theodore Roosevelt was even opening the White House to him—and the Czarist government was alarmed. Having failed to get Gorky barred from American shores as an anarchist, the Russian Embassy in Washington shrewdly decided to have him ostracized as a libertine. In the press, Maria Andreyeva had been identified as Mme. Gorky, the celebrated author's wife, and, indeed, she was so registered at the Hotel Belleclaire. Now the Russian Embassy let the truth be known. The real Mme. Gorky was in Russia. She had been separated from the author for years, but had refused him a divorce. Maria Andreyeva's "relations with the author had not been sanctioned by the clergy." She was his mistress, and had been such for three years.

The Russian Embassy correctly assessed American reaction to this flagrant immorality. The scandal was front-paged in most of the press. The *New York World* published pictures of the real Mme. Gorky and of the "so-called Mme Gorky, who is not Mme

Gorky at all but a Russian actress, Andreyeva, with whom he had been living since his separation from his wife a few years ago."

In 1675, Nell Gwyn had been cheered for admitting that she was a mistress. In 1906, Maria Andreyeva was crucified. The adulterous couple was evicted from the Hotel Belleclaire, then from the Brevoort and the Rhinelander, quitting the last in the middle of the night. President Roosevelt expeditiously forgot about the White House reception. Except for Edwin Markham and John Dewey, American celebrities backed away. William Dean Howells withdrew from a dinner at which he was to preside. Mark Twain ran for cover. Lecture dates were canceled. In Boston, one retreating hostess explained: "I do not want to judge Mr. Gorky, but apparently his views on morality and ours somewhat differ. . . ." Newspapers were elated. Unanimously, they rejoiced that "the purity of our inns" was no longer being defiled by a fallen woman. Gorky retired to Russia, where he finally obtained his divorce and legalized his union with the actress. During these same years, he expressed his opinion of the United States in a series of acid short stories.

These two episodes—the public's happy acceptance of Nell Gwyn and its angry rejection of Maria Andreyeva—merely illustrate how far, in less than two and a half centuries, the position of the mistress had declined in public esteem. In the seventeenth century, the mistress had reason to be proud of her vocation. In the first half of the twentieth century, she had been reduced to the dismal camouflage of good friend, constant companion, and call girl.

Today, while prostitution still exists and promiscuity is more prevalent than ever, the ancient station of mistress is without honor—a station to which few aspire, and one which is slowly but certainly becoming extinct. There remain mistresses, of course, in every civilized nation of the Western world, but no longer do they thrive. Among older people they dwell now amid whispers, scandal, censure, while the young enjoy something called "living together." But it was not always so.

Before this most remarkable mutation of the female species becomes extinct, she deserves to be awarded her niche in history. Too little has been recorded of too few of her, although she has given more pleasure to the human race than have generals, and often has accomplished more for the common welfare than politicians or statesmen. As a class, she deserves greater and more sympathetic recognition.

What is a mistress? Almost all dictionaries are in accord. In the New English Dictionary on Historical Principles she is "a woman who illicitly occupies the place of wife." In the New Standard Dictionary she is "a woman who unlawfully or without marriage fills the place of a wife." In Webster's Second New International Dictionary she is "a woman with whom a man habitually cohabits unlawfully as his paramour."

Since the mistress, for a week, a year, or a lifetime, with a lover married or unmarried, simulates the role of wife, or performs the primary duty of wife, she might better be understood if one first understands the meaning of matrimony. "Marriage is generally used as a term for a social institution," writes Edward Westermarck in *A Short History of Marriage*. "As such it may be defined as a relation of one or more men to one or more women which is recognized by custom or law and involves certain rights and duties. . . . Marriage always implies the right of sexual intercourse; society holds such intercourse allowable in the case of husband and wife, and, generally speaking, even regards it as their duty to gratify in some measure the other partner's desire."

Marriage originated in the dim recesses of savage or primeval society. First, groups of men mated with groups of women, often exchanging partners, and almost always rearing their offspring in common. "This habit was sanctioned by custom, and afterwards by law," writes Westermarck, "and was thus transformed into a social institution." Eventually, monogamy replaced polygamy and polyandry in the Western world. With the acceptance of marriage to but one person at a time as the social norm—a principle endorsed by the highly civilized ancient Greeks—the mistress was ready to make her entrance into history.

While the monogamous wife gained, by law, certain privileges and degrees of security, she was left vulnerable to the competition of other women. She learned, soon enough, that nature was the enemy of monogamy. When she menstruated, or was in an advanced state of pregnancy, she could not satisfy the sexual demands of her husband. As the years wore on, and her beauty faded, she could not prevent her husband's search for his own lost youth in the youth of other women. While the passage of time improved her standing as a companion, she found that too often

it dulled her husband's sexual appetites, and that he chafed for
novelty and variety that might stimulate him afresh. When, as in
so many cases, she was wedded for her dowry—property and mon-
ies, position and authority—she realized that her husband might
seek sexual love elsewhere from the beginning. The monogamous
wife had her husband's name and his protection, but she had not
the assurance of his presence in the nuptial bed. Her predominant
fear was well-founded—for monogamy had indeed created the
woman "who illicitly occupies the place of wife."

Through the centuries, the illicit wife of a married, or sometimes unmarried, man has had many names and faces: adulteress,
common-law wife, concubine, demirep, courtesan, cocotte, harlot,
hetaera, strumpet, demimondaine, paramour, doxy, *fille de joie*,
kept woman, bawd, *femme entretenue*, slut, lady of easy virtue.
All these, with but slight variations in function and performance,
have described the same woman—the mistress.

Almost all mistresses, however, fall into one of several specific
categories. The adulteress, without whom novelists from Stendhal
to Tolstoi would have been far less prolific, represents a special
type of kept woman. She is a woman who undertakes an affair
with another man while still legally married to her husband. The
married woman commits adultery; the unmarried, fornication.

When Moses proclaimed, as one of his Ten Commandments,
"Thou shalt not commit adultery," he was largely protecting husbands from property damage and spiritual hurt. In Old Testament times, the adulteress was stoned to death. In a later age,
Jesus tempered this severity. Confronted by the Pharisees, who
brought before him an adulteress they thought should be stoned,
He replied, challengingly, "He that is without sin among you, let
him first cast a stone at her."

While many adulteresses have sought, by their transgressions,
to improve their financial status or social position—among these
may be included the demireps of eighteenth-century England,
married women of the respectable middle class who bartered their
bodies for the pleasure to be obtained from material comfort—the
majority became involved in illicit relationships because they
sought love. There are hundreds of examples of the latter. A typical case is that of Marguerite de Bonnemains.

Mme. de Bonnemains, a magnificent blue-eyed blonde in her

early thirties, was well married to the Vicomte Pierre de Bonnemains, an army lieutenant, when she first met General Georges
Boulanger, then France's Minister of War. The two were introduced at a dinner given in Paris by an old convent girl friend of
Mme. de Bonnemains. They fell in love at that moment and,
while she lived, were never apart.

They had four years together, and in those years General Boulanger's star rose and fell. In 1887, backed by Royalists, Boulanger
conspired to establish a dictatorship. and for this he was exiled to
the provinces by his superiors. Returning to Paris in disguise, he
formed the Nationalist party, then resigned from the army to lead
the party. His antidemocratic campaign swept preliminary elec-
tions, and split France into two camps. Anatole France backed
Boulanger; Zola fought him. Hero worship ran high. But it was
Mme. Arman de Caillavet who, after having Boulanger as a guest
at a party, remarked dryly, "He is not a lion, he is only a fox."
The fox had not the lion's courage. When his moment of decision came, and he could have had his coup d'état, he faltered.
While Boulanger wallowed in indecision, the existing government, sensing his weakness, acted. It was preparing to try him for
conspiracy, when he fled to Brussels.

Through those fateful years, Mme. de Bonnemains was beside
him. Though Boulanger had long been separated from his wife,
his mistress still had a husband. She obtained a civil divorce, but
it was not enough. She was a strict Catholic. She petitioned the
Vatican for an annulment of her marriage. She did not get it,
and so she accepted the role of adulteress. She followed Boulanger
to his earliest exile at Royat, a French spa, where he was under
military house arrest. Learning of her arrival, Boulanger went
over the wall of his prison, dodging sentries, to keep their first
assignation. Soon, in an atmosphere of secrecy and danger, they
were together daily. Dressed in lace and satin evening gowns,
Mme. de Bonnemains played the piano for her general, read to
him from military works, and made love to him. In a short time
she was pregnant, but lost the child after a fall, while in her
fourth month.

When Boulanger fled to Brussels in 1889, with his eighteen
aides and servants, Mme. de Bonnemains accompanied him, with
her sixty dresses. In Brussels she contracted pleurisy, and when
the pair moved to London, this illness was compounded. While

Boulanger took opium pills to settle his nerves, and persistently intrigued to return to Paris, his mistress toiled incessantly to raise funds to keep them alive. Soon they were nearly bankrupt. They moved to the chillier, more economical St. Helier, on the isle of Jersey. Here Mme. de Bonnemains suffered terrible coughing spells. Unable to retain food, she was reduced to a human skeleton, slowly wasting away from consumption. Once, she dragged her exhausted body to Paris to collect an inheritance that had come too late. After returning to Brussels and Boulanger in 1891, she died.

On her tombstone, Boulanger carved her given name, "Marguerite," and beneath it the simple promise, "See you soon." He kept his word. Two and a half months later, standing before her grave, he shot himself. His tombstone was erected beside hers, and it bore the inscription he had requested. First his given name, "Georges." And then, below, the chiseled lover's question, asked in wonder and apology, "Could I really live two and a half months without you?"

Among the various categories of mistress, the two least illicit— if one may be permitted to make so fine a distinction—were the position of concubine, a type of sex partner widely accepted until the Middle Ages, and the position of common-law wife, a sex partner widely tolerated and often legally recognized even in more modern times.

The concubine has been known longer to history than has the wife. In the beginning she was usually a prize of war, a slave held by her owner for his own uses. She had to perform as a wife would in later times, in bed and out, to love her master and obey him, and be faithful to him. Lack of faithfulness was an offense usually punishable by death. And neither the concubine nor her children possessed the rights of inheritance or citizenship. The concubine was recognized by the Christian Church for seven centuries after Constantine, and approved of by leaders ranging from Demosthenes to Thomas Aquinas.

The successor to the concubine, in a sense, has been the common-law wife. According to the Encyclopedia of the Social Sciences: "A common law marriage is one which has not been solemnized in any particular form, being based only upon the mutual assent of the parties. It is thus a marriage which does not depend for its validity upon any religious or civil ceremony. It is an unlicensed, an unrecorded and non-ceremonial marriage." The rights of the common-law wife were recognized in Rome, they were recognized in England until 1753, and they were, until recently, recognized in almost half of the states of the United States. Yet, the common-law wife is not a legal wife. She is a mistress.

Such a mistress was Léonie Léon, an attractive French girl of twenty-four who contracted a common-law union with Léon Gambetta, the one-eyed French statesman. Mlle. Léon, the daughter of a French colonel, left home to make her way in Paris after her father's death. She was employed to tutor the children of an important government official. Eventually she was seduced by this official. She left his household, filled with guilts, to dwell alone and eke out a livelihood as best she could.

One day, in 1869, she attended the *corps législatif* to hear the great Gambetta speak. An eloquent lawyer and member of the Assembly, it was he who proclaimed the fall of the Emperor Napoleon III after Sedan and who founded the new republic and determined to fight on against Bismarck after escaping Paris in a balloon. Mlle. Léon, tall and beautiful, watched him with growing excitement from her gallery seat. When Gambetta's eye met hers, he faltered momentarily in his address. The moment the speech was done, he publicly scribbled a note and sent it up to her in full view of all. Affronted, she tore it up and fled. Not until two years later did they meet again, this time at the home of a mutual friend. He followed her into the street, cornered her, and proposed marriage.

She became his mistress, but she would not become his wife. She was Catholic. Only a marriage inside the Church could be a real marriage in her eyes. Gambetta, on the other hand, was the leader of the anticlerical party in France. He could not undergo a religious ceremony without endangering his career. Nevertheless, he proposed it. Léonie Léon would have none of it. She suggested a compromise. "Let us be formally betrothed by the exchange of rings," she suggested, "and let us promise each other to marry in the future." Thus she became his common-law wife.

Although she maintained her own home, they lived together. She was the love of his life and his inspiration, and it was her encouragement that led him to become President of the Chamber of Deputies in 1879. Three years later, discouraged by a defeat

in the Chamber, Gambetta resigned from public life and planned
to formalize his union with Léonie Léon. With his last twelve
thousand francs, he purchased Balzac's old estate at Les Jardies,
and set a date for the wedding. But shortly before the wedding,
he accidentally shot himself in the hand with a dueling pistol that
he was cleaning. Although the wound was not serious, blood
poisoning set in, and Gambetta was dead on New Year's Eve of
1882. His common-law wife first went into a convent, and then
into a Parisian garret where she was supported by her lover's followers until her death in 1906. To the end, she preserved a scrap
of poetry Gambetta had written, more treasured perhaps than a
marriage contract:

> *To the light of my soul; to the star of my life—*
> *Léonie Léon. Forever! Forever!*

Among all the variations of kept woman, the courtesan is the
one that comes closest to the public's conception of mistress. More
than any mistress, the courtesan possesses independence. She has
full freedom of choice in selecting the lovers she prefers. And she
is not fettered by the obligations of marriage or pseudo marriage.
In her lifetime she may have one liaison—or she may have one
hundred. She may live and sleep with a man of her choice for a
day or a year, or for as long as she wishes. She may seek, in each
choice, love or security or both. She is—ambition and economics
aside—her own woman.

Many of her liaisons, remarks Dr. Joseph Tenenbaum in *The
Riddle of Woman,* have been "built on a solid basis of love and
erotic affinity. Perhaps just because they were voluntary and ter-
minable, they often proved more lasting than many a conventional marriage." What impels a woman to become a courtesan?
Sometimes it is an economic need. A woman born in poverty, in
periods when there are no careers beyond marriage, might seek
to improve her lot by marketing a beautiful face and figure or a
sensual manner. Sometimes it has been a will to gain power. A
woman born in the comfortable middle class or lesser aristocracy
might wish to rise to the highest circles of royalty or wealth and
by trading her comeliness, wit, and charm, know the intoxication
that comes from wielding authority. Sometimes it has been a psy-
chological necessity. A woman might reach maturity, harboring
excessive sexual desires or even nymphomania. She might desire

many men or a variety of men, might lose herself in lust, forever
unsated, because she blindly sought the love she had not received
from her parents or because an unsatisfactory father relationship
had encouraged a continuing hostility toward men.

In history's gallery of courtesans there are many striking figures.
But there was only one Anne de Lenclos, known then, and to
all men and times thereafter, as Ninon. She, if any, was the classic courtesan. She was small in height, with a perfectly propor-
tioned body. Her hair was red-gold, her eyes large and dark, her
lips full and provocative, and her complexion peach-fair. She was
graceful, intelligent, witty, and accomplished at music, literature,
and sexual intercourse. She lived eighty-five years, and she lived
a hundred lives.

She was born in Paris during May of 1620. Her mother was a
forbidding, religious household drudge who tried to instill in
Ninon a fear of God. Her father, according to Voltaire, was a
poorly paid musician who supplemented his income by pimping.
Knowing the tastes of men, he worked to make her a worldly,
sophisticated child. By the time she was twelve she had learned to
dance, could play the harpsichord, and had read Montaigne. Her
father extolled the virtues of hedonism, and this lesson Ninon
learned well.

Both of Ninon's parents died before she was twenty. She was
left a small inheritance, which she invested wisely, and this gave
her an income for life. Before her father's death, she had met
many of his friends—authors, soldiers, minor nobility—who con-
gregated in the suburbs of Paris. Now, left to her own devices,
she invited their attentions.

Her affairs were legion. Her first was with the young Comte
Gaspard de Coligny. She followed this by simultaneously consorting with the Abbé Dessiat and the Maréchal d'Estrées, and
when she became pregnant, both men claimed the honor of having accomplished the impregnation. They settled the paternity of
the expected child by throwing dice, and Ninon's first son was
raised by the Maréchal d'Estrées. Ninon's affairs, and her appearance, stimulated an invitation from Cardinal de Richelieu.
He wished for her body; she wished only his platonic friendship.
Neither one was successful. Instead, Ninon delivered her best
friend, Marion Delorme, to the cardinal, and Marion was more

than receptive to the ecclesiastic's advances and the fifty thousand crowns he paid for the privilege of enjoying her charms.

Soon Ninon had the best-attended salon in Paris. Renowned visitors came to view her and succumbed. Ninon divided them into three classes: "the payers, the martyrs, and the favored." Saint-Évremond was her lover and her friend. La Rochefoucauld was another, and the Marquis de Sévigné and the Duc d'Enghien were satisfied to share her. The Marquis de Sévigné's son succeeded his father to her bed, but briefly. The youth was quickly dismissed by Ninon because, she remarked, he had "a soul of boiled beef, a body of damp paper, with a heart like a pumpkin fricasseed in snow." Her longest liaison was with the Marquis de Villarceux, who moved her to his estate in the country for three years. When he left her for a married woman, Ninon went briskly on to an affair with M. de Gersay, who gave her a second son.

Although her general aspect was one of cool indifference, she came alive during the act of love and demanded the same warmth from her lovers. "One needs a hundred times more esprit in order to love properly than to command armies," she remarked. On another occasion she elaborated: "Love without grace is like a hook without bait." When the Comte de Choiseul was too casual in his lovemaking, she sent him packing with a quote from Corneille: "Oh, Heaven, what a lot of virtues you make me hate."

Once, in the early stages of her affair with the Marquis de Sévigné (who would later lose his life in a duel), she poured out her feelings on being in love, and thus tried to define the emotion:

"Love! I feel thy divine fury! my trouble, my transports, everything announces thy presence. Today a new sun rises for me; everything lives, everything is animated, everything seems to speak to me of my passion, everything invites me to cherish it. . . . Since I loved you, my friends are dearer to me; I love myself more; the sounds of my theorbo and of my lute seem to me more moving, my voices more harmonious. If I want to perform a piece, passion and enthusiasm seize me; the disturbance they cause interrupt me every minute. Then a profound revery, full of delight, succeeds my transports. You are present to my eyes; I see you, I speak to you, I tell you that I love you. . . . I congratulate myself and I repent; I wish for you, and wish to fly from you; I write to you and tear up my letters; I reread yours, they seem to me now gallant, now tender, rarely passionate and always too short. I consult my mirrors, I question my women about my charms. In brief, I love you; I am mad; and I do not know what I shall become, if you do not keep your word with me this evening."

Few men could resist such giving.

Ninon's wit, also, was much admired, and she was sharpest when stung into retaliation. Once, the queen regent, Anne of Austria, became offended by Ninon's scandalous salon. She ordered Ninon to a religious house. Ninon was agreeable. "The Monastery of the Grands Cordeliers?" she suggested sweetly. This monastery, as all Paris knew, was not only inhabited by Franciscan friars—but friars noted for their debaucheries. On another occasion, one of her lovers, the Marquis de la Chastre, refused to take a business trip unless Ninon signed a contract pledging fidelity while he was gone. Annoyed, Ninon signed. The moment la Chastre departed, Ninon took up with a series of new lovers, mystifying each, as she reclined, with her laughing exclamation, "Oh, that delightful guarantee I gave la Chastre!"

The greatest people came to pay court. Molière, Scarron, Mme. de Maintenon, the thirteen-year-old Voltaire (to whom Ninon willed two thousand francs for the purchase of books), and Queen Christina of Sweden. In her salon, Ninon permitted no drunkards, and herself shunned alcohol. She scoffed at chastity, but allowed no vulgar conversation. And she was the soul of honesty. A nobleman, forced to flee Paris, divided his savings of twenty thousand crowns between a clergyman and Ninon, and begged them to hold the money for him. When he was at last able to return, the nobleman was dismayed to learn that his clerical friend had given his half of the savings to the poor, to gain a reputation for charity. The nobleman was certain that he faced bankruptcy. "If this is what I get from a saint," he groaned, "what can I hope from the sinner?" To his amazement, Ninon was waiting cheerfully with his ten thousand crowns intact.

By the time she had passed her fortieth birthday, Ninon was regarded as France's foremost authority on the subject of lovemaking. She was considered by one and all, as Horace Walpole would remark some decades later, "a veritable Notre-Dame des Amours." To supplement her income, Ninon decided to put this reputation to practical use. And thus, she established her School of Gallantry—a polite euphemism for School of Lovemaking.

The classroom was her home. The students were young aristocrats enrolled by their mothers to learn the requisites of manhood. The curriculum covered by Ninon in her talks included the care and handling of a mistress or wife, the psychology of women, the correct approach to courting and seduction, the acceptable ways of ending an affair, and the physiology of artful sex. Ninon's school was an immediate success.

While no formal record was kept of the proceedings in her classes, many of the things that she said—in the form of advice, answers to questions, aphorisms—were remembered and repeated by her male pupils and became widely known. Herewith a sampling of Ninon the Educator:

"It is all very well to keep food for another day, but pleasure should be taken as it comes. . . . Talk to your woman continually about herself, and seldom about yourself. Take for granted that she is a hundred times more interested in the charms of her own person than in the whole gamut of your emotions. . . . Remember, there are moments when women would rather be treated a little roughly than with too much consideration; men are more often defeated because of their own clumsiness than because of a woman's virtue. . . . Should you be the one who ceases to love first, let the woman have the advantage of making the break and appearing cruel. . . . A woman who is through with a man will give him up for anything except another woman."

Often, Ninon listened privately to the specific problems of her young men and then advised and guided them. On several occasions, when words would not do and more earthy instruction was required, Ninon took her young men to bed to demonstrate the techniques of foreplay and sexual intercourse. One student so favored was Philippe de Courcillon, the Marquis de Dangeau, who enjoyed the laboratory training conducted by his teacher in her bed. Later, he put his practical knowledge to good use in two marriages with wealthy and high-placed ladies, and in his *Memoirs*, a history of the French court.

Many young women of noble blood envied the instruction enjoyed by Ninon's male pupils, and they sought her out, begging for advice, also. While Ninon would not conduct classes for women, she tried to help them whenever she could. It is recorded that one well-bred girl came to Ninon and inquired, "How large should a woman's breast be to attract a lover?" To this, Ninon replied simply, "Large enough to fill the hand of an honest man."

When she reached her sixties, Ninon abandoned her formal classes, but she continued to receive socially the young men whose families sent them to her salon to acquire sophistication and manners. While the story may be apocryphal, it was said that one of these young men was the Chevalier de Villiers, Ninon's natural son. She received him on the condition that his father, M. de Gersay, keep her true relationship to the youth secret. But because he was her son, she favored him over all others, and like all others, the boy regarded her not as a son would but as a lover. When the boy declared his passion, Ninon sent him away. He returned, more ardent than ever. Ninon was harsh with him. "Look at me. It is sixty-five years since I came into the world. So you think at this age I can listen to a declaration of love? Can you not see that your passion is ridiculous?" With this she sent him off again, but she could not keep him away. At last she determined that she must disclose her secret. She summoned him. He arrived, assured he had won her favor at last. Before she could speak, he began to make passionate overtures. Angrily she stopped him. "This dreadful love cannot go on. Do you realize who you are and who I am?" And with that, she told him. He was stricken. She embraced him maternally. He stared at her, murmured the word *Mother* twice, and fled into the garden where, using his sword, he committed suicide.

After that, Ninon was old. No longer would she permit visitors to call her by her nickname. Henceforth she was Mlle. de Lenclos. According to Voltaire, her last days were spent in peace: "Some lovers, many friends, a somewhat sedentary life, reading, agreeable supper parties and that completes the end of her story." She expressed bitterness only once. "If I were told I had to go over again the life I have led," she said to Saint-Évremond, "I would hang myself tomorrow." But that was only a fleeting mood. Generally, she was serene as she recalled her past. For, as Saint-Évremond reminded her in one last letter, "I consider you, in full life as you are, the happiest creature that ever was. You have been loved by the most honorable men in the world, and have loved often enough to leave nothing untasted in pleasures. . . ."

Dying, in October of 1705, Ninon was resigned. On her death-bed she composed one final verse:

> *I put your consolations by,*
> *And care not for the hopes you give:*
> *Since I am old enough to die,*
> *Why should I longer wish to live?*

The courtesan, as exemplified by Ninon de Lenclos, differs from the prostitute mainly in the area of free and independent choice of mate. "The prostitute," writes William Tait in *Magdalenism*, "is generally a person who openly delivers herself up to a life of impurity and licentiousness, who is indiscriminate in the selection of her lovers, and who depends for her livelihood upon the proceeds arising from a life of prostitution." An elaboration may be found in the Encyclopedia of the Social Sciences, where prostitution is defined as being "characterized by three elements: payment, usually involving the passing of money, although gifts or pleasures may constitute equivalent consideration; promiscuity, with the possible exercise of choice; and emotional indifference, which may be inferred from payment and promiscuity." In short, the prostitute is not merely one who employs her sex to make a living, but she is one who has a multiplicity of lovers, she is one who is notoriously promiscuous, and she is one who indulges in what the Romans have called "passion without delight."

Prostitutes are as old as the Bible. A harlot watched the walls of Jericho tumble down. And whores long ago peddled their bodies on the crooked streets of ancient Egypt, of Persia, and of Greece. Largely a city phenomenon in modern times, they exist by the thousands in New York, London, Paris, Rome, and Berlin. They are there because men need them. Just as monogamy created the mistress in general, so the chivalric concept of love has fostered and maintained the prostitute in particular. The romantic restrictions on the act of love in many marriages—the obligations to be gentle, kind, diplomatic, persuasive, and unselfish—thwart man's selfish, irrational, brutally primitive sexual urge. The act of love, in prostitution, does not throw up such barriers. Man may, for his hour, be an animal, coarse, unrestrained, utterly self-gratifying. And after his hour, he may depart without obligations, emotional, economic, or social.

What makes women turn to prostitution? There have been countless surveys. In one of these, only 2 percent of the prostitutes questioned claimed they had become prostitutes solely because they needed money. Many were lazy or mentally retarded girls who regarded prostitution as easier than working behind a ribbon counter or a desk. Many were amoral, and considered sexual variety a lark. Many hoped, optimistically, to meet a man of a higher class who might take care of them. Many were lured into it by husbands, seducers, pimps. Many were encouraged to go into it by environmental immorality; many to escape parental neglect or abuse. Many were just plain lonely.

These are the reasons articulated, for a century, by the prostitutes themselves. But psychiatrists, today, give more penetrating reasons. The prostitute is a girl who was once disillusioned by reality. In excessive sexual activity, she has her small triumph. She achieves value and identity. And, above all, she has her revenge. For, terrified of her father in childhood, she has come to hate all men. Now these men whom she has feared are humbled by her, for they need her. These men are symbolically castrated and debased by her, for she knows they can never satisfy her. This would seem to be unconscious sadism, yet the prostitute is in fact a masochist. "As a matter of record," writes Dr. Joseph Tenenbaum, "it is usually impossible to rescue a prostitute from her misery just because misery is what she craves most of all." She despises her profession, yet she would not abandon it. For, every hour of every night she attains her debasing victory.

Unlike Ninon de Lenclos and her sister courtesans, prostitutes rarely become famous enough to have their lives recorded. Most have, of necessity, lived shadowy lives, in dim places and in secrecy. But a handful have brazened it out, have become notorious enough because of their talents and patrons, to defy anonymity. One of these was Catherine Maria Fisher, known to students of harlotry and nursery rhymes as Kitty Fisher.

Kitty was born in the Soho section of London, in 1738, of poor German parents. As she approached maturity, she was apprenticed to a milliner. In that period, milliners' shops were, like the theater, showcases for pretty young girls who were potential prostitutes or courtesans. Kitty was, indeed, pretty. She was a small girl, almost delicate, with light blue eyes, a turned-up nose, and a generous mouth. She was intelligent, clever, gay. She had the outward dignity and poise of a well-bred lady, yet one sensed at once the promise of attractive vulgarity beneath. She was not long behind the milliner's counter. The son of an English merchant, an army ensign named Anthony Martin, dazzled Kitty with gifts and extravagant promises, and soon she was ensconced in his apartments as his mistress. However, young Martin was parsimonious, and when, at last, he was shipped abroad, Kitty was not displeased. At any rate, she had found her profession.

Patrons quickly beat a path to Kitty's door. Thomas Medlycott, heir to a great estate, introduced her to fine attire, the opera, and the Islington Spa. Augustus Keppel, a naval officer with the best of connections, introduced her into high society. And society produced new admirers in the forms of Admiral Lord George Anson, General John Ligonier, and Edward, Duke of York, brother to the future George III.

Kitty Fisher did not sell herself cheaply. The price for her favors was one hundred guineas a night. Once, the Duke of York, after having slept the night with her, handed her a fifty-pound bank note before taking his leave. Kitty, who would brook no bargain hunter, was deeply offended. With admirable contempt, she placed the fifty-pound bank note on her bread-and-butter and ate it for breakfast. And then she barred the duke from her bed forever.

She was a celebrity and she could do no wrong. And all that she did was news. When she had tea served in her box at the theater during a performance, no one was surprised. When she ordered fresh strawberries in the winter, at twenty guineas a box, all of London was delighted. When a baronet commissioned Joshua Reynolds to paint her, it seemed only natural. Later, Reynolds painted her again, as Cleopatra, and reproductions were hawked throughout the metropolis. When she was entertaining the dwarfish Lord Montfort, and was notified that Lord Sandwich, a rival for her affections, was about to appear, she shoved her pigmy peer under her hoopskirt and walked him safely out of the room, and all of Parliament roared with pleasure at the story. When she fell off a horse, while riding in St. James's Park, it inspired wide concern in the English press and resulted in a verse in the *Universal Magazine*:

> *Dear Kitty, had thy only fall*
> *Been that thou met'st with in the Mall,*

> *Thou had'st deserved our pity;*
> *But long before that luckless day,*
> *With equal justice might we say,*
> *Alas! poor fallen Kitty!*

After six years of popularity, during which period she met King George II, William Pitt, and Casanova, she fell ill and retired from her profession. In 1765, she met John Norris, Jr., whose grandfather had been a vice admiral in the British Navy, whose father was an important landowner, and who was himself a member of Parliament. A year later, Kitty married Norris in Scotland, much to the horror of his family. Several months passed before her father-in-law, after considerable soul-searching, sent for her, received her in the manor house in Kent, and approved of the match. That winter she was very happy and very ill, and five months after her wedding day she was dead. She was only twenty-nine.

"Sexual desire, which is the source of the feeling of love, remains a virtually unchanging instinct; it varies as little as human bodies," wrote André Maurois in *Seven Faces of Love*, "but the manifestations of this instinct, which are the ways of loving, become modified in the course of centuries." To observe best the evolution in the ways of loving, and to observe the changing attitudes toward those who made the art of loving their careers, one need only follow the peregrinations of the mistress from her first entrance into society until modern times.

The rise of the mistress began, quite logically, in the enlightened civilization that was ancient Greece. Monogamy was in force, but this did not guarantee widespread joy to women. The Athenian wife was little more than a chattel. She dwelt in the rear of the house, secluded from all male visitors, without freedom of movement, without legal or inheritance rights. It was even thought that she did not play a role in conceiving offspring, because "seed" was believed to be produced exclusively by the male. Birth control was popular. Since she was not allowed to encourage a large family, the Athenian wife rubbed oil of cedar and ointment of lead on the opening to her uterus to prevent conception. She loved, honored, and obeyed, and was herself honored, but it was not the most exciting of lives. If she sought romance elsewhere, she risked her life, for if she was discovered, her husband had the legal right to kill her.

No wonder, then, that so many Athenian women remained unfettered, and that so many of these undertook the often happier role of mistress. Of the various types of mistress, the *porne* or prostitute was the least respected. She worked in houses recognized, and taxed, by the government, and there, often clad in little more than a veil, she stood for examination by prospective customers. However, because she supplied so much revenue to the state, her lot was generally improved through the years. Above the prostitute, in social station, was the *auletris*, a trained entertainer who was expert with the flute, in the suggestive dance, and at lovemaking. But above all free women, in Greece, stood the *hetaira*, or courtesan.

The Athenian courtesan was usually a highly cultivated, highly attractive young woman, with dyed blonde hair, and small breasts. She attired herself in a flowery robe prescribed by law. While she possessed no civil rights, and was barred from entering any temple other than her own, she remained a free citizen. Her average fee was five hundred gold drachmas a visit. Many of these courtesans became as renowned as generals, philosophers, playwrights or Olympic heroes. There was Clepsydra, who kept an hourglass beside her bed, and dismissed her lovers when the sands ran out. There was Cyrene, who was much in demand when word spread that she knew twelve different ways of performing sexual intercourse. There was Theoris, who gave the playwright Sophocles an illegitimate child in his old age. (When Sophocles' legitimate son, fearing he might lose his inheritance, took his father to court for mental incompetence, the old man proved his sensibility by rising to read the latest of his 113 plays.) There was Lamia, who demanded that Demetrius Poliorcetes, King of Macedon, pay her 250 talents, or $300,000, for her favors. He agreed, and raised the money by levying a soap tax, which provoked one Athenian wit to remark that since Lamia required so much from soap, she surely must have been dirtier than everyone thought. But foremost among all the courtesans in Greek history were Aspasia, Lais, and Phryne.

Of Aspasia's physical attractions little is known, except that her hair was golden, that her voice was silvery, and that her foot was agreeably small. It is thought that she posed for her friend Phidias

when he created his *Athene of the Parthenon.* Socrates admired
her eloquence. And it is said that she wrote several of Pericles'
orations, notably the memorable funeral address he made at the
outset of the Great Peloponnesian War.

She was born in Miletus, managed a brothel in Megara, and
arrived in Athens in 450 B.C. to conduct a school for elocution
and philosophy, intended principally for young ladies. It is possible that she continued to run a brothel as a sideline. At any rate,
Socrates, Anaxagoras, and Euripides joined the ladies attending
her classes. When Pericles, the high-domed dictator of Athens,
also attended and was enchanted, Aspasia's future was made, and
she forthwith withdrew from the profession of teaching to resume
her role of courtesan.

It is thought that Pericles was forty years old, and Aspasia
twenty-five, when they met. He was at the height of his popularity. He had democratized parts of Greece, and ennobled its
culture. He was married, keeping a courtesan from Corinth, and
he had two adolescent sons. Now he discarded both his wife and
his Corinthian to devote his full energies to his new mistress, who
was already pregnant by him. Having arranged another marriage for his former wife, Pericles brought Aspasia into his house.
Since she was not an Athenian citizen, he could not marry her.
But he willed his fortune to their son, Pericles II, and soon neglected his followers and the council hall for her caresses.

Pericles' enemies, and even some of his supporters, resented
Aspasia, and especially the part she played in political affairs.
They conspired to destroy her. Led by one Hermippus, a playwright, they accused Aspasia of impiety toward their gods, and of
acting as a procuress who supplied young freeborn Athenian
ladies to satisfy Pericles' lust. The trial was held in 432 B.C., before a jury of fifteen hundred men, and Aspasia, as a foreigner,
was not allowed to speak in her own defense. When Pericles
realized that the evidence was going against his beloved, and that
the penalty would be death, he appeared to defend her in person.
Though known for his phlegmatic, judicial, aloof manner, Pericles opened his heart to the jurors. His voice quavered with emotion. He broke down and wept. And the jurors, irrationally
moved, voted for acquittal.

But Aspasia's detractors were not done. Aristophanes, who detested her, held her responsible for instigating the costly Pelopon-

nesian War. He insisted that she was still in the brothel business, that two high-spirited officers from Megara had kidnapped two of her most valued prostitutes, and that, as a result, she had urged Pericles to attack Megara. While it is more likely that Pericles had started the conflict to secure his control of the Aegean Sea, popular feeling against Aspasia mounted.

When Pericles pulled his citizenry behind the walls of Athens, hoping that his navy might be sufficient to bring about victory, misfortune struck in the form of a plague. One out of every four Athenian soldiers died, and Pericles lost his two legitimate sons. When the war ended, Pericles was accused of having bought the peace through misappropriation of funds from the public treasury. He was convicted and fined over a quarter of a million dollars. Nine years later he was back in power. One of his first acts was to force the legislature to legitimize his son, Pericles II, by then an Athenian general. Shortly after, Pericles was dead in his sixties. As for Aspasia, a month later she was consoling herself with a wealthy sheepdealer named Lysicles.

The second great courtesan of ancient Greece was Lais, born in Sicily, brought to Corinth as a slave, and discovered by a painter, who purchased the youthful girl for a model. For three years the artist trained her in the social graces, permitting her to work in a brothel when he could spare her, and then he set her free. She was, Athenaeus remarked, "superior in beauty to any woman that had ever been seen."

It was natural that she should move to Athens to pose for the great sculptors, and to offer herself as a mistress to the greatest of them. The elderly artist, Myron, who had done the classic *Discus Thrower*, hired her first. When she removed her veils, and stood naked before him, preparing to pose, the old man was stunned. At once he offered her a fortune, the entire contents of his studio, to stay the night with him. She studied the old man's tangled gray hair and beard, his unkempt garments, turned, snatched up her veils, and walked out. The following day, the frenzied Myron had his hair cut and trimmed, his beard shaved off, his cheeks rouged, his new scarlet robe perfumed. Then, wearing a chain of gold, and jeweled rings, he sought out Lais and told her that he loved her. She studied him as before, and was amused. "My dear friend," she said, "you are asking of me what I refused your father yesterday."

She gave herself only to those she loved. When Demosthenes offered her ten thousand drachmas for a single night, she sent him away. Yet, when the impoverished philosopher and searcher for an honest man, Diogenes—who is said to have dwelt in a barrel—indicated interest, she gave herself to him for nothing. Aristippus, the philosopher, paid her such huge sums for her affection, that she was able to contribute generously to charities and temples.

When her money was gone, and her beauty too, she continued to offer her body now at bargain prices. Epicrates recorded the last years of her life:

"Lais is idle and drunken. She comes to wander among the tables. To me, she is like one of those birds of prey which, in the strength of youth, hurl themselves from the summit of mountains and carry off young goats, but which, in old age, perch languidly on the pinnacles of temples, where they live, consumed by hunger, a sinister augury. Lais, in her springtime, was rich and superb. . . . But now, her winter is coming; the temple is fallen in ruins and opens easily; she stops the first comer to drink with him; a stater, a three-oboles piece, are a fortune to her. Young and old, she takes all the world; age has so softened her humor that she extends her hand for a few pieces of money."

At the age of seventy, she fell passionately in love with a youth in his twenties. She followed him to Thessaly, and then into the Temple of Venus, where she profanely offered herself to him. Women nearby, repelled by the sight, stoned her to death. In Athens she was not forgotten, and there a mighty tomb rose to honor her memory.

But it was the third of the great courtesans of Athens who is best remembered. Her name was Mnesarete, but for the yellowish cast of the skin covering her perfect body she was called Phryne. She was born in the small town of Thespiae. With maturity, she became possessed of so shapely a body that it was inevitable she must go to Athens. There she became the mistress of Apelles, who used her as the model for his *Aphrodite Anadyomene,* and then she became the mistress of Praxiteles, who posed her for his two Aphrodites, one version nude and the other clothed. When Praxiteles offered her, as a token of his love, any one of the priceless sculptured pieces in his studio, she was at a loss and begged him to make the choice for her. He refused. A few days later she rushed up to him in the street, shouting that his studio was ablaze. He groaned. "I am lost if my *Satyr* and my *Eros* are burned." Phryne then admitted the fire was a hoax, chose the *Eros,* and presented it to her native Thespiae. There, it remained a tourist attraction until years later, when Nero confiscated it only to lose it himself when Rome burned.

Among all the Greek courtesans, Phryne was the most modest. She was always fully clothed in public, favoring a tight-fitting chiton. She never attended the public baths. And when she made love, it was always in darkness. Only twice annually, at the Eleusinian and Poseidonian festivals, did she stand in the portico of the temple, strip to the flesh, and walk in nudity through the gaping thousands to enter the sea and pay homage to the gods.

It was said that no man could resist her charms. Yet, some said there was one. They pointed to Xenocrates, the philosopher who governed Plato's Academy for a quarter of a century. He was a man of virtue, without a fleshly desire, his entire waking day given over to intellectual preoccupations. Phryne was intrigued. What about his nights, she wondered. He was, after all, a mere man. She wagered that she could seduce him in a single evening. The wager was accepted by his admirers. Wearing her jeweled ornaments, and dressed in the thinnest of veils, she rapped on his door one night. Xenocrates opened it, and Phryne hastily entered. She said that she was being pursued by thieves, and begged for refuge until morning. Xenocrates, ever the perfect host, told her to sleep on the bench, and returned to his bed. Phryne disrobed, and slipped into bed beside him. He remained unmoved. She embraced him savagely. He did not respond. She shrieked with despair, and fled into the night. But she would not pay her bet. "I wagered that I would render a man, not a statue, sensible," she explained.

More responsive lovers lavished wealth upon her. When Alexander the Great brought down the walls of Thebes, Phryne offered to rebuild them. There was one condition. On the new walls must hang a plaque bearing the words: "Thebes was overthrown by Alexander and rebuilt by Phryne." The Thebans refused her offer.

Quite naturally, the wives of Athens resented her. They encouraged one of Phryne's unsuccessful suitors, Euthias, to bring her to judgment for "having profaned the majesty of the Eleu-

sinian mysteries by parodying them, and of being constantly occupied with corrupting the most illustrious citizens of the republic by seducing them from the service of the fatherland." On
trial for her life, she induced the renowned orator, Hyperides, to
undertake her defense in return for her becoming his mistress.
His conduct of her case was brilliant, but the cause seemed hopeless. The death penalty appeared inevitable until Hyperides, in a
moment of inspiration, led Phryne before her judges, yanked her
garments from her shoulders, and pulled them down to her waist.
She stood with her faultless breasts exposed. The judges stared at
her in wonder. This was not a woman. This was a divinity. So
perfect a body could not hide an imperfect soul. Confused by
their superstitious reasoning, the awed judges voted for acquittal.

Phryne retained this beauty to the end. In her later years she
invented a cosmetic that prevented wrinkles, and with its help
she continued to thrive. Her death was honorable, and her monument was a golden statue in the Temple of Diana of Ephesus.
The statue was fashioned by Praxiteles, who remembered.

Less than three centuries later, there appeared the next of the
great mistresses. She was a Macedonian, but the land of her origin was Egypt. Her name was Cleopatra, and, at the age of seventeen, she had ascended the throne of the Ptolemies in Alexandria,
the city founded by Alexander the Great, and had undertaken the
rule of one million subjects. In the beginning she had ruled
jointly with her younger brother, Ptolemy XII, and was by decree his legal wife. After Ptolemy XII was "accidentally" drowned
in the Nile, she was married to her brother, Ptolemy XIII. Before
she was widowed a second time, she was already carrying a child
by Julius Caesar, and in this heir she saw the fulfillment of her
lifelong ambition. For, with the advent of Caesar, Egypt had become no more than a Roman colony, garrisoned by Roman troops.
Cleopatra meant to change all that.

She did not have the armies to enforce her ambition. She had
only herself. And she knew that Rome was ruled by men. Her
confidence in the power of her attractions amazed many, for she
was not beautiful. Most historians believe that she was a brunette
(though she is said to have dyed her hair red), with large blue
eyes, prominent nose, finely shaped mouth, and well-rounded
chin. She was probably small of stature, with pear-shaped or coni-

cal breasts, and with a complexion fairer than that of most of her brown-skinned subjects. Her countenance, thought Plutarch, was not "such as to strike those who saw her." Yet, there were other assets. She had charm, manners, breeding, intelligence, and individuality. There was about her an air that was erotically exciting. Although never promiscuous, she gave promise of sensuality. She had an instinct for flattering and satisfying a man, and the chameleonlike ability to be either retiring or aggressively passionate, as the occasion demanded.

When Julius Caesar had first arrived in Alexandria, Cleopatra saw her chance. Whether Caesar secretly sent for her because she had been banished by her brother's regent, or whether it was she who determined to see Caesar and enlist his aid, is not known. She reached the Alexandria wharves in a small boat, accompanied by a friend and servant named Apollodorus. Then, fearing her brother's assassins, she had herself rolled inside several blankets and had these secured by rope. Thus did Apollodorus carry her into Caesar's presence. When the bundle was unrolled, his astonishment turned quickly to admiration, and before many days she was his mistress and, soon, again the mistress of all Egypt.

During his prime, the handsome, ruthless Caesar had seduced many women—among them Pompey's wife and Cato's half sister—but Cleopatra seemed to be his most enduring love. Even though a wife and political unrest awaited his attentions in Rome, he lingered on in Alexandria, receiving Cleopatra almost daily, and often kept her with him until dawn. The product of their companionship was a son, Caesarion, who became Ptolemy XIV, and it seems evident that Caesar meant to make him the next Emperor of Rome.

After putting down an African revolt instigated by Cato and Scipio, Caesar returned in triumph to Rome in 46 B.C. A short time later, he sent for Cleopatra and their son. She arrived with a vast retinue of eunuchs and slaves, and was established in a huge house on the right bank of the Tiber. Their reunion was short-lived. For the Ides of March had come. And Caesar, surrounded by conspirators, was stabbed again and again, a total of twenty-two times—in the neck, in the back, in the side, in the groin. While defending himself ineffectually with his *stilus*, he cried in wonder at Brutus, "You too, my child?", then fell dead at his friend's feet.

The throne of Rome was vacant. Who was to rule? Cleopatra approached the muscular, earthy, good-natured Marc Antony and pleaded the cause of her child by Caesar. But by then Caesar's foster son, a relative he had adopted—the nineteen-year-old Octavian—had arrived to plead his own case. To avert civil war, Antony advised Cleopatra to return to Egypt and wait. And this she was forced to do.

Presently a triumvirate—Antony, Octavian, and Lepidus—held power. To assert the new order of things, Antony began a goodwill journey through the East. Halting in Tarsus, he sent for Cleopatra. She arrived not as a suppliant with a cause to plead, but as a queen. She headed toward the quays in a gilded vessel, rowed by silver oars and driven by wind-filled purple sails. Her most beautiful female slaves, attired as sea nymphs, lined the railings. Her royal orchestra, with its harps, pipes, flutes, played exotic music. And on a couch, beneath a great gold awning, reclined Cleopatra. Clothed lightly in the shimmering veils of Venus, she was fanned by young boys dressed as Cupids, and was surrounded everywhere by clouds of smoke from fragrant incense.

She invited Antony to dine with her. He came, with a large following, and was again dazzled by the gold and purple tapestries, the flower-strewn floor, the dozen triple couches surrounding the tables laid with gleaming golden platters. When Antony exclaimed in admiration, Cleopatra made him a present of the room's furnishings and appointments.

There were two more dinners, and Antony, at forty-two, found himself in love with Cleopatra, who was twenty-nine. He followed her to Alexandria, and spent the winter in her palace and in her bed. They drank together, and laughed, and hunted, and fished, and continued to make love. Once, Cleopatra wagered her lover that she could drink the equivalent of nearly half a million dollars' worth of wine in a sitting. He made the bet. She poured a glass of vinegar wine, dropped two pearls worth ten million sestertia into it, and drank it down. It was all amusing, but Antony was worried about Octavian, and restless. By spring he was on his way back to Rome, leaving behind a promise to return soon, and by autumn Cleopatra had borne his twins, a boy and a girl, whom she named after the sun and the moon.

Antony was gone four years. In that time he played politics. He married Octavian's virtuous sister, and drew up plans to make himself the conqueror of Parthia. At last, to solidify his authority, he set out on world conquest. Parthia proved a disaster—Antony lost fifty thousand men—but he celebrated it as a triumph in Alexandria. There, once again under Cleopatra's spell, he divorced his wife, and in 36 B.C. he married his Egyptian queen. He named their twins rulers of the Eastern provinces, and Cleopatra and her son Caesarion the rulers of Egypt and Cyprus. And then he settled down to a few years of relaxation. But Octavian would not have it. He took Antony's will from the Vestal Virgins and read it to the Senate. It stated that Antony's children by Cleopatra were to be his heirs and that he was to be buried in Alexandria. Rome was incensed. The moment had come. Octavian declared war—not on Antony, but on Cleopatra—and sent an attacking fleet under the command of Agrippa.

In 31 B.C., Cleopatra and Antony arrayed their five hundred top-heavy ships against Agrippa's four hundred light vessels off Actium. When the battle went against Cleopatra, she withdrew her sixty Egyptian ships. It is not known whether an accident of signals or some personal panic prompted her action. At any rate, she fled, and the day was lost.

Later, hearing that Cleopatra was dead, Antony bared his chest and stabbed himself. Only after the mortal wound was inflicted did he hear that the rumor was false, that Cleopatra still lived, hidden in a mausoleum. He ordered himself carried to her. When he was brought in, she laid her tearful face upon his bloodied body, and moaned her love.

He requested a cup of wine, drank it, and died.

When Cleopatra finally faced the victorious Octavian, she faced him alone.

Although she was resting on her bed, naked, when her conqueror made his sudden entrance, she made no attempt to seduce him. Rather she covered herself with a garment, then tried to soften Octavian by showing him letters that his foster father, Julius Caesar, had once written her. But she could not soften him, and later she learned that he was going to transport her to Rome in three days' time, there to display her as a captive. She was still a queen and she would not have it. It is thought that she kept a small, gray mud asp secreted in a vase, or that she had one smuggled to her in a basket of figs. Holding the snake, not to her breasts but to her arm, she let it bite her. Octavian hastened to have the poison sucked from her wound, but the venom had already done its work. She was buried beside Antony. Her son by Caesar was slain. Her twins by Antony were sent to Rome to be raised by Antony's former wife. And soon Cleopatra was legend.

Under Octavian, who became Augustus Caesar, and under the numerous Caesars who ruled briefly and were deposed after him, immorality flourished in Rome and the marriage bed too often remained empty. There were legal *meretrices* or prostitutes, who were permitted to work outside the city walls but only by night. They wore distinctive long robes and charged the standard fee of one obolus, or three cents, a visit. There were concubines, like Nero's faithful Greek, Claudia Acte, and Commodus' less faithful companion, Marcia, a conspirator in his murder, who were little more than slaves. There were courtesans, who enhanced their dark, delicate beauty with masses of curled hair which was made blonde through use of German dyes, and who encouraged admirers by wearing transparent silken dresses. But most of all, in later Rome, there were the adulteresses. "Pure women are only those who have not been asked," observed Ovid wryly. Apparently, a great number of married women were asked. And though the law threatened the unchaste wife with the death penalty, and her lover with mutilation, many married women circumvented this danger by registering as prostitutes under fictitious names. The most incredible and notorious of these adulteresses was Valeria Messalina, who became the third wife of the Emperor Claudius of Rome.

Her father was a senator who believed in the domestic and virtuous woman. But her mother was not a domestic and virtuous woman, and so Messalina was raised in an atmosphere of moral laxity. She was wedded, at sixteen, to an older cousin, Claudius, the forty-eight-year-old grandson of Antony. Three years later, when Caligula was deposed, Claudius was found trembling behind a curtain and named emperor by the Praetorian Guard. And thus Messalina, though only nineteen, found herself Empress of Rome.

She enjoyed her new power, but had only contempt for her husband. In truth, Claudius was not a prepossessing figure. He was tall, thin, stooped, and paunchy. He walked with a limp, his head shook, he stuttered and dribbled at the mouth, and his nose ran. His mother had called him "a little monster," and his relatives thought him a fool. Actually, he was anything but a fool. In his lifetime Claudius wrote twenty books relating to Etruscan history, eight books on Carthage, a play in Greek, and eight volumes of autobiography. He wrote learned papers on gambling and on the Roman alphabet, to which he added three new letters. Too, his tastes in sex, if excessive, were normal. Unlike his predecessors, he had no perversions. "Of the first fifteen emperors," wrote Gibbon, "Claudius was the only one whose taste in love was entirely correct."

Messalina could not appreciate his virtues. She was bored by the doddering, scholarly, drunken old man. Having given him a daughter and a son, she dispensed with wifely duties and sought romantic pleasures elsewhere. She began with the palace courtiers, moved on to the entertainers, and to all of this the emperor was blind. She fell in love with the handsome actor, Mnester, and demanded that he leave the stage to become her full-time lover. When he refused to comply with her wishes, Messalina made it known to the emperor that the actor would not obey certain of her commands. The emperor ordered the actor to obey any royal order. Loyally, Mnester quit the stage to serve his empress. She loved him savagely, as he would testify three years later when he dared to display the scars on his body, and she built a bronze statue to honor his talents.

In A.D. 43, Claudius led his troops to Britain, and Messalina was left behind to indulge herself in the wildest of sexual excesses. Encouraged by her conquest of Mnester, she next invited highborn Romans to enjoy her favors. Those who refused were charged with crimes against the state. Eventually she became dissatisfied with these relatively tame palace affairs. She decided to solicit new adventures in the most common parts of the city. Juvenal, and others, have left us a picture of her at this time: the curly, yellow hair piled high on a small, flat head; the low forehead; the large eyes set too close together; the small, thin-lipped mouth.

With a veil draped over her head, she entered taverns and alleys, searching for men. On one such excursion, filled with wine, she danced naked on a wooden platform in the Forum. Another time, she redecorated a bedroom of the palace to resemble a brothel, hung the name of Rome's most renowned prostitute on the door, then disrobed, gilded the nipples of her tiny breasts, and invited the male public to enter and be entertained at no more than the legally regulated fee. Emboldened by the heavy traffic, she challenged a particularly noted prostitute of Rome to a contest, insisting that she could entertain more men in twenty-four hours than her rival. Pliny the Elder tells us that she "surpassed" her rival, "for within the space of twenty-four hours she cohabited twenty-five times."

When Claudius returned from Britain, he knew nothing of these indiscretions. He celebrated his young wife's faithfulness by permitting her to ride beside him in the triumphal procession. For three years more, Messalina continued to dupe her mate. And then, at last, in a frenzy of love, she went too far. When the emperor decided to enjoy the mineral baths at the seaport of Ostia, Messalina remained in Rome to pursue a young, aristocratic nobleman named Gaius Silius. She had already showered Silius with gifts of jewels and slaves, and had convinced him that he must divorce his wife. Now, in the emperor's absence, she went further. She promised Silius the throne of Rome if he would marry her. She moved him into the imperial palace, had the ceremony publicly performed, and then celebrated with him the Bacchanalia, the festival of the vintage. While Messalina led nude dancing girls in rhythmic movements among the wine presses, Silius, wearing an ivy crown, watched and dreamed of glory. At the end of the intoxicating dance, a bed was placed before the assembled guests, and on it Messalina and Silius performed the act of love.

Neither the bigamous marriage nor the Bacchanalia disturbed Claudius' followers. What did trouble them was the possibility that Silius might depose Claudius and rule in his stead. One of the emperor's loyal retinue, a freedman named Narcissus, who resented Messalina for having had his best friend executed, went to one of Claudius' favorite mistresses and asked her to carry the word to her master. In Ostia, this mistress threw herself at the emperor's feet, blurting out the news: "Messalina is married to Silius!" The extent of Messalina's adultery was quickly revealed, and Claudius was horrified. He ordered his chariot, and headed back to Rome.

Warned of her emperor's approach, Messalina abruptly terminated her celebration. While Silius fled to the Forum, and guests dispersed to their houses throughout the city, the empress summoned the Vestal Virgins and marched to the city's entrance. The emperor's chariot rushed into sight, slowed in front of her, and then rolled on. Messalina hastened to her private gardens, and there, with her mother beside her, she awaited her fate.

Meanwhile, Claudius passed the death sentence on Silius and Mnester. Heavy with wine and mellowing, he now hesitated. He decided he would sleep first and consider Messalina's punishment the following day. Narcissus, sensing that delay might work in the empress's favor and endanger his own life, informed the guards that the emperor had passed the death sentence on Messalina and commanded that her execution be carried out immediately.

The guards found her in her garden, and informed her of the emperor's decision. Her mother gave her a blade. She tried to kill herself, but faltered. A guard stepped forward and plunged his sword into her bosom. She died at once. The following evening, Claudius, somewhat sobered, appeared at dinner and noticed that Messalina's place was empty. He began to eat, then almost absently inquired, "Where is the empress tonight?" He was told. He listened thoughtfully, nodded, and returned to his food and wine.

Soon the Dark and then the Middle Ages supplanted the corrupt and decayed Roman Empire. The Middle Ages, generally agreed to cover those years between the fifth and fifteenth centuries, served as the bridge between ancient and modern times. During this period, Christianity was on the ascendancy, and celibacy was the order of the day. Not only was the mistress frowned upon, but even the sex act in marriage was damned. Since procreation was necessary to propagate the Faith, it was allowed but every means was used to keep it from being pleasurable. This attitude, according to G. Rattray Taylor in *Sex in History,* "reached its crudest expression with the invention of the *chemise cagoule,* a sort of heavy nightshirt, with a suitably placed hole, through which a husband could impregnate his wife while avoiding any other contact." Because of these pressures, the Church and its children, during the Middle Ages, were obsessed with sex, and the mistress continued her rise.

The clergy set the moral standard for the period. St. Augustine

had confessed that, before embracing Christianity, he had possessed "an insatiable appetite" for sex and had "boiled over in . . .
fornication." Whereas St. Augustine overcame his weakness of
the flesh, his successors to the cloth were less resolute. They
erected statues of saints with abnormally large phalli, and in
many communities these phalli were sheathed in leather and used
by brides before entering the marriage bed. The Bishop of Liège
was said to have fathered sixty-five illegitimate children. A Spanish abbot at St. Pelayo was known to have kept, during his lifetime, seventy mistresses. In Switzerland, married men, to protect
their wives from seduction in the confessional, petitioned author-
ities to allow their priests to keep one mistress apiece. In Salzburg,
a priest who limited his philandering to one mistress was considered a candidate for sainthood.

This sexual license was but a reflection of conditions at the
Vatican in Rome. In the city of Rome, some seven thousand
prostitutes played hostess to the parishioners. In the Holy See,
doors were opened to mistresses of every kind. At the beginning
of the tenth century, Marozia, the daughter of a papal official,
had Pope Sergius III for her lover and her pawn, and in A.D. 931
she conspired to have her illegitimate son named Pope John XI.
In the years between, Marozia's mother, Theodora, had been the
mistress of Pope John X. Numerous infamous women surrounded
Pope John XII, who was eventually tried for "sacrilege, simony,
perjury, murder, adultery, and incest." And his successor, Pope
Leo VIII, expired of a stroke suffered while committing adultery.

Among the last of the great mistresses to frequent the Holy See
during the Middle Ages were Vanozza dei Cattanei and Giulia
Farnese, both kept by the remarkable Pope Alexander VI, father
of the infamous Borgias. Vanozza, a native of Spain, first met
Alexander VI while he was a lawyer in Valencia and still known
as Rodrigo Borgia. When Borgia's uncle, Pope Calixtus III,
brought him to Rome, and made him notary in the Vatican,
Vanozza followed. She saw her lover rise to the rank of cardinal, and then to Pope. In those years she gave him four children—
one was Cesare Borgia and another was Lucrezia Borgia—and
when he attained the papal chair, she was nearby. To camouflage
their liaison, Alexander VI found her three different husbands.
When she started her menopause at forty-four, she was retired on

a pension, and Alexander VI turned to Giulia Farnese, who was only seventeen.

Giulia was sent to the Pope by her brother, Alessandro Farnese, who had been exiled for a series of crimes and now sought a pardon. When Alexander VI laid eyes upon the exquisite Giulia, he at once issued the pardon to her brother. She had been married to an Orsini for two years. Now, the Pope persuaded her to leave her husband and move into his apartments. Even though he loved her, his orgies continued. In 1501, she was witness to one of them —fifty nude prostitutes crawled among lighted candles, picking up chestnuts, and later serviced a group of men, with prizes offered to the most durable of the male participants. Giulia Farnese gave her elderly lover—he was forty years her senior—three children. When he died, his infamy was his monument. When she died, two representations of her beauty remained as her memorials. For, while mistress of the unsaintly head of the Roman Catholic Church, she had posed for both Pintoricchio's *Madonna* and Guglielmo della Porta's *Truth,* the last a marble nude which still reclines atop the tomb of her brother, Pope Paul III.

Midway in the medieval epoch there appeared the most beloved and delightful mistress of them all, the learned and witty Héloïse, who also found her love in one highly placed in the clergy. Héloïse had been orphaned in her infancy. An uncle in Paris, Fulbert by name, a canon at Notre Dame, undertook to support her. He had her educated at the convent in Argenteuil, where she amazed the nuns with her grasp of Latin and Hebrew, and then he brought her to Paris. She was sixteen, a small, well-formed, enchanting creature, when she first met Pierre Abélard.

The meeting was inevitable. Abélard and Héloïse's uncle were fellow canons at Notre Dame. But Abélard, at thirty-six, was more than a mere canon. He was a national figure. Born in Brittany in 1079, the oldest of the four children of a small estate owner, he grew up to be a handsome, amusing, conceited young man. Steeped in the disciplines of theology and liberal philosophy, he arrived in Paris to lecture at Notre Dame. Thousands heard him and were impressed, and it was even predicted that the brilliant young orator might eventually attain the papal seat. And then it was that Abélard saw Héloïse and, temporarily, his ecclesiastical career was forgotten.

He was, he admitted, "aflame with passion" for her. He must

possess her, and he was confident he would succeed. "Indeed the thing seemed to me very easy to be done," he later wrote. "So distinguished was my name, and I possessed such advantages of youth and comeliness, that no matter what woman I might favor with my love, I dreaded rejection of none." He conceived a scheme whereby he might seduce the chaste young girl. He knew her uncle was a man of "avarice." He told Fulbert that he would like to take rooms in his household, and he offered a small monetary recompense as well as instruction in several languages for Fulbert's niece. The money appealed to Fulbert, but the instruction even more. He invited his fellow canon to move in. Héloïse's lessons began at once, but they were not linguistic. "We were united," said Abélard, "first in the dwelling that sheltered our love, and then in the hearts that burned within us. . . . Our kisses outnumbered our reasoned words; love drew our eyes together. . . . The pleasure of teaching her to love surpassed the delightful fragrance of all the perfumes in the world."

The instruction proceeded, and soon Héloïse was with child. Abélard sent her off to his sister in Brittany, and faced her irate uncle with the truth. He proposed that he would marry Héloïse, on the condition that the marriage be kept secret, so that it might not endanger his future in the church. Fulbert was agreeable. Héloïse, returning to Paris with her infant son Astrolabe, was not agreeable. She would be Abélard's mistress, but not his wife. In marriage, she feared their love might grow "stale and insipid," but "tasted sparingly" it might survive. Too, she felt a family would divert Abélard's energies from his career, and that in turn might hinder his advancement. Nevertheless, Fulbert prevailed. The marriage was secretly performed, after which the couple was forced to live apart.

But news of Héloïse's child got out, and to defend her virtue, Fulbert revealed the marriage. At once, hand on the Bible, Héloïse denied it. She insisted, before the world, that she was Abélard's mistress, not his wife. In a fury, Fulbert punished her. In an equal fury, Abélard kidnapped her, spirited her back to the convent in Argenteuil, requesting her to assume a nun's garb and remain in hiding until he summoned her.

Now occurred an epic misunderstanding. Fulbert assumed that Abélard had wearied of Héloïse, and had retired her to a convent so that he might philander with other women. He assumed, also, that Abélard had made his wife a nun so that he might again be eligible for the priesthood. Fulbert determined to have his revenge. He hired four disreputable men taken from the streets of Paris, then bribed Abélard's manservant to let them enter his bedroom one night. There three of them bound Abélard to his bed, while the fourth wielded a razor. "They cut off those parts of my body," wrote Abélard, "whereby I had done that which was the cause of their sorrow." News of the castration swept Paris, and history records that the women of the city wept. Three of the assailants were captured. Two of them, said Abélard, "suffered the loss of their eyes and their genitals," the third was sent to prison, and Fulbert was deprived by a church court of all his earthly goods.

Despite Héloïse's entreaties, Abélard felt that his church career was ended, and his marriage, too. He ordered Héloïse to enter a nunnery and take the veil. She obeyed. He, himself, took the vow of a monk at St. Denis. Later he wrote his candid autobiography, and legend has it that when Héloïse read his words, she began a correspondence with him that was to become part of the literary heritage of the Western world. Her sensual love had survived the years of religious dedication. She would still be his mistress, she said, preferring "love to matrimony, freedom to a bond." Nor need he be jealous of any other mortal man. "It is God alone that takes Héloïse from you," she assured him: "Yes, my dear Abélard; He gives my mind that tranquility which a quick remembrance of our misfortune would not suffer me to enjoy. Just Heaven! What other rival could take me from you? Could you imagine it possible for any mortal to blot you from my heart? Could you think me guilty of sacrificing the virtuous and learned Abélard to any one but God?"

Unfortunately, this famous correspondence probably was not written in Héloïse's time. Scholars have since agreed that the letters are a brilliant forgery perpetrated a century after Héloïse's death.

In his later years, Abélard was accused of heresy for his bold writings and unorthodox teachings. He undertook a journey to Rome to defend himself before the Pope. At the priory of St. Marcel, near Chalon-sur-Saône, he fell ill and died while in his sixty-third year. Héloïse had his body interred in the gardens of the Paraclete, a priory of which she was the abbess, where she could visit him and look after his grave. She survived him by twenty-two years, not dying until 1164. Seven centuries later the pair were reburied in Paris in the Père-Lachaise Cemetery, where to this day they rest, side by side, beneath an ornate canopied stone tomb.

Although Héloïse symbolized a more refined and romantic type of mistress than had been known previously, the age in which she lived was still licentious and profligate. Customs and dress had changed, but not morals. And so the rise of the mistress was not impeded. The courtesan and the prostitute also flourished. Three hundred such Frenchwomen attended the Crusaders at the siege of Acre. Where nudity had once been fashionable, men and women sleeping naked and bathing in the nude together, the fashion now demanded that they wear clothing. But the garments worn proved more provocative than nakedness. Men attired themselves in short doublets, which focused attention on their private parts. The genitals were encased in *braguettes,* pouchlike containers that were the medieval version of the modern-day trouser flap. Women attired themselves in long linen dresses. These were laced high under the bosom to dramatize the breasts, and had holes in the bodice to reveal the nipples. Skirts were drawn skin-tight at the hips, to flaunt sex further.

Then gradually, after the peak of the medieval period, a significant change took place in the general attitude toward sex. This was the growth, in France, Italy, Germany, and England, of courtly or romantic love, and the harbingers of this love were the troubadours. These wandering singers gave to their centuries good manners, and grace, and chivalry. Their foremost patron was Eleanor of Aquitaine, who became Queen of France by marrying Louis VII and later Queen of England by marrying Henry II, and who, along the way, managed to have affairs with a wide variety of men ranging from an uncle to a Saracen slave. But while the troubadours sang of love, few of them desired it. Rilke is said to have remarked "that the troubadours feared nothing so much as the success of their wooing." Yet, it was enough that the troubadours spread the propaganda for romantic love. The knights, the roaming noblemen of medieval times, were to put it into practice.

The worship of womanhood was the contribution of the troubadours to an ancient world emerging into modern times. This, and a new word. For the troubadours originated the word *mistress*, employing it to mean the woman to whom they gave "the vassalage of love-service." But with the end of medievalism, it was to denote the woman who "illicitly occupies the place of wife."

The rebirth of civilization, the Renaissance, finally came. The mistress had her name, her identity, and her place, and she was ready to step into the pages of history.

The years of celebrity and esteem for the mistress spanned four centuries, those years between 1500 and 1900. After that, she declined. But in the four centuries of her triumph, she served with honor and distinction, and often she made her mark in politics and the arts.

Many great mistresses adorned the modern world. The need for these women remained constant decade after decade. Only the morality of each ensuing period, its ideals of beauty, the customs, the fashions changed. Each of these women was, in a sense, one woman—of infinite variety. But the backdrops, against which she played out her roles, were many.

In the years between 1610 and 1793, from Louis XIII to Louis XVI, in France, there was widespread tolerance of the mistress. She was as much a part of the aristocracy as those born to the blood. Sometimes she ruled from Versailles. Often, with shadows painted under her eyes to make her appear interesting and exhausted, she received male visitors while reclining in bed or changing her clothes. Filmy lingerie was yet unknown. Generally, linen undergarments were worn beneath dresses. Drawers were not in use. The mistress doused herself with perfumes and oils, but she did not bathe in water.

The position of the mistress was all the stronger because marital ties were so weak. Noble houses married off their children young, and these convenient, loveless unions remained marriages in name only. On reaching maturity, most titled husbands and wives went their separate ways. Adultery was quite acceptable. When the Maréchal de Richelieu came upon his wife in bed with another man, he had only one complaint. "Really, madame, you should be more careful," he protested. "Suppose it had been someone else who had found you like this?" Again, when Casanova met Marie Fel, the singer, he became aware of three young boys playing about her skirts. He was surprised that they bore no resemblance to one another. "Of course not," said Mme. Fel. "The eldest is the son of the Duc d'Annecy, the second of Comte Egmont, and the third is the son of Comte Maisonrouge." Casanova apologized. "Forgive me, madame. I had thought they were all your children." Madame smiled. "So they are," she said. It was the Abbé de Bernis who summarized the fashion: "When I entered life, it was thought ridiculous for a husband to love his wife, and vice versa. Marital constancy savored of the bourgeoisie."

Indeed, the bourgeoisie, the wealthy tradesmen and the middle classes, took a dim view of the mistress. Though some men of this station tried to imitate their betters, most chose to uphold fidelity. The French clergy and the poor, however, found much to admire in Versailles. The lower classes, when possible, found women in the cheaper cabarets, cafés, and bistros of the cities and towns, and in Paris a guidebook was published yearly listing the leading brothels, as well as the names and addresses of the outstanding courtesans.

Though from 1649 to 1658, under the puritanical influence of Oliver Cromwell, the mistress suffered in England, she quickly recovered after the Restoration. Between 1660 and 1685, with the encouragement of Charles II, she attained new heights of respect and power. Cromwell had inveighed against the "sins of incest, adultery and fornication." A woman caught in adultery suffered death; in fornication, a prison sentence of three months. With the return of Charles II, most penalties were lifted. And England rejoiced in a new sexual freedom.

The Restoration mistress wore low-cut gowns, hoopskirts, and high heels. The cult of the bosom was at its height. Since most Englishwomen were small-breasted, artificial breasts made of wax were introduced, and these were draped with kerchiefs or veils. Too, contraceptive devices had their first popularity. They had been introduced back in 1560 by Dr. Gabriello Fallopio, but his were crude sheaths of linen, and too uncomfortable to gain wide usage. Now a Dr. Conton, from whose name was derived the word *condom*, created less constricting contraceptives made of fish bladder and lambskin. Young rakes used them to prevent venereal disease, and mistresses passed them out to their lovers to prevent conception. Soon they were being openly advertised in the public press, and sold in all brothels, and the lot of the mistress was made easier.

There was little modesty: In England, the mistress might leave her carriage to relieve herself at the wayside, in full view of her retinue; in France, she might sit side by side with male friends, in the lavatory, conversing.

Since they had received the blessings of their sovereign, courtesans became national celebrities, and acceptable in all loftier society. In some homes, they were brought in to dwell under the same roof with the wife. Among the masses, prostitution mushroomed everywhere. One census credited London with fifty thousand whores, and Paris with eighteen thousand, though both figures were probably exaggerated. The trade was so profitable that entire families turned to it. In one instance, a Mrs. Leah Davis trained thirteen of her daughters to be prostitutes. Eventually, however, the market became so glutted that a night with a virgin brought only five pounds instead of the earlier price of fifty.

From 1799 to 1815, under Napoleon Bonaparte, the mistress again stood in official favor. In France, she wore loose garments, with the waist high and the bodice low. She wished to emphasize her bosom and minimize her waist. She used little makeup, and combed her hair with studied untidiness. She received male callers while arranging her toilette, and she did not trouble to hide her liaisons. In England, she was even more provocative, the most fashionable costume being "a thin transparent muslin veil" and nothing more. The mistress advertised her wares frankly, and had her affairs openly.

From 1852 to 1870, under Napoleon III—Napoleon the Little, as Victor Hugo called him—the mistress had her last moments of dazzling splendor. She was scandalous, but eagerly welcomed in the best circles. She was often showered with wealth. She set the fashion. She traveled widely and frequented the best spas. Rarely did she look toward England. For there, as she must have known, her obituary was being written.

Queen Victoria was on the throne, her reign covering the years 1837 to 1901. Sex continued to be enjoyed, of course, and the mistress, too. Like the early Christians, the Victorians were obsessed with sex, simply because they tried to repress it. Women's garments no longer fired the imagination. They became mounds of crinoline, steel-hooped skirts, petticoats, corsets, pantalettes. The middle class was dominant and prudery was its bulwark. Direct references to the human anatomy were reacted to with neurotic shock. In shops, displays of underclothing were folded to hide the portion that covered what extended below the waist. Women attended their physicians not with vaginal complaints but with liver trouble. Chicken breasts were referred to as bosom of chicken. This madness stretched across the sea to America, where a piano leg became a limb, and where a man's trousers became his lower garment. In the United States this folly of discretion was best reflected in the pages of *Godey's Lady's Book*, where the perfect hostess was advised "that the works of male and female authors be properly separated on her bookshelves." It was not an atmosphere in which the mistress might thrive. And when, at the turn of the century, Victoria died, the mistress all but died with her.

"The twentieth century," wrote Lesley Blanch in *The Game of Hearts*, "cast a long shadow before it, ominous and forbidding, and *la vie galante*, high gallantry, and the courtesan were all doomed."

Doomed in the twentieth century? The courtesan?

Not quite. Almost, but not quite.

But before anticipating and entering into the present, it might prove both illuminating and entertaining to continue this excursion through the scandalous past.

II

The Unfaithful
Wives

One exists with one's husband—
one *lives* with one's lover.

—HONORÉ DE BALZAC

THROUGHOUT HISTORY, the law has been relentlessly
severe in its punishment of the unfaithful wife. Undoubtedly,
the reason for this is that the law was written by men, for men,
to protect what all men esteemed highly—namely, private property.
Women were regarded as simply a special form of private property.
And on those occasions when this animate property wished to
disengage itself from its owner, the male spokesmen for order
and justice were deeply outraged.

In Athens, the statutes of Solon permitted a husband to rid
himself—in any way he wished—of a wife caught committing
adultery. In Rome, the robust, industrious Emperor Septimius
Severus, who was obsessed by the subject of adultery—although
his sons were permitted to scandalize the city with their debaucheries—ordered three thousand trials for this crime alone. As

in Athens, the injured husband was given the option of personally killing his erring wife, or of allowing the court to banish her from the country. With the growth of Christianity, the Bible became the last word in judgment on the fallen wife. The biblical edict was also harsh: "Such is the way of an adulterous woman; she eateth, and wipeth her mouth, and saith, I have done no wickedness." Early Christians informed the adulteress that she had indeed "done wickedness" and must be punished with death. The Puritans and the Pilgrims brought the same attitude of righteousness to the New World. The earliest American adulteresses were put in stocks or forced to wear a scarlet letter A, and, in 1638, three women in Massachusetts Bay Colony were condemned to death for committing the sin of adultery.

In almost all past ages and places, the married woman turned mistress had no voice and was given no mercy. In later, more enlightened times, the unfaithful wife was no longer put to death but, instead, made to suffer the bleak exile of social ostracism. Yet, many of these women deserved better from their contemporaries. When one searches into their lives, marriages, hearts, one feels obliged to sheathe the sharp edge of severity. For in knowing these women, in trying to understand the outer pressures or inner needs that drove them to revolt against law and society, one is tempted more often than not, to view them with a growing tolerance.

Adulteresses have abounded in every stratum of society. But three ladies in particular are memorable. Ranking among the most prominent in their groups, they possessed both wealth and high station. Not only did they lead colorful lives, but their lives were often exposed to public view, and so the details of their indiscretions are well-known to later generations. However, for every one of these, there were perhaps hundreds more whose notoriety was short-lived. The annals of adultery are crowded with the faded names of women almost lost to history. Before proceeding to the tales of prominent adulteresses, it might be useful to tarry briefly over the case of one typical fallen wife who enjoyed the limelight for a short period and was then quickly forgotten. She was Mrs. Catherine Earle, whose infidelity might have gone unproved but for a hole in the wall.

In the latter half of the eighteenth century, all of London was regaled by the divorce trial of Catherine Earle, who stood charged with adultery by her legal mate. She had been wedded to William Earle in 1750, and had brought him a sizable dowry. The dowry was not needed. Earle was wealthy, with an income of three thousand pounds a year, but money was not sufficient to satisfy his wife. One evening, while watching a play, she fell madly in love with Charles Holland, the leading man. In a frenzy of uninhibited passion, she wrote him, offering to become his mistress. The actor was astounded, but amenable. Gallantly, he accepted her offer.

To promote their love, the pair used the home of a Miss Gilbert, one of Catherine's friends. When William Earle became suspicious of his wife's protracted nocturnal visits to the spinster, he persuaded the mercenary Miss Gilbert to spy for him. In a moment of erotic inspiration, Miss Gilbert drilled a hole in the wall of her guest bedroom. Then, one winter's night in 1765, when Catherine and Holland had been given use of this bedroom, Miss Gilbert and a lady friend indulged in a rewarding session of voyeurism. At the trial, Miss Gilbert admitted that from her peephole she had seen "Holland kneel in front of Mrs. Earle, raise her skirts and kiss her knee." She described the act of adultery that followed in joyful detail. This unchaste activity was further corroborated by Catherine's maid. Once she had stood by at the theater while Catherine retired "for ten minutes to an adjoining bedroom" with the gifted actor. Understandably, the peers of the realm were sympathetic to William Earle. Quickly, he was returned to the happier state of single life. And almost as quickly, his faithless wife returned to the anonymity she had so recently desired.

Of more enduring memory as as adulteress, in the eyes of the English public, was Elizabeth Milbanke, known to history as Lady Melbourne. Her lineage was venerable. Her father was Sir Ralph Milbanke, descendant of a fine Yorkshire family. At seventeen Elizabeth was married to Sir Peniston Lamb, who was to become Baron Melbourne. He brought to their marriage a large fortune, which he had always used lavishly and now continued to squander; a mistress named Mrs. Sophia Baddeley, with whom he continued to correspond; and a passion for the hunt, the inevitable bottle of port, and the game of faro. Although he sat in Parliament forty years, he made but one speech. He was interested in neither current events nor advancement; his wife, on the other hand, was exceedingly interested in both.

The dark-eyed, shapely, companionable Lady Melbourne set up a fine house in London, conducted a brilliant salon, with herself as its center, and proceeded to devote herself to the opposite sex. Men were her study and her vocation. Save for her husband, none of them bored her. She was everything a man could wish for: attractive, amusing, intelligent, admiring, passionate, and compliant. While her husband busied himself at Almack's Club, she gave herself to many of her suitors, less for pleasure than to promote her social station and to improve the lot of her children. She had an affair with the popular Lord Coleraine. Gossip had it that he sold her to George Wyndham, third Earl of Egremont, for thirteen thousand pounds, and that she received a portion of this amount. Lord Egremont, who bred horses and collected art, later married another woman at the suggestion of Lady Melbourne. Eventually, she met the young Prince of Wales, who would become George IV, and danced with him—"in the cow style," an observer remarked, "but he was in ecstacies with it"—and briefly became his mistress. As a result of this affair, she was able to have her husband promoted from baron to viscount, and then, ironically, appointed lord of the bedchamber.

About London, Lady Melbourne's six children, four sons and two daughters, were known as the "Miscellany" due to their uncertain paternity. Her second son, William, was undoubtedly sired by Lord Egremont, her fourth son, George, by the Prince of Wales, while her first daughter, Emily, was by a lover whose identity remains unknown. Despite, or perhaps because of, her scandalous conduct, her friends included Fox, Sheridan, and, above all, Lord Byron. It was Byron whom she chose to advise when he had an affair with her son William's wife, Lady Caroline Lamb, and this advice was repaid by the poet's affection. "The best friend I ever had in my life and the cleverest of women," he wrote of her. "If she had been a few years younger, what a fool she would have made of me had she thought it worth her while."

Lady Melbourne died in 1818, far too soon to witness what might have been her greatest triumph—that of seeing her son William Lamb, the second Viscount Melbourne, become Prime Minister of England. Long after, William was seen nodding over a portrait of her. "A remarkable woman, a devoted mother, an excellent wife," he muttered, "but not chaste, not chaste."

At the time of Lady Melbourne's greatest infidelity, another lady of higher birth and rank was outdoing her in adulterous adventures, first as Princess of the Asturias and then as Queen María Luisa of Spain. She had been born a princess of Parma, and Carlos III, who had once ruled there, remembered her when he sought a bride for his son and heir, who was to become Carlos IV. Her adultery began before her husband ascended the throne, and was apparent to all except her royal mate. Once her husband, while still a prince, discussed adultery with his father. Said young Carlos, "It's difficult for a woman of royal rank to commit adultery. They have little opportunity because there are so few people of equal rank." Carlos III was incredulous, and could only reply, "What an ass you are, Carlos, what a blind ass."

It was not María Luisa's beauty that attracted lovers. Goya has pictured her for all time: the small, beady eyes; the beak of a nose; the shrewish mouth. Years later Napoleon Bonaparte would look into this dissolute face, and then comment, "María Luisa has her past and her character written on her face. It surpasses anything you dare imagine." Yet, though without grace, she was vital and clever. She was also lustful. Her lovers could never satisfy her, and, with one exception, each came to hate her in the end.

When her husband at last ascended the Spanish throne as Carlos IV, María Luisa already had a remarkable record of infidelity behind her. Kingship did nothing to enhance Carlos in María Luisa's eyes. He was a kindly, sentimental, overweight, sedentary man, possessed of an elongated nose. He was more attentive to his violin than to his wife, and he was, indeed, as his father had remarked, "a blind ass." María Luisa had, as early as the age of eighteen, been unfaithful to him with the youthful Conde de Teba. Next, for a brief period, she was the mistress of the aged Don Augustin Lancaster. Then followed Don Juan Pignatelli, whose father had been one of the Duchess of Alba's lovers. After Don Juan came Luis de Godoy, a musically inclined guardsman, who lasted until he introduced her to his younger brother. From that day on, the younger brother, Don Manuel de Godoy, a towering, dark-eyed, easygoing, uncommonly well-made provincial child, dominated the field.

In the period following December 1788, when María Luisa became queen, the young Godoy, sixteen years her junior, became the great love of her life, and he rose rapidly from the mean rank of army private to that of prime minister. But by then unfaithfulness had become a habit. Even as she submitted to Godoy, she sought new sensations elsewhere. One alternate favorite was Don Luis de Uruijo, secretary to a minister in the government. Uruijo, a fanatic Francophile, was made the head of state for a brief time, to appease Napoleon. Another favorite was an attractive guardsman named Don Manuel Mallo, upon whom the queen showered expensive gifts. Once, Mallo, in a magnificent carriage, passed beneath the balcony where Carlos IV, María Luisa, and Godoy stood. The king was astonished. "How can that fellow afford better horses than I?" The queen flushed. "I'm told that he has a fortune from the Indies." Godoy was amused. "Well, that's not what I've heard," he said. The king wanted to know exactly what he had heard. "Why," said Godoy solemnly, "I've heard that Mallo is kept by a very wealthy and very ugly old woman, whose name I cannot remember." Godoy could dare such insolence. For though María Luisa had many lovers, it was he that she truly loved.

Even in his most splendid hour, Godoy was known to the people as *El Choricero*, "the sausage maker" or "the pork butcher," for having been born in Estremadura, that province where the pigs of Spain were raised. At seventeen, the son of a noble, impoverished family, he came to Madrid to join the Royal Bodyguard. When María Luisa met him, his destiny was determined. He received from her a coach and six horses, and the rank of general. Curiously, his next promotion was not due only to the affection of his mistress. The king met and adored him. And in 1792, at the age of twenty-four, Don Manuel de Godoy was Duke de la Alcudia and Prime Minister of Spain.

Politically, Godoy was a disaster. Among other things, he challenged Napoleon, with the usual results, then joined Napoleon against Great Britain, and lost Trinidad for his country. His private life was equally hectic. Not only was he the queen's lover, but he maintained a mistress of his own choice. She was Josefa Tudo, and she gave him two sons. Eventually, he was also forced to take a wife because the king, showing a paternal interest in him, suggested that he marry. Godoy thought it politic to follow his sovereign's suggestion, and so in 1797 he was wedded to María Teresa de Vallabriga, the king's niece.

When Godoy encouraged the French to enter Spain, he helped fan the fires of a popular revolution. In 1808, after barely escaping with his life, he reached Bayonne with the aid of the French and was cordially received by Napoleon. Five days later Carlos IV and María Luisa, deposed, arrived. The ex-king's first words in exile were "Where is Manuel?" The three, husband, wife, lover—and soon a fourth, the lover's mistress—retired to Rome. In January 1818, María Luisa died. Three weeks later the king followed her to the grave. Next, Godoy's wife died, and his mistress, tired of exile, left him. He was alone and destitute. He moved to Paris and subsisted, in a second-floor apartment, on a pension of six thousand francs a year which was given him by King Louis-Philippe, a fellow Bourbon. Godoy devoted most of the forty-eight years of his loneliness to petitioning succeeding Spanish governments for restoration of his estates and to entertaining the French children who played in the Tuileries. Few of the youngsters imagined that this amusing, shabby old man had once opposed Lord Nelson, treated with Napoleon, and been the paramour of a powerful and faithless queen.

Although Napoleon Bonaparte had not respected María Luisa, he had been kind to her. But in Switzerland, during this period, dwelt an adulteress whom Napoleon respected but abhorred. She was known as Mme. de Staël, and Napoleon despised her for her aggressiveness, a characteristic the consul did not appreciate in women, and he persecuted her for her political meddling.

She was born Anne Louise Germaine Necker. Her father, Jacques Necker, a native of Switzerland, was one of the richest men in Europe (he had loaned the French government two million francs), and had been King Louis XVI's director of the treasury. Her mother Suzanne, a writer and the daughter of a Swiss Calvinist clergyman, was fair enough to have been loved by Gibbon. While working as a lady's companion in Paris, she had stolen her mistress's fiancé, none other than M. Necker. Raised in the sprawling château Coppet, on Lake Geneva, in an atmosphere highly charged and persistently intellectual, Germaine was a precocious child. At the age of five, invading her mother's salon, she cornered the ancient Duchesse de Mouchy and piped, "Madame, what are your views on love?"

With her parents, Germaine commuted regularly to Paris during her adolescence. There, at the age of fourteen, she first met Eric Magnus, Baron de Staël-Holstein, who was seventeen years her senior. He was the Swedish chargé d'affaires in Paris, and he was poor. Necker thought that he might make a good son-in-law, and bought him the post of ambassador for the next twelve years to make him more eligible. At the age of twenty, Germaine Necker became Baronne de Staël-Holstein—although she was known as Mme. de Staël—and from the very beginning she was unenthusiastic.

Since she had literary ambitions, she buried herself in writing. Two novels were quickly produced and published, and were dismissed by one biographer as "filleted Rousseau." In 1788, when she was twenty-two, Mme. de Staël produced her first political tract, *Lettres sur Jean-Jacques Rousseau*. Unfilleted Rousseau, it described Jean-Jacques Rousseau as a genius who "walked through life like a blind man" and had to be "guided like a child and listened to as an oracle." About this time, a daughter she had had by Baron de Staël died in infancy. Following her period of grief, Mme. de Staël temporarily neglected her husband and literature to devote herself to adultery, and not with one man but with several.

Physically, she was not attractive. Except for her large eyes and buxom figure, she was plain. She had, Gouverneur Morris decided, "very much the air of a chambermaid." She knew it, and pretended not to care, but she did care. For, she would later write Mme. Recamier: "I would gladly give half of the wit with which I am credited for half of the beauty you possess." But she did not need beauty to seduce men. She was clever, vivacious, aggressive, self-assured, thoroughly liberated, and possessed of the confidence of a daughter who is loved by her father.

Mme. de Staël was an energetic adulteress. Successively, she gave herself to Charles de Talleyrand, the Duc de Montmorency, and most often to the Comte de Narbonne, who she sometimes thought was the only man she ever loved. Narbonne, said to have been the illegitimate son of King Louis XV, was an army officer on active duty. This did not deter Mme. de Staël. Once, disguised in male uniform, she visited him in his tent. The by-products of their affair were two bastard sons and one novel, *Zulma*, written out of venom after Narbonne had left her. In her novel, she castigated him, writing, "He passed for a man of honor, because he was only perfidious and cruel in his relations with women." Yet, despite all of this extramarital activity, she found the time to bear her husband three children.

In 1794 she met the man who was to dominate the rest of her life. Her husband was in Sweden, and she was in Switzerland when she encountered Benjamin Constant, a twenty-seven-year-old Swiss who had been educated at Oxford and Edinburgh and who was to make his name as a writer and politician in France. Constant was tall, awkward, redheaded, and at first his appearance, Mme. de Staël admitted, "filled me with an insurmountable physical repulsion."

Apparently, this repulsion proved surmountable, after all. For, a short time after they met, their love affair began, and both were ecstatic. "One who has met her," said Constant, "can expect no greater happiness anywhere." It is thought that Mme. de Staël had a daughter by Constant, and that she was delivered of the child in her husband's Swedish Embassy in Paris.

Meanwhile, Mme. de Staël had fixed her sights on another male, but this one was less submissive to her will. The future Napoleon I was still only General Bonaparte, and in Italy, when he received a worshipful letter from Mme. de Staël. She lauded him for being "a Scipio," and she reproved him for his marriage to Josephine, writing him that "the union of such a genius with an insignificant little Creole unworthy to appreciate or understand him is a monstrosity." Napoleon brushed her letter aside with the comment, "The woman must be mad."

Thereafter, she persisted in her pursuit of Napoleon. Her real purpose was to impress her political ideas upon him—such as her opposition to his plan to overthrow the government of Switzerland —rather than make herself his mistress. But she was not above trying to bring him to her bed. Followed by her lover, Constant, she returned to Paris where she rejoined Baron de Staël and used her connections to meet Napoleon. When she finally met him, she experienced "a difficulty of breathing," and could hardly speak. However, by the time she encountered Napoleon a second time, she had found her voice. She tried to discuss politics, but admitted afterwards that this subject "wiped out all expression from his eyes, so that they might have been carved in marble." On the next occasion, she was more feminine and seductive. Unable to melt him, she said teasingly, "You are, then, not fond of women?" To which Napoleon replied, stonily, "I am fond of my wife."

Still, Mme. de Staël would not give up. Once, according to Paris gossip, she entered Napoleon's house in search of him. She prowled through the house, and located him alone in the bathroom. Napoleon roared out in protest against this assault on his privacy and modesty, and she replied coolly, "Genius has no sex."

In the end, she turned upon her hero. She began writing books attacking Napoleon's policies. He endured this, but when he heard that Mme. de Staël was conducting a salon where Constant, and others, voiced their sentiments against the first consul, his patience ran out. He decided to banish her from Paris. Immediately, she received an official order commanding her to withdraw at least forty leagues from the city. As for Constant, who had been elected to the Chamber of Deputies, he was to relinquish his seat at once. Mme. de Staël tried to persuade Napoleon to rescind the decree. He refused, announcing, "If Madame de Staël would be either a Royalist or a Republican, I would have nothing against her. But she is a perpetual-motion machine, stirring up the salons." And this was unforgivable.

However, Napoleon was not the only person Mme. de Staël had offended. By now, her husband, Baron de Staël, had also lost his patience with her behavior. He would not be cuckolded any longer, he told her, and they agreed upon a separation. When, in an effort to assert his manhood, the baron took a mistress, Mme. de Staël was not annoyed. But when he lost his ambassadorship, she cut off his allowance. Only upon learning that he was seriously ill did Mme. de Staël rejoin her husband, and she was present when he died in a provincial inn outside Paris.

After Mme. de Staël and Constant had been driven out of Paris by Napoleon, they devoted their exile to writing and traveling. They went to Weimar. Goethe thought her clever. Schiller had a reservation. "The only defect in her," he complained, "is her overpowering volubility." Finally, Goethe concurred, saying, "Her great ambition is to subjugate political men and to impress upon them the ascendency of her opinions."

She was writing at a relentless pace again. In fact, when her complete works were published in Paris thirteen years after her death, they ran to seventeen volumes. Her greatest success throughout the Continent was her romantic novel, *Corinne*. Lord

Byron, who had become Mme. de Staël's friend, told her, tongue in cheek, that it was a "very dangerous" novel "to be put into the hands of young women." He remembered that he then told her "that all the moral world thought, that her representing all the virtuous characters in 'Corinne' as being dull, commonplace, and tedious, was a most insidious blow aimed at virtue, and calculated to throw it into the shade. She was so excited and impatient to attempt a refutation, that it was only by my volubility I could keep her silent. She interrupted me every moment by gesticulating, exclaiming—'*Quel idée!*' '*Mon Dieu!*' '*Écoutez donc!*' '*Vous m'impatientez!*' . . . I was ready to laugh outright at the idea that *I*, who was at that period considered the most *mauvais sujet* of the day, should give Madame de Staël a lecture on morals; and I knew that this added to her rage."

On another occasion, approving of one of her books, Lord Byron wrote of Mme. de Staël: "She is sometimes right, and often wrong, about Italy and England; but almost always true in delineating the heart, which is of but one nation. . . ." Lord Byron appreciated her. As he told Lady Blessington, "Madame de Staël was certainly the cleverest, though not the most agreeable woman" he had ever known. And then he added, with full understanding of her, "She *thought* like a man, but, alas! she *felt* like a woman. . . ."

When she was not writing, she was *feeling*, continuing her emotional and erratic affair with Constant. She was never unaware of the importance of love. Her most widely quoted line was "Love is the whole history of a woman's life, it is but an episode in man's." She and Constant were rarely apart, and Constant was tiring of it. He could not be without her, yet he could not bear her domineering manner. Not only had she the arrogance of wealth—her father's will had left her three million francs—but she possessed the arrogance that comes with intellectual superiority. Constant was one of the few men who could match her in the drawing room, but the strain was telling. In his journal he noted: "I have never seen a better woman nor one with more grace and devotion. At the same time I have never seen a woman whose exigencies, without her being conscious of it, are more continuous, who absorbs more of the lives of those about her. . . ."

After her husband's death, Constant, exhausted, had asked her to marry him if "only to go to bed early." She had refused. Following her beloved father's death, Constant finally broke away from her, and she wrote him a distraught note which ended: "Farewell, my dear Benjamin, I hope that you at least will be near me when I die. Oh, I did not close my father's eyes; will you close mine?"

In 1809, Benjamin Constant secretly became the third husband of Charlotte von Hardenberg. But this was not long kept hidden from Mme. de Staël. Hearing of Constant's marriage to—as she put it—"some German woman," she threatened to demand repayment of a sum of money he had owed her father. In the end, she did not act upon her threat.

She consoled herself by writing another book, De l'Allemagne —Napoleon condemned the whole printing of ten thousand copies because it was "not French"—and by taking up with a devoted Italian army officer named Albert-Jean-Michel Rocca, whom she called John. The Italian was twenty-three years old and soon consumptive and Mme. de Staël was forty-five and soon pregnant. In 1813, three years before she would marry Rocca, she whisked him off with her on a triumphal tour of Russia, Finland, Sweden, England. In Russia, Mme. de Staël summoned Czar Alexander to discuss with her "the great issue of European policy." She wanted the czar to resist Napoleon's armies. She met with no success in this, for the czar and Napoleon had enjoyed a warm meeting at Tilsit earlier. One result of this meeting was that the czar confessed to an "infatuation" for Napoleon, and Napoleon said of the czar, "Had he been a woman, I would have made love to him." Nevertheless, Mme. de Staël emerged from her last great tour with many forensic victories, sufficiently so that Mme. de Chastenay was inspired to remark, "In the Europe of today there are three powers: England, Russia, and Madame de Staël."

After Waterloo, Mme. de Staël was back in Paris again, permanently, and once more presiding over a lively salon. Her health deteriorated steadily, and in Paris, during July of 1817, she died. She had been "torn to pieces," one biographer wrote, "by the furious struggle to be in herself . . . both the mistress and master of men." She was buried at Coppet, in Switzerland, at her father's feet. For, in truth, he had been the only man whom she had ever loved selflessly and without reservation.

III

The Portrait
by Romney

What else am I but a girl in distres—
in reall distress?

—LADY EMMA HAMILTON

EMMA HAMILTON, Maria Walewska, Pauline Bona-
parte, although of three different nationalities, had two things
in common. They were, all three, products of the same period in
history and they were typical of the unchaste wives of that period.
Of these three, there was one whose principal liaison made her
the most prominent and most spectacular adulteress of the eighteenth century. This was the woman born Emma Lyon, later to
be known as Emyly Hart, and finally as Lady Emma Hamilton.

She first met her great love, Lord Horatio Nelson, in 1793.
Lord Nelson was bewitched at once. He wrote to his wife: "I
hope one day to be able to introduce Lady Hamilton to you. She
is one of the most remarkable women in the world."

He did not mention that she was also one of the most beautiful.
Almost all men praised Emma's comeliness. She was tall and

full-bodied, yet possessed of delicate features. Her auburn hair, when let down, fell almost to the floor. Her forehead was wide, her eyes gray, her nose and mouth perfectly shaped. Goethe met her and reported that she was "exceedingly beautiful and finely built," and Sir Gilbert Elliott thought her appearance "incomparable." Gainsborough, Reynolds, and Lawrence concurred, and put her on canvas for posterity. Romney painted her many times, and, in 1791, he wrote: "Here is a young female of an artless and playful character, of extraordinary elegance and symmetry of form; of a most beautiful countenance, glowing with health and animation, turned upon the wide world." One of the few dissents came from Lord Fitzharris. She was "the most coarse, ill mannered, disagreeable woman" he had ever known, he said, but then he was referring to her character and not to her physical attributes.

Emma Lyon was born in May 1765 at Great Neston in Cheshire. Her father, a blacksmith, died when she was a child, and she was boarded out with her grandmother at Hawarden. At thirteen she was placed as a nursemaid in a doctor's family, but two years later she accompanied her mother to London to work successively as a clerk for a greengrocer, a domestic for a doctor, a companion for a wealthy woman, and a barmaid for a wine merchant. Shortly after this last employment, there occurred the incident that was to make Emma aware of the possibilities of bartering her feminine desirability in exchange for security. One of Emma's numerous cousins had been seized by the press-gang of a warship and forced into service, and his impoverished wife and child had turned to Emma for help. When Emma learned that her cousin's release could be obtained only through the recommendation of the ship's captain, she went to see the captain. He was John Willet-Payne, a young and emotional naval officer, later to become a rear admiral. He was moved by Emma—though less by her plea than by her physical charms. He made her a blunt offer. If she would become his mistress, he would free her cousin. Within the week her cousin was freed. Emma was seventeen when she gave birth to a daughter. The busy captain provided for the child for a few months, then forgot about both his offspring and her mother. The child was christened Emma, discreetly turned over to country relatives named Connor, and was supported for years through the charity of her mother's lovers.

Having employed her body once to good effect, Emma now employed it regularly. For a short time, she worked in a house of prostitution in Arlington Street. Then she worked for that shrewd but unstable medical quack, Dr. James Graham, an attractive Scot who conducted a Temple of Health in which the gullible might find rejuvenation through the use of "milk baths, balsamic tonics, dry friction, a magnetic throne, and a celestial bed for those who thought they were sterile." Emma posed, unadorned, as the doctor's Goddess of Health. She performed erotic dances in the nude around the Oriental celestial bed. This canopied bed, supported by twenty-eight glass pillars, was rented out for fifty pounds a night to those who sought cures for impotence as well as sterility. The naked Goddess also demonstrated the rejuvenating effects of Dr. Graham's mud baths.

Emma advertised her employer's wares effectively, and her own even more effectively. While Horace Walpole came to scoff—"the most impudent puppet show of imposition I ever saw, and the mountebank himself the dullest of his profession"—there were others who were more impressed. Titled young bloods flocked to the Temple for a glimpse of Emma, and one of them, Sir Harry Fetherstonhaugh, removed the Goddess of Health to his country home in Sussex.

Under Sir Harry's protection, Emma lived the fast life of the sporting set, until one day she met a house guest who seemed strangely retiring in this company of extroverts. He was the Honorable Charles Francis Greville, a phlegmatic dilettante, interested in antiques and art and the very antithesis of the young sports that had surrounded her. Emma was fascinated. She devoted herself to Greville, and earned the condescension of his love. Sir Harry was not amused. Emma was evicted and she was penniless. She dispatched a hysterical letter to Greville: "What else am I but a girl in distres—in reall distress? For God's sake, G. write the minet you get this, and only tell me what I am to dow. Direct some whay. I am allmos mad. O for God's sake tell me what is to become on me. O dear Grevell, write to me. Write to me. G. adue, and believe yours for ever Emly Hart." Perhaps Greville was as desirous of correcting Emma's orthography as improving her situation. At any rate, he could not resist. He brought her to London to become his full-time mistress.

They were together four years, during which she loved him

madly. As Greville's Galatea, she learned to dress and walk properly, to appreciate art and music, to converse with her betters, to act as hostess at his table. She sat for George Romney, who did one portrait after another of her. His obsession intrigued society, and a cult sprang up that was devoted to her beauty.

It was around 1783, when he was forty-nine years old and she was eighteen, that George Romney first set eyes on Emma. He had abandoned his wife and children in their country village twenty-one years earlier to seek his fortune as an artist in London. After an interlude of study in Italy, he had returned to London and had become as sought-after a portraitist as Joshua Reynolds. In this period, he saw Emma and was instantly smitten. He painted her as Venus, Circe, Mary Magdalene, Cassandra, Joan of Arc and as herself. She was, he admitted, the inspiration of all that was most beautiful in his art. "Her fascinations," according to one source, "had their share in aggravating that nervous restlessness and instability, inherent in his nature, which finally ruined both health and mind." Finally, three years before his death, morbid and depressed, Romney returned to his wife and family after a separation from them of thirty-seven years.

Despite his vast popular appeal, art critics and historians took a jaundiced view of Romney's talent and of his endless Emmas. One of the most respected, R. H. Wilenski, regarded Romney as "a neurotic with weak will, who longed to make the imaginative contribution which was actually made by Blake, took the line of least resistance and painted hack portraits all his life. Falling in love with Lady Hamilton, he told the world that she was a graceful creature with wet red lips and lustrous eyes and he painted her time and again with pictorial effects stolen from Reynolds."

But although Romney had the pleasure of Emma's presence as a model, and the opportunity to capture her on canvas, he never won her heart. For, at their first meeting, she still belonged to Charles Francis Greville, and in the years to come she would continue to be beyond the touch of all but Romney's brush.

Meanwhile, Greville knew that he had a good thing in Emma, and it is doubtful that he would have let it go had he not been in financial want. Since he was not a rich man, he could ill afford an extra mouth to feed. More important, he could not afford to neglect his future. His future lay in the hands of a wealthy uncle,

the aging Sir William Hamilton, Ambassador to Naples. When
Hamilton returned to London for a vacation, Greville determined to secure his position as the heir most likely to inherit the
old man's fortune. He did this by treating his relative to Emma.

It was during an afternoon in 1785 that Greville first introduced Emma to his uncle. Emma was then twenty, and Sir
William Hamilton was fifty-five. Sir William was a lean, healthy,
handsome, scholarly gentleman. He had puttered in the ruins of
Pompeii and studied the crater of Vesuvius, ascending that volcano
twenty-two times. He immersed himself in poetry and philosophy,
and he collected Roman coins and rare vases (the Portland vase
was one of his acquisitions). His hobby was classical beauty.
Emma was classical beauty incarnate, and Sir William was immediately interested. Greville could not have been more pleased. Sir
William's rich and religious Welsh wife of three decades had died
three years before. This could put Greville next in line for the
Hamilton estate—that is, if he could see to it that his uncle did
not marry again. The best way to assure this, Greville reasoned,
was to give the old gentleman a mistress. So he gave him Emma,
in return for a piece of property at Pembroke and a preferred
place in his uncle's will.

Emma was not informed of the bargain. She knew only that
she and her mother had been invited to Naples to be Sir William's
guests. She agreed to make the trip, if Greville would follow. In
1786 she went to Naples. Greville did not follow. Bewildered,
Emma begged him to rescue her, since her host's patronage was
becoming less platonic. Greville seemed unconcerned. And then,
at last, she understood. Emma was too well armed to be so coldly
bartered. She planned for herself a neat revenge. A year later, after
accompanying Sir William to London as his mistress, she made
him her husband, and ended forever Greville's dreams of inheritance.

As Lady Hamilton, Emma was not acceptable to the English
court, but she was welcomed with open arms in the court of
Naples. There, Marie Antoinette's sister, Queen Maria Carolina,
a domineering and licentious woman, and a fanatic Anglophile,
ruled. She took Emma under her wing, and they became the closest of friends. For seven years, Emma lived a contented life. She
did not love Sir William, but she respected him. She was the perfect hostess at their Palazzo Sessa on the Mediterranean and at

their seaside villa at Posillipo. They had their box at the San
Carlo Theater, their cabinets of Sir William's volcanic specimens,
their cosmopolitan friends, their festive life at the royal court. The
routine was regular, relaxing, thoughtless. There was sun all the
time, and passion hardly ever. And then, in 1793, when Emma
was twenty-eight, there arrived in Naples the British captain,
Horatio Nelson, and the lives of the Hamiltons were never to be
quite the same again.

Nelson was already an important personage but not yet an au-
thentic hero. He was a frail, shy, little man, wedded to a former
widow in London. He guided his ship, the *Agamemnon,* into the
Bay of Naples, and disembarked to deliver diplomatic messages to
the British ambassador. He took to Sir William at once. But he
was even more enchanted by the beauty, gaiety, and intellect of
Sir William's young wife, and deeply appreciative of the consideration she showed for his stepson Josiah, a midshipman on the
cruise. The visit was brief, but neither Nelson nor Emma forgot it.

Five years later, while in pursuit of the French, Nelson reached
the vicinity of Naples and tarried for a reunion with the Hamiltons. By now, he was a living legend. He had lost an eye and an
arm. These anatomical subtractions seemed to add to his heroic
stature. He had been victorious at the Nile, was a peer of the
realm and an admiral of the Royal Navy, and his name was on
the lips of all. Naples was agog. Emma, wearing a blue shawl
enbroidered with anchors, went aboard the *Vanguard* to welcome
him. But the sight of his living presence was too much. She
gasped, "Oh God, is it possible?"—and fainted into his remaining
arm.

When Emma recovered, she and Sir William staged a festive
dinner for Lord Nelson. Though there were eighteen hundred
guests in attendance, Emma was aware only of Nelson. He was
overwhelmed, both by her sincere admiration and her flawless
beauty. Other dinners followed, and after one Lady Minto would
report: "He is devoted to *Emma,* thinks her quite an *angel* and
talks of her as such to her face . . . and she leads him about like
a keeper with a bear. She must sit by him at dinner to cut his
meat, and he carries her pocket-handkerchief."

For Nelson, at forty, the discovery of Emma Hamilton provided
emotional fulfillment. He had not found this fulfillment in the
Norfolk parsonage where he had been raised with his ten brothers

and sisters, or in the affection given him by Frances Nisbet, the doctor's widow whom he had married when he was twenty-nine. Despite the belated honors heaped upon him by his country, he was a lonely and ingrown man. He needed an outgoing woman for reassurance and companionship. Emma was such a woman. When he found her, Nelson gave up his campaign against the French to further his alliance with the ambassador's wife.

While Nelson dallied under Sir William's roof, the French were on the move. Soon Nelson was forced to help evacuate Naples. Four weeks before the French reached the city, he embarked for Palermo, taking with him the Hamiltons and the king and queen. From Palermo, even as he awaited recall to England, Nelson took off on a five-week pleasure cruise with the Hamiltons. It was during this sea change that Nelson and Emma, forgetting their respective mates, began their historic affair. What made them determine to flout convention? Nelson was blindly in love with a woman who fed his ego. Emma, tired of obscurity in Italy and a sixty-eight-year-old husband, enjoyed the glory of being loved by a living legend. The consequences? Perhaps they thought they were above them. "In Nelson's mind," wrote C. S. Forester in *Lord Nelson*, "had begun to creep the faint idea that the ordinary laws of society did not apply to him . . . that this marvelous romance which held him enthralled was not one of the vulgar intrigues of which society rightly disapproved, but something of a far different quality, which he expected everyone, including his wife, to applaud and forward. . . . Emma's experience had hardly been one which would develop rigid ideas of chastity." By the time they returned to Palermo, Emma was pregnant.

The Hamiltons—and Nelson—decided to travel overland to England. In Vienna, Emma sang the "Nelson Aria" to Franz Josef Haydn's accompaniment, but in Dresden she and Nelson were cut dead by the elector and his court. In November 1800, they were in London. Gossip had preceded them. Scandal was in the air. While the Hamiltons settled in Piccadilly, Nelson returned to his own home to face his wife's wrath. Lady Nelson was concerned less with her husband's victory at the Nile than she was with his conquest of Emma. For weeks, insensitively, immaturely, Nelson tried to reconcile his wife with his mistress. He had the Hamiltons to his house; he suggested they move in under his roof.

He was appalled when Emma made it clear to him that Lady Nelson bore her an "antipathy not to be described."

The showdown came quickly. On a January morning in 1801, the Nelsons were breakfasting with their attorney. Nelson, as usual, was blithely praising or quoting his beloved Emma. Suddenly his wife stood up. "I am sick of hearing of dear Lady Hamilton, and am resolved that you shall give up either her or me!" Nelson stared at her, embarrassed and annoyed. "Take care, Fanny, what you say. I love you sincerely, but I cannot forget my obligations to Lady Hamilton, or speak of her otherwise than with affection and admiration." Trembling, Lady Nelson said that her mind was made up. She stalked out of the room, and forever out of Nelson's life.

The quartet was now a trio again. Only Lord Hamilton stood between Emma and Nelson. Although Emma was in her ninth month of pregnancy, her husband remained blissfully unaware. For one thing her condition was hidden by her regular attire—she favored full flowing Grecian garments—which resembled maternity clothes. For another, her husband, even when not ailing and in bed or fishing in the Thames or attending an art auction, was rarely with her and almost never in her bedroom.

But before the child could be born, Nelson was appointed vice admiral under Sir Hyde Parker and sent north to the Baltic. In his cabin, sitting before a framed portrait of Emma, Nelson employed his busy pen to scratch out more love letters than battle orders. He promised her that in eight weeks the campaign would be over. Then he would marry "the most beautiful woman of the age." They would have "peace in a cottage, with a plain joint of meat, doing good to the poor, and setting an example of virtue, even to kings and princes." At last the happy word came from Emma. She had borne him a daughter. He wished the girl named Emma, but Emma named her Horatia. The birth had been kept secret, and three days afterward, Emma was not only on her feet but on her husband's arm at a concert sponsored by the Duke of Norfolk. In letters sent by ordinary post, as a measure of safety against prying eyes, Emma and Nelson pretended that Horatia had been born to an imaginary couple named Thompson. (Later, Thompson would "die," and Emma would undertake the care of the child, and Nelson would legally adopt her.)

Nelson was ecstatic. When upon occasion he found a trustworthy messenger who would deliver a letter personally by hand, he gave full vent to his feelings. Addressing Emma as his "own dear wife," he wrote: "I love you, I never did love any one else. I never had a dear pledge of love till you gave me one. You, my beloved Emma, and my country, are the two dearest objects of my fond heart." And then a postscript: Kiss and bless *our* Horatia—think of that!"

For six months he dreamed of Emma, but he tried to concentrate on battle also. At Copenhagen, he reacted quickly and well. When, in the midst of an attack on the city's defenses, his superior officer, Sir Hyde Parker, signaled a retreat, Nelson brought his telescope to his blind eye and then reported that he could not see the signal. Nelson defeated the Danes. Parker was recalled, and Nelson was made a viscount. His task done, he hastened back to his increasingly corpulent Emma.

In London, Nelson went to see his blonde, blue-eyed daughter, who was being boarded with a widow named Gibson. Encouraged by this view of his offspring, he tried to persuade Emma to bear him another child. She protested that her health was failing. Frustrated, he diverted his energies into the purchase and furnishing of Merton Place, a country house in Surrey, for Emma and himself—and Lord Hamilton. Even though Hamilton was irritated by the nightly dinner parties and befuddled by Nelson's attentiveness to his wife, he never once doubted "the purity" of his host's friendship.

After the trio had lived in Surrey five months, Nelson's friend, Lord Minto, came visiting, and recorded a fair insight into Emma's hold on her lover. "She is in high looks, but more immense than ever. She goes on cramming Nelson with trowelfuls of flattery, which he goes on taking as quietly as a child does pap. The love she makes to him is not only ridiculous, but disgusting; not only the rooms, but the whole house, staircase and all, are covered with nothing but pictures of her and him, of all sizes and sorts, and representations of his naval actions. . . ."

A similarly harsh view of Emma, in this period, was held by William Beckford, a cousin of Sir William Hamilton and one of the true eccentrics in English history. Beckford, who never went to school because his mother did not believe in formal education and who inherited one million pounds from his father, had learned to speak Arabic and Persian from an Orientalist and to play the piano from Wolfgang Mozart. He published ten or eleven books, two under the pen names of Lady Harriet Marlow and Jacquetta Agneta Mariana Jenks. His masterpiece, admired by Lord Byron, was a romantic allegory set in Arabia and written in French. Its title was *Vathek*, and its plot revolved around a caliph who had built five palaces, each devoted to one of the five senses.

On a trip to Italy in 1780, Beckford amused himself in Venice with an elderly mistress who had earlier entertained Casanova, and then he went on to Naples to make the acquaintance of his cousin, Sir William Hamilton. Ten years later, in Naples again, Beckford had a reunion with Sir William during which he met the ambassador's fiancée, Emma Lyon, and he entertained the pair in England after their marriage. When Lord Nelson entered the picture, and was preparing to travel with the Hamiltons through the West Country, Beckford tendered another invitation. He addressed Emma as "the tutelary divinity of the Two Sicilies" and the "lovely and generous-minded Being." Emma replied in her usual flirtatious style. "How we often wished for you at Naples, for, believe me, Sir William loved you dearly; as to myself, I will not tell you whether I do or not, it will be a great pleasure for you to find out." But Beckford had something else in mind. As a commoner, he had been obsessed throughout his life with becoming a peer of the realm. Now, he offered Sir William and Emma an income of two thousand pounds a year for life, and Emma a five-hundred-pound lifetime annuity after Sir William's death, if she would use the Hamilton family's influence to gain him a peerage. The offer appealed to Emma, who wrote the queen suggesting it. The queen did not reply. Learning of this, Beckford remained undiscouraged.

"We must not give up easily," he wrote Emma. "If baffled one day—rise again the next and pursue your object with those omnipotent looks, words and gestures, with which Heaven has gifted you." Then, once more, Beckford pressed his invitation upon the Hamiltons and Lord Nelson.

The trio accepted, because an invitation to Beckford's estate at Fonthill in Wiltshire promised a bizarre adventure. Fonthill Abbey was the wonder of the English countryside. A decade before, Beckford had hired the leading architect of the day, James Wyatt, to build him the tallest private residence in all Europe.

First, a wall twelve feet high and seven miles in circumference was constructed to keep out sightseers. Next, Beckford's residence, the Great Tower, built by five hundred laborers employed in two shifts, half toiling by sunlight and half by torchlight, began to rise. Recently, the flimsy timber-and-cement structure, its central portion three hundred feet high and set on a narrow base, had been completed. This section contained eighteen cramped, unventilated rooms, all unmirrored (Beckford had an aversion to mirrors), all connected by corridors with niches for the maids to hide in when the master passed (Beckford had an aversion to most women). It was to this monstrosity, which would break in two and tumble to the earth in a windstorm some time later, that Beckford had summoned the Hamiltons and Lord Nelson to enjoy "a few comfortable days of repose—uncontaminated by the sight and prattle of drawing-room parasites."

In December of 1800, Emma and Lord Nelson, with Sir William trailing after them, arrived at Fonthill Abbey. They were greeted by a band playing "Rule Britannia," and led to their quarters by a Spanish dwarf in livery. Despite their host's promise to protect them from "drawing-room parasites," there were many other guests on hand, including Benjamin West, the American painter. During the two-day stay, Emma sang for the guests "in her expressive and triumphant manner"—as a London periodical reported—and then performed one of her skits in which she played "the character of Agrippina."

This meeting did nothing to further Beckford's chances of becoming a peer. Three years later, upon Sir William's death, Beckford gave up all hope for a title, and no longer pretended that he had any interest in Emma. In fact, with time, his aversion to her paralleled his feelings toward his household maids.

On one occasion, when asked if he had not thought Emma Hamilton fascinating, Beckford replied:

"I never thought her so. She was somewhat masculine, but symmetrical in figure, so that Sir William called her his Grecian. She was full in person, not fat, but *embonpoint*. Her carriage often majestic, rather than feminine. Not at all delicate, ill-bred, often very affected, a devil in temper when set on edge. She had beautiful hair and displayed it. Her countenance was agreeable, —fine, hardly beautiful, but the outline excellent. She affected sensibility, but felt none—was artful; and no wonder, she had been trained in the court of Naples—a fine school for an English woman of any stamp. Nelson was infatuated. She could make him believe anything. . . ."

And back in London, Nelson did believe anything his Emma said to him, and his idyll with his mistress continued as before. Only the frail presence of Sir William Hamilton disturbed the lovers. In April 1803, this presence was removed by death. It is doubtful that Hamilton had ever suspected that his wife's relations with Nelson were other than platonic. He could not have imagined, when once a small child was brought to Merton Place and introduced as the offspring of a Mrs. Thompson, that this was the product of Emma's infidelity.

In 1803, England declared war on France, and Nelson was given the Mediterranean command. Emma was left behind to run Merton Place on a small income willed her by Hamilton, and twelve hundred pounds a year given her by Nelson. She surrounded herself with rakes and bohemians and disreputable characters like the Duke of Queensberry, entertained constantly and lavishly, gambled steadily, and all but existed on champagne. After two years spent chasing the elusive French fleet across the Atlantic and back, Nelson returned to Emma, and was quick to disapprove of her extravagances and her friends. She won him over again, and in short days he was introducing her as his wife. "Unfortunately," he would add, "she is not yet Lady Nelson."

They had three weeks left. The French fleet had been located, and Nelson was recalled to duty. The night that he was notified, he and Emma had guests to dinner. Emma would not eat, but wept through the entire meal. Later, Nelson knelt before his sleeping five-year-old daughter and prayed for her. He kissed Emma and was gone. From his ship he sent a last message: "With God's blessing we shall meet again. Kiss dear Horatia a thousand times." Emma replied: "May God send you victory, and home to your Emma, Horatia, and paradise Merton, for when you are there it will be paradise."

On October 21, 1805, Nelson engaged the French at Trafalgar. During the battle, while pacing his quarterdeck with his flag captain, Thomas Hardy, Nelson was struck in the back by a French sniper's bullet. His shoulder was shattered and his spine broken. He was carried below, suffering great agony. For three hours, fingering the miniature of Emma around his neck, he lay dying.

He learned that the French had been crushed. But his mind was on his beloved. "Take care of my dear Lady Hamilton, Hardy," he begged his captain. "Take care of poor Lady Hamilton. Kiss me, Hardy." The captain kissed him on the cheek. Nelson looked at his doctor. "Remember that I leave Lady Hamilton and my daughter as a legacy to my country—never forget Horatia."

Nelson's doctor wrote of his death to Emma's mother, who in turn relayed the catastrophic news to Emma. She collapsed, crying, "My head and heart are gone," and was too ill to view the body when it lay in state at Greenwich Hospital or to be present when it was interred in St. Paul's.

She was alone with Horatia, and Nelson's child was not enough. She found solace in wine and gambling. The five-hundred-pound annuity Nelson had left her was attached to pay her mounting debts. She sold Merton Place to an Abraham Goldsmid for thirteen thousand pounds, but soon that money was dissipated in a round of wild parties. Mere survival became a problem, and at last she sold off Nelson's relics.

Nelson had left his mistress as a legacy to his country. His country could not have cared less. In 1813, swollen and shapeless, Emma Hamilton was arrested for debt and sentenced to one year in prison. After she had endured nine miserable months of confinement, an old friend of Nelson's, a sugar refiner named Joshua Jonathan Smith, bailed her out, gave her fifty pounds, and saw her off with her daughter to France.

She rented a farmhouse two miles out of Calais, struggled to send Horatia to an English day school nearby, and lived only that she might see her daughter "well settled." Her exile lasted seven months. She became increasingly ill, and, as Horatia recalled, "the baneful habit she had of taking wine and spirits to a fearful degree, brought on water on the chest." She died January 15, 1815, at the age of fifty.

Horatia was returned to England and placed with friends. She would later learn that Nelson was her father, but she was never to know that the fat, alcoholic, middle-aged lady with whom she had lived in France was her mother. And so, most objectively, she could compose Emma's obituary. "With all Lady H's faults,—and she had *many*—," Horatia would write, "she had many fine qualities, which, had [she] been placed early in better hands, would have made her a very superior woman."

IV

The Polish
Countess

I saw no one but you, I admired no one but
you, I want no one but you.

—NAPOLEON BONAPARTE

THERE WERE many victims of Trafalgar. Emma Hamilton, who lost her lover, Lord Nelson, was but a minor victim. A far greater victim was Napoleon Bonaparte, who lost control of the seas to the English. Yet, for Napoleon, there were some gains. Forced to pursue his conquests on land, Napoleon won victories over the Austrians and Prussians—and, incidentally, over Maria Walewska.

Although Maria Walewska's adultery was as well-known as any scandal in her time, her personal reputation suffered comparatively little. Other adulteresses who knew men illicitly used them largely to promote their own welfare or for sensual pleasure. Maria's scandalous conduct was largely selfless and romantic. She knew only one man illicitly, and when she submitted to him she was thinking of her country's welfare. She succumbed not out of need for security or love, but after acceding to the persistent logic of politics and patriotism. She was seduced by diplomacy. Love came later.

She was born Maria Laczinska in Poland during 1789. Her family was noble, ancient, and poor. She was raised in a dilapidated mansion, on a run-down estate, by a widowed mother. There were six children, including an older brother with gloomy prospects, and various sisters. When Maria was fifteen she came to the attention of Count Anastasio Colonna Walewski, an extremely wealthy landowner and master of a great castle at Walewice, near Warsaw. Count Walewski, a man of cheerless disposition, twice a widower, and sixty-eight years of age, began to court Maria. While Maria's mother was impressed, Maria was less intrigued. She wrote to a girl friend in Paris: "Walewski continues to bore me with his attentions." Maria's mother, aware that the choice was between poverty and a son-in-law whose youngest grandchild was ten years older than her daughter, pleaded with Maria to be practical. In 1805, at sixteen, Maria became the Countess Walewska. Her mother's debts were paid, the family estate restored, and her brother was sent to France to study.

Maria accompanied Walewski on an Italian honeymoon, found him "good and kind," returned to the castle to serve as wife-secretary, and gave him an ailing boy child. Dutifully, she devoted herself to motherhood and to campaigning for the freedom of Poland, a country which had already been twelve years in bondage to Russia, Austria, and Prussia.

In the bitter cold December of 1806, Napoleon Bonaparte, his star still in its ascendancy, arrived in Poland to do battle with the Russians and Austrians. Every Pole looked upon him as the country's liberator. Among these was Maria Walewska. In the village of Bronia, before Warsaw, she joined the hundreds of her countrymen who lined the streets to welcome the emperor. While Napoleon's horses were being changed, he gazed out at the cheering multitude. And then he saw Maria. She was seventeen and, according to the Napleonic scholar Frédéric Masson, "fair-haired, with big blue eyes full of simplicity and tenderness, and a smooth skin, and all rosy with the freshness of a tea-rose blushing with shyness." Napoleon removed his cocked hat, and tendered her a bouquet from the flowers that filled his carriage. And then he rode on in pursuit of the enemy.

After driving the Russians out of Pultusk—they escaped him in the heavy weather—he returned to Warsaw to await the spring thaw, while his troops made winter quarters on the right bank of the Vistula. He had time on his hands, and then he remembered the girl on the roadside in Bronia. He made inquiries. "Talley-rand got her for me," he said later. Through Prince Joseph Poniatowski, head of Poland's provisional government, Maria was invited to attend a formal ball Napoleon was giving at the Blacha Palace. Some instinct made her decline. But Polish patriots, and finally her husband, prevailed upon her to accept. Nothing must be done to irritate the liberator.

She arrived at the ball on her husband's arm. She wore an embroidered white tunic over her white satin gown. She wore no jewels. She was pale. Napoleon hungrily watched her every move. Finally, he sent an emissary to request a dance. She sent back word: "I do not dance." Annoyed, Napoleon crossed the room, brushing past guests, to confront her. She lowered her eyes. He stared at her, then suddenly blurted, "White does not go well on white, madame." She did not reply. He moved closer. "Why would you not dance with me? I had expected a far different welcome." He turned on his heel and left. Maria hurried home.

The following morning there were flowers and a note:

> I saw no one but you, I admired no one but you, I want no one but you. Answer me at once, and assuage the impatient passion of
>
> N.

Napoleon's blunt declaration both repelled and frightened Maria. She told the messenger that there would be no answer to the note. The following morning Napoleon wrote again. Maria would not open his letter. But already word of the emperor's desire was out. Prince Poniatowski appeared, opened the letter, and read it to her:

> Did you not like me, madame? I had reason to hope you might. Or perhaps I was wrong. While my ardor is increasing, yours is slackening its pace. You are ruining my repose! Ah! grant a few moments' pleasure and happiness to a poor heart that is only waiting to adore you. Is it so difficult to let me have an answer? You owe me two.
>
> N.

Still Maria would not reply. The emperor persisted. But now, shrewdly, he struck at Maria's most vulnerable defenses. He promised more than love. He hinted that Maria's response might determine his interest in Polish liberation. He wrote:

> There are times—I am passing through one now—when hope is as heavy as despair. What can satisfy the needs of a smitten heart, which longs to throw itself at your feet, but is held back by the weight of serious considerations, paralyzing its keenest desires? Oh, if only you would! No one but you can remove the obstacles that keep us apart. My friend Duroc will make it quite easy for you.
>
> Ah! come! come! You shall have all you ask. Your country will be dearer to me, once you have had pity on my poor heart.
>
> N.

Through his aide, General Géraud Duroc, Napoleon let the contents of his latest appeal be spread among the members of the Polish provisional government. Their reaction was precisely what he had expected. They saw at once, in the person of the reluctant Maria, a means of obtaining the restoration of their nation. Dozens of these aristocrat patriots called upon her. She refused to see them, pleading illness. They begged Count Walewski to intervene. What the aged nobleman's true feelings were in this affair cannot be known. Did he attempt to resist the pleas of his countrymen? Did he yield, hoping Napoleon's interest in his wife was merely platonic? Or did he agree to sacrifice his wife's honor for the sake of Polish autonomy? Whatever he felt as a husband, Count Walewski forced his wife to receive the Polish patriots.

They begged Maria, on behalf of twenty million Poles, to visit Napoleon. She was too distraught to be evasive. She demanded to know whether they were asking her, in so many words, to become the emperor's mistress. They replied that they were asking nothing of the kind. They wanted her to visit Napoleon so that she could plead personally and persuasively for Polish independence. But if it were necessary to become his mistress to help her country's cause, she must be prepared to make the sacrifice. They produced a written petition, signed by all the members of the group. One of them read it to her:

"If you were a man you would give your life to the just and

noble cause of the Fatherland. As a woman there are other sacrifices you can make and which you should force yourself to make,
painful as they may be.

"Do you think Esther gave herself to Ahasuerus because she
loved him? The terror he inspired in her was such that she fainted
at his glance. Was that not proof that love had no part in that
union? She sacrificed herself to save her nation—and she had the
glory of saving it.

"May we be able to say the same for your glory and our happiness!"

Broken and miserable, Maria agreed to see Napoleon. One
imagines she did not look at her husband.

The first intimate meeting with Napoleon was a surprise.
She did not know what to expect, but certainly she did not expect
compassion. As a matter of fact, Napoleon's mood was anything
but gentle. For years he had merely snapped his fingers to be served
a woman of his choice. Maria's melancholy beauty, her perfect
figure, her imperfect French, her very resistance, inflamed him.
"The day after the ball he kept getting up, walking about the
room, sitting down and getting up again," recalled Constant, his
valet. Learning that two of his young aides had been seen flirting with Maria, he promptly transferred them to the front lines.

When, at last, he saw her alone in a private room of the palace,
and she sat in an armchair before him, he struggled to restrain
himself. He knelt before her and kissed her hands, then took her
in his arms and kissed her until she tore free and made for the
door. But he caught her, forced her back to the chair. He declared
his love. She wept. He was responsive to her fears, and suddenly
all gentleness. He spoke to her of her beloved Poland and his
plans to make it independent again. He questioned her about
Count Walewski. Why had she wed so old a man? She made her
last protest against committing adultery: "What has been joined
together on earth can be severed only in Heaven." Luckily, Duroc
appeared too soon. "Already?" asked Napoleon. Then, to Maria,
"Well, my sweet and plaintive dove, go home and rest. Do not
fear the eagle. . . . In time you will come to love him, and in all
things you shall command him."

Thus, unscathed, Maria returned to Count Walewski. But unscathed for one night only. The next morning she woke to a bou-

quet of diamonds, a bouquet of flowers, and a new plea from the emperor:

> Maria, my sweet Maria, my first thought is of you, my first desire is to see you again. You will come again, won't you? You promised you would. If you don't, the eagle will fly to you! I shall see you at dinner—our friend tells me so. I want you to accept this bouquet: I want it to be a secret link, setting up a private understanding between us in the midst of the surrounding crowd. We shall be able to share our thoughts, though all the world is looking on. When my hand presses my heart, you will know that I am thinking of no one but you; and when you press your bouquet, I shall have your answer back! Love me, my pretty one, and hold your bouquet tight!

> N.

Maria reacted with anger. All thoughts of patriotism vanished. The diamonds were too obvious a payment for her body. She returned them, and the flowers. Duroc came pleading, with lofty promises of Poland's freedom. She did not trust him. Left alone, she considered suicide, then flight. She dashed off a note to her husband. She told him that she had seen Napoleon. She added: "I came out unharmed, promising to return this evening. I cannot keep that promise, for now I know too well what would happen."

She did not deliver the note. She did not run away.

That evening she attended Napoleon's dinner, and throughout the meal she avoided his gaze and exchanged no words with him. When it was over, and the guests had been sent home, she was asked to remain. She was led to a private room. Presently Napoleon appeared. His face was clouded, and his manner brusque. "I scarcely expected to see you again," he said. "Why did you refuse my diamonds and my flowers? Why did you avoid my eyes at dinner? Your coldness is an insult which I shall not brook." She had confirmed his low opinion of her people. She was exactly like all the other Poles, proud, superficial, emotionless. But he had not given up. "I will have you know that I mean to conquer you. You shall—yes, I repeat it—you shall love me! I have made your country's name live once more. The Polish race still exists because of me." He pulled free his pocket watch and held it up. "See this watch which I am holding in my hand? Just as I dash it to fragments before you, so will I shatter Poland if you drive me to desperation by rejecting my heart and refusing me your own." With that, he slammed the watch to the floor, smashing it into a hundred pieces. Maria screamed, and fainted.

When she recovered consciousness, and found that her clothes were in disarray, she realized that she had been violated. Napoleon was ashamed and apologetic. She lay too stunned to hate. Later, Duroc was summoned, and he carried her to a palace suite. For a while, she slept. When she awoke, Napoleon was waiting. Thereafter, he was thoughtful and tender. He spoke sincerely of himself, his hopes and dreams, and of Poland.

Incredibly, in the days that followed, her affection for him grew. She no longer thought of her husband and her shame. She began to look forward to visiting Napoleon. At eighteen, she had known only the love of a man who was seventy. Napoleon, at thirty-seven, was virile, though lacking a well-developed physique. "Napoleon's hands and feet were extremely small," wrote Dr. C. MacLaurin in *Post Mortem*, "his skin was white and delicate; his body had feminine characteristics, such as wide hips and narrow shoulders; his reproductive organs were small. . . . There was little hair on the body, and the hair of the head was fine, silky, and sparse."

In Paris, the Empress Josephine, that faithless forty-three-year-old Creole who had not given Napoleon an heir, heard of the affair. She wrote that she would join him. He wrote that he would not think of it. The climate was not right for her—as indeed it was not. "I am more disappointed than you," he told Josephine. "I should have liked to pass the long nights in this season with you." But to his friends he wrote in a different tone, hinting at the source of his new high spirits. To Joachim Murat he wrote: "My health has never been so good, so much so that I have become more gallant than in the past."

When the Russians mobilized troops in East Prussia, Napoleon hastily returned to the field. While he battled the enemy to a stalemate, he found time to send daily messages to Maria, who had traveled with her mother to Vienna for a rest. Another winter had come. Napoleon took up quarters at the fortified Prussian castle of Finckenstein. He was nervous and lonely. He sent for Maria. Escorted by her brother, a captain in the Polish lancers, she came to him.

She had her own bedroom, with a huge fireplace and a four-poster, adjoining Napoleon's bedroom. While Napoleon worked, she read or did embroidery. When he was free, they dined together, talked unceasingly, and made love. She enjoyed the power that she held over Europe's leading figure. "It is my great privilege to be a leader of nations," he said to her. "Once I was an acorn; now I am an oak. Yet when I am the oak to all the others, I am glad to become the acorn for you." The pretense that their affair was based on politics was abandoned. Although Napoleon helped create a new Polish ministry and reestablish a Polish army, he confessed that he could not liberate Poland. But Maria's affection for him did not diminish. "I love your country . . . but my first duty is to France," he told her. "I cannot shed French blood in a foreign cause." When he left her in the spring, after two and a half months together, she gave him a ring which was engraved inside: "When you have ceased to love me, remember that I love you still."

They were not long apart. Even though he had several casual affairs, he missed Maria. When he learned that she was pregnant, he summoned her to Paris. She arrived in January 1808, accompanied by her brother and her maid. Napoleon settled her in a house at 48 Rue de la Victoire, and ordered his doctor to examine her daily. She lived quietly, never using the box he had reserved for her at the Opéra. When she went out, usually at night, it was to visit with him in the Tuileries. The idyll was happy but brief. Her pregnancy ended in a miscarriage, and soon Napoleon was on the move again.

After crushing Austria at Wagram, Napoleon took up residence in the palace of Schönbrunn in Vienna, and before long sent for Maria. He found her a cottage nearby, and for three months he saw her almost every night. It was their last period together as lovers, and when it had ended Maria was once more pregnant.

Returning to Paris, Napoleon was obsessed with the idea of having a legitimate heir. In 1807, to prove that the failure was Josephine's and not his own, he had produced a natural son by one Mlle. Denuelle de la Plaigne, a woman who read aloud to his sister Caroline. The boy grew up to become Count Léon and die a pauper in 1881. Now, Maria Walewska's pregnancy held promise—yet, he must have a legitimate heir. Impatiently, he thrust aside Josephine, and in April 1810 he married Marie Louise, the tall, brown-haired, cowlike daughter of the Emperor of Austria. He was delighted with his Hapsburg from the start. "You should all marry Germans," he advised his circle. "They are gentle, good, unspoiled, and as fresh as roses."

No sooner had Napoleon remarried than he heard from distant Walewice that on May 4, 1810, Maria had borne him a son, Alexandre Walewski, whom Napoleon would make a count. Excited by the news, Napoleon asked Maria and the boy to visit him. He received them in the Tuileries, affectionately held the child, spoke of making him King of Poland one day, and conferred upon his mother a pension of ten thousand francs a month. Maria and Alexandre were next presented to Marie Louise, who, not knowing that they were Napoleon's mistress and natural son, greeted them with indifference. From Malmaison, the discarded Josephine sent word that she would like to meet Maria and see Alexandre. Maria obliged.

In the four years that followed, Maria returned to Poland, effected a reconciliation with Count Walewski, and resumed her old life at Walewice. Throughout her homeland she was a legend —Napoleon's "Polish wife"—and even the great patriot, Thaddeus Kosciusko, called upon her to pay homage. In the spring of 1811 she heard that Marie Louise had given Napoleon his long-desired legitimate heir—Joseph Charles, later Duke of Reichstadt—who would be known as L'Aiglon, and die of tuberculosis at the age of twenty-one. In 1812 Napoleon was faced with a debacle in Russia. Fleeing the Cossacks outside Warsaw, he considered halting to visit Maria. But the instinct for self-preservation overcame this romantic notion. In 1814 he abdicated and went into temporary exile on the island of Elba.

He had been on the island five months when Maria disembarked from an English vessel to visit him. She was accompanied by their son, four-and-a-half-year-old Alexandre, and her brother and sister. Napoleon kissed her hand warmly, bounced his son on his knee, and assigned them to rooms in his cottage while he slept in a nearby tent. He would permit Maria only two days on Elba for fear that her presence might give Marie Louise an excuse not to join him. He had pleasure watching the lively boy play games with his grenadiers. Once he asked him what he wanted to be when he grew up. The boy thought he wanted to be a warrior like Napoleon. He added that he loved Napoleon. "Why do you love him?" asked Napoleon. The boy had his answer: "Because he is my papa, and Mama told me to love him." As for Maria, she gave Napoleon gossip about the new French government and the public dissatisfaction with it, and she offered him all her jewels. He refused to take them. In fact, he gave her a gift of sixty-one thousand francs, since the royal pension he had granted her was no longer being honored. On their last night, he hugged Alexandre, whispering, "Good-bye, dear child of my heart." And then, through his telescope, he watched Maria's ship sail for Leghorn.

There followed his return to the mainland, and the Hundred Days. In Paris, he received Maria Walewska for the last time. Ahead lay Blücher and Wellington—and Waterloo. He spoke to Maria privately, and then publicly he held her hand in a final farewell.

After his defeat at Waterloo, Napoleon abdicated his throne, and threw himself upon the mercy of his British captors. The British shipped him off to the lonely island of St. Helena in the South Atlantic. There, in October of 1815, Napoleon began an exile that would end only with his death six years later.

Napoleon's empress, Marie Louise, had refused to share his earlier exile on Elba. Instead, she had returned with their son to her native Austria. When Napoleon threatened to have her kidnapped and brought to him, she determined then never to see him again. After being told the news of his current exile to St. Helena, she merely nodded and said, "Thanks. By the way, I should like to ride to Markenstein this morning. Is the weather good enough to risk it?" During her husband's second exile, Marie Louise became deeply involved in a love affair with Adam Albrecht, the Count von Neipperg, who originally had been assigned to guard as well as spy on her. This one-eyed Austrian had once received a decoration from Napoleon, whom he detested. Marie Louise dwelt with Neipperg in the toy kingdom of Parma —and was to give him three children—while on St. Helena, Napoleon excused her adultery and commanded that, upon his death, his heart be preserved in spirits of wine and sent to his "dear Marie Louise."

He might better have given his heart to Maria Walewska, for she loved him to her last hour. Napoleon had been on St. Helena a year when he heard that Maria Walewska, finally widowed, had remarried in Brussels. Her new husband was General d'Ornano, a French officer, a Corsican and a distant cousin of Napoleon's who had served in the Imperial Guard at one time. Napoleon was pleased for her and for their son. He would have been even more pleased to know that his son Alexandre would one day be appointed France's Minister of Foreign Affairs by Napoleon III.

Although Maria Walewska's love for Napoleon remained steadfast, she had great affection for General d'Ornano. She gave d'Ornano a son, but knew only a year of marital happiness. In 1817, aged twenty-eight, in the house in Paris that had been the emperor's gift, she died. The last word on her lips was—"Napoleon."

V

The Canova
Model

With the finest and most regular features imaginable she combined a most
shapely figure, admired (alas!) too
often.

—COUNTESS POTOCKA

OF NAPOLEON BONAPARTE'S three sisters—"the three
crowned courtesans," they were called—only one stood by his side
during his first exile, on Elba, and only one persistently petitioned the British government for permission to live with him
during his last exile on the isolated isle of St. Helena. This sister
was Pauline Bonaparte.

Her loyal devotion to her brother, her willingness to share his
martyrdom, amazed those who had known Pauline well. For her
life, until then, had been a monument to self-indulgence and
frivolity. Unique among the adulteresses of the period, she had
an attitude toward the marriage tie and infidelity that was re-
freshing. She performed without any feeling of guilt. She was as
amoral as a cat.

Her physical beauty, the fulcrum of her existence, was preserved for posterity by Antonio Canova, an Italian sculptor who rose from a poor family of stonemasons to become the Marquis of Ischia. Canova, whose chief patron was Pope Clement XIV, had executed some commissions for Napoleon in Paris. It was quite natural that Canova immortalize Napoleon's sister Pauline in marble. To this work, evidently, Canova brought not only his hands but his heart. Of all Canova's outstanding pieces of sculpture—and many grace the Louvre, the Pitti Palace, the Vatican, the Hermitage in Leningrad—it was his nude sculpture of Pauline that brought him the most renown.

Canova's Pauline, representing a taunting, sensuous Venus, described in one guidebook as "pensive, a little amused," may still be found reclining in a roped-off area of the Villa Borghese in Rome. Canova's Pauline seems to belong to the days of the Caesars. Perhaps her nose is too straight and prominent and her chin too sharp, but the full female body—from the graceful neck and shoulders to the perfect curve of the breasts to the generous fleshy hips is magnificent.

"No one would have ventured to contest her right to the apple which, it is said, the sculptor Canova handed to her after he had seen her unclothed," stated Countess Potocka. "With the finest and most regular features imaginable she combined a most shapely figure, admired (alas!) too often." Her nakedness so stimulated Canova that he had difficulty finishing the task of pressing wet clay to her body. Her willingness to pose nude shocked many of her contemporaries. One lady asked how she could bear to do it. "Why not?" replied Pauline. "It was not cold. There was a fire in the studio."

All who knew her agreed that her small body was without blemish. If faults were to be found, they were to be found in her character. According to the poet Arnault: "She was an extraordinary combination of perfect physical beauty and the strangest moral laxity. If she was the loveliest creature one had ever seen, she was also the most frivolous. She acted like a schoolgirl. . . ." She enjoyed mimicking famous personages, she loved jokes and horseplay, and she despised intellectual conversation, especially when it concerned history, music, or painting. Her cult was her flesh, and with admirable generosity she deprived few admirers of sharing its delights with her.

Napoleon had long been aware of his sister's amiable and obliging nature. She had hardly attained maturity when she had fallen in love with a man much older than she was, and she had also flirted with most of Napoleon's General Staff. She was sixteen when Napoleon determined to remove her from temptations that could precipitate a scandal. He cast about for an eligible husband and settled upon one of his trusted aides, twenty-four-year-old General Victor Emmanuel Leclerc, a blond, clean-cut, humorless young man of substantial wealth. Leclerc, blindly devoted to Napoleon, was given to imitating his master's walk, talk, and dress. He was pleased by the opportunity to become Napoleon's brother-in-law, and enchanted by Pauline. They were married in June 1797. A year later Pauline bore a son whom Napoleon named Dermide, after a character in the poems of Ossian. The boy Dermide would die at the age of four.

Shortly after their son was born, Leclerc and Pauline were ordered to the West Indies by Napoleon. There, in the Caribbean, the distant French colony of St.-Domingue—later to be known as Haiti—was in a state of turmoil. The prosperous tropical colony, which produced sugar, coffee, cotton, was inhabited by French planters, Negro slaves, mulattoes, and a minority of native Indians. When the French government had granted the mulattoes certain political privileges, as well as the right to acquire land, the French planters in Haiti resisted. As allies in this resistance, the planters called in English and Spanish troops. Immediately, a former black slave who had become a physician, and then turned soldier and statesman, François Dominique Toussaint L'Ouverture, had determined to free his fellow blacks from slavery by attempting to overthrow the French planters and drive out the English and Spanish soldiers. Napoleon had sided with Toussaint, and the revolution was successful. One problem remained: Napoleon felt that his black partner had saved the island for France; Toussaint believed that he had rescued Haiti from all foreign white domination.

When Toussaint made himself governor of Haiti, declaring that he was "the Bonaparte of Santo Domingo," the real Bonaparte of France was less than flattered. Fearing that the colony might be lost to France, Napoleon acted with dispatch. He gave his brother-in-law, General Leclerc, the assignment of crossing the Atlantic with twenty-five thousand troops to restore French control and revive the institution of black slavery. As Leclerc prepared to leave for Haiti, Pauline was ordered by Napoleon to accompany her husband. To Pauline, whose fidelity to a husband or to any one man always took second place to her comfort, the idea of leaving Paris for some hot primitive pesthole was unthinkable. She refused to go along. In a temper, Napoleon had her locked in a litter, guarded by six grenadiers, and carried aboard Leclerc's ship by force.

Surprisingly, once she arrived on Haiti, Pauline enjoyed the island. She found that she could give parties and balls, and behave just as she had in France. Thus insulated inside her Paris-away-from-home, Pauline had little interest in the violence raging outside her door. Leclerc and his French soldiers were engaged in a fierce struggle with Toussaint and his blacks over control of the sweltering, fever-ridden island. At last, Leclerc suggested a truce, and he persuaded Toussaint and his followers to lay down their arms temporarily while talks were held. The moment that Toussaint was disarmed, he was placed under arrest by Leclerc, shipped off to France, and locked up in the prison of Joux for life. In his jail cell, betrayed and starving, Toussaint died in 1803.

Meanwhile, in Haiti, General Leclerc reigned as master of a portion of the island and prepared to colonize the Territory of Louisiana in America. But soon, General Leclerc was faced with an enemy more formidable than Toussaint had ever been. Yellow fever raged through the French colony, and even Pauline abandoned frivolity to enlist in helping nurse and transport her husband's ailing soldiers. Finally, Leclerc himself was stricken by the fever. His illness was fatal. Pauline was beside him every moment of the week before his death. Immediately following his death, in the emotion of utter grief, Pauline cut her long hair and covered Leclerc's body with it. Then she had him embalmed and laid in a costly lead coffin, ready for burial when she reached France. She accompanied the body from Haiti to Toulon to Paris, where the funeral Mass was reported to have been one of the most magnificent of its day.

Once back in Paris, and with her husband's remains laid to rest, Pauline abruptly ended her mourning. There were beautiful men everywhere, and Pauline wanted to enjoy them, one and all. She resumed the flirtatious behavior that had preceded her marriage. Her lovers were a roll call of royalty and the celebrated, among them François Talma, the tragedian of the Théâtre Français de la Richelieu and one of Napoleon's favorite actors.

Again, to preserve her reputation, if not her chastity, Napoleon sought a husband for his acrobatic sister. A prospect soon appeared in the person of Prince Camillo Borghese. The prince proved to be a charming, brainless twenty-eight-year-old Italian Croesus who had recently inherited a great fortune as well as one of the world's finest diamond collections and the art-crammed Villa Borghese in Rome. Pauline was intrigued. Napoleon approved. Onlookers, who knew Prince Borghese for a nitwit and nothing more, could not understand. Said the Duchesse d'Abrantès of Prince Borghese, "To give oneself to him was to give oneself to nobody." Pauline apparently decided to overlook Prince Borghese's shallowness and concentrate on his most attractive attribute—his wealth. The marriage took place at Mortefontaine on November 6, 1803, and was attended by Pauline's mother, her sister-in-law Josephine, and her uncles Joseph and Louis. The marriage brought Pauline not only a husband but an annual allowance of seventy thousand francs, a portion of the Villa Borghese in Rome in her own name, two carriages, and numerous other material advantages.

No sooner was she the wife of Borghese than Pauline entered upon the most extravagant and licentious period of her life. She bounced from bed to bed. Observers coupled her name with that of Messalina. Why did she so quickly commit adultery? It has been suggested that Prince Borghese was sexually impotent—or incompetent. General Paul Thiebault insisted that it was the former. A biographer of the Bonapartes, David Stacton, thought that it was neither. The problem, wrote Stacton, was that Prince Borghese "somewhat disappointingly had a very small penis. Pauline, whose nymphomania was periodic but intense, scorned all but very large ones." Still, one senses that—impotency, incompetency, diminutive penis aside—had Prince Borghese been a Casanova, it would not have been enough. Pauline was sexually insatiable. She needed many men, and needed to be constantly reassured that they all thought her ravishing. Within a year, after she had openly had an affair with a French count, she and Borghese were separated. Napoleon would not countenance a divorce.

Few women, before or since, have lived as luxuriously or as sensuously. She had six hundred dresses, millions of dollars' worth of jewels, and she traveled from spa to spa in a carriage drawn by six horses. When she settled in Neuilly, Napoleon gave her 130,000 francs a month to add to the Italian fortune she already possessed.

Unlike most Frenchwomen, Pauline made a fetish of the bath. Her garments were so transparent, and her body so frequently exposed, that she felt that cleanliness was a necessity. She bathed every morning in a tub filled with twenty liters of milk mixed with hot water. Daily, after disrobing, she had her young Negro servant, Paul, carry her to the tub and place her in the milk and water. When friends thought this intimate exposure to a Negro indecent, Pauline replied, "But why not? A Negro is not a man." To quell such gossip, she arranged to have Paul marry one of her white kitchen maids—but continued to have him carry her to and from her bath. Lolling in the tub, she often received male admirers, and was pleased to have them stare at her exposed breasts. Clothed in only a flimsy chemise, she would spend hours in the presence of male guests having her hair coiffured, and her rouge and rose perfume applied.

In 1806, she had an affair with an intellectual, which in itself was an unusual diversion for her. The cultured Nicolas Philippe Auguste de Forbin, aged thirty, a society painter who had been a pupil of David, possessed a muscular physique but small income. Pauline remedied this financial embarrassment by appointing him her chamberlain. However, what appealed to Pauline was not her chamberlain's intellectual endowments as much as his physical endowments, which were uncommon. In contrast to Prince Borghese's "very small penis," M. de Forbin possessed a huge organ of copulation. For a year, Pauline cherished her lover, and their passion was total—so much so that Pauline's doctors, and her gynecologist in particular, became concerned. Pauline's health had declined. She appeared worn and drained, and suffered severe vaginal distress. Her condition, stated one biographer, "was based on nothing but undue friction, mostly brought on by M. de Forbin, who was endowed with a usable gigantism and very hard to get rid of."

When Pauline's illness intensified, one of her doctors addressed a consultant as follows:

"Her general appearance indicates acute depression and exhaustion. The womb was still sensitive, but somewhat less so;

and the ligaments still exhibited signs of the painful inflamma-
tion for which we prescribed baths last Thursday. The present
condition of the uterus is caused by a constant and habitual ex-
citation of that organ; if this does not cease, an exceedingly dangerous situation may result. . . . I blamed the internal douches,
and spoke in general of anything, of whatever nature, that stimulated the abdomen; I think she understood. . . . The douche
and its tube cannot always be held responsible; one is bound to
assume a continuous cause for such exhaustion in the case of a
young and beautiful woman in her state of life. If there is anyone
who shares the fault for these indulgences, this person would not
accuse himself. We would be blamed for seeing nothing and permitting everything. . . . If we cannot speak as masters, the only
thing to do is withdraw."

Unable to speak as masters to Pauline, the physicians finally
confided their concern to her mother and the rest of the family.
With some difficulty, her relatives persuaded Pauline to discontinue her relationship with the "person" who shared "the fault for
these indulgences."

After a gradual recovery, Pauline departed for Nice without
M. de Forbin. But for her, abstinence was impossible. Presently,
she hired an interesting young violinist named Blangini as con-
ductor of her orchestra. Of course, she had no orchestra. She had
her bed, and in it she and Blangini enjoyed their duets.

Next, Pauline's gaze fell on Armand Jules de Canouville, one
of the four aides to Marshal Berthier, Napoleon's chief of staff.
Canouville's military career had been brilliant, and at twenty-
five he was a colonel. He was also a vain dandy who enjoyed
boasting of his numerous conquests. He was as frivolous and
foolish, in many ways, as Pauline herself, and she adored him.
Their love affair was soon public knowledge.

One incident, particularly, made all of Paris laugh. Pauline,
suffering a toothache, summoned a dentist, one Bousquet, to
Neuilly. Upon arriving, the dentist found a rumpled young man
in a silk dressing gown consoling Pauline. The young man was
begging Pauline to have her tooth extracted. "For the past three
nights you have done nothing but cry," he told her, "so that neither
of us has had a wink of sleep. Why not have it over with?" Pauline
resisted, until the young man allowed Bousquet to pull out one of
his teeth. Impressed by this grand gesture, Pauline submitted to

the extraction. Shortly after, when the transgressions of royalty were being discussed in the presence of Bousquet, the dentist mentioned Pauline as an exception. "I was at Neuilly the other day and saw her in private with her husband. They were a model pair. It is a happy marriage." Bousquet was stricken when he learned that the young man in attendance had been Canouville—and that Prince Borghese was barred from even entering Neuilly.

Napoleon was not amused by the dentist's revelation. Canouville was suddenly sent with the French legions to Russia. At Moscow, he was killed. Pauline sobbed over his gifts and letters, and plaited a bracelet out of locks of his hair.

After Elba—and Pauline shared four months of Napoleon's exile there—Prince Borghese, who had comforted himself with a mistress in Florence, found the courage to sue for divorce. Pauline fought the action, and won a legal separation instead—as well as twenty thousand francs a year, ownership of the Palazzo Borghese, and the right to her own separate apartments in the Villa Borghese. By the time her marital problems were resolved, she was almost forty years old, and unhappy about her age. She wore ten strands of pearls to hide the lines around her neck, and she ordered Canova's nude statue of her put in storage, so that detractors could not "see how the poison works in me." There was one more lover, her last, the young and gifted Sicilian composer, Giovanni Pacini, whose opera, *Slave of Bagdad*, she had had performed in her palazzo.

Then she was alone, and she was ill, dying of cancer. The six physicians who attended her could not console her. She wanted her husband back. Pope Leo XII, it was said, brought about a reconciliation between Pauline and Prince Borghese. If so, it was short-lived. On June 9, 1825, flanked by her husband and her youngest brother, Jerome, Pauline Bonaparte, aged forty-five, completed her last will and testament, lingered briefly, and then died —a mirror in her hand.

Her deathbed wish had been that her coffin not be opened at her funeral. For those who desired to see her, she had said, there was the Canova sculpture. Her wish was respected. The coffin remained closed. The Canova nude was brought out of storage and placed on public view. And Pauline Bonaparte was young once more.

VI

The Byron Lover—

English Style

If there is one human being whom I do
utterly *detest* and *abhor* it is she. . . .

—LORD BYRON

IN 1816, after signing the deed of separation demanded
by his wife, George Gordon Byron, aged twenty-eight, left London and England for a self-imposed exile in Switzerland, Italy,
and Greece. Lord Byron departed from his native England, which
he would never see again, for many pressing reasons: the unpleasantness of his separation, the scandal created by his suspected incestuous affair with his half sister, the inconsiderate
attitude of his creditors, and the unpopularity of his politics.

Possibly, too, there was one additional irritant that put him to
flight. This irritant was Lady Caroline Lamb, wife of a future
prime minister. She had recently been Byron's first prominent
mistress.

In a gallery of adulteresses, Lady Caroline would be deemed the
most difficult. When Byron wished to end their stormy affair, he

told her that he must do so in order to cease making "fools talk, friends grieve, and the wise pity." In June 1814, he wrote her mother-in-law, Lady Melbourne, that he "would sooner, much sooner, be with the dead in purgatory, than with her, *Caroline* (I put the name at length as I am not jesting), upon earth. . . . I am already almost a prisoner; she has no shame, no feeling, no one estimable or redeemable quality. . . . If there is one human being whom I do utterly *detest* and *abhor* it is she, and, all things considered, I feel to myself justified in so doing."

Yet, not too long before, he had written to Caroline herself: "I never knew a woman with greater or more pleasing talents. . . . You know I have always thought you the cleverest, most agreeable, absurd, amiable, perplexing, dangerous, fascinating little being that lives now, or ought to have lived 2000 years ago. I won't talk to you of beauty; I am no judge. But our beauties cease to be so when near you, and therefore you have either some, or something better. And now, Caro, this nonsense is the first and last compliment (if it be such) I ever paid you. . . ."

The woman who inspired in Byron such violently contradictory feelings was born Caroline Ponsonby in November 1785. Her father was the third Earl of Bessborough. Her mother, Lady Bessborough (Lady Blarney, Byron called her), had occupied her mature years by amorously subduing the British statesman Lord Granville, while in turn fending off the advances of the obese Prince of Wales. When Caroline was three, her mother suffered a slight stroke. Caroline was packed off to Italy with a nurse for six years. She was then turned over to her aunt, the attractive Duchess of Devonshire, to be raised with cousins in a London household that also included the Duke of Devonshire and his mistress Lady Elisabeth Foster.

Caroline's early years, filled with extravagance, were bewildering. In company with her cousins, she ate all her meals off silver plates. "We had no idea that bread and butter was *made;* how it came, we didn't pause to think, but had no doubt that fine horses fed on beef," wrote Caroline. "At ten years old, I couldn't write . . . I spelt not, but made verses that all thought beautiful." Servants were her only mentors. She had no formal schooling, since doctors had advised against it, insisting that she was too high-strung. She was an unbridled, nonconforming tomboy until fifteen when, all at once, she discovered she could easily master French, Italian, Greek, Latin, and realized that she was talented in music, art, theatricals, and conversation. About this time a family friend, William Lamb, fresh from Cambridge and about to be called to the bar, first laid eyes upon her. A more original creature he had never seen. "Of all the Devonshire House girls," he said, "that is the one for me."

Lamb courted her for three years. Though elusive, she was interested. They made a contrasting pair. She was bright, vivacious, shocking. She had the face of an impudent angel, with a mop of curly blonde hair cut short, and wide round hazel eyes. She was small, boyishly slender, and affected a fashionable lisping drawl. Friends called her "Squirrel" and "Ariel" and "the Sprite." A few even called her "Young Savage." William Lamb, with his mocking smile and his cultivated air of bored indifference, was a studied dandy, ingrown, intelligent, easygoing, the detached observer personified. "William was born to be her victim," wrote David Cecil in *Melbourne*. "His sceptical, sophisticated spirit was at once entertained and invigorated by her naturalness and her certainty." They were married on an evening in June 1805. Throughout the ceremony Caroline was all nerves, and at its end, unaccountably offended by the officiating bishop, she suddenly ripped the front of her wedding gown and fell into a faint. Thus unconscious, the new bride was carried through the great throngs of curious spectators waiting outside and placed in her honeymoon carriage.

The first four years of their marriage were reasonably happy. They occupied one floor of the elegant Melbourne House in London; Caroline's mother-in-law, Lady Melbourne, had the other floor. They had guests morning, afternoon, and night. On the rare occasions when they were alone, they discussed politics and classical literature, and found time to produce three children. Of these, the first, Augustus, grew to manhood a hopeless imbecile and died at the age of twenty-nine; the other two children died in their infancy. When the novelty of marriage wore off, Caroline became restless. The routine and banality of wifehood bored her. She loved her husband, but loved herself far more. She required direction and restraint, but these Lamb could not supply. Her dream world of wedded ecstasy had become tiresome; she determined to discover new dream worlds that would provide continuous excitement and sensation.

She began with a salon to which only the most creative and outrageous personalities were invited. Among the male callers she received was Samuel Rogers, the banker-turned-poet whose work, *The Pleasures of Memory*, had gone into fifteen editions; among her female callers was Lady Oxford, who had made a career out of her highly advertised sensuality. When conversation became as wearisome as marriage, Caroline decided to experiment in adultery. For her lover she chose Lady Holland's first husband, Sir Godfrey Webster, a jaunty, empty-headed libertine. She made no secret of their affair and often appeared with Webster in public. Her family and friends were appalled. Only her husband was tolerant. Patiently, Lamb waited for the tawdry adventure to end. Soon it did end—but a more scandalous entanglement lay ahead, one that would scar Caroline emotionally for the remainder of her life.

It was March 1812, and the twenty-four-year-old Lord Byron had awakened one morning to find himself famous. Until then, Byron had been an undistinguished minor poet. His manner was anything but agreeable. His background—a violent and drunken mother, a haphazard and debt-ridden childhood, a stupid nurse, and a medical quack who tried to correct a right leg made lame by a "hemorrhage on the surface of the infant's brain" during birth—had made him sensitive, moody, defensive, almost antisocial. Yet, he was attractive. His face possessed a classic beauty. His attitude was romantic. And, in 1809, after taking his seat in the House of Lords, he had invoked this romanticism while traveling to Albania, Greece, and Turkey. On this trip he had composed the first part of *Childe Harold's Pilgrimage*, and it was published in March of 1812—a few days after he had made a spectacular maiden speech in the House against capital punishment for workingmen who sabotaged machinery—and overnight he was famous. The Duchess of Devonshire reflected the popular reaction: "The subject of conversation, of curiosity, of enthusiasm of the moment is not Spain or Portugal, warriors or patriots, but Lord Byron! . . . The poem is on every table and himself courted, flattered, and praised whenever he appears . . . he is really the only topic of every conversation—the men jealous of him, the women of each other."

Caroline Lamb had borrowed the advance proofs of Byron's book from Samuel Rogers. She read it with mounting enthusiasm, and immediately sought out Rogers. "I must see him—I am dying to see him!" she exclaimed. Rogers was amused. "He has a club-foot and he bites his nails," he said. Caroline did not care. "If he is as ugly as Aesop, I must see him!"

A few days later she saw him. At Lady Westmoreland's ball he was drawn away from a circle of feminine admirers and led up to Caroline. After the introduction, he suggested that he would like to call upon her. She stared into his face; then, theatrically, without a word, she turned on her heel and walked away. That night, in the privacy of her boudoir, she wrote in her journal: "Mad, bad, and dangerous to know." Shortly after, she would pen one more line: "That beautiful pale face is my fate."

Two days later, at Holland House, they met again. Remembering her previous performance, he quickly remarked, "This offer was made to you the other day. May I ask why you declined it?" Her reply remains unrecorded, but it is known that she invited him to her home and that he accepted.

The following morning Byron called upon her in the upstairs private apartments at Melbourne House. "Rogers and Moore were standing by me," Caroline remembered. "I was on the sofa. I had just come in from riding. I was filthy and heated. When Lord Byron was announced, I flew out of the room to wash myself. When I returned, Rogers said, 'Lord Byron, you are a happy man. Lady Caroline has been sitting here in all her dirt with us, but when you were announced, she flew to beautify herself.' Lord Byron wished to come to see me at eight o'clock, when I was alone. . . . I said he might."

Their affair had, in effect, begun. Yet, it was strange, for she was not his type. Months later he would write Lady Melbourne: "C. herself (as I have often told her) was *then* not at all to my taste, nor I (and I may believe her) to hers. . . ." During his travels to the Near East, Byron had found that he liked voluptuous and uncomplicated females. Slender women reminded him "of dried butterflies." Caroline was both thin and complex. "I am haunted by a skeleton," he said of her, but he could not resist. Her cleverness, her high station, her nervous sexuality, above all her ready availability, intrigued Byron. His taste and good sense were temporarily suspended. He gave way to his emotions.

Caroline began to receive him regularly in her rooms at Melbourne House. He arrived late in the morning and stayed the day.

Mostly, he talked and she listened. Both were deeply in love, but neither moved to consummate this love. Byron proceeded warily in the early stages. If her talents were pleasing, they were, as he told her, "unfortunately coupled with a total lack of common conduct. . . . Your heart, my poor Caro (what a little volcano!), pours lava through your veins." When she offered him her jewels to relieve his debts, he declined by sending an unusual rose and a note reading: "Your Ladyship, I am told, likes all that is new and rare—for a moment." But this nonsexual friendship could not go on indefinitely. Before many weeks had passed, they were lovers.

Once toward the end of their affair, when she had treated him coldly, she recollected the warm beginning of their love. "Was I cold when first you made me yours—" she asked Byron, "when first you told me in the Carriage to kiss your mouth & durst not—& after thinking it such a crime it was more than I could prevent from that moment—you drew me to you like a magnet & I could not indeed I could not have kept away—was I cold then—were you so? . . . Never while life beats in this heart shall I forget you or that moment when first you said you lov'd me—when my heart did not meet yours but flew before it—& both intended to remain innocent of greater wrong."

Whatever would happen later, he loved her passionately at the start. When Caroline, suffering from the censure of mother and relatives, questioned his faithfulness after five months, he replied: "If tears which you saw and I know I am not apt to shed,—if the agitation in which I parted from you,—agitation which you must have perceived through the *whole* of this most *nervous* affair, did not commence until the moment of leaving you approached,—if all I have said and done, and am still but too ready to say and do, have not sufficiently proved what my real feelings are, and must ever be towards you, my love, I have no other proof to offer. . . ." They sealed their love by exchanging vows in a mock marriage ceremony, giving each other rings, and jointly autographing a book (her signature read "Caroline Byron").

And what of William Lamb during all of this? Byron was not unmindful of the injured husband. He regarded Lamb highly and thought of him as being "as much above me as Hyperion above the Satyr." Lamb did not reciprocate this high regard. While admitting that Byron was attractive and clever, he thought him a poseur. In the presence of an enraged Caroline, he enjoyed ridiculing Byron's romantic airs. But he would do nothing to check his wife's infidelity, and constantly reassured relatives that the errant pair would not run off together. "They neither wish nor intend going," he would say, "but both like the fear and interest they create."

Caught up in the throes of her grand passion, Caroline lost all restraint. If she found herself at the same party with Byron, she would openly leave on his arm. If he were at a party to which she had not been invited, she would wait outside, among the linkboys and drivers, until he emerged, and go off with him in his carriage. If a single day elapsed without a visit from him, she would disguise herself as one of her pages, even donning pantaloons, and force her way into his quarters.

She conformed to his every wish. He asked her to give up her salon, and she did so. He told her he detested the waltz, which had recently become popular, and she gave up dancing. When both her mother and her father-in-law, Lord Melbourne, tried to bring an end to the affair by making her go abroad, she threatened to elope with Byron. In a temper, her father-in-law shouted, "Go and be damned—but I don't think he'll take you." With a hysterical sob, she rushed out of the house and fled down Pall Mall. After hiding in a chemist's shop, she took a coach to Kensington. There she pawned an opal ring for twenty guineas, took a room in a surgeon's house, and made plans to continue on to Portsmouth where she intended to book passage on the first ship bound in any direction. Late in the day, Byron, who had been summoned by Caroline's family, traced her through the coachman and forcibly took her from the surgeon's house. She was returned home after Lamb had promised to forgive her.

Byron was becoming weary of Caroline's hysterical antics and her frenzied possessiveness. He determined to make a break, and to do it rudely and dramatically. He plunged into an affair with Caroline's onetime friend, forty-year-old Lady Oxford, whose erudition and easy virtue were a relief after the convulsive months with Caroline. Byron would always remember Lady Oxford with affection. "A woman is only grateful for her *first* and *last* conquest," he wrote. "The first of poor dear Lady Oxford's was achieved before I entered on this world of care; but the last, I do flatter myself, was reserved for me, and a *bonne bouche* it was."

Stunned, Caroline bombarded Lady Oxford, whom she addressed as "My dearest Aspasia," and Byron, with angry letters.

Exhausted, determined to end the relationship, Byron, perhaps in collaboration with Lady Oxford, wrote Caroline a vicious farewell:

> Lady Caroline,—I am no longer your lover; and since you oblige me to confess it, by this truly unfeminine persecution . . . learn that I am attached to another. . . . I shall ever remember with gratitude the many instances I have received of the predilection you have shown in my favour. I shall ever continue your friend, if your Ladyship will permit me so to style myself; and, as a first proof of my regard, I offer you this advice: correct your vanity, which is ridiculous; exert your absurd caprices upon others; and leave me in peace.
>
> Your most obedient servant, Byron

For Byron it was done. For Caroline it would never be done. Her emotions seesawed between hate and love. On her servants' new livery, she had buttons sewn that were inscribed "Ne crede Byron" ("Do not believe Byron"). She forged a letter imitating Byron's hand and sent it to his publisher in an attempt to obtain a portrait he had long refused her. She offered her favors to young London rakes if they would challenge Byron to duels on her behalf. At Brocket Hall, in a ceremony before village girls attired in white gowns, she burned Byron in effigy, and then consigned to the flames the books he had given her, locks of his hair, and copies of his letters (she carefully preserved the originals). In London, she laid siege to his rooms. "She comes at all times, at any time," Byron complained, "and the moment the door is opened in she walks."

Once, entering Byron's rooms, she found them empty. On a table lay a copy of Beckford's *Vathek*. Picking up the book, she scrawled across the flyleaf: "Remember me!" Returning home, Byron found the open book and Caroline's inscription. In a fit of anger, he sat down and dashed off an eight-line poem:

> *Remember thee! remember thee!*
> *Till Lethe quench life's burning streams*
> *Remorse and shame shall cling to thee*
> *And haunt thee like a feverish dream.*

Remember thee! Ay, doubt it not,
Thy husband too shall think of thee,
By neither shall thou be forgot,
Thou false to him, thou fiend to me!

He did not send it to Caroline. But years later he gave a copy of the verses to Shelley's cousin, Tom Medwin, in Italy, and after Byron's death Medwin published them in his *Conversations with Lord Byron*. When the poem appeared, Caroline—who had not known of its existence—almost lost her mind. Pathetically she wrote Medwin: "Byron never could say I had no heart. He could never say, either, that I had not loved my husband. In his letters to me, he is perpetually telling me I love him the best of the two; and my only charm, believe me, in his eyes was, that I was innocent, affectionate, and enthusiastic."

Still upset by Medwin's memoir, Caroline summoned Byron's friend, John Cam Hobhouse, to her Melbourne House bedroom. After two hours, Hobhouse went away and made a memorandum of their conversation: "She is in the utmost rage at Medwin's *Conversations* representing her as not having been the object of Byron's attachment and she showed me a very tender letter of his which she wished to publish. She told me that her brother William Ponsonby was not against the publication as he thought with her that no imputation was so dreadful as that of not having been loved by her paramour. . . . She is certainly very mad."

Indeed, Caroline was mad enough actually to publish the proof of Byron's love for her. She wrote Medwin: "I have had one of his letters copied in the stone press for you; one just before we parted." What Medwin received was a lithograph copy—Caroline had posted dozens to Byron's friends—of one of Byron's last letters to her. It read, in part:

"You know I would with pleasure give up all here and all beyond the grave for you, and in refraining from this, must my motives be misunderstood? I care not who knows this, what use is made of it. . . . I was and am yours freely and most entirely, to obey, to honour, love,—and fly with you when, where, and how you yourself *might* and *may* determine."

With this, Medwin was persuaded to retract. In his second edition of the book, Medwin charitably deleted the painful verses.

But all this furor came later. For when Byron originally wrote the offensive verses after Caroline inscribed his copy of *Vathek* —when he scrawled "thou fiend to me!"—his love had curdled into hatred and Caroline's damaged pride was continuing to make her publicly vindictive.

The climax to Caroline's hysteria was reached the evening of July 5, 1813, during a great ball given for Lady Katherine Heathcote. At this social event, Caroline and Lord Byron suddenly came face to face. The orchestra was playing a waltz. Remembering his ban on dancing, Caroline said to Byron, "I presume *now* I am allowed to waltz." He replied cuttingly, "With everybody in turn"—though the following day he told Lady Melbourne he had actually suggested that Caroline waltz "because she danced well, and it would be imputed to *me*, if she did not." Finishing her dance, she moved near him. He was conversing with a lady, but he turned to whisper to Caroline, mockingly, "I have been admiring your dexterity." He started to leave, but then, as he recalled, "she took hold of my hand as I passed, and pressed it against some sharp instrument, and said, 'I mean to use this.' I answered, 'Against me, I presume?'" As he walked away, she cried, "Byron," then ran into the supper room and began to slash at her arms with the sharp instrument—a fruit knife.

Horrified guests rushed to stop her. When she was about to faint, someone handed her a glass of water. Quickly she smashed the glass on a nearby table, and now tried to gash her wrists with the broken fragments. Eventually, subdued, she was taken home. Byron insisted that he did not know of the scandalous occurrence until the next day. "I am quite unaware of what I did to displease; and useless regret is all I can feel on the subject," he wrote Lady Melbourne. "Can she be in her senses?"

She had her senses sufficiently under control to predict—when Byron married her cousin Annabella Milbanke in 1815—that "Byron would never pull together with a woman who went to church punctually, understood statistics, and had a bad figure." Her prediction was correct. In 1816, legally separated from his wife, Byron left England forever. He was in Geneva when Caroline, still smarting over his rejection of her, had her literary revenge. She published a melodramatic novel, *Glenarvon,* in which Byron, Lady Oxford, William Lamb, and she herself were all thinly disguised as fictional characters. In it Byron was portrayed as a minor monster. She prayed he would read her book. He did.

"Madame de Staël lent it me to read from Coppet last autumn," he wrote Thomas Moore. "It seems to me, that if the authoress had written the *truth*, and nothing but the truth—the whole truth —the romance would not only have been more *romantic*, but more entertaining. As for the likeness, the picture can't be good—I did not sit long enough."

After that, her total disintegration began. Lamb, disgusted by the novel, left her. Alone in Brocket Hall, the Melbourne country house, she tried to recreate her Byron romance with a series of illicit affairs, each more degrading than the former. Her parade of lovers—one of the last was the bewildered twenty-one-year-old Edward Bulwer-Lytton, who would become renowned for *The Last Days of Pompeii*—was subjected to wearing Byron's ring, listening to her organ recitals, and enduring her mercurial passions. Following a visit to Brussels, where she nursed her brother Frederick who had been wounded at Waterloo, she went on to Paris to meet the hero of the hour, the Duke of Wellington, and she attempted to seduce him but without success.

Once, after Lamb had temporarily returned to her, she met in her daily ride a funeral procession wending its way to Newstead. That night, from her husband, she learned it was Byron's cortège. Her disintegration was now complete. Thereafter, she took to drugs and brandy. Her mind constantly verged on insanity. She was abusive to visitors, she broke dishes, she stayed awake entire nights, she gave up regular meals and all semblance of maintaining an orderly house. Often, she retired drunkenly to her room, to sob beneath a portrait of Byron that hung next to a crucifix on the wall.

In 1825, Lamb made their separation a permanent one. Two years later Caroline fell seriously ill of dropsy. She was moved to Melbourne House. Sinking, she implored her family to bring her husband. "He is the only person who has never failed me." Lamb arrived, sat at her bedside, and spoke kindly to her. She could not know that her dear William, who had recently inherited the title Lord Melbourne, would in six years be Prime Minister of England and after that become the tutor and confidant of Queen Victoria. She could only know that there had never been a more decent, more patient, more understanding mate. His last act of tenderness was all that she had been waiting for. She lingered on another day, but then closed her eyes and was freed from her tortured mind forever.

Perhaps William Lamb himself summed it all up best in his cool, detached rhetoric. Whether he was referring to Caroline and Byron, or to Caroline and himself, is not known, but this is what he wrote: "Neither man nor woman can be worth anything until they have discovered that they are fools. This is the first step toward becoming either estimable or agreeable; and until it is taken there is no hope."

VII

The Byron Lover—
Italian Style

I doubt her liking anything for very long,
except one thing, and I presume she will
soon arrive at varying even that.

—LORD BYRON

CAROLINE LAMB had been in her grave five years when
the Countess Teresa Guiccioli arrived on her initial visit to England. If, in terms of a sustained relationship, Caroline had been
Lord Byron's first mistress, then Teresa Guiccioli had been his
last. To be sure, there had been affairs in between: Claire Clairmont, Mary Shelley's stepsister, who gave Byron an illegitimate
daughter; Marianna Segati, the wife of his landlord in Venice;
Margarita Cogni, a sharp-tongued Italian tigress; and many more
of slight importance. But with Teresa's arrival in England to make
a pilgrimage to Byron's final resting place and to Newstead Abbey, to visit her lover's surviving friends, to sell his manuscripts,
the full circle of Byron's romantic life was completed.

Teresa Guiccioli, accompanied by her elder brother, Vicenzo,
and with some knowledge of conversational English, fared well

during her brief visit to Byron's homeland. She was the center of interest at Lady Blessington's fashionable salon. She was wined and dined by her poet's publisher, John Murray. She had tea with Byron's tutor at Harrow. And, above all, she satisfied a long-standing curiosity when she met Byron's half sister, Augusta Leigh, with whom he was alleged to have had an incestuous affair. This meeting lasted three hours. The sole subject of conversation was Byron. Augusta was pleased with Teresa, and Teresa thought Augusta "the most good-natured, amiable person in the world."

The climax of Teresa's tour was a visit to her lover's grave. After Byron's death, he had been refused burial in Westminster Abbey. His coffin was then lowered into the family vault in the little church at Hucknall Torkard near the village of Newstead, and there Byron was left to rest beside his mother's coffin. Now, eight years after Byron's burial, his last mistress arrived at Hucknall Torkard, closely observed by members of the press. "The lady went into the church alone," reported *The Dial*. "From the door, and before even there was time to close it, the attendant saw the visitor prostrate herself on the flags which covered the remains of Byron. . . . She remained thus alone in the church, while the servant and the attendant waited outside for no very brief space of time—for an hour or more, I believe."

Bidding farewell to Byron's remains and his surviving friends, Teresa left behind her in England many who were favorably impressed. Yet, those in London who had known Caroline Lamb, and who had just met Teresa Guiccioli, may have been disconcerted by a certain similarity between the two. On the face of it, their manners and characters were far apart. Unlike Caroline, Teresa had self-restraint, strength, direction. Yet, beneath this, lurked that nagging similarity. Byron had seen it at once and confided it to his friend Douglas Kinnaird: "She is a sort of Italian Caroline Lamb, except that she is much prettier, and not so savage. But she has the same red-hot head, the same noble disdain of public opinion, with the superstructure of all that Italy can add to such natural dispositions." Byron had begun with Caroline Lamb—and, in a sense, ended with her, too.

His Italian Caroline was born in Ravenna in 1800. As the most promising of Count Gamba's five daughters, Teresa was educated at the modern Convent of Santa Chiara in Faenza. At eighteen—with the appearance, someone observed, of "a healthy, rosy, jolly-looking milkmaid"—she was forced to marry the wealthy, red-bearded, myopic, fifty-seven-year-old Count Alessandro Guiccioli.

The groom was not new to the state of matrimony. In *The Last Attachment*, Iris Origo has quoted a biographical inquiry into the count's life made by the vice legate of Ravenna for the Austrian Police. He had first "married the Contessa Placidia Zinanni, who made up for the disparity of her age—much greater than that of the Cavaliere—and for her physical imperfections, by a very large dowry. . . . He used to keep in his house a series of maids, whom he seduced and then discharged and sent away, according to circumstances and to the greater or lesser resentment of his wife." With one of these maids, Angelica Galliani, a brunette with soulful eyes, he had a more enduring affair, which produced six illegitimate children. After his wife died—or was removed by the skillful administration of poison—Count Guiccioli married his mistress. In 1817, she, too, died, and in 1818 the count took Teresa for his third wife. Later, Byron would hear that the count was the author of "two assassinations"—the murder of Domenico Manzoni, a wealthy landowner, and that "of a commissary who had interfered with him."

Three days after her marriage in Ravenna, Teresa met Lord Byron at the house of the Countess Albrizzi in Venice. She was too nervously exhausted to be impressed by anyone. But less than a year later, again in Venice, at a party given by the Countess Benzoni in April of 1819, Teresa saw Byron a second time, and by then she was ready. Her marriage to Guiccioli was proving singularly unsuccessful. She slept in a separate bedroom, addressed her husband as "Signore," and had learned that no vows of love could bridge the thirty-nine years that gaped between them. Her gentle and romantic nature was offended by his autocratic manner and predisposition toward violence. She was ready for the traditional and socially acceptable *cavaliere servente,* the lover who would unobtrusively wait on her hand and foot.

Byron answered her need. "His noble and exquisitely beautiful countenance, the tone of his voice, his manners, the thousand enchantments that surrounded him, rendered him so different and so superior a being to any whom I had hitherto seen, that it was impossible he should not have left the most profound impression upon me." And, of course, Byron was impressed by Teresa: her auburn hair falling in ringlets, her pretty face, her voluptuous bust. All in all, she had a well-rounded figure, one that was marred only by buttocks too ample and legs too short. Her movements were sinuous, her eyes inviting. What followed was inevitable.

As Teresa confessed it to her husband later: "I then felt attracted to him by an irresistible force. He became aware of it, and asked to see me alone the next day. I was so imprudent as to agree, on condition that he would respect my honour: he promised and we settled on the hour after dinner, in which you took your rest. At that time an old boatman appeared with a note, in an unknown gondola, and took me to Mylord's gondola, where he was waiting, and together we went to a *casino* of his. I was strong enough to resist at that first encounter, but was so imprudent as to repeat it the next day, when my strength gave way— for B. was not a man to confine himself to sentiment. And, the first step taken, there was no further obstacle in the following days." They had ten days before the count spirited his adulterous wife out of the city. To the physical consummation of their love, Byron would write Kinnaird, they devoted "four continuous days."

Before the affair began, Byron had complained to John Cam Hobhouse of Teresa's frankness: "She is pretty, but has no tact; answers aloud, when she should whisper—talks of age to old ladies who want to pass for young; and this blessed night horrified a correct company at the Bensona's, by calling out to me *'mio Byron'* in an audible key, during a dead silence of pause in the other prattlers, who stared and whispered to their respective *serventi*." But now that she was his mistress, and out of reach, all was forgiven. From Venice he wrote her: "You sometimes tell me that I have been your *first* real love—and I assure you that you shall be my last Passion."

From Venice to Ravenna he sent her further reassurance of this passion: "My sweetest treasure—I am trembling as I write to you, as I trembled when I saw you—but no longer—with such sweet heartbeats. I have a thousand things to say to you, and know not how to say them, a thousand kisses to send you—and, alas, how many Sighs!" Yet, there was more to tell her. As a footnote he added: "How much happier than I is this letter: which in a few days will be in your hands—and perhaps may even be brought to your lips. With such a hope I am kissing it before it goes. Good-bye—my soul."

Letters were not enough for Teresa. Despite the fact that her brother warned her against "a man so strange . . . of so doubtful a reputation . . . a Pirate," Teresa could not endure separation. She fell ill. She begged Byron to come to Ravenna and attend her in her husband's house. Again, Byron was shocked by her boldness. "The Charmer forgets that a man may be whistled any-where *before*, but that *after* . . . She should have been less liberal in Venice, or less exigent at Ravenna." Nevertheless, her feverish sensuality exerted a strong appeal. He thought about her further and then came running.

Byron moved into the vast Palazzo Guiccioli, where Teresa lay weak and coughing. She "has been very unwell," Byron wrote Kinnaird, though "not ill enough to induce any amatory absti-nence." Byron confirmed their lovemaking in a letter to Alexander Scott. "The G. is better—and will get well with prudence—our amatory business goes on *well* and *daily*." Byron quoted his doctor as remarking that "she may be cured if she likes. Will she like? I doubt her liking anything for very long, except one thing, and I presume she will soon arrive at varying even that. . . ."

In Ravenna, Teresa's role as mistress was secured. It would last five years, until Byron left on his final journey. Recovered from her illness, she attired herself in "high hat and sky-blue rid-ing habit," and galloped with her lover through the pine forest, irking him only when she allowed her horse to run after his and "to bite him." He enjoyed the affair and he hated it. One day, coming across her favorite novel, Mme. de Staël's *Corinne*, the thick edition "in small print and bound in purple plush," resting in her sitting room, he wrote in the margin of the index page:

"My dear Teresa—I have read this book in your garden;—my love, you were absent, or else I could not have read it. It is a favourite book of yours, and the writer was a friend of mine. You will not understand these English words, and *others* will not understand them—which is the reason I have not scrawled them in Italian. But you will recognise the handwriting of him who passionately loved you, and you will divine that, over a book which was yours, he could only think of love. In that word, beauti-ful in all languages, but most so in yours—*Amor mio*—is comprised my existence here and hereafter. I feel I exist here, and I fear that

I shall exist hereafter—to *what* purpose you will decide; my destiny rests with you, and you are a woman, seventeen years of age, and two out of a convent. I wish that you had stayed there, with all my heart,—or at least, that I had never met you in your married state.

"But all this is too late. I love you, and you love me,—at least, you *say so*, and *act* as if you *did* so, which last is a great consolation in all events. But *I* more than love you, and cannot cease to love you."

Weeks later, Byron would inform Hobhouse: "Better be an unskilful Planter, an awkward settler . . . than a flatterer of fiddlers, and a fan carrier of a woman. I like women—God he knows—but the more their system here developes upon me, the worse it seems. . . . I have been an intriguer, a husband, a whoremonger, and now I am a Cavalier Servente—by the holy! it is a strange sensation."

But fan carrier of a woman and *Cavalier Servente* he remained. On September 15, 1819, with the blessings of the now remarkably lenient Guiccioli, Teresa and Byron left for Venice. En route they visited the ruins of Petrarch's house, recited his sonnets, and signed their names in the guest book. They visited Teresa's relatives at Filetto, tarrying to observe an eclipse of the sun through smoked glasses, to bowl on the green, and to catch fish in nets. They dwelt placidly in and out of Venice. Then Guiccioli had a change of heart, brought on no doubt by Byron's refusal to lend him one thousand pounds and Byron's inability to acquire for him a consular post. There was a triangular emotional scene. Teresa chose lover over husband. Eventually, the Pope was asked to intervene. His Holiness abetted true love. He awarded Teresa a legal separation, two hundred pounds a year alimony, and admonished her to confine herself to her father's roof.

Thereafter Teresa and Byron were almost never apart. They settled into a comfortable domestic routine that resembled the security and monotony of marriage. In some ways, however, the liaison was more difficult than marriage. The "humiliation and vexations" of being a mistress, Byron told Lady Blessington, "cannot fail to have a certain effect on her temper and spirits, which robs her of the charms that won affection; it renders her susceptible and suspicious, her self-esteem being diminished, she becomes doubly jealous of that of him for whom she lost it, and on whom she depends." Her lover, Byron concluded, "must submit to a slavery much more severe than that of marriage, without its respectability."

Occasionally, his thoughts turned to marriage, and he fantasized over the possibility. Writing to his half sister Augusta, he confided:

"I can say that, without being so *furiously* in love as at first, I am more attached to her than I thought it possible to be to any woman after three years—(*except one & who was she can YOU guess?*) and I have not the least wish nor prospect of separation from her. . . . If Lady B. would but please to die, and the Countess G.'s husband (for Catholics can't marry though divorced), we should probably have to marry—though I would rather *not* —thinking it the way to hate each other—for all people whatsoever."

During their long days together, Teresa loved to observe Byron at work. She was with him when he created a portion of *Don Juan,* and she recounted later a scene between them:

"His pen moved so rapidly over the page that one day I said to him, 'One would almost believe that someone was dictating to you!' 'Yes,' he replied, 'a mischievous spirit who sometimes even makes me write what I am not thinking. There now, for instance—I have just been writing something against love!' 'Why don't you erase it, then?' I asked. 'It's written,' he replied, smiling, 'the stanza would be spoiled.' And the stanza remained."

Teresa enjoyed Byron's friends, especially Shelley, whom she found "rather Spirit than man." She had heard that "in his adolescence he was beautiful," but she thought his appearance now did not suggest this, disfigured as it was by bad teeth, abundant freckles, and uncombed, graying hair. "He was also extraordinary in his dress, for he generally wore a schoolboy's jacket, never any gloves, and unpolished shoes—and yet, among a thousand gentlemen, he would always have seemed the most accomplished." Shelley, in turn, thought her "a very pretty, sentimental, innocent, superficial Italian" who would one day "repent her rashness" in entrusting her life to Byron. Teresa lived through all the drama of the Pisa circle—the appearance of Trelawny ("You will not like him," Byron warned her), the death of Byron's natural daughter Allegra, and the terrible drowning of Shelley. And finally she watched Byron sail off forever.

When Byron first told her of his impending departure for Greece, she could not accept it. She would go with him. Or at least she would go to Genoa and await his return there. Else, she would lose her sanity. Byron dreaded the final scene. As he confided to Kinnaird: "If she makes a scene (and she has a turn that way) we shall have another romance, and tale of ill-usage, and abandonment, and Lady Carolining, and Lady Byroning, and Glenarvoning, all cut and dry. There never was a man who gave up so much to women, and all I have gained by it has been the character of treating them harshly."

When the moment of separation came, there was no scene. Teresa spent two hours with Byron, watched him go aboard his brig, and with Mary Shelley she stood sadly waving as her lover sailed for Greece, where he hoped to help the Greeks gain their independence from Turkey. She lived with her father, and she lived for Byron's letters. In October 1823, he was writing her: "I was a fool to come here; but, being here, I must see what is to be done." And later: "You may be sure that the moment I can join you again, will be as welcome to me as at any period of our recollection."

Byron's last letter to Teresa was dated March 17, 1824: "The Spring is come—I have seen a Swallow today—and it was time—for we have had but a wet winter hitherto—even in Greece. We are all very well, which will I hope—keep up your hopes and Spirits." A month later, he was dead. Guiccioli's great-grandson, a boy of eighteen, brought her the news. "It was in the morning and she was still in bed. She turned away for a moment—was silent a little—and that was all."

She would live fifty-five years more. She returned to her husband for five months. The myopic, violent old man, cohabiting with a Venetian prostitute when he could, had not changed. Teresa obtained another papal decree which restored her alimony, and then she left him forever. In a year she was in the midst of an unhappy affair with a young Englishman who, like Byron, was handsome and lame. This was Henry Edward Fox, son of Lady Holland. Byron had met him once. "He appears a halting angel who has tripped against a star." In his journal, young Fox noted: "I was not prepared for the extreme facility of the conquest, which (such is the perverseness of one's nature) scarcely gave me pleasure. She is too gross and too carnal. . . . She tries and believes she is in love for a short time, but it is alarming when she talks and expects a constancy of five years. She has a pretty voice, pretty eyes, white skin, and strong, not to say *turbulent* passions." The affair was passionate and angry, and at last, because Teresa was "jealous" and "troublesome," and because of "various quarrels and hysterics," Fox broke it off with the comment: "Poor Ld Byron! I do not wonder at his going to Greece!"

In the years that followed, Teresa devoted herself to becoming a monument to Byron's memory. She visited England several times. She cooperated with the many biographers—Lamartine, Lady Blessington, Medwin, Moore—of her lover. She stood as defender of the faith against detractors, notably the malicious and wounded Leigh Hunt. When Hunt's *Lord Byron and Some of His Contemporaries* appeared in 1828, she said, "Everything in this book breathes hostility, calumny, falsehood." She wrote a book of her own, *Vie de Lord Byron,* which sought to transform her Byron into a waxen puritan, and their love into a discreet parlor flirtation.

In 1847, at the age of forty-seven, she married the Marquis de Boissy, a wealthy nobleman and persistent suitor, in Paris. The ghost of Byron rounded out their luxurious household. The marquis was proud to introduce his Teresa as "my wife, Madame la Marquise de Boissy—formerly mistress of Lord Byron." A full-length portrait of Byron hung over the drawing-room mantel. Teresa would show it to guests, exclaiming, "How beautiful he was! Heavens, how beautiful."

The marquis died in 1866. Later, after attending a spiritualist's séance, Teresa claimed that she had spoken both to her husband the marquis and to Lord Byron, and was pleased that "they are together now, and are the best of friends." Teresa, grown plump and gray, lived out her last seven years in her husband's villa near Florence. A mahogany box, which contained relics of a grand passion, was beside her when she died. In it were found a lock of Byron's hair, a handkerchief he had carried, and a copy of the novel *Corinne,* with Byron's inscription to *"Amor mio"* in its margin.

VIII

The Nympho

It is now a month and twenty days since Medjuel last slept with me! What can be the reason?

—LADY ELLENBOROUGH
(at the age of seventy-three)

THE SEXUAL ODYSSEY of one of the most attractive and
glamorous nymphomaniacs in modern times began on that day,
late in the autumn of 1829, when Lady Ellenborough, the beautiful twenty-two-year-old wife of Great Britain's lord of the privy
seal, fled her enraged husband, her agitated family, and her gossiping friends in London, and soon thereafter arrived in Paris to
meet her Austrian lover.

As Lady Ellenborough remained in complete seclusion in a
Paris apartment awaiting the birth of her lover's child, the English House of Lords began a pitiless public debate on a scandal
that had long titillated London society. For on March 9, 1830,
Lord Ellenborough had presented to his fellow peers a bill entitled
"An Act to dissolve the Marriage of the Right Honourable Edward Baron Ellenborough with the Right Honourable Jane Eliza-

beth Baroness Ellenborough, his now Wife, and to enable him to marry again: and for other Purposes therein mentioned."

Since at the time this bill was presented, the consent of both houses of Parliament and of the king was required to obtain a divorce—an average of two divorces being granted annually—the indiscretion committed by Lady Ellenborough was aired openly, not only in England but throughout the continent of Europe.

The marriage between Lord Ellenborough and Jane Elizabeth Digby—"a noble lord and his faithless lady," Lord Ellenborough's counsel called them—had survived for four years. During that time Lord Ellenborough, an unpopular, imperious, and ambitious man, had devoted most of his energies to Tory politics. With his encouragement his youthful mate had busied herself with the frivolities of London's most sophisticated set. The husband and wife had not, according to Lady Ellenborough's old governess and companion, "slept together for a very long time." When Prince Felix Schwarzenberg, a dashing attaché in the Austrian Embassy, came along, it surprised no one that Lady Ellenborough was soon involved in an illicit love affair. What did surprise everyone was Lady Ellenborough's indiscretion. According to the witnesses who appeared before the House of Lords, and later the House of Commons, Lady Ellenborough had made little effort to keep her unfaithfulness a secret.

On April 6, 1830, Lord Ellenborough was granted his divorce. He did not, however, emerge unscathed. In the House of Commons, Joseph Hume, that highly moral member from Montrose, had at one point voiced a minority opinion: "Ought not the charge be read as one of criminality against Lord Ellenborough, who had permitted and even encouraged his wife's association with the persons responsible for her downfall, rather than one of marital infidelity against an unfortunate lady whose youth and immaturity ought to have been safeguarded by her natural protector?"

But in the end, the one to suffer longest was Lady Ellenborough. The scandal, a cross she carried for life, branded her as easy prey in the years to come. This, combined with her incredible beauty, her impulsive nature, her never-ceasing desire for sexual satisfaction and emotional security, started her on a romantic career seldom equaled in the history of errant females. In her seven decades, she acquired at least four husbands, and possibly as many as nine, each married in a different capital of Europe or the Near East. As to her affairs, there is documentary evidence of at least twelve lovers—French, German, Italian, Greek, and Arab—but it is more likely that she enjoyed three times that number.

While many of Lady Ellenborough's lovers were men of great renown, wealth, and title, perhaps the most gifted was the massive, red-faced Honoré de Balzac, regarded by fellow writers in the more than a century since (among them Henry James and W. Somerset Maugham) as literature's foremost novelist.

At the time that she was publicly divorced and disgraced, Lady Ellenborough was living with Prince Schwarzenberg in Paris, expecting the birth of their child. She hoped to marry the prince, but there were difficulties. His domineering sister in Vienna, as well as his rigidly Catholic family, objected to his union with a divorcée, and his political mentor, Prince Esterhazy, indicated that the marriage would be harmful to his political future. While the prince went about pursuing his career, both diplomatically and socially, Lady Ellenborough continued to be confined by her pregnancy and the scandal. Among the few friends the couple shared were the Count and Countess de Thurhein. And it was through the Countess de Thurhein that Jane Ellenborough became acquainted with Balzac.

The affair between the prince and the Lady, which had lasted a year and a half in London and continued another year and a half in Paris, began to fall apart even before Lady Ellenborough gave birth to their daughter. Lady Grenville, wife of the British Ambassador to France, wrote friends across the channel: "Poor Lady Ellenborough is just going to be confined. Schwarzenberg going about flirting with Madame Oudenarde."

Early in 1831, probably because Lady Ellenborough was creating scenes over his philandering, Prince Schwarzenberg secured a transfer back to Vienna, and thence to a post in Berlin. In short, he deserted her completely. "Felix avenged most awfully Heaven's outraged laws," Lady Ellenborough wrote years later. The Austrian Embassy in Paris, in an effort to protect Schwarzenberg's name, let it be known that the good prince abandoned his lady only after sufficient provocation. According to a member of the embassy staff, twenty-seven-year-old Count Rudolf Apponyi, Schwarzenberg and a cousin had continued to escort Lady Ellenborough about. But then: "This cousin discovered once that Milady was receiving in her house an Ancien of the Garde du Corps [a former bodyguard of the king's]. The cousin spoke to her about this, telling her that if she did not break off, he would be obliged to inform Schwarzenberg. Lady Ellenborough promised, but did not keep her word. Schwarzenberg was informed at once. This decided him to leave Paris within forty-eight hours. Lady Ellenborough wept more or less, but kept her body-guard. However, happiness of this type cannot last long. The body-guard was soon replaced by another one—I do not know who; finally, from successor to successor . . ." Count Apponyi's gossip has the ring of truth. It is likely that Lady Ellenborough did have an affair with a French soldier, but she probably did so in retaliation for Schwarzenberg's unfaithfulness.

Jane Ellenborough was deserted in a Paris seething with revolution. Mobs marched through the streets, and stormed the bishop's palace, in reaction against the unpopular King Charles X. Trapped in the midst of this national upheaval, and suffering from personal loneliness, Lady Ellenborough turned to one of the few friends she truly admired. She turned to Honoré de Balzac.

Their love affair was brief in duration—no more than two months—but four years later it was to produce a belated offspring. In 1835, as a result of the union, Balzac gave birth to a magnificent brainchild—Lady Arabella Dudley, beautiful and scandalous English nymphomaniac of *Le Lys dans la vallée*.

At first glance, Lady Ellenborough and Honoré de Balzac made an unlikely couple. She was tall and stately, with firm breasts and long, slim legs. Her hair was a soft, golden blonde, her eyes large and blue, her complexion creamy and flawless. "One of the most beautiful women I ever saw," Count Apponyi reported after he first met her. Count Alexandre Walewski concurred. She was the most "divinely beautiful" woman, he said, that he had ever laid eyes upon.

Balzac, on the other hand, was physically repulsive. A short man, he was absurdly fat—and no wonder. At a single meal he had once consumed twelve cutlets, one duck, two partridge, one sole, one hundred oysters, twelve pears, and several desserts. His everyday fare was not much lighter. His hair was black, his nose wide, and his lips thick. He affected blue coats with gold buttons, trousers with pleats, patent-leather shoes, and a turquoise-studded cane.

But they had much in common. Both were emotional, passionate, adventurous and extravagant. As a child, Jane Ellenborough had run off with a band of gypsies, and later tried to elope with her father's groom. As a young wife, she had had love affairs with her grandfather's librarian, her cousin, and Prince Schwarzenberg before she was twenty-one. Balzac's romantic involvements, if not as numerous, were equally impulsive. He had several mistresses, among them Mme. de Berny, who was more than twenty years his senior and the mother of nine children, and Countess Eveline Hanska, who dwelt on a fifty-thousand-acre Ukrainian estate with her large family and gave Balzac one stillborn child.

Whereas Lady Ellenborough actually lived her adventures, Balzac sublimated his desire for adventure in his creative work. He had quit the practice of law to take up the writing of historical potboilers in a Paris garret, publishing many under pseudonyms that were anagrams of his name. The very year he met Lady Ellenborough, he launched the first in a series of novels, which were sensuous studies of French life. These he called *La Comédie humaine*.

Balzac was a Spartan about work. Daily, from twelve to twenty hours at a stretch, his raven's quill scratched out his fiction, and in this fiction he lived an entire second life. For the characters he created were as real to him as his friends—George Sand, Victor Hugo, Alexandre Dumas—or his mistresses. Once while immersed in the novel in which he portrayed Lady Ellenborough and which was narrated by his anemic hero, Félix de Vandenesse, Balzac startled his family with the announcement: "Do you know who M. Félix de Vandenesse is marrying? A Mlle. de Grandville. The match is an excellent one. The Grandvilles are rich, in spite of what Mlle. de Belleville has cost the family." On his deathbed—it is said—he cried over and over again, "Send for Bianchon—he can save me!" Bianchon was the fictional doctor Balzac had invented for his *Comédie humaine*.

This complete immersion in his work may account for the brevity of Balzac's romance with Lady Ellenborough. During their few months together, she must have pleased him. She was witty, intelligent, attractive. And, apparently, she was passionate enough to encourage the creation of what one biographer has called "the most erotic heroine in the whole *Comédie humaine.*"

Yet it is quite possible that he did not fully please her. Lady Ellenborough's first fifty years were dominated by a search for peace of mind and body. She demanded a man who could supply full-time emotional security, and this Balzac was not capable of doing. Now at the height of his productivity, he had little time to spare from his writing labors. Even as he made love to Lady Ellenborough, he busily warded off the suspicions of his mistress in the Ukraine with volumes of letters. At the same time, he indulged in all sorts of fanciful money-raising schemes—from manufacturing paper to growing hothouse pineapples to locating the buried treasure of Toussaint L'Ouverture. This he did in an effort to pay for his extravagances which included the constant attendance of cook, valet, and groom, as well as the frequent presence of innumerable guests (once he refurnished his entire dining room to entertain at a single dinner party).

Lady Ellenborough needed days of affection. Balzac had only hours to give. Furthermore, she wanted to escape from the painful memories of Paris and forget the nearness of London. She was restless, yearning for fresher, more vitalizing scenes. In the spring of 1831, she acted. She moved on to Munich, there to become the mistress of that lovable classicist, King Ludwig I of Bavaria, and there to camouflage the royal affair by eventually marrying a wealthy court official, the red-headed Baron Carl Venningen. It was in the third year of her second marriage, at a time when she had briefly settled down as Baroness Venningen, that Honoré de Balzac finally decided to include her in the next volume of his *Comédie humaine.*

A dozen volumes of the series were devoted to "Provincial Life," and the third in this group was *Le Lys dans la vallée,* or *The Lily of the Valley.* Balzac conceived the novel and began writing it early in 1835, while staying at the Hotel zur Goldenen Birne in Vienna. Though he was visiting his wealthy mistress and future wife, Eveline Hanska, and her husband, he worked steadily on the book. "It is called *Le Lys dans la vallée,*" Balzac wrote the Marquise de Castries, an exasperating, aristocratic blonde whom he had failed to seduce. "Perhaps I deceive myself, but I imagine it will draw forth many tears. I have surprised myself in tears while writing it."

Balzac penned the first chapter in Vienna, where his preoccupation with Mme. Hanska limited his work schedule to twelve-hour days. He mailed the chapter off to F. Buloz for serialization in the *Revue de Paris,* devoted more time to Mme. Hanska, and finally hastened back to France and the book. "I worked night and day in Paris, only sleeping two hours in the twenty-four," he told Mlle. Zulma Caurraud. "I thus brought in the *Lys.*" Swathed in a silk-lined white cashmere robe, Balzac would begin his toils every morning at two o'clock. He wrote on a table illuminated by green-shaded candles, while he consumed coffee by the gallon—it is said he died of "fifty thousand cups of coffee." Previous books he had written hastily, feverishly, but this book was, by his own admission, one of his "most polished stones . . . slowly and laboriously constructed."

By July 1835, Balzac had finished *The Lily of the Valley*. Most of the installments ran in the *Revue de Paris*. But when the periodical fell into a disagreement with Balzac, he refused to give them the last chapters. A lawsuit occurred. Balzac won, published the remainder of his story in another periodical, and "his adversaries put themselves hopelessly in the wrong by reviewing the termination of the book, when it appeared elsewhere, in a strain of virulent but clumsy ridicule."

The Lily of the Valley was, for Balzac, a departure from his previous writing. For, while its prose was full of shrewd observation, of encyclopedic detail, of crude but poetic style, it avoided the vulgarisms, cynical realism, and sensuality of his other works. Critics disagreed on it then, as they continue to disagree on it to this day. George Saintsbury thought *The Lily* "of a somewhat sickly sweetness." But a later critic, Peter Quennell, found it "extraordinarily fresh and clear and brilliant," and he praised "its elegant workmanship—so unlike the haphazard workmanship of his other books."

It is more than possible that in 1836, there were as many readers who bought *The Lily* for the titillation of guessing the originals of Balzac's characters as there were those who purchased it for the pleasure they derived from Balzac's style. Balzac was notorious throughout his life for borrowing from the living for the personae of his fiction. After he wrote *Beatrix,* he frankly admitted to Mme. Hanska that he had employed Marie d'Agoult and George Sand as his models. Though, almost at the same time, he reassured George Sand that the characters were entirely imaginary, which provoked Sand to reply: "Please don't worry yourself over my susceptibilities. . . . I am too used to writing novels not to know that the novelist never indulges in portraiture, that, even if he would, one cannot copy a living model. Heavens! where would art be if one did not invent, for good or bad, three quarters of the characters in whom the stupid, inquisitive, public likes to think that it can see originals who are known to it?"

Nevertheless, *The Lily of the Valley* was filled with realistic portraiture. And among the most realistic characters in the book was the hero's elegant mistress, Lady Arabella Dudley—one of Balzac's most "fascinating" creations, Peter Quennell has called her. And she, of course, was Lady Jane Ellenborough.

Most contemporaries of Balzac correctly identified Lady Dudley as Lady Ellenborough. And later, the thorough researcher, Elinor Mary O'Donoghue, who wrote about Lady Ellenborough under the name of E. M. Oddie, concluded: "That Lady Arabella Dudley, however exaggerated a figure she cuts in *La Lys dans la vallée,* a novel which idealized a very different type of mistress, was the living human Jane and not the creation of Balzac's fertile brain, is certain. The fabric of the chapters in which she figures are shot with the gold of her personality, and the clues to her identity are many and unmistakable."

If there were no other evidence beyond *The Lily of the Valley* itself, it would still be clear that Balzac had borrowed heavily from Jane Ellenborough's personality and background. In the book, Lady Arabella Dudley abandoned two sons in England for the gay life of Paris; Lady Ellenborough left behind one son, a year and a half old, upon her flight to Paris. In the book, Lady Dudley rode an Arabian horse to her nocturnal meetings with her French lover; Lady Ellenborough, when known as Baroness Venningen, galloped on an Arabian steed to secret meetings with her Greek lover. In the book, Lady Dudley's husband was "one of the most eminent old statesmen of England . . . stiff, full of conceit, cold, with the sneering air he must have worn in Parliament"; and Lady Ellenborough's husband was "a vain man, too masterful and overconfident" and, in an opinion expressed by Lord Melbourne to Queen Victoria, "an unpopular man . . . his manners have been considered contemptuous and overbearing."

In the book, Balzac derived Lady Dudley's married name from

Lady Ellenborough's little boy, Arthur Dudley. The hero-narrator of the story, Félix, was derived from Prince Felix Schwarzenberg, the Austrian who was one of Lady Ellenborough's earliest lovers. But the best internal evidence of all was Balzac's description of his fictional nymphomaniac, a description that tallied precisely with Lady Ellenborough:

"This beautiful lady, so slim, so frail, this milk-white woman, so languid, so delicate, so gentle, with such a tender face, crowned with fine, fawn-colored hair, this creature whose brilliancy seems phosphorescent and transient, is an organization of iron. However fiery it may be, no horse resists her nervous wrist, this apparently weak but tireless hand. She has the foot of a roe, a small, hard, muscular foot, under an indescribably graceful exterior. . . . Her body knows no perspiration, it inhales the warmth in the atmosphere, and lives in the water for fear of dying. Her passion, too, is quite African."

The real Lady Arabella Dudley was born in England on April 3, 1807, and christened Jane Elizabeth. Her father was an admiral, Sir Henry Digby, who had gained wealth capturing Spanish ships, and fame fighting under Nelson at Trafalgar. Her mother was the attractive Jane Coke, daughter of the renowned Coke of Holkham. Originally, her mother had married Viscount Andover. But he had died early without heir, and after six years of widowhood her mother married Admiral Digby, though she persisted to the end of her days in using the title Lady Andover.

Jane was the first child produced after Lady Andover's remarriage. There were also two brothers by the time Jane was four, but her striking appearance made her the family favorite. When she was thirteen, a relative observed her studying with her cousins at Holkham, and reported that he had seen "little Miss Digby—oh! so beautiful."

It was this beauty that encouraged her mother to push her into an early debut in London. The Digbys took a residence at 78 Harley Street and sponsored Jane's coming-out. She was only sixteen when, at her coming-out party, she first met thirty-three-year-old Edward Law, Lord Ellenborough.

The son of a lord chief justice, Ellenborough had already attained the distinction of being one of the most disliked men in England. Educated at Eton and Cambridge, he now served in Parliament as the Tory member from St. Michaels. His star had risen when he married Lady Katherine Octavia Stewart, sister of the powerful and detested Lord Castlereagh. After Lord Castlereagh, oppressor of the English masses, died by his own hand, slashing his throat with a penknife, crowds of impoverished Londoners had stoned his coffin as it passed toward Westminster Abbey. Even though Lord Ellenborough had broken with his brother-in-law before the latter's suicide, and aligned himself with the Duke of Wellington, the people of England refused to forget his earlier relationship with Castlereagh. Too, Lord Ellenborough's personality had made him countless enemies. He was egotistical, pompous, ambitious, though undeniably a man of political ability.

When he met Jane Digby, he had been a widower four years. Lady Katherine Octavia Ellenborough had died in 1819, at the age of twenty-six. Despite his unattractive appearance—Lord Ellenborough was stodgy, flabby, and old for his years—he still had the reputation of being a roué. He was a wealthy man, with estates in Hertfordshire and an income of ten thousand pounds annually. And it was generally felt that he would rise high in government.

He fell in love with Jane Digby at first sight. In his eyes, she was desirable in every way. She came of a good family. She was the season's youngest and prettiest debutante. Above all, she might give him an heir. After several months' acquaintance, he proposed marriage. For Jane, he was somewhat less than desirable. She wanted a Byron, and she was in effect getting a businessman. She wanted a gay, young lover, and she was getting a stuffy politician seventeen years her senior. But Jane's parents regarded him as the perfect catch. His station would give her luxury and position. His maturity would curb her childishly romantic impulses.

The marriage was hurriedly arranged. Family friends were skeptical. Jane, they felt, was too young in experience, and Ellenborough too old. One observer, Thomas Creevey, noted in his diary: "Lady Anson goes to town next week for the wedding of the niece the pretty Aurora [after Aurora Raby, a heroine of Lord Byron's Don Juan]—Light of Day—Miss Digby, who is going to be married to Lord E. It is Miss Russell who refused Lord E. as many others are said to have done. Lady Anson will have it that he was a very good husband to his first wife, but all my impressions are that he is a damned fellow."

The couple were married on September 15, 1824, at Admiral

Digby's house in London, with Lord Ellenborough's uncle, the Bishop of Bath and Wells, performing the ceremony. Lord and Lady Ellenborough then went to Brighton for their honeymoon. The honeymoon, as revealed later, was "a flat failure." Whether or not this was attributable to Ellenborough's impatience with his inexperienced young wife is not known. But it is known that in the first days of his marriage, he cast an amorous glance elsewhere. Joseph Jekyll, a gossipy friend of the lord's, mentioned seeing "the pastry cook's girl at Brighton, whom Ellenborough preferred to his bride. Very pretty."

Back in London, Lord Ellenborough was soon deeply involved in politics. He had little time for bestowing affection or providing companionship. He left his young bride to her own devices. Long after, when Edmond About, the lively French journalist and novelist, met her in Greece, and discussed her first marriage with her, he noted:

"A little more than twenty years ago, she was, like most unmarried girls, a book bound in muslin and full of white pages. She was awaiting a husband with character and wit to influence her for good or for bad. This is the story of all women; they are what they are made. Ianthe [Greek for Jane], who was not wealthy, accepted what was considered a good match; she married Lord Ellenborough.

"When it came to love, Lord Ellenborough was a fairly satiated gourmet. He must have found this pink and white beauty terribly appetizing to undertake a marriage so disproportionate to his age. He married for his personal pleasure and treated his wife like something for which he had paid a great price. He was soon punished for this."

Confused and dismayed by her husband's attitude toward their marriage, Jane Ellenborough quickly entered into the whirl of London's international-society set, which was then dominated by the Princess Esterhazy, wife of the Austrian ambassador. At the weekly balls Jane Ellenborough's breath-taking beauty attracted the attention and flattery of dozens of polished young diplomats. They ridiculed her faithfulness to an older, preoccupied husband. Yet, for over two years Jane did not weaken. And when she finally did, it was not with a foreign diplomat, but with a scholarly English librarian.

In March of 1827 a twenty-seven-year-old employee of the

British Museum, Sir Frederick Madden, was summoned to classify the extensive Greek library belonging to the English agricultural reformer, Coke of Holkham. Shortly after Madden's arrival, he noted the advent of Coke's granddaughter in his diary: "Lady Ellenborough, daughter of Lady Andover, arrived to dinner, and will stay a fortnight. She is not yet twenty, and one of the most lovely women I ever saw, quite fair, blue eyes that would move a saint, and lips that would tempt one to forswear Heaven to touch them." Ten days later, Madden forswore heaven. There was a late game of whist, and after it, he noted: "Lady E lingered behind the rest of the party, and at midnight I escorted her to her room. . . . Fool that I was! I will not add what passed. . . . Gracious God, was there ever such a fortune!"

If Jane regretted the interlude, it was but briefly for she soon took up with her young cousin, Colonel George Anson, and their affair became the talk of Mayfair. Meanwhile, Lord Ellenborough had stirred himself sufficiently to have hopes of seeing an heir. In February 1828, Jane did bear him a son, Arthur Dudley, who died two years later when she was in Paris. It was after the birth of the boy that Lord Ellenborough ceased sharing his bed with his wife. For Jane, this was of no consequence. She had already met Prince Felix Schwarzenberg.

Prince Schwarzenberg was twenty-eight years old when he left his diplomatic mission in Brazil and sailed for Falmouth, England, to serve as special attaché to Prince Esterhazy, Ambassador to Great Britain. Schwarzenberg was a handsome man, tall and thin and stiff, with an angular face, penetrating eyes, long, straight nose, and a great black mustache. His court biographer in Vienna insisted that he possessed mystical powers: "The excessive life-force of the Prince is illustrated by the fact that he had a magnetic influence over women—not in the romantic and figurative way, but actually and medically. His sister was supposed to come especially to visit him and touch his hand to acquire more strength."

Magnetic force or no, he was a compelling person. His manner was, his contemporaries insisted, "artless . . . kind and friendly." His interests were broad—he studied anatomy and wrote musical comedies—and he conversed on all subjects with wit. His background was cosmopolitan. He had been a cavalry captain in Vienna when Metternich determined to convert him into a diplomat. He served in St. Petersburg, Paris, and Rio de Janeiro before arriving in London. His one weakness as a career diplomat was his undeniable susceptibility to attractive women.

While attending a British Foreign Office reception, shortly after his arrival, he saw Lady Ellenborough. They met, they danced, and their passion was immediate and mutual. Within short weeks, they were lovers. At first Jane was cautious, but soon she did not care. As Edmond About reported it: "One fine morning she climbed up on the roofs, and distinctly shouted to the whole United Kingdom, 'I am the mistress of Prince von Schwarzenberg!' All the ladies, who also had lovers, but did not tell it, were horribly shocked."

In Harley Street, close by the Digby residence, Schwarzenberg took rooms which he shared with a count from the embassy. Jane found an opportunity to visit Harley Street almost every afternoon, when the count was out and the prince was in. Usually she dismissed her groom and green carriage at the corner, and walked to Schwarzenberg's rooms. He was always eagerly waiting, his door already ajar.

What transpired thereafter was explained to the House of Lords in excruciating detail by one John Ward, a "gentleman's gentleman," who was employed in lodgings directly across the street. Mr. Ward became curious about the lady who appeared almost daily at the prince's doorway.

"Do you recollect," Mr. Ward was asked, "seeing the lady in the drawing room on the first floor in the company of Prince Schwarzenberg?"

"Frequently."

"And do you recollect seeing anything particular occur between them?"

"Yes."

"What was that?"

"I once saw Prince Schwarzenberg lacing her stays."

But as it developed, Mr. Ward's constant watchfulness had been rewarded by an even greater sensation. Once the lovers, caught up in their passion, did not bother to draw the bedroom blinds, and so Mr. Ward had clearly seen them in bed together.

Soon, afternoons were not enough. Jane and Schwarzenberg began to meet evenings, although this was more dangerous. On one occasion they arrived separately, and alone, at a house party in Wimbledon. When the evening was over, they left a few minutes apart, in different carriages. At Putney Heath her carriage drew abreast of his. Then the two coachmen reined in their horses so that she could descend from her vehicle and join the prince. They rode off together. When this evidence was presented to the House of Commons, one member, Mr. Hume, saw nothing wrong in Jane's action. "Would anybody believe," he asked, "that a lady dressed to go out to dinner could be guilty of anything improper?" This question, according to the official record, was "met with a laugh, as if the Members were astonished at Mr. Hume's simplicity."

All through 1828 Jane continued to arrive at parties and balls unescorted to be followed shortly by Prince Schwarzenberg. Count Rudolf Apponyi kept a record of the night he first met her under such circumstances. He had attended the theater, and then gone to a late dance given by a Mrs. Michels.

According to Apponyi, "We arrived at one A.M. There was already a large crowd on the stairs. Among all these people, one lady attracted me most. She was Lady Ellenborough, one of the most beautiful women I ever saw, blonde haired, lovely complexion, large blue eyes, only nineteen and with the figure of a nymph. She is the one Schwarzenberg adores and I did not fail to have myself introduced. Intellectually, she did not enchant me, I must admit, but all things cannot be found in one person. Her expression is sweet, as is the sound of her voice, and there was an air of modesty and innocence about her that charmed me.

"The coldness and ceremony of a first acquaintance did not last long between us. She spoke to me with great frankness of her husband, whom she charged with being jealous and unkind to her. But actually, I believe that Lord Ellenborough, occupied as he is with the duties of his exacting position, has no time to give good advice to his young wife. . . . I had already danced with Lady Ellenborough, when Schwarzenberg arrived. Milady did not mention to him that she had already danced with me. She asked him to request, from me, the pleasure of the first waltz. . . ."

The blatancy of the affair set off a whispered scandal. When rumors of the liaison sifted down to Margaret Steele, Jane's one-time governess, she begged her former charge to desist. Jane ignored her pleas. Then Miss Steele, all moral indignation and anger, went to Lord Ellenborough. She tried to warn him, she later told the House of Commons, that his young wife was "associating with bad companions . . . persons of rank." When Miss Steele was asked why she objected to her mistress's associating with persons of rank, she snapped, "Because I knew them by repute to be gay and profligate men." She was then asked, "What did Lord Ellenborough do when you warned him?" Miss Steele replied, "He laughed. . . . I was shocked."

Lord Ellenborough laughed because he did not believe the innuendos of a foolish spinster. On February 6, 1829, when his wife asked permission to take their son to Brighton for some fresh sea air, Lord Ellenborough saw no reason to object. He was now busier than ever. Under the sponsorship of the new prime minister, the Duke of Wellington, he had been appointed lord of the privy seal. His political diary reveals that on the day his wife, son, and his son's two nurses traveled to Brighton, Lord Ellenborough was occupied with a debate in the House of Commons and with a meeting involving the prime minister.

In Brighton, Jane took a suite in the exclusive Norfolk Hotel, where she had previously honeymooned with Lord Ellenborough. Shortly after she had packed her son off to bed, Prince Schwarzenberg arrived at the hotel in a yellow carriage. His carpetbag, plainly initialed F.S. and marked by an imperial crown, was delivered to his suite. He summoned a waiter, William Walton, and asked whether any other new guests had arrived that day. The waiter replied that there had been only one other, a Lady Ellenborough. Prince Schwarzenberg thought he knew her, and sent his card. As Mr. Walton delivered the card, he tried to read it. But it was in a foreign language.

At midnight, when the hotel was still, the prince emerged from his suite, moved softly toward Lady Ellenborough's rooms, and entered. Unfortunately, he was seen. A night porter, Robert Hepple, who had remained awake to admit a family that had gone to the theater, observed the furtive entry of the "foreign gentleman." Mr. Hepple, concerned only with the high moral tone of the hotel, as he later explained, approached Lady Ellenborough's door and put his eye to the keyhole. It was blocked by a key. Undiscouraged, he then placed his ear to the keyhole. "What did you hear?" he was asked by the House of Lords. "Kissing," he replied. Anything else? "The creaking of a bed," he replied. At three o'clock Prince Schwarzenberg left for his own quarters, and Mr. Hepple salvaged the remnants of his night's sleep.

Three months later it became apparent that Lady Ellenborough was in an advanced stage of pregnancy. Since her husband had not slept with her in more than a year, her condition would provide an increasing embarrassment. She had to speak to someone, and so she spoke to Margaret Steele, her companion. "God knows what will become of me," she said. "The child to which I shall soon give birth is Prince Schwarzenberg's."

The scandal had already spread so far that it had reached the ears of Lord Ellenborough's uncle, the Bishop of Bath and Wells. Like Miss Steele before him, the bishop tried to warn Lord Ellenborough. Whether or not his warning would have had any effect will never be known. For in the meantime Jane Ellenborough had decided to unburden her heart to her husband. On the evening of May 22, 1829, she revealed to Lord Ellenborough the full consequences of her love for the prince. The shock of revelation, however, was not sufficient to keep Ellenborough from his duties that same evening. "Dined at Lord Hill's," his diary notes. "A party chiefly military." But it is significant that for the following day there is no entry at all in Lord Ellenborough's diary.

During the weeks that followed, the three parties to the triangle were in a state of perpetual emotion. At the instigation of his benefactor, Prince Esterhazy, Schwarzenberg was hustled across the Channel, to circumvent the embarrassment of either a duel or a lawsuit. Jane, in retreat at her mother's, busied herself with packing, and preparing a farewell note to her husband:

> I hardly know what or how to write you. I dare not use the language of affection. You would think it hypocrisy. But though my family naturally wish that all should be again as it once was between us, those feelings of honour which I still retain towards you make me still acquiesce in your decision. God bless you, dearest Edward.
>
>   JANE

Dearest Edward's decision was, of course, divorce.

While Jane left for Paris to meet Schwarzenberg, Lord Ellenborough remained in London to face the notoriety that accompanied a debate in Parliament over his private life. Ellenborough's counsel opened the proceedings by touching briefly on Jane's sins, and then he went on: "I have seldom, my lords, been engaged in a case in which so distinctly has been brought home the criminality of the parties. The unhappy lady herself acknowledges her fault. I engage to show all these circumstances, if your lordships think it necessary. I hope, however, you will not require such proof. I am not anxious to feed the appetite which now rages in this country for slander and censure of persons moving in the highest ranks of society."

Counsel's hope was in vain. Their lordships required full proof.

Thereafter, a long file of witnesses—grooms, waiters, maids, valets—appeared before the House of Lords and the House of Commons to delineate the extent of milady's disgrace. Lord Ellenborough's handful of friends valiantly defended his goodness. Sir Henry Hardinge remarked that Ellenborough had been a thoughtful and considerate husband, and then read aloud the contents of a letter from Jane's own mother in which she had stated her gratitude to her son-in-law for his kindness to her daughter.

But Lord Ellenborough did not escape from the proceedings unblemished. He was chastised, in both Houses, for having "neglected, abandoned and sacrificed" his young wife. Lord Radnor, pointing out that Ellenborough had allowed his wife to go to bed alone almost every night, misquoted sonorously from St. Matthew: "'He that putteth away his wife for any cause other than adultery, causeth her to commit adultery.'"

Outside the halls of Parliament, the press had a circus. One newspaper published a sketch of Jane, her breasts bare, captioned by the poem:

> Never fancy time's before you,
> Youth believe me will away
> And then, alas, who will adore you
> Or to wrinkles tribute pay.

Such admonitions to Jane, implying criticism of her conduct, were rare in the press. For the most, the London newspapers sympathized with Lady Ellenborough and laid full blame on her husband. The tone of the press was such that Lord Grey was moved to write Princess de Lieven, "I think the attack upon Ellenborough rather hard, though *he* will not meet with much compassion. I feel very indignant at the articles which are directed against the upper classes generally."

Somehow, Lord Ellenborough survived the scandal. From the day the divorce was granted over shouts of "Not content," he never mentioned Jane's name again. Nor did he remarry. Instead, he built a memorial to his first wife, and lived on alone and unpopular until his death in 1871, by which time he had gained great honors both as Queen Victoria's Governor General of India and as First Lord of the Admiralty.

For Jane, the reunion with Prince Schwarzenberg in Paris was an unhappy one. She successfully gave birth to their daughter, but the love child became a symbol of their folly. When the prince left her, she permitted him to take their child and raise it as he wished. It was more than twenty years before she saw Schwarzenberg and her daughter again. By that time, she was the wife of a Greek, and the mother of a son she adored. Schwarzenberg, still a bachelor, was a major general in the Austrian Army, assigned to the court of the King of Naples. He came to Naples, from Turin, bringing with him Jane's grown daughter and his sister. Jane arrived in Naples with her boy. She met Schwarzenberg. What transpired between them is not known. Isabel Burton, wife of the translator of the *Arabian Nights*, insisted long after that Jane had loved Schwarzenberg to the day of her death. "It was easy to see that Schwarzenberg had been the love of her life," Mrs. Burton wrote, "for her eyes would light up with a glory when she mentioned him and she whispered his name with bated breath." From all other evidence, Mrs. Burton was romanticizing. In the letters Jane wrote in the half century after he left her, she plainly regretted her affair with Schwarzenberg and displayed no signs of affection for him.

After breaking with Jane in Paris, Prince Schwarzenberg had gone on to spend six years in Germany and ten years in Italy, before becoming Premier of Austria. As for Jane, though stranded in Paris after their separation, she was financially comfortable. She had three thousand pounds annually, for life, from Lord Ellenborough, as well as other income. She had her brief affair with Balzac and would achieve immortality in the pages of *La Comédie humaine*.

However, three English writers—all women—had utilized Jane

as the model for characters in their fiction, by the time Balzac's book appeared.

In 1826, Jane's relative, Marianne Stanhope, published a three-decker novel about London society, *Almack's,* in which the heroine was partially drawn after Jane. In 1830, Lady Charlotte Bury, who had been twice widowed and had served nine years as lady-in-waiting to Queen Caroline, brought out *The Exclusives.* In it she portrayed Jane's affair with Colonel George Anson, but defended Jane—or Lady Glenmore, as she called her in the novel—because she had been "thrown alone in the midst of the most dangerous class of the most dangerous society in London."

Then, in 1835, just before Balzac's *The Lily of the Valley* appeared, Lady Marguerite Blessington crucified Jane in *The Two Friends,* a best seller of the period. In this book Jane was represented as the spoiled, immoral Lady Walmer, who betrayed her husband by seducing first a young Englishman and then an Italian nobleman. Edward Bulwer-Lytton, who had helped arrange for the book's publication, wrote Lady Blessington that he thought her characterization of Lady Walmer "a very harsh but a very true portrait."

Lady Blessington was, of course, the last person on earth with the right to look virtuously down her nose at anyone. After a miserable marriage to a sadistic Irishman, she had had an affair with an English army officer, and been bought out of it for ten thousand pounds by her second husband, the Earl of Blessington. After the earl's death, Lady Blessington began a liaison with her stepdaughter's husband, a weak, charming French count named D'Orsay. *Fraser's Magazine,* in reviewing Lady Blessington's malevolent portrait of Jane, took her severely to task for her intolerance: "We have many allusions . . . to the story of Lady Ellenborough whom the authoress has caused to sit for her sketch of Lady Walmer and whom as such, she takes care to discredit and punish after a fashion which is more creditable to her morality than to her good taste and charity. . . . It is a sad doom to shadow forth for a fellow creature not more guilty than many of her old companions, but only more unfortunate in the emblazonment of her guilt. The misdeeds of her past life and probable miseries of her future were no fitting theme for a female novelist."

Such miseries as there would be in Jane Ellenborough's future, however, were not too readily apparent when she determined to leave Paris for Munich in the early summer of 1831. Munich was then a lively Teutonic Athens, ruled over by the eccentric, versifying aesthete, forty-five-year-old King Ludwig I of Bavaria.

King Ludwig was a remarkable man. At an early age he had fallen in love with the antiquities of Greece and Italy, and had decided to superimpose that antiquity upon Munich, much to the confusion of the good burghers of Bavaria. Parsimonious in his personal affairs—he wore frayed suits, made his children eat black bread to save money, denied his servants onions because they were expensive, and gave his mistresses nothing more than poems— he nevertheless lavished a fortune on palaces, churches, museums, Hellenic temples, and on archeological excavations in Greece and Rome. His mania was for beauty—in architecture and in women. Though married to Theresa of Saxe-Hildburghausen, an attractive "hausfrau who was to give him seven children and never a moment of anxiety," he changed mistresses more frequently than he did his linen. It was poetic justice that a beautiful woman caused his downfall.

When Ludwig was sixty years old, he received a request from a dancer newly arrived in Munich, who wished his permission to perform in the royal theater. When he refused to receive her to discuss her request, she forced her way into his study, then tore open her bodice, exposing her breasts to his gaze. The king not only permitted her to appear in the royal theater, but promptly took her for his mistress. This dancer was the twenty-eight-year-old Lola Montez, born Marie Gilbert in Ireland, who had acquired a few Spanish dance steps, a mantilla, and some castanets to help promote her international career. Her atheistic sentiments, and intrusion into Bavarian politics, irritated the local Jesuits, who incited riots against the king and Lola Montez. Once when a mob of students gathered outside her dwelling to heckle her, Lola appeared on the second-story balcony and poured champagne over their heads. In the end, Lola was forced to flee Munich for Switzerland, and the king was forced to abdicate his throne. He died in Nice, and Lola Montez died in Brooklyn, both shorn of their earlier power.

But fifteen years before Lola Montez, it was Jane Ellenborough who shared the king's bed and his favor. When Ludwig heard of Lady Ellenborough's beauty, he arranged to meet her.

The moment she was presented, King Ludwig commanded his court painter, Carl Stieler, to preserve her classic features for the Schönheits-Galerie—the Gallery of Beauty—located in the Residenz. In this gallery there hung portraits of all the beautiful women King Ludwig had loved or at least had coveted. There were thirty-six portraits of fresh, bosomy young women from every station in life, including ones of the daughter of the royal butcher and the Archduchess Sophie—and Jane Ellenborough. Jane was depicted in portrait as all the others had been—ringlets, big eyes, ivory complexion, well-exposed bosom. Several times a week the king wandered through his gallery, studying the beauties, seeking inspiration for what one biographer has called his "execrable verse."

The affair between Jane and King Ludwig progressed pleasantly. He was clever, learned, kindly, and naïve. He called her Ianthe and she called him Basily, both Greek names. From Ludwig she gained a renewed self-confidence, a brief sense of peace, and a lasting interest in painting and in ancient history. The affair eventually became quite public and was quite accepted. In 1835, Joseph Jekyll wrote Lady Sloane Stanley that a friend of his had just returned from Munich, where he had seen Lady Ellenborough: "Her liaison with the King is never denied. The King is a man of talents. My friend saw in one of his palaces a fine painted ceiling of the 'Triumph of Neptune' and among the sea nymphs discovered the portrait of Lady Ellenborough, which the King of Bavaria had given orders to introduce, and which the guide had reported readily."

A little over a year after she had become the king's mistress, Lady Ellenborough suddenly married a tall, redheaded official in the Munich court, Baron Carl Venningen, whom she had met earlier while out horseback-riding. Since she gave birth to a son just six weeks after her marriage, it was generally thought that the child was King Ludwig's and that he had forced her to wed to avoid scandal. According to Joseph Jekyll, as he related it in another of his letters to Lady Stanley, Queen Theresa had insisted upon Lady Ellenborough's marriage:

"Volume the second of the ci-devant Lady Ellenborough.

"'My dear Queen,' said His Majesty of Bavaria, 'I wish you would permit her to be presented.'

"'My dear King,' said the Queen, 'it is impossible. Consider her position with respect to yourself. Why don't you get her married, and then she would be presented of course.'

" 'That may be difficult,' quoth the King.

" 'Not in the least,' rejoined Her Majesty. 'Order one of your Marshals or Barons, and the man will be flattered by the mark of your favour.'

"The thing was done. A Baron was instantly found; old loves preserved; and three people made happy!"

Even though Baron Venningen's Catholic family tried to prevent the union, the baron married Jane in Italy during November of 1832. It is more than likely that Jane was still seeing King Ludwig, who was also in Italy at the time. But soon Ludwig was left to contemplate his Gallery of Beauty alone. For Jane, now the Baroness Venningen, found Carl Venningen a "most admirable man" in what was to be a long lifetime of men.

Jane remained faithful to Venningen for almost three years. They divided their time between the estates the baron owned in Munich and Baden, and took occasional trips to Sicily. There was one cause for constant disagreement. Venningen wanted his wife to become a typical German hausfrau. She had given him two children, but he hoped for more. The prospect of being permanently pregnant, as well as remaining anchored to the baron's estates and his small Bavarian circle, appalled Jane. She dreamed of new faces, new adventures, new sites. This insistence on her playing hausfrau, even though on a regal scale, was a growing source of irritation. Still, Jane had great affection for Venningen, and the marriage might have lasted many more years if Count Spyridon Theotoky had not appeared on the scene.

Indirectly, it was King Ludwig who was responsible for the entrance of Count Theotoky into Munich society and hence into Jane's life. While importing Greek culture to Bavaria, Ludwig had in 1832 exported his seventeen-year-old son Otto to Athens. There the Teutonic youth reigned as modern Greece's first king. Many old Greek families thought it wise to send their sons to Munich for education in the ways of their new ruler. Among the first of the Greeks to arrive was Count Spyridon Theotoky, who wished to study German military techniques. He was tall and slender, with a mop of black hair, curling mustache, and finely chiseled features. What he lacked in money, he made up for in manners, charm and gaiety.

The two, Jane and Theotoky, met at a royal ball given by King Ludwig in honor of the monarch of Prussia. Before the evening was over, Jane was calling her new friend Spyro, and when the evening was ended, they left the ball together. Their love for each other was spontaneous and immediate. She was utterly entranced, not only by Theotoky's physical charms but by his romantic references to his home in Corfu and his father's residence on the Aegean island of Tenos. Theotoky begged her to run off with him. She could obtain an easy divorce in Greece and then marry him.

While accompanying Venningen on a trip to Baden, she was torn by indecision. Count Theotoky followed, blindly, recklessly, finding quarters in Heidelberg. In Baden, Jane took great risks. When the baron slept, she would slip out late at night, lead her Arabian horse from the stables, and ride to a rendezvous with the count. One evening while her husband was away on a short business trip, Jane went to a dance Theotoky was attending. They left in a carriage together. Baron Venningen, returning home earlier than expected, passed the carriage. He had heard rumors about his wife and the Greek, but had tried to discount them. Now, seeing the pair together, he found his suspicions confirmed. He ordered his coachman to wheel about and give chase. Jane and Theotoky, aware that they had been discovered, fled for the French frontier. But at the frontier they were delayed by border guards, and there Venningen caught up with them.

Quite naturally enraged, Venningen insisted upon immediate satisfaction. An impromptu duel, with pistols as the weapons, was arranged in a wooded area off the highway. The coachmen acted as seconds. The baron and the count paced off, pivoted, and the more experienced Venningen fired first. The bullet imbedded itself above Theotoky's heart. He sagged to the grass and lay apparently dying in his own blood. Hysterically, Jane threw herself upon him. A frontier physician, hastily summoned, pronounced the wound a mortal one. According to Count Apponyi, Theotoky believed he had but a few hours to live. "He then declared to the husband that he was innocent and the victim of the most infamous calumny. He insisted that between him and the Baroness there had never been anything beyond a deep and sincere friendship. Then he clasped the hand of his friend, and, with a deep sigh, shut his eyes. Fortunately for him, he did not shut them forever."

Carried to the Burg Venningen so that he might die in bed, Count Theotoky became an immobile embarrassment by persistently remaining alive. Within a few weeks he was well, and the disposition of Jane had to be considered again. While all Bavaria buzzed with the story of the three of them—husband, wife, and lover—confined under one roof, Jane asked Venningen for her freedom. Graciously, he gave it. He saw Jane and Count Theotoky off to Paris, and retained for life Jane's gratitude and her two children. Baron Venningen, until he died of a heart attack while horseback-riding in Munich forty years later, corresponded regularly and affectionately with Jane. Mostly he wrote her of their son Heribert, who grew up to marry a girl half English (who gave Jane three grandchildren), and of their daughter Bertha, who went insane and died in an asylum.

It was five years before Jane saw either Theotoky's Greece or his wedding ring. In this interval they lived, as lovers, in France and Italy. When Jane was not socializing in Paris with Theotoky, she was shopping against the day they would be married and could set up a house in Greece. But the wedding could not occur until Jane obtained her divorce from Venningen, and was admitted into the Greek Orthodox Church. "In order to marry her dear Count," Edmond About noted, "she adopted the Greek religion. You know, of course, that Greek baptism is performed by dipping. That is why the Greeks call us ill-christened dogs. The Countess was baptized in a bathtub."

In 1841, when Jane was thirty-four, she finally became the Countess Theotoky. Immediately after the ceremony in Paris, she set out to meet her father-in-law, Count Joannes Theotoky, who was governor of the isle of Tenos.

The old count awaited Jane's arrival on Tenos with nervous expectancy. He had been told only part of her background. He knew nothing about Schwarzenberg, Balzac, King Ludwig or her marriage to Baron Venningen. He thought that she had just recently deserted Lord Ellenborough for his son. But even this was enough to make him apprehensive. One of his guests at the time, on the cramped and stony isle, was apprehensive about Jane's arrival for a different reason. This guest was a fifty-year-old French archeologist named Alexandre Buchon.

Buchon knew somewhat more of Jane's actual history, and could not imagine her dwelling on the treeless, perpendicular isle of Tenos. He noted that the island had twenty-one thousand peasants who lived in crude stone houses, but he could find few assets beyond the natives' lacework, their antique jewelry, and a church that had been built on the spot where a local priest once saw the Virgin Mary. Even his host's house, in which Jane was expected to settle down, was small and inconvenient, and located on a narrow, twisting lane, without a view of either the mountains or the sea.

During his stay at the house, Buchon saw Jane's most recent purchases, just shipped from Paris, being unpacked. An incredulous Buchon recorded the sight in his private journal: "I can't imagine what stories Theotoky could have told Lady Ellenborough to have convinced her to settle in a country so completely devoid of any comfort, convenience, beautiful scenery or decent conversation. That she should send saddles to a country where horses cannot walk and where even mules have difficulty retaining their footing on the slopes and slippery rocks, shows a complete ignorance of the land where she will live. She will be sadly disappointed when she sees Tenos as it is—a Governor's house, an army garrison, a naval station, a village, and a piece of landscape. It will be a bitter expiation of the follies of her youth, a folly that will end in the greatest of all her follies."

Buchon was off on a side trip to some of the other Cyclades Islands when Jane finally disembarked at Tenos. When the French archeologist returned, four months later, he realized at once that his attempt at prophecy had been a failure. For Jane was neither disappointed nor dismayed by the island.

Indeed, she seemed to thrive on the vigorous, primitive pleasures provided by Tenos. Perched on muleback, she led Buchon, and two of his French friends, on a harrowing climb to the picturesque village of Kardiani. During early mornings, she often hiked to the ruins of Exoburgo Castle. Sometimes she was accompanied by her father-in-law, whom she had completely captivated, as well as by her husband. Frequently, she entertained the local Italian doctor and the Greek priest at dinners when she served lamb roasted on stones, pickled doves, and Malmsey wine.

Eventually she moved to Dukades, Theotoky's estate on Corfu. Here she busied herself with making the new home attractive.

She gave her husband an English library and herself a French drawing room, and in the spacious, untended grounds she laid out a garden and planted a cypress tree, which may still be seen today. There were constant parties with nights of eating, drinking, singing, and Jane was happy. Then, suddenly, Count Spyridon Theotoky was promoted to a colonelcy in the Greek Army, appointed aide-de-camp to King Otto, and ordered to Athens. And the marriage fell apart.

In Athens, which young King Otto had made the new capital of Greece, replacing Nauplia, Jane built a house and stables and entertained lavishly. She gave birth to a son named Leonidas. Of the six children that she had in her lifetime, by both husbands and lovers, Leonidas, a blond, gentle child who resembled her, was her favorite. She adored the boy, and took him, dressed in suits trimmed in gold lace, on a vacation to Italy. One day while she was chatting with Italian friends in her villa near the Lucca Baths, little Leonidas tried to slide down the second-story banister. He slipped, plunged to the marble floor below, and was instantly killed.

Shortly after, Jane divorced Theotoky. The child had been their last bond. They had been together fifteen years, five years as lovers, ten years as husband and wife, but they had gradually gone their own ways. Theotoky had become increasingly careless with Jane's income and increasingly attentive to other women. After the divorce, he went on to marry three more times before his death in Russia. As for Jane, months before her marriage was officially severed, she had turned to another lover. Years earlier, in Munich, she had been the mistress of King Ludwig. Now, in Athens, she became the mistress of his son, King Otto.

King Otto was his father's son in one respect: He was a classicist. But when England, France, and Russia assented to King Ludwig's proposal that Otto occupy the Greek throne, it was an unfortunate compromise. The trouble was basic. King Otto was interested in Greece's past; the Greek people were interested in their present. Athens, a crude village of perhaps twenty thousand, was impoverished. The wealthiest families subsisted on vegetables, the poorest on salted fish. "If you stop a workman on the promenade," said Edmond About, "and ask him if he would sell his shoes for a reasonable price, you can bet ten to one he'll walk home barefooted."

While his lack of interest in the national economy annoyed the Greeks, King Otto provoked antagonism for other reasons. He was a Roman Catholic, which the Orthodox Greeks resented. He was a Bavarian, loading his court and army with Germans imported from Munich, and this the Greeks resented even more. Worst of all, he was a weakling. Though not without charm, his manner was unfortunate. "It is practically impossible not to laugh before His Majesty of Greece," confessed Édouard Thouvenal, a French diplomat. "Instead of speaking, he swallows his saliva with infinite difficulty for five minutes before giving birth to a sentence." Actually, King Otto's domineering wife did most of his speaking, writing, and thinking for him. She had been the Princess Amalie of Oldenburg. The royal marriage, prearranged, was barren of both children and love. The joke around Athens at the time was that the king read everything without signing it and the queen signed anything without reading it.

Queen Amalie disliked Jane for her beauty, her conversational ability, her dancing skill, and her horsemanship. And she despised Jane for taking away her husband. Jane reciprocated this feeling of hostility. In 1854, when revolution was brewing throughout Greece and flight by the royal couple seemed inevitable, Jane received the news in Syria and exclaimed with pleasure: "So then my wish is granted and my rival the Queen is annihilated." However, Jane's wish was not fully granted until eight years later when the royal couple was finally forced to escape from Athens on a British warship, a year after a student tried to assassinate the queen.

Jane was eight years older than King Otto, but her beauty was well preserved. Edmond About met her in Athens in 1852, when the affair was still in progress, and considered her striking: "Ianthe is a wonderful example of health and physical beauty. She is tall and slender without being thin. If her waistline were a bit lower, it would be impossible to find a woman with a better figure. . . . Her complexion has preserved that milky whiteness that blooms best under English fogs. But at the lightest emotion she blushes. You might say that this fine transparent skin is little more than a net which imprisons her passions. You can see her passions, agitating, coloring, as they move about their jail."

Once when she was having tea with the youthful About, Jane referred indirectly to her affairs with King Ludwig and King

Otto. She asked About, "Do you believe in fortune-telling by cards? Long ago, I consulted Mademoiselle Lenormant and she told me I would turn many men's heads—"

About interrupted gallantly: "It would require no sorceress to predict that."

"—particularly three crowned heads."

"Have you found them?"

"I looked thoroughly, but to date I found only two."

"That is because the third one is yet to come," he assured her.

This conversation took place at the Pentelikon residence of the remarkable, eccentric, expatriate Frenchwoman who had brought Jane and About together. This Frenchwoman was the wealthy Sophie de Barbe-Marbois, the Duchesse de Plaisance. She had been born in Philadelphia, married one of Napoleon's generals, become a lady-in-waiting to the Empress Marie Louise, and finally had retired to Athens to found a new religion. She resided in a home she would not finish building—"through the superstitious fear of dying when she had completed anything," About thought. The duchess dwelt in isolation, a tiny, crusty, white-haired old lady, protected by six huge Irish wolfhounds. One of her few friends, perhaps her oldest friend, was Jane Ellenborough.

Jane needed the duchess desperately. For consorting with King Otto and subsequently with one of his generals, she was ostracized not only by the Athens court but by Greek society at the instigation of Queen Amalie. Only the Duchesse de Plaisance defended Jane's affairs, calling each a "free union."

But the companionship of the duchess was not enough. Without a real man's love, Jane was unhappy and unfulfilled in hostile Athens. Already weary of King Otto, she determined to travel in search of she knew not what. She went to Turkey, Italy, Switzerland. The mysterious months she spent in those countries remain the least-known period of her entire life. She left behind her, especially in Italy, a trail of gossip and rumor that has confounded biographers for almost a dozen decades. Many writers of the time, more interested in sensation than in fact, chose to believe that she had cavorted about Rome like a reincarnated Jezebel. A Vienna correspondent in the Near East reported to his paper: "She went to Italy where, as she told me herself, she was married six times in succession." Others echoed this report and

credited Jane with five Italian husbands as well as a Spanish one.
More conservative writers contended that she had taken many
lovers in Italy, but only two husbands.

However, the Italian husbands, whether two or five, remain
undocumented by either Jane's written words or official records.
The lovers are another thing. It is highly probable that Jane had
a number of indiscriminate affairs in this period. One story that
persists involves her with three Italian suitors simultaneously. At
a ball given in Rome by the Princess Corci, Jane met an Italian
artillery officer. She succumbed to his flattery, accepted his gift of
a diamond necklace, and was considering his proposal of marriage. Then another suitor, an Italian army captain, told her that
her prospective groom was an impoverished scoundrel who had
cheated a jeweler out of the necklace. This charge proved to
be true. The artillery officer went to jail, and the captain was
prepared to lead Jane to the altar. But by then she had turned to
a young diplomat, the son of an Italian ambassador. Infuriated,
the captain challenged the diplomat to a duel. Both assumed that
she would marry the survivor. The duel was fought with swords.
The diplomat, though badly slashed across the face, ran the captain through. When the diplomat thereupon demanded Jane's
hand, and she refused him, he killed himself, or so the story goes.

The overemotionalism of the Latins and the chaos of her social life in Rome were far from soothing. She returned to Athens,
took up with King Otto again briefly, and then, one day, she met
General Xristodolous Hadji-Petros and forgot all about the king.

Jane had gone on a tour of northern Greece. There the men
of the mountains—thin, nervous, silent men—were called palikars,
"the brave ones." Half patriots, half bandits, these palikars had
fought valiantly to help Greece win its independence. The leader
of these mountain men was seventy-year-old General Hadji-
Petros. He was tall for his race, and young for his years, and
brigand that he was, he reigned as an absolute sovereign over
his people. In addition, for his service to the cause of liberation,
he had been appointed governor of the province surrounding
Lamia.

Jane saw him first in the city of Lamia. He wore a red cap,
gold jacket, pleated white skirt, and sat gracefully astride a horse,
on a silver-trimmed saddle. Though he was twenty-five years older
than she, Jane was entranced. She managed an introduction,

then accompanied him into the hills with his troops. She became his mistress at once, slept with him before campfires under the stars, ate bread and cheese, and drank red wine from goatskin containers.

She learned that the general was a widower, and the father of an attractive son named Eirini. She enjoyed being treated as a bandit queen. "She imagined she was born a Palikar," Edmond About reported. "She ruled over Lamia. The whole city was at her feet. When she went out for her walk, the drums beat out a greeting."

The drums were heard in Athens, too. Queen Amalie, who had not forgiven Jane, saw a way to get her revenge. She signed an order reproving General Hadji-Petros for immorality, and temporarily suspended him from the governorship of Lamia as well as his command of the palikars.

The general was distressed. He promptly protested to the queen in a most unfortunate bit of prose. "Your Majesty has dismissed me," he wrote, "undoubtedly because I am living with the Countess Theotoky. But whatever my enemies may have told you, I can assure you on my word of honor as a soldier that if I am this woman's lover, it is not for love's sake, but purely for self-interest. She is rich and I am poor. I have a position to maintain and a child to educate."

In an effort to humiliate Jane further, Queen Amalie made the letter public. Curiously, Jane did not seem perturbed. She was convinced that the general had written the letter merely to regain his position as governor of Lamia. She suggested that they return to Athens together. The general agreed. Jane rented two bungalows, connected by a garden, in the suburbs. In one she lived with her young French maid, Eugénie, whom she had brought from Paris after she married Theotoky; in the other she established the general and his retinue of faithful palikars. But a bungalow proved too small and uncomfortable for Jane. She was as out of place in her little house, About remarked, "as a portrait by Lawrence hanging in a kitchen."

She contracted to have a huge mansion built at Piraeus, a small, primitive village four or five miles from Athens, so that she and the general could live more expansively. Her bedroom was built like a throne room. The general had his private suite.

His palikars had a barracks among the almond trees at the rear. And, of course, Jane had her stables. It was a paradise.

But soon there was trouble in this paradise, too. The elderly general was increasingly crotchety and uncommunicative. He smelled of garlic and took to cuffing Jane about. All of this she endured, as long as she felt that Hadji-Petros loved her. But when she learned that he was also sleeping with her maid Eugénie, her disillusionment was complete.

Sick at heart, she cast about for an escape. And then she thought of the ruins of ancient Palmyra, deep in the Syrian desert far from both Baghdad and the Mediterranean. She had heard about Palmyra first from King Ludwig. And then she had heard more about it from Theotoky and King Otto. Suddenly it seemed to her the haven she so much needed. She left Athens by ship for Alexandretta, Syria, with a minimum of preparation. She said only that she was going to buy Arabian mares in the East.

Actually, this was the turning point in her life. Without realizing it, though perhaps she sensed it, she was moving closer to that which she had always sought. Few of those who knew her, even those closest to her, really understood what Jane Ellenborough was after. Many dismissed her as a nymphomaniac, one of those frenzied females who constantly demand new bed companions in their search for continual sexual gratification. That Jane possessed a consuming and persistent need for—and enjoyment of—sexual love, there can be little doubt. But was Jane Ellenborough a nymphomaniac?

Modern psychologists tell us there are two concepts of what constitutes a nymphomaniac. By clinical definition, the true nymphomaniac is one step away from a mental ward, a female who cannot control her desire for sex, whose need is unquenchable, whose compulsion for sex is irrational, and who always feels degraded by her performances. The popularly accepted definition of a nymphomaniac is a woman who is sexually permissive beyond the standards acceptable to her society. As Dr. Albert Ellis and Edward Sagarin put it in a recent study: "What is often termed nymphomania is *usually* promiscuity, relatively well controlled, probably highly selective, and of a nature that would be considered relatively normal if found in almost any male in our society."

That Jane Ellenborough was, clinically, a nymphomaniac seems unlikely. But she does fit the popularly accepted definition since she was promiscuous, although in a controlled and selective way. Jane's desires exceeded mere sexual gratification. For, in addition to the transitory pleasures of sex, Jane needed the peace of mind that comes from being wanted, being secure, belonging to somebody. She felt that she would find this peace if she found the right mate in the right place. In Syria, she found the place. And there, also, she found the mate. And her long journey came to an end, but it did not happen all at once.

First, there was Saleh. This was "selective" sex or "promiscuity" and little else. She met him in May of 1853, while riding along the Jordan en route to Jerusalem and Palmyra, accompanied by a contrite Eugénie and an Arab escort. She noticed a thoroughbred mare and asked who owned it. She was told that the mare belonged to a Bedouin sheik who lived nearby. He turned out to be a young, attractive Arab, and his name was Saleh.

As Jane recounted the story of the meeting to the Duchesse de Plaisance in Athens later, Jane tried to buy the mare and Saleh refused to sell. "Unfortunately, this horse cannot be tamed," he said. "But even if she could be tamed, I would not set a price on her. I value her more than anything in the world, even more than my three wives."

"A fine horse is a treasure," Jane agreed, "but so are three wives, if they are beautiful. Bring your horse to me, and let us see if she can be tamed."

Saleh signaled two of his tribesmen, who brought forth the rearing animal. With some difficulty, the mare was saddled. Jane mounted her, stayed with her, gentled and gradually subdued her. Saleh's gaze had not been on the horse, but on Jane. When she dismounted, he went to her. "Woman often succeeds where man fails, because she knows when to yield. The mare is priceless, now that you have tamed her. If you still want her, you may buy her—but not with money."

According to Jane, she studied Saleh's handsome face and well-developed physique for a moment, and then accepted Saleh's terms. "I will pay for your horse the price you expect," she said. "I did not come all this way to bargain. But one thing you must know—in my country, women are too proud to share a man's heart. They enter his tent on the condition that they reign in it alone. I will pay the price you wish for your horse, but only if you send away your harem."

Saleh quickly replied, "The men of my country have as many women as they can afford. I should look like a twelve-hundred-franc employee if I sent away my harem and lived with one woman. Too, I must obey my religion, set an example for my followers, and follow the custom of the Turks. To us, polygamy is necessary."

Soon, however, Saleh's passion overcame his scruples. By late afternoon he had sent away his harem, and by evening Jane had entered his black tent.

The affair continued with great intensity for several months. Jane was sufficiently satisfied with Saleh's virility to wish it to continue indefinitely. Toward this end, she decided to return briefly to Athens and settle her affairs. But first she must see Palmyra. She left Saleh with regret and pushed on to Jerusalem and Damascus.

Damascus, capital of Syria, was a complete surprise. Jane was stimulated and excited by the Moslem religious center. As she rode up the crooked Street Called Straight, she was not offended by the reeking piles of refuse, the hawkish desert Arabs, the chanting merchants. She saw only what Kinglake had seen earlier: "This 'Holy' Damascus, this 'earthly paradise' of the Prophet, so fair to the eye that he dared not trust himself to tarry in her blissful shades—she is a city of hidden palaces, of copses, and gardens and fountains, and bubbling streams." It was with difficulty that she shook off the spell of the fragile minarets and domes and began to think of Palmyra.

When the English consul heard of her plan to visit Palmyra, he was horrified. He warned her that it was a dangerous ten-day trek on horseback across hot sands, through bandit-infested country. Jane ignored his warning. She was determined to arrange for a caravan at once.

Jane made inquiries. She learned that two Arab tribes, the Shammars and the Anazehs, each with twenty-eight thousand tents, controlled the Syrian desert beyond. Among the Anazehs was a trustworthy group, the Mezrabs, with a hundred tents. They could be depended upon to guide her, find the hidden water holes, fight off raiders. Jane asked the Mezrabs to send an emissary to discuss price.

And thus she met Medjuel. She could not know then that it was the most important meeting with a man in her entire life. Her mind was still on Saleh. And Medjuel's appearance was not such as to make her forget her Bedouin lover. Medjuel was a short, leathery, bearded man. Isabel Burton called him "that dirty little black . . . much darker than an Arab generally is." Lady Anne Blunt, Lord Byron's granddaughter, described him more accurately: "In appearance he shows all the characteristics of good Bedouin blood. He is short and slight in stature, with exceedingly small hands and feet, a dark olive complexion, beard originally black but now turning grey, and dark eyes and eyebrows."

Medjuel's real attraction, however, had nothing to do with his appearance. He was an erudite and cultured man, with a knowledge of desert lore, and he had several languages at his command, although English was not one of them. Lady Blunt thought him "well bred and agreeable." And Isabel Burton grudgingly admitted that, despite his color, he was "very intelligent and charming."

His background was as aristocratic as Jane's. His family was one of the four noble first families of the desert. He had been the second of nine sons, and was in line to succeed his childless brother, Sheik Mohammed, as head of their clan. It was his linguistic ability that had secured him the assignment of bargaining with the wealthy Englishwoman about her caravan.

If Jane was unimpressed by him, Medjuel certainly was aware of her. As a matter of fact, he was struck dumb by her beauty. He agreed to the first price she offered him—eight thousand francs— for providing her with a caravan and escorting it to Palmyra. When Medjuel returned, still dazed, to his tribe, he expected to be chastised for the poor bargain he had made. But his brother was unconcerned. For his brother had made a better bargain with the Gomussa, an allied clan. The plan was that the Mezrabs would lead Jane into a mock Gomussa ambush. She would be kidnapped and held for ransom, or else be robbed of the money she carried with her and then abandoned. Either way, a large sum of money would then be divided between the two tribes.

When Medjuel objected to this plan, he was ridiculed into silence. The tribe was poor. The golden opportunity must not be lost. The caravan, with Medjuel in charge, was quickly prepared, and soon was on its way to Palmyra. Since Jane spoke no Arabic, the only person she could communicate with was Medjuel, who knew French. She asked him about Palmyra. He told her stories of the walled city's heyday in A.D. 250, under the rule of the half-Greek, half-Arabic eighteen-year-old Queen Zenobia. He told her of Queen Zenobia, astride a camel, challenging the might of the Roman Empire, and of the siege that forced her to flee, and of her eventual capture and death in chains. Jane was fascinated, not only with the history but with Medjuel's presentation of it. She confided her past to him, and described her present affair with Saleh. He told her of his wife and two sons. He did not tell Jane that he was deeply in love with her.

Medjuel was riding beside her when they moved into the pre-arranged ambush. Suddenly, from every direction, Gomussa raiders, shrieking and screaming, lances held high, charged in. Medjuel's instructions were to offer a halfhearted sham defense, and then abandon Jane. But he could not bring himself to do it. Rallying his followers, he plunged, flaying about him, into the mass of startled attackers. After a short, sharp struggle, during which Medjuel would not give ground, his confused allies and fellow conspirators turned tail and fled into the dunes.

Jane was impressed and grateful. The caravan continued to Palmyra and there camped among the two thousand broken marble columns. Medjuel led Jane around the remains of the seven-mile wall that had once protected the oasis, showing her the sites of the ancient palaces and temples.

On the way back to Damascus, just outside the gates, Medjuel summoned up the courage to propose marriage. He told Jane that he was in love with her. He said that he would divorce his wife for her. Jane would not have it. She liked Medjuel, liked his dignity, manners, humor. But she would not permit him to leave his wife. Besides, though she did not speak of it, her mind was on Saleh. Medjuel did not press his suit. He left her without once holding her hand or attempting to kiss her.

It was late in 1853 when she came back to Athens. She stayed just long enough to rearrange her financial affairs and pack her effects. She was anxious to return to Saleh. When the Duchesse de Plaisance, who disapproved of Jane's affair, could not dissuade her from leaving, she quarreled with Jane, so that she would be sure not to miss her. Jane returned to Saleh. But so had his three wives. The bargain was broken.

Angrily, Jane left for Baghdad. As her guide, she hired Sheik El Barrak, a hot-tempered, brutal, animal man. He had heard that she had been Saleh's mistress, and he had taken the job only to seduce her. The moment that they were on the road, he began making advances. She disliked El Barrak and tried to reject him. Eventually, because of her utter weariness and his insensitive persistence, she gave in and slept with him.

By the time they reached Mezrab territory, they were no longer speaking. She had fed a starving camel out of their food supplies, and he had ranted at Jane over such waste. She despised him. Then, realizing that she was among the Mezrabs, Jane remembered Medjuel, remembered his kindness and sweetness. She began to inquire after him. And suddenly, one afternoon, he appeared. Medjuel had heard of her arrival, and as a gift he brought her a young Arabian mare. Overwhelmed by his gift and by the sight of him, she knew that she was finally in love.

Jane dismissed El Barrak, and happily rode to Damascus with Medjuel. He told her that he had divorced his wife, returning her to her family with her dowry, but he had kept his sons, Japhet and Schebibb. Now, once again, he asked Jane to marry him. This time, filled with excitement, she accepted.

There were immediate obstacles. Medjuel's entire family opposed the marriage. Her blood was not as blue as his, her faith was not Mohammedan, her background was not the right background for the desert. Jane met equal opposition from the British consul in Damascus. He could not believe his ears when he heard that she wanted to marry a Bedouin. He reminded her that she was a Digby, an Ellenborough, an English subject who would by this marriage become a Turkish national, since Medjuel and all Syrians were subjects of Turkey's Ottoman Empire. He told her that it was sheer madness, that he would have her declared a lunatic rather than cooperate. But in the end he cooperated, as did Medjuel's family. Medjuel owned a small house in Homs. There, in 1855, Lady Ellenborough became Jane Digby el Mezrab. She was forty-eight and her husband was forty-five. The marriage, as it turned out, was her last, her longest, and her best.

A compromise about their mode of living was effected at once. Six months of each year were to be spent, Western style, in her Damascus villa, and the other six months would be spent, Bedouin style, in his desert tent. This hastily arrived at compromise lasted the entire twenty-six years of their marriage and was entirely satisfactory to both of them.

Except for Medjuel's brief forays into the desert, when he joined his fellow tribesmen in fighting their enemies, the Shammars, the two were separated but once. A year after their marriage, Jane decided to return to England for a visit. She had not seen her homeland for a quarter of a century, not since the day in 1829 when she had fled her noble lord and her family to join Schwarzenberg in Paris.

The decision to bridge the broken years and ignore the wreckage and scandal of her past was a difficult one to make, but her father had died and there were family matters to be settled. Yet there may have been even more at stake. She had taken up a life so different from that which she had known in her early years—a life involving a relationship considered insane and bizarre by family and friends—that she may have wanted to test her own feelings. Perhaps there would never be peace for her in the desert, until she had laid the ghost of English respectability. And so, for the last time, she went back to her English home.

Surely there is the perfect subject for a drama in Jane Digby el Mezrab's return. She walked down the gangplank at Folkestone, dressed in the height of Paris fashion, on December 19, 1856. Jane Steele, the sister of Jane's childhood governess, was on hand to greet her. The two women embraced, wept a little, and then drove to Tunbridge Wells.

Jane's mother, Lady Andover, now a corpulent eighty, was waiting, full of warmth, as was Jane's old governess, Margaret Steele. Jane's brother Edward came to visit for three days. But when she tried to show him her watercolors of Palmyra, a sudden coolness set in. The family did not wish to hear of her marriage to an Arab, and Margaret Steele persisted in referring to her as Mme. Theotoky. For a few brief moments she was depressed. "My family ties burst asunder; no children; no English home!" she noted. "I am not gay as I gaze around and think of what might have been and what is." But then her beloved younger brother, the Reverend Kenelm Digby, appeared full of questions about Medjuel and the desert, and suddenly Jane was happy again and she knew what was right. The East was her home and Medjuel was her husband—and she wrote him, quite incredulously: "I in England!"

There was a surreptitious visit to London to see old friends. It has been claimed that Jane's entire visit to England was made furtively, because one condition of Lord Ellenborough's alimony agreement had been that she never return. More likely, Jane kept her visit quiet for fear of embarrassing her family. For England had changed. Fornication was no longer in fashion. Victoria was on the throne.

After a fiftieth-birthday party and four months spent with the remaining members of her family, she departed from England forever. In Paris, she bought a piano and painting supplies, and a month later she was in Damascus. "With beating heart I arrived," she said. "Then he arrived, Medjuel, the dear, the adored one, and in that moment of happiness I forgot all else."

For the most part, her life in Syria was serene. Her sprawling villa outside the Damascus gates was furnished in the comfortable Arabic manner, except for her private rooms, and these were filled with French furniture, English books received regularly from London, and her own watercolors of Palmyra and Greece. The grounds were large enough for a lily pond, a garden in which Jane planted seeds imported from England, and a stable for her Arabian horses. Her pets roamed everywhere, among them a gazelle, a turkey, a pelican, and at least a hundred Persian cats. Here, according to Isabel Burton, "she led a semi-European life. She blackened her eyes with kohl, and lived in a curiously untidy manner. But otherwise was not in the least extraordinary."

Isabel Burton was wrong. When Jane accompanied Medjuel into the desert, she was quite extraordinary, as Mrs. Burton later admitted. "When she was in the desert," wrote Mrs. Burton, "she used to milk the camels, serve her husband, prepare his food, wash his hands, face and feet, and stood and waited on him while he ate, like any Arab woman, and gloried in so doing." She loved the desert and played Bedouin to the hilt. Because her light hair was considered bad luck by the tribesmen, she dyed it black and wore it in braids. Dressed in a pale-blue cotton gown and often barefoot, she worked and she rode. The Mezrabs adored her, called her Mother of Milk because of her creamy complexion, and White Devil because of her courage. When the tribes moved south to graze their camels, this courage was needed. There were constant battles over grazing areas. Once when a band of Shammars swooped down on the Mezrab tents, many of Medjuel's tribesmen fled. Jane snatched up a rifle, and with her first shot killed the approaching sheik. The attackers broke and retreated.

Occasionally throughout the long years of her marriage, Jane's happiness was sorely tried. In the beginning, religion had been no issue. While Medjuel was devout and turned his face toward Mecca five times each day, Jane remained disinterested in any orthodox faith. Her attitude was changed by the infamous July massacres of 1860. Fanatical Syrians, infuriated by the efforts of foreign missionaries to convert Moslems and inflamed by the incident of an infidel murdering a Druse, rose in revolt. Blood was let throughout Syria, and three thousand Christians died violently. Mobs stormed into the European quarter of Damascus, burning houses, killing the Dutch consul, wounding the American consul. Christian corpses littered the streets. While Jane took in refugees, Medjuel stood guard over her with a gun. But no Arabs entered her villa. All regarded her as one of their own. When the massacres were over, Jane did not forget their horror. Defiantly, she returned to her Protestant faith, even going to the extreme of attending church twice every Sunday.

The greatest problem in her marriage, as it turned out, did not concern her being an infidel, but rather it concerned her husband's infidelity. When she married Medjuel, she had made a rash statement to him. Moslem men, she knew, were permitted to possess more than one wife. Jane had told Medjuel that if ever, in the years to come, he felt that he required another woman, he might take one, as long as he kept her existence a secret. With the years, this promise came to haunt Jane. Twice, when he rode off into the desert to fight or to look after his herds, she heard rumors that he was visiting another wife, whom he kept hidden. On each occasion, tortured by jealousy, she accused Medjuel of unfaithfulness, and each time he proved to her satisfaction that he had not seen another woman, that he had no other woman, that he wished none.

Jane's fears were renewed when one of Medjuel's sons died and the boy's widow was brought into the house to live with them. The widow was a dazzling young Bedouin girl named Ouadjid. For many years, Jane feared that Medjuel had quietly married the girl or had taken her as a mistress. Jane ached with the realization that Ouadjid was young and she was old. A single thought oppressed her: if only she had her youth again, if only Medjuel had known her as she was when Schwarzenberg and Balzac and King Ludwig had known her, if only she had met Medjuel long before. It was the one time she hated aging. And even after her suspected rival died in 1880, Jane confessed, "I am jealous of her memory."

On the other hand, she was still sufficiently beautiful, and also rich enough, to attract other men, and the proposals made to her were a constant source of annoyance to Medjuel. When she was fifty-one, Sheik Fares ibn Meziad tried to win her away from her husband, but failed. When she was seventy-one, her young drago-man, Anton, tried to sleep with her, but was rejected. During her entire life in Damascus, her legendary past made her a target for romantic adventurers, foreigners who wished to build reputations as lovers by reporting that they had seduced Lady Ellenborough. Typical among these was a Bavarian-born English citizen, Carl Haag, who was one of Queen Victoria's favorite court painters. He hired Jane and Medjuel to guide him about the desert, and when he returned to London, he hinted that he had been her lover—this in an effort to publicize the products of his brush. De-spite all the gossip, it is unlikely that Jane was ever unfaithful to Medjuel. She loved him too much, and she never tired of his at-tentions. In her seventy-third year, when her husband was him-self seventy, she complained, "It is now a month and twenty days since Medjuel last slept with me! What can be the reason?"

Proof of the constancy of Jane's devotion to Medjuel, as well as the fullest picture of her last years, may be found in the writings of the many travelers she received and entertained in Damascus. One of the most vivid of these accounts was set down by Lord Redesdale, after visiting Jane in 1871:

"I found Lady Ellenborough—Mrs. Digby as she now called herself—living in a European house, furnished so far at any rate as the rooms in which we were received were concerned, like those of an English lady; in the desert with the tribe she would be altogether Arab. Her tables were covered with the miniatures, knick knacks and ornaments, indigenous to Mayfair—quite out of tune with Damascus. The owner was, like her belongings, a little old-fashioned, and very nice to look upon, as she had the re-mains of great good looks, and the most gracious and beautiful old world manners.

"She was very much interested in hearing about England, and

asked many questions about friends she had known in the old days. She seemed to think that the world had stood still since she left it, for she spoke of people who, if not dead, were quite old folk, as if they were in the hey day of blooming youth. She asked after the old Lord Chantallam—grandfather of the present Earl. How was he? 'Wonderful,' I said, 'cutting us all out skating at Highclere two or three months ago.' Lady Ellenborough looked puzzled. 'But why should he not?' she asked. 'Well,' I answered, 'you must remember that he is past seventy years of age.' 'Dear me, is that possible, that handsome young man?' Her old friends remained in her mind just as she had known them—Lady Palmerston, Lady Jersey, Lady Londonderry, still reigning beauties, still queens of Almack's.

"It was strange to hear a delicately nurtured English lady talking of her life in the desert with 'her' tribe. She told us how, the summer before, a hostile tribe had raided them and stolen some of their mares, and how, this next summer, they must ride out to avenge the outrage, and get back the lost treasures. There would be fierce fighting, she said, and she must be there to nurse the chief should anything happen to him. 'In fact,' she added, 'we have our foot in the stirrup, for we must start for the desert tomorrow morning.'

"We had a long talk, for she was a keen questioner, and then she insisted on taking me to an adjoining paddock to see the horses. There we were joined by her husband, Sheik Medjuel, the brother of the head of the clan, Mezrab, a branch of the Anazeh tribe. The sheik was not an imposing personage—indeed anything but one's idea of a great lord of the desert. Nevertheless she seemed very fond and proud of him, and evidently between this wild nomad life between the desert and Damascus, she had found a happy haven of rest, after the adventures of her stormy youth."

Six years later, when Jane was sixty-seven, Sir Edwin Pears met her and found her still content with her life in the desert. Sir Edwin was a distinguished foreign correspondent who represented the London *Daily News* in Constantinople. He had heard about her, years before, from Carl Haag, the painter. He knew she would not see reporters, so he had not attempted to interview her. One day, however, he met her banker in Beirut, a man named Heald, who traveled to Damascus twice a year to deliver to Jane her three-thousand-pound income. Sir Edwin begged Heald to take him along on his next visit, and Heald obliged.

The day after arriving in Damascus, the two men called upon Jane at her villa. "We were shown into a long sala or drawing-room," Sir Edwin Pears recalled later. "A few minutes afterwards I saw a tall woman enter, who at once gave me the impression of having been strikingly handsome; but a black cloud was over her when she saw that my companion, who had come to pay her the money, had with him a stranger." Embarrassed, Heald explained that he was traveling with a friend and had felt it would be impolite to leave him outside. He offered to return another day. Relenting, Jane decided that would not be necessary. She suggested that Sir Edwin go to the far end of the room while she transacted her business with Heald. Sir Edwin quickly obliged, and occupied himself with studying her watercolors until Heald had delivered her money. When she rejoined Sir Edwin, Jane asked whether he was interested in art. He mentioned their mutual acquaintance Carl Haag, the painter, and then volunteered that he was planning to remain in Damascus a week. As he was speaking, Medjuel entered, took a liking to Sir Edwin, and offered to guide him about the mosques during this stay. Now, Jane softened completely and invited Sir Edwin to tea.

Sir Edwin Pears saw her four times in all. He was most curious about life in a Moslem harem. Did Jane know anything about harems? As it turned out, Jane knew a great deal:

"The women of the harem, she said, had about them the delightfulness of children. . . . The worst side of their character related to their sensuality. They had no pleasures corresponding to those found in European society, no music, no literature, no social intercourse with men. The result was that even amongst the most respectable classes there was a gross sensuality, which showed itself in the language which well-dressed harem ladies would employ. Subjects were spoken of even in the presence of children about which all Christian races agree to be silent."

Eventually, Sir Edwin took the liberty of asking her personal questions. He wanted to know about her relationship with her husband's tribe. She told him it was excellent and recounted several anecdotes to prove it. One in particular showed how the tribe felt about Jane, and Sir Edwin carefully recorded it:

"On one occasion, by mistake, the whole of her husband's tribe flocked into Damascus and took possession of her home, sleeping on the stairs, the landings, and anywhere they could lie down. She was the only woman in the house, and could not get into communication with her husband. I made some remark, which I forget, intimating that she must have been alarmed with the crowd of these wild fellows. She immediately retorted that she was greatly alarmed, but not, as I appeared to think, at anything which her husband's tribe would do. Her fear was that some of the many Turkish soldiers near her would make some remark derogatory to her, in which case, she said, not a Turk in the neighborhood would have been left alive."

Of all the visitors Jane entertained during her twenty-six years as Medjuel's wife, the most notorious, by far, was Sir Richard Burton, the quite incredible Burton of Arabia. He was Captain Burton when he arrived, fresh from four years in Brazil. And he was now to serve as the new British consul in Damascus. He was a tall, powerful, bearded man, robust and athletic. He was a great scholar, explorer, writer, and lover. He was a rebel and iconoclast, a smasher of idols. If Jane knew nine tongues, he knew more, including Jattki, a Sindhi language dialect used in India, as well as an Afghan dialect for which he had prepared a written grammar.

The new British consul, as Jane soon learned, had led an adventurous life. After being sent down from Oxford, he had served with the British Army in India. There he was nicknamed "White Nigger" because of his practice of disguising himself as a native and wandering about the bazaars. In 1853, he determined to visit the birthplace of the Prophet. After dying his skin, studying the intricate Mohammedan ritual, and having himself circumcised (a painful operation for an adult male in those days), he became the first Englishman to survive the pilgrimage to Mecca. In Africa, he had been badly wounded in Somaliland, but recovered and went on to discover Lake Tanganyika. In America, he took a covered wagon from Missouri to Utah in 1860, to observe polygamy at first hand. When he asked Brigham Young whether he might become a member of the church, the wily old Mormon replied, "No, Captain, I think you have done that sort of thing before."

Burton was in constant conflict with authority. When British Intelligence asked for a report on life in Karachi, Burton supplied them with a detailed account of Indian sex perversions. When Queen Victoria ordered him to talk the African King of Daho-

mey out of the practice of human sacrifice, Burton informed her
that he thought the customs of Dahomey no more revolting than
those of England. When his wife begged him to write a "nice"
book, Burton told her that he was preparing *The Scented Garden*,
which dealt with "female circumcision" and "the Fellahs copulat-
ing with crocodiles."

Jane was intrigued with Burton. Night after night, Jane and
Medjuel entertained him in the villa, and Burton thought her
quite "the cleverest woman" he had ever met. Since he was obsessed with the subject of sex, most of his questions concerned the
love life of Arabian women. He was, at the time, preparing his
epic translation of *The Arabian Nights*. In his Terminal Essay to
the book—an essay which was later expurgated since it openly discussed the erotic habits of all nationalities—he drew heavily on
the material Jane had given him. Such was their admiration for
each other that one of Burton's biographers remarked that had
Jane "been thirty years younger, there might have been much between her and Richard Burton."

Three months after Burton's arrival in Damascus, his plump
wife appeared on the scene with her English maid, her St. Bernard, and her aggressive Catholicism. Isabel Burton was a snob.
She was impressed by titles and Jane had a title. Consequently,
Isabel took to Jane at once. Medjuel was another matter. Where
her husband appreciated Medjuel for what he was, Isabel was
repelled by his dark skin. When she saw Jane and Medjuel together, she recoiled.

"What was incomprehensible to me," wrote Isabel, "was how
she could have given up all she had in England to live with that
dirty little black—or nearly so—husband. I went to see her one day
and when he opened the door to me I thought at first he was a
native servant. I could understand her leaving a coarse, cruel husband, much older than herself, whom she never loved (every
woman has not the strength of mind and the pride to stand by
what she has done); I could understand her running away with
Schwarzenberg; but the contact with that black skin I could not
understand. Her sheik was dark—darker than a Persian—much
darker than an Arab generally is.

"All the same he was a very intelligent and charming man in
any light but that of a husband. That made me shudder. It was
curious how she had retained the charming manner, the soft
voice, and all the graces of her youth. You would have known her

anywhere to be an English lady, well-born and bred and she was delighted to greet in me one of her own order."

It was partly due to Isabel's intolerance that Burton lasted less than two years as British consul in Damascus, and that Jane was unhappily deprived of his friendship. Burton's appointment to Damascus was resented from the outset because of his circumventing the taboo against infidels entering Mecca. Isabel simply compounded this resentment. She, who had seen tears on her plaster Madonna, was determined to convert all of Damascus to Catholicism. An energetic and overwhelming woman, she pounced upon the Moslem poor and, with gifts of food, tried to bribe them into embracing the Church of Rome. She nursed dying Arab children, then baptized them over the protests of their mothers. Once, while showing titled English visitors through a mosque, she ordered a praying Moslem to move aside, since he was blocking the view of a tomb. When he did not move, she hit him across the face with her riding whip.

Meanwhile, Burton, attempting to halt corruption in Damascus, cracked down on influential financiers, involved himself in a Greek riot, and tried to purchase land to establish a colony for his wife's Arab converts. Protests poured into the British Foreign Office in London, and overnight Burton was dismissed.

He noted in his diary: "18th August. Left Damascus forever; started at three a.m. in the dark, with a big lantern; all my men crying. . . . Dismissal ignominious, at the age of fifty, without a month's notice, or wages, or character." Shortly after, Isabel followed Burton. Jane rode with her to the city gates. "The parting with Lady Ellenborough affected me greatly," Isabel wrote. "I was the poor thing's only woman friend."

If this was the last Jane was to see of Isabel Burton, it was not the last she was to hear of her. The following year—during which the Burtons, after a vacation in Iceland, took over the British consulate at Trieste—Jane returned from a tribal war in the Syrian desert to find herself declared dead.

She read her obituaries with amazement. The most sensational one, which raked up the scandals of Jane's past, appeared in *La Revue Britannique*. Published in Paris during March 1873, it was reprinted throughout Europe. "A noble lady, who had made a great use—or abuse—of marriage, has died recently," the obituary began. "Lady Ellenborough, some thirty years ago, left her first husband to run off with Count von Schwarzenberg. She retired

to Italy where she married six consecutive times." The obituary
went on to report that Jane had died a widow, since her husband,
"a camel driver named Sheik Abdul," had preceded her to the
grave.

With mounting disbelief, Jane awaited the ensuing installment
of this fiction. The very next issue of *La Revue Britannique* carried a long letter sent to the editor from Trieste, a defense and
eulogy written by none other than Isabel Burton:

"I lived for two years as an intimate friend of Lady Ellenborough in Damascus, where my husband, Captain Burton, was
Consul. Since she knew that, after her death, all sorts of false-
hoods, painful to her family, would appear in the papers, she
asked me to write her biography, and for an hour a day she dictated the good and the bad with equal frankness. I was pledged
not to publish this until after her death and that of certain near
relatives.

"As to what has been written about her marriage to a 'camel
driver' probably taken from the gossip of some dismissed servant,
I can easily give a brief summary of the story of her sojourn to
the East from the time when, some sixteen years ago, Lady Ellenborough, who was tired of Europe, decided to imitate what Lady
Wortley-Montague and Lady Hester Stanhope had done before
her."

Then, after offering a few inaccuracies of her own about Jane's
marriage to Medjuel, Isabel Burton concluded:

"She was an exquisite woman, not only because of her wit and
manners, but because of her good heart. She spoke French, Italian, German, Spanish, Russian, Greek, Turkish and Arabic as
easily as her mother tongue. As an artist she was a painter, sculptor, musician. But she loved the outdoors as well, growing flowers,
breeding horses, taking care of fowl.

"*Bon sang ne peut mentir*—True blood will always tell. I never
met a nobler heart, nor one more charitable to the poor. She fulfilled all the duties of a good Christian lady and an Englishwoman. All those who knew her in her last days will weep for
her. She had but one fault in Europe (and who knows whether
it was really her fault) but she made up for it in the East through
fifteen years of virtue and repentance. She is departed. Be the
world kind to her."

More in annoyance than anger, Jane advised the press that she was very much alive and in the best of health. She firmly denied having ever dictated a single word to Isabel Burton for a so-called projected biography. It was true, of course, that many people had wanted her to publish her story. When Sir Valentine Chirol had asked why she did not set down her memoirs, she had replied, "I just couldn't. The list of my husbands and lovers would read like a naughty edition of the Almanach de Gotha." What had happened most probably, in the case of Isabel Burton, was that she had wanted to write a book about Jane. Since she knew Jane would not cooperate on such a project, Isabel had instead made detailed notes after evenings spent conversing with her. The moment that she thought Jane was dead, she had attempted to establish her exclusive rights to the potential best-seller by announcing to the world that Lady Ellenborough's intimate revelations had been dictated to her. Jane's resurrection intimidated Isabel into silence forever after.

Jane Digby el Mezrab survived her obituaries by eight full years. She became more and more a recluse, spending her time with Medjuel and a few close friends, until the day she was confined to her Damascus bedroom by an attack of dysentery. She succumbed to the illness during August of 1881. Medjuel watched her burial, in the Protestant plot of the Jewish Cemetery, from the saddle of her favorite white mare. The cross on her grave bore only two words in English: *Madam Digby*. And beneath, carved in Arabic script by Medjuel's own hand, was a quotation from the Koran.

Her will left two thousand pounds and some diamonds to her favorite child, Baron Heribert Venningen, a turquoise ring and inkstand to her favorite brother, Kenelm, but all of her other earthly possessions—house, stables, gardens, jewels, money—went "to my husband, as a token of my respect and regard." Medjuel received the monetary bequest in a group of neat packages, each containing five hundred sovereigns, and after he died, several of these packages were found unopened beneath his bed. He never remarried. Jane had been his life.

In the Jewish Cemetery of Damascus, she lay at rest.

In the pages of Balzac, Lady Arabella Dudley continued to pursue her tumultuous existence. But Jane Ellenborough had at last found peace in the grave where Madam Digby slept for all eternity.

Book Two

THE HEROINE
AS A SCANDAL

IX

The Real-Life

Emma Bovary

Why not write the story of Delamare?

—LOUIS BOUILHET to
GUSTAVE FLAUBERT

GUSTAVE FLAUBERT'S Mme. Emma Bovary—"the most complete woman's portrait I know in the whole of literature, including Shakespeare and including Balzac," literary critic Émile Faguet has called her—was inspired by an incident that occurred when the author was thirty years old and uncertain of his literary future. Until then his career had been confused and unpromising. "I went to school when I was only ten," he would say, "and I very soon contracted a profound aversion to the human race." During his formative years he suffered falling in love with a married woman almost twice his age, he suffered studying law in Paris, and he suffered a fit of epilepsy.

Shortly after his father, Dr. Achille-Cléophas Flaubert, a successful Rouen surgeon, purchased Croisset, a two-century-old mansion on the Seine, young Flaubert turned his full-time attention to writing. For nine months a year, he wrote six hours daily in the study overlooking the river. The other three months, he spent in Paris seeking experience.

One Parisian experience, the most involved he was to have with a woman, began when he met Louise Colet, a poet. She was extremely attractive, with her fair hair that fell in long curls and her large, soft eyes and her throaty voice, and she had a husband and a lover at the time Flaubert met her. In a month she became Flaubert's mistress—though the anticipation of her submission had delayed Flaubert's ability to consummate the union for some time. Thereafter, for several years Louise was Flaubert's faithful correspondent, literary conscience, and, in the end, the bane of his existence.

In 1851, following a trip to Egypt, Palestine, and Greece, Flaubert penned the first draft of *The Temptation of St. Anthony.* Upon its completion, he sent for his two closest friends, Maxime du Camp, editor of the *Revue de Paris,* and Louis Bouilhet, a shy peasant poet. Flaubert told them that he was going to read to them from the manuscript of his newest work. For almost four days, reading aloud eight hours a day, Flaubert went through *The Temptation.* He completed his reading on a midnight, and waited for the verdict. One of his listeners said bluntly, "We think you ought to throw it in the fire and not speak of it again."

The following afternoon, deeply discouraged, Flaubert joined du Camp and Bouilhet in his garden. He complained to them about his artistic barrenness. He had several new historical ideas in mind, but he was not confident that any of them had value. He had no desire to return to the desk in his study. What he needed, he thought, was a fresh subject.

At this point Maxime du Camp cautioned him, "As soon as you feel irresistibly drawn toward this poetic soaring, you must choose a subject in which it would be so absurd that you will be forced on your guard and compelled to drop it." Then du Camp added, "Take some workaday subject, one of those episodes bourgeois life is full of, and compel yourself to handle it in a natural tone."

Flaubert retorted that he knew of no such episodes of bourgeois life. Suddenly Louis Bouilhet interrupted. "Why not write the story of Delamare?" he asked.

Flaubert sat up. "Now, that's an idea!" he exclaimed.

Bouilhet continued speaking. He had intended for some time

to mention the Delamare idea to Flaubert. It had first struck him when he called upon Flaubert's mother, while Flaubert was abroad. On arriving at Croisset, Bouilhet had found another guest, an elderly, sorrowful provincial woman who was introduced to him as Mme. Delamare. She dwelt in dire poverty in a nearby village, caring for herself and a very young granddaughter who had been left in her charge. Her son had recently committed suicide, and since this son had once studied under Dr. Flaubert, she was seeking consolation from the great surgeon's widow. Even as they were introduced, Bouilhet located the old lady in his memory, recalled the tragedy of the Delamares, and thought what a fine, realistic piece it might make for Gustave Flaubert's pen.

Bouilhet wondered: Did Flaubert fully remember the tragedy? Flaubert replied: He did, indeed.

Thus, Maxime du Camp's recollection, thirty years later, of the day Flaubert was given the idea for the creation of *Madame Bovary*.

However, in her 1966 biography of Flaubert, Dr. Enid Starkie, after a study of Flaubert's correspondence, concluded that he had read his *The Temptation of St. Anthony* to du Camp and Bouilhet in 1849, not 1851. But Dr. Starkie agreed that it was not until Flaubert had returned from abroad that the Bovary story "seemed to him a possible topic for him." Assuredly, by the summer of 1851, Flaubert had heard of Delphine Delamare—and to her he and literature would owe much of the character of Emma Bovary.

Sometime before he began the actual writing of *Madame Bovary* in September of 1851, and possibly during the four and a half years in which he wrote the novel, Flaubert appears to have researched deeply the background of his real-life prototype.

What, then, did Flaubert learn?

Eugène Delamare had been a plodding medical student, studying surgery at the Rouen hospital under Flaubert's father. He was a mediocre undergraduate. He failed in several critical examinations, and he did not have the funds to obtain special tutoring or to extend his training time in the hospital. Unable to earn his diploma as a full-fledged physician, Delamare became a licensed medical officer, an *officier de santé*.

Shortly after, Delamare married a widow older than himself

—an act with much precedence in the French provinces—and took a job as health official in a rural community called Ry. When his wife died, Delamare was left alone. He longed for another mate. Then, he met an attractive seventeen-year-old named Delphine Couturier.

Delphine had smooth blonde hair which she parted in the center, eyes which a neighbor said seemed "to change to deeper colors according to the lighting," and a shapely figure. Flaubert described her more fully, and probably from firsthand information, when he depicted her fictional counterpart: "The thing about her that was beautiful was her eyes; although they were blue, they looked black because of her lashes, and her glance met yours frankly with a candid assurance. Her hair, in two . . . bands, each of which looked like a single piece, was parted in the middle in a fine line which deepened slightly, following the curve of the skull; and, barely revealing the tips of the ears, was drawn back in a loose knot at the back, with a wavy effect at the temples which the country doctor saw for the first time in his life. Her cheeks were pink."

Delphine was the youngest daughter of one of Delamare's patients, a well-off farmer who owned property at neighboring Blainville-Crevon. She had been educated by the Ursulines at a convent in Rouen, and her head was filled with reveries evoked by romantic novels and popular magazine serials. On August 7, 1839, over the objections of her father ("who preferred a son-in-law endowed with more worldly possessions," said a friend), Delphine Couturier became the second Mme. Delamare.

At the start, Delphine had been excited by the achievement of marrying a mature medical man. Soon she found Delamare a bore and the small community of Ry oppressive. Flaubert sensed, or mirrored, Delphine's feelings exactly when he showed Emma Bovary's growing distaste for Dr. Charles Bovary. Mme. Bovary had envisioned for herself an impulsive, stimulating lover, set against a world of gondolas and tropical vistas. Instead she had wed a dullard whose conversation was "as flat as a street pavement. . . . He could not swim, he could not fence, he could not handle firearms. . . . His ardors had become regular; he embraced her at certain times. It was a habit among others, and like a dessert predictable in advance after the monotony of dinner." And dinner, and what followed it, were becoming unbearable. "One after the other he would tell of all the people he had met, the villages to which he had been, the prescriptions he had written and, pleased with himself, he would eat the leftover beef, finish off his cheese, crunch an apple, empty his decanter, then go to bed, lie on his back and snore."

Frequently, when alone in the afternoons, she "would reiterate to herself: 'Why, dear God, did I get married?' She wondered if there might not have been some means, given other combinations of chance, of meeting another man; and she tried to imagine those events which had not occurred, that different life, that husband whom she did not know. No one, as a matter of fact, bore any resemblance to that man. He would have been handsome, witty, distinguished, attractive, as those men undoubtedly were whom her former classmates at the convent had married. What were they doing now? In the city, with the sounds of the streets, the confused murmuring of theaters, and the highlights of balls, they led the sort of existence in which the heart dilates, the senses expand. But life for her was cold as an attic whose window faces north, and boredom, a silent spider, spun its webs in the shadow of every corner of her heart."

What to do? "Was this misery to last forever? Would she never emerge from it? She was just as good as all the women who led happy lives! At Vaubyessard she had seen duchesses with thicker waists and more common manners, and she cursed God's injustice; she would rest her head against the walls and weep; she coveted tumultuous living, nights of masquerade, insolent pleasures with all the passions she had not experienced, and which they must give. . . . Her innermost heart, however, was waiting for something to happen. Like shipwrecked sailors, seeking some white sail in the far mists of the horizon. . . . But nothing happened to her; God had willed it so! The future was a dark corridor, with its door at the end shut fast."

All of this was derived from Flaubert's knowledge and perception of Delphine Delamare, and he understood her exactly. Yet Delphine, in real life, refused to let the door at the far end of the dark corridor remain shut. She determined to pry it open and escape. In contrast to her growing contempt for her bourgeois husband and the dull life he offered her, Delphine valued highly her own intellect and beauty and believed in the possibilities of making her daydreams come true. Recklessly, she determined that she would discover a more stimulating and fulfilled existence.

She began to spend money extravagantly on clothes, and Delamare, without being aware of it, was soon deeply in debt. When this orgy of buying lost its first excitement, she openly invited the attentions of other men. First, she committed adultery with a neighbor named Louis Campion, then with a sturdy farmhand, then with a gentlemanly notary clerk, then with many "young clerks," then—with anyone. As Flaubert wrote of her fictional counterpart: "She recalled the heroines of the books that she had read, and the lyric legion of these adulterous women began to sing in her memory." Secretly, in fields, hotels, and back rooms, Delphine Delamare accepted the attentions of lover after lover, desperately searching for the ideal that did not exist. She neglected her husband, her little daughter, her friends and neighbors, her attendance at Mass, as she indulged herself in sensuality.

Old Mme. Delamare tried to warn her son. But he adored his young wife and paid no attention to his mother's broad hints. Although Delphine's extravagance and nymphomania continued, she began to have trouble finding lovers, and those she did find were increasingly disappointing. Delphine sought to fill her empty hours in many ways. As one neighbor remembered, "She chose a day, Friday, to play the grande dame. She closed the curtains, lit the candles, and waited for visitors who did not come." The dreariness was closing in on her again.

At last, during the early dawn of March 6, 1848, in the ninth year of her marriage, when her husband's credit was ruined and her appearance attracting fewer and fewer admirers, Delphine Delamare took a fatal dose of arsenic. As one story has it, her daughter was awake at the time. When her daughter wanted to know what she had done, Delphine "refused to say what poison she had swallowed," but when "her little girl allegedly implored her on her knees . . . then Delphine told the truth." After that, her death came quickly.

Dr. Starkie has questioned this version of Delphine Delamare's death, implying it was one more case where life was made to imitate art. In other words, once Emma Bovary's fictional suicide became widely known, literary historians then agreed that her prototype must have ended her earthly existence in the same way. "There is no proof whatsoever that Delphine Delamare committed suicide," wrote Dr. Starkie, "though all accounts now state that she did. The death certificate was published in *La Normandie Médicale*, and no cause for her death was given. It is dated 7 March 1848 and merely states that she had died at Ry at 3 A.M. on the previous day, at the age of twenty-seven. There was no inquest; no paper mentions the possibility of suicide; and the priest allowed the body to be buried in consecrated ground."

Several months after Delphine's death, the grief-stricken Eugène Delamare finally learned the full extent of his wife's extravagances, and he also heard for the first time the details of her infidelities. Shocked beyond reason by her excesses, he killed himself, leaving the small daughter he had adored to the care of his impoverished mother.

On the day that Bouilhet originally reminded Flaubert of this provincial tragedy, Bouilhet had been able to give his friend many more particulars. As Francis Steegmuller recounted it: "He reminded him of the black-and-yellow striped curtains in young Madame Delamare's parlor, which had first caused her to be thought pretentious and extravagant by her mother-in-law and her neighbors and had been gossiped about all over Normandy; of the way she had instructed her peasant servant to address her in the third person; of her prettiness, her chic, her haughtiness and nervousness, her at-homes on Friday afternoons which she herself was the only one to attend, the unpaid bill she had left at a lending library in Rouen. He recalled Delamare's heavy appearance and manner, his good-natured stodginess, his satisfaction with his situation in life, the confidence, almost the affection, with which he was regarded by his country clients."

Flaubert was convinced that the Delamare story was the perfect vehicle for his talents. He hated the destructive romanticism and mediocrity of the bourgeois in the provinces. He knew Normandy and he knew these people. But two things bothered him. The story was vulgar and the characters commonplace. Nevertheless, Flaubert could not resist it. Heeding his mother's entreaties that he refrain from ever mentioning that he had used the Delamares as his models, for fear the elderly Mme. Delamare might be hurt, Flaubert proceeded to mold Emma and Charles Bovary out of the lives of Delphine and Eugène Delamare—with a touch of Louise Colet added to Emma.

The novel went slowly, six pages a week. "I itch with sentences that never appear," he told Louise. "What a heavy oar the pen is." He worked seven hours a day, every day, for fifty-five months. Even as he toiled, he continued to research every scene of the story—here, studying romantic novels of the kind that Emma Bovary might have read—there, trying to learn the actual effects of arsenic poisoning. At times, his work made him ill. He recalled: "When I was describing the poisoning of Emma Bovary, I had such a taste of arsenic in my mouth and was poisoned so effectively myself, that I had two attacks of indigestion, one after the other—two very real attacks, for I vomited my entire dinner." Other times, he was emotionally upset by his own creation. "Last Wednesday I was obliged to get up and look for my handkerchief; tears were streaming down my face. I had moved myself deeply as I wrote." The original scrawled manuscript, now in the Municipal Library at Rouen, attests to the labor: 1,788 written and rewritten pages of foolscap, and a final draft of 487 pages.

Flaubert allowed Maxime du Camp to publish the result as a six-part serial in the *Revue de Paris* between October and December of 1856. The publication churned up a tempest. "As soon as the first chapters had appeared," said du Camp, "our subscribers rose in wrath, crying that it was scandalous, immoral. They wrote us letters of doubtful courtesy, accusing us of slandering France and disgracing it in the eyes of the world. 'What! Such women exist? Women who deceive their husbands, pile up debts, meet their lovers in gardens and hotels? Such creatures exist in our lovely France, in the provinces where life is so pure? Impossible!'"

The public furor was primarily over the novel's realism.

Flaubert objected. "Everyone thinks I am in love with reality, whereas actually I detest it. It was in hatred of realism that I undertook this book. But I equally despise that false brand of idealism which is such a hollow mockery in the present age."

Unimpressed, the idealists urged the French government to suppress the book. And so Flaubert, and two of the men connected with its publication, were brought to trial for having written and published a pornographic and antireligious work. The hearing was brief, and the court determined "that it is not sufficiently proven" that Flaubert and his two fellow defendants "are guilty of the misdemeanor with which they are charged; the Court acquits them of the indictment brought against them, and decrees a dismissal without costs."

Madame Bovary was free, and now Michel Lévy offered to publish the novel in a two-volume edition. During April 1857, the first book edition of *Madame Bovary* appeared, and it sold fifteen thousand copies in sixty days. There was some critical carping. Louise Colet, who had by then quarreled with Flaubert, announced that the book read as if it had been written by a traveling salesman. And a reviewer for *Réalisme* felt the novel reminded one "of a geometrical drawing . . . all in right angles and, finally, dry and arid." But, for the most part, the critical acclaim was unanimous. Sainte-Beuve announced, "He has style." Charles Baudelaire thought the novel "a marvel." Victor Hugo sent his congratulations.

For much of this acclaim, Flaubert owed a huge debt to the obscure Delphine Delamare. Yet, he would not pay this debt by publicly acknowledging the role she had played in his success. Persistently, he denied Delphine credit as his inspiration. "No model sat for me," he stated. "There is nothing in *Madame Bovary* that is true." In a letter to Mlle. Leroyer de Chantepie, he wrote, "Madame Bovary has no foundation in fact. It is an entirely fictitious tale." In another letter, this one to a M. Cailleteaux, he wrote, "No, sir, I had no model before me. Madame Bovary is pure invention. All of the characters in the book are completely fictitious. . . . Though this has not prevented people here in Normandy from discovering a host of allusions in my novel." Once, in utter exasperation, he growled, *"Madame Bovary, c'est moi"*—"I am Madame Bovary!"

But he was not Madame Bovary, and neither was anyone else, except Delphine Delamare. Perhaps Flaubert refused to acknowledge his real-life model because he felt that such an admission might impugn his creative ability. Or perhaps, and this is more likely, he refused to credit Delphine because he still did not wish to offend his mother—who had once begged him to be discreet, in order to protect the elderly Mme. Delamare and her grandchild.

Nevertheless, Flaubert certainly did not forget what Bouilhet had once told him. With Delphine Delamare "the essence of the tragedy was her disgust with the surroundings in which she found herself, and beyond which she had somehow learned, however futilely, to look; it was the infection of romanticism"—and

this infection of romanticism was what killed Delphine Delamare and gave life to Emma Bovary.

Though Flaubert, in his crotchety and lonely old age, tired of
his novel's continuing notoriety—"I should like to find some way
of making a lot of money so that I could buy up every copy of
Madame Bovary in existence, throw them all into the fire, and
never hear of the book again"—the novel went into edition after
edition and attained the stature of an established classic.

Today, in the village of Ry, postcards are hawked which immortalize an erring daughter named Delphine Delamare. And
today, in the Museum of Rouen, hang two portraits of a striking
young woman painted by the artist Court. One is called *Rigolette*
and the other *Venetian at the Masked Ball,* and both, according
to tradition, represent Delphine Delamare.

Delphine Delamare could not know it, but in her death she
had finally achieved her most romantic dreams.

X

The Lady

of the

White Camellias

So you are in love with me? Say it straight
out, it is much more simple.

—MARIE DUPLESSIS

AT ALMOST the same time that the provincial adulteress who inspired *Madame Bovary* was struggling to escape from the captivity of her mean village in Normandy, a more worldly courtesan was struggling to maintain her precarious position in Paris. Marie Duplessis, the original model for Marguerite Gautier, heroine of *La Dame aux camélias*, started lower and rose higher than did Delphine Delamare.

The prototype for the lady of the camellias was born Rose Alphonsine Plessis in the village of St.-Germain-de-Clairfeuille, in Lower Normandy, on January 15, 1824. On her father's side, her grandmother had been a streetwalker and her grandfather a licentious priest. Her father, Marin Plessis, a peddler of gadgets and almanacs who later opened a draper's shop in Nonant, was a drunkard and a brute. Her mother, Marie-Louise Deshayes, came from a more respectable background. It was in the second year of what proved, not surprisingly, to be an unhappy marriage that the girl who was to be known as Marie Duplessis was born. Eventually, Marie's mother left her father, obtained employment as a maid for an English family in Paris, and placed Marie and her sister with a cousin who owned a farm.

When Marie was eight, her mother died. Marie remained with her mother's cousin, who permitted her to roam about the farm and neighborhood unrestrained and wild. At the age of twelve, Marie became enamored of a young farmhand, and a short time after, it was said, she "left her virtue, together with her petticoat, underneath a bramble bush in a hedge." Learning of the episode, her relative-guardian promptly returned her to the custody of her father.

Marie was thirteen, and working as an apprentice to a laundress, when her alcoholic father became aware that she had the face of an angel and the body of a Salome. He decided to capitalize on these commodities. For a small sum of cash he turned her over to a wealthy, lecherous bachelor friend, Plantier, aged seventy, who used her as he wished for a year and then sent her back to her parent. For a while she was a tavern maid, then an employee in an umbrella-manufacturing establishment, until her father shed any further responsibility for her by depositing her with distant relatives who owned a grocer's shop in Paris. Presently, she acquired shabby lodgings of her own among the dissolute students living in the Latin Quarter. She supported herself as a messenger for a corset maker, as a clerk in a hat store, and as a girl of the streets.

There exists a picture of her in this period, as recalled by a young playboy and theater manager named Nestor Roqueplan. One evening, ascending the steps of the Pont Neuf, he saw standing before a vendor of fried potatoes "a pretty girl, of delicate appearance and very dirty. She was munching a green apple which she did not seem to care about. Fried potatoes were what she wanted. I bought her a bag of them." Less than two years later Roqueplan saw the girl again. She had been transformed into a splendid young lady, and was escorted by the handsome Duc de Guiche-Gramont, who was to rise to a cabinet position in France. "He had with him, hanging on his arm, a very charming lady, most elegantly dressed, who was no other than my little *gourmande* of the Pont Neuf. She was now known as Marie Duplessis."

She would later explain her change of name from Rose Alphonsine Plessis into Marie Duplessis to a friend from her home village. "I chose Marie because it's the name of the Virgin," she said. And she chose Duplessis because it sounded more aristocratic than Plessis and because she remembered a grand estate known as the "du Plessis estate" back in Nonant and hoped to have money enough one day to buy it.

But the real change, the transformation from street urchin into brilliant courtesan, was more remarkable.

"At sixteen," wrote Jean Prastau, one of her many French biographers, "she was just a rough peasant girl, said by the villagers to have been sold for debauchery by her father who had the evil eye. She could barely read and write. At twenty she had become a woman of refinement, an arbiter of taste in frivolous, *blasé* Paris: she ran her household with six servants; she read Hugo, Eugène Sue and de Musset; she entertained Paris society; she created a stir in the *salons* of the Faubourg Saint-Germain and she ruined the richest men in France."

How had this spectacular rise come about?

It had its real beginnings on a Sunday in Marie's sixteenth year, when she accompanied two girl friends on an outing to St.-Cloud, and they stopped on the way for a snack in a cheap restaurant near the Palais-Royal. The proprietor of the restaurant, a fat widower named Nollet, was dazzled by Marie's beauty. He invited her to return the following week—alone. Soon she was his mistress, installed in an apartment of her own in the Rue de l'Arcade. For the first time, she had the necessities of life. In short months, she would have its luxuries, too.

One evening she was seen at the theater by Count Ferdinand de Monguyon, and overnight she abandoned her restaurateur for the nobility. Next, she was seen at a dance by the wealthy young dandy, Agenor de Guiche, later the Duc de Guiche-Gramont and eventually France's Foreign Minister under Emperor Napoleon III. Guiche made Marie a better proposition than the Count's and whisked her off to the spas of Germany for the summer. It is thought that she had a child by Guiche, a boy delivered in Versailles in 1841, and that Guiche promptly placed their offspring with foster parents. According to Joanna Richardson, an

English biographer: "In 1869, a man of about twenty-seven called on Marie Duplessis's elder sister and asked to see the portrait of Marie. When he went away, he left a card: 'Judelet. Employé de Commerce, Tours.' His face was remarkably like the face in the picture."

After the interlude with Guiche, in order to gain her material goals more rapidly, Marie Duplessis accepted lovers in great numbers. According to the newspaper *Figaro*, she was at one time supported by a syndicate of seven ardent admirers. The seven gentlemen pooled their money to keep her, and each was given a separate night of the week to visit her. "They symbolized their collective devotion by combining to present her with a magnificent dressing-table containing seven drawers."

Marie Duplessis, who had long graduated from the Latin Quarter, was finally established in a lavish suite of rooms at 11 Boulevard de la Madeleine. The rooms, with their walls decorated in heavy silk, were exotically and romantically furnished in the style of Louis XV. In the anteroom were rare plants growing out of lacquered boxes; in the salon were pieces of rosewood furniture, the "sofas covered in Beauvais tapestry," as well as Venetian mirrors, ornaments of solid silver, and a magnificent Pleyel piano; in the dining room, surrounding the carved oak table which was covered in green velvet, were rare tapestries and Dresden china; in the boudoir or dressing room were the seven-drawer dressing table, leather-bound volumes of Molière, Lord Byron, and Abbé Prévost, velvet and satin drapes, and a great wardrobe filled with gowns designed by Mme. Palmyre. Most important, there was the *chambre à coucher*—Marie's place of business and pleasure—with its oversized rosewood bed resting on a floral-patterned carpet. Across from the bed was the gilded bronze antique clock ornamented with porcelain birds, which was said to have originally belonged to Mme. Pompadour.

By 1844, when Marie was twenty, there were still multiple lovers, but one man in particular was paying for the luxuries on the Boulevard de la Madeleine. Marie had met the Count de Stackelberg at the baths of Bagnères. He had been the Russian Ambassador to Vienna. He was married, wealthy, and eighty years of age. He was later represented in the novel *La Dame aux camélias* by the character of the elderly Duc de Mauriac. In the novel, he befriended Marguerite Gautier and sponsored her be-

cause she so closely resembled a daughter he had lost. Their
fictional relationship was platonic. Dumas made it clear that this
was not so in fact: "The story of the consumptive daughter whose
double the Duke discovered in Marie Duplessis is sheer invention. The Count, in spite of his great age, was not an Edipus
looking for an Antigone, but a King David looking for a Bath-
sheba."

Though the discreet old Russian paid the bills, imported carriages and horses for Marie from England, and rented boxes for
her at all the best Parisian theaters, he was not able to give her
the love she desired. To satisfy this facet of her needs—her extreme romanticism and intense sensuality—she looked elsewhere.
Foremost among her young lovers was the witty Viscount Édouard de Perregaux, who had been a member of the French
cavalry in Africa and was now a member of the Jockey Club
in Paris, and who attended her regularly when the Russian was
occupied with his wife.

Many descriptions of Marie Duplessis, as she was in her twentieth year when she was one of the two-star sights of Paris, still
exist. Jules Janin remembered, after her death, that she "was tall,
very slight, with black hair, and a pink and white complexion.
Her head was small; she had long enameled eyes, like a Japanese
woman's, but they were sparkling and alert. Her lips were rud-
dier than the cherry, her teeth were the prettiest in the world; she
looked like a little figure made of Dresden china." For all her
excesses, her lovely young face retained the look of a startled virgin. Dumas recalled it well when he wrote in *La Dame aux
camélias*: "How it was that her ardent life had left on Marguerite's face the virginal, almost childlike, expression which characterized it, is a problem which we can but state, without attempting
to solve it."

A more complete picture of Marie in her prime survives in the
the words of an actress, Judith Bernat, one of the leading players
of the Théâtre des Variétés, who was admired by Marie and who,
in return, became her friend.

"She had an incomparable charm," Judith Bernat wrote in her
memoirs. "She was very slim, almost thin, but wonderfully delicate and graceful; her face was an angelic oval, her dark eyes
had a caressing melancholy, her complexion was dazzling, and
above all her hair was magnificent. Oh! That fine, silky dark hair!"

When the actress wondered why Marie Duplessis had "taken up prostitution," Marie "hid her face" and then, repeating the question, tried to answer it: "Why do I sell myself? Because the labor of a working girl would never have brought me the luxury for which I've had such an irresistible craving. Despite appearances, I swear to you that I'm neither covetous nor debauched. I wanted to know the refinements and pleasures of artistic taste, the joy of living in elegant and cultivated society. I've always chosen my friends. And I've loved. Oh, yes, I have loved sincerely, but no one has ever responded to my love. That is the real horror of my life. It's wrong to have a heart when you're a courtesan. You can die from it."

Men were moved by her candor, her flashes of gaiety, her tact, her graceful fragility, and, above all, her world-weariness, brought on by the pointlessness of her existence and her increasingly frequent spells of weakness from tuberculosis. Yet, she enjoyed her clothes and servants, her two spaniels, her carriage outings to the country, her visits to the opera and the theater. She enjoyed, too, gambling at cards, drinking, and off-color stories. She gave dinners attended by Eugène Sue, Honoré de Balzac, Théophile Gautier—and an occasional celebrated visitor to Paris like Lola Montez. Still, secretly, she desired solitude, security, and true love—but these she never had for any length of time.

It was stated that she "made vice decent, dignified and decorous." Her trademark of purity, of elegance, of beauty, was the white camellia. She had a fresh vase of camellias placed in her apartment daily, and she had them made into small bouquets to carry when riding in the Champs-Élysées or to hold while sitting in the Opéra.

Alexandre Dumas *fils* saw her first in 1842, when he was eighteen and unsuccessful and she was eighteen and infamous. He was strolling in the Place de la Bourse one afternoon when a rich blue carriage, drawn by two splendid bays, halted at the curb. She stepped down and entered a shop. She wore an Italian straw hat, a cashmere shawl, an India muslin dress. She had her spaniels on leashes, and a bouquet of camellias in a gloved hand, and she had a wondrous smile. He was instantly smitten.

But he held little hope for his chances. She was the plaything of millionaires, the beloved princess of pleasure enthroned by the mighty. He was the illegitimate son of a great father, and nothing more. He was struggling to become a writer in the shadow of his fat, childlike parent. The elder Dumas was prodigious. He boasted that he had produced five hundred children, fought twenty duels, written enough to fill twelve hundred volumes (including *The Count of Monte Cristo* and *The Three Musketeers*), and earned and spent the equivalent of five million dollars. Alexandre Dumas *père* would have known how to manage Marie Duplessis. Alexandre Dumas *fils* was helpless.

However, within two years he had met Marie and made her his mistress, and through her found his fame and fortune. "On a fine day in September, 1844, I had been to Saint-Germain-en-Laye to see my father," young Dumas recalled afterwards. "On my way there I had met Eugène Dejazet, the son of the famous actress. We had ridden together in the beautiful forest of Saint-Germain, and returned to Paris for dinner, and gone to the Variétés, and were seated in the stalls. Marie Duplessis was in the stage box on the right-hand side. She was alone there, sniffing at a bouquet, nibbling sweets from a bag, hardly listening to the performance, looking about her in all directions, exchanging smiles and glances with three or four of our neighbors, leaning back from time to time, to chat with an invisible occupant of her box, who was no other than the aged Russian Count S."

Then Dumas had a stroke of luck. Marie waved to a stout woman sitting in a box opposite hers. This was Clémence Prat, a hatmaker who dwelt near Marie Duplessis and who often served as Marie's procuress. Dumas's companion, Dejazet, knew Mme. Prat and went to speak to her. He returned with exciting news. After the theater, Count de Stackelberg was taking Marie directly to her suite. He planned to leave immediately. They would wait in the street, and then enter and join Marie and Mme. Prat for supper.

It was midnight when Dumas and his friend entered the elaborate salon. Marie Duplessis, in a brocade gown, was at the piano. Champagne was served, and then supper. Mme. Prat told a coarse story. Marie laughed, fell into a fit of coughing, and rushed into her bedroom. Dumas followed. When he realized how ill she was, he told her that if he could continue seeing her he would take care of her. What transpired next Dumas reported faithfully, word for word, in his novel. Marie, or Marguerite, considered his proposal and then studied him.

"So you are in love with me? Say it straight out, it is much more simple."

"It is possible; but if I am to say it to you one day, it is not today."

"You will do better never to say it."

"Why?"

"Because only one of two things can come of it. . . . Either I shall not accept: then you will have a grudge against me; or I shall accept: then you will have a sorry mistress; a woman who is nervous, ill, sad, or gay with a gaiety sadder than grief, a woman who spits blood and spends a hundred thousand francs a year. That is all very well for a rich old man like the duke, but it is very bad for a young man like you, and the proof of it is that all the young lovers I have had have very soon left me."

Their turbulent affair lasted one year, and it ended as she had predicted. After a few months of escorting her to dances and gambling casinos, and of buying her expensive gifts, Dumas was almost out of funds. He tried his luck at baccarat to recoup, and lost the little that remained. He borrowed and he fretted. He became insanely jealous of her Russian count and insisted that she give him up. She said she would if Dumas paid all the bills. Thereafter he was bitterly silent.

Meanwhile, her consumption had grown worse. She had tried hypnotists, among them the renowned Dr. David-Ferdinand Koreff, an engaging quack who had treated Stendhal and George Sand, and had met Heine and Delacroix, and whom Talleyrand called a "devil" who "knows everything, even a bit of medicine!" But Dr. Koreff's strange prescriptions, and treatments involving animal magnetism and hypnosis, were to no avail. Then, at Dumas's insistence, Marie gave up night life and champagne, and went on summer picnics with him and drank goat's milk. Once, she even accompanied him into the countryside, but within a week, the quietness and the fresh air and closeness of nature bored her. She hastened back to Paris, to her old dissipations, and one evening, after she had complained that she was too exhausted for company of any kind, Dumas watched a new lover enter her rooms.

In a cold fury, Dumas sat down and wrote her a note:

My Dear Marie,

I am neither rich enough to love you as I could wish, nor poor enough to be loved as you wish. Let us forget, therefore, you a name which must be very nearly indifferent to you, I a happiness which has become impossible for me. It is superfluous for me to tell you how sorry I am, for you know how much I love you. Good-by, then. You have too tender a heart not to understand why I am writing this letter and too much intelligence not to forgive me for writing it.

Mille souvenirs. A.D.

Long after Marie's death, Dumas recovered this letter at an auction. He presented it to Sarah Bernhardt, who had portrayed Marguerite in his play, and with it he gave her a copy of the novel that he had based on his relationship with Marie Duplessis. "This particular copy," he wrote Bernhardt, "is unique because of the autograph letter that you will find opposite page 212, and which is almost identical with the printed letter on that page. This letter was written by the real Armand Duval, nearly forty years ago. . . . This letter is the only tangible thing that is left of that story. I feel that it should come to you by right, since you have through this piece of the past, brought back to me my youth and life."

When Marie Duplessis received the original letter from Dumas, she did not reply. And she was soon too busy, and too ill, to care. She had seventeen months of life left. She lived them to the hilt.

Franz Liszt, at thirty the toast of Europe, was in Paris for a series of concerts. In the lobby of a theater, between acts, Marie saw the musician and introduced herself to him. They remained in the lobby chatting throughout the third act. A friend of Liszt's, witness to the meeting, reported that the musician was enchanted by her. He listened to her "with rapt attention," enjoying "this fine flow of talk, full of ideas, this manner of speech that was so sonorous, eloquent and dreamy all at the same time." Later, Marie insisted that her doctor, who knew Liszt, bring him to one of her receptions. The doctor obliged, and Liszt came, and by the end of the evening he was her latest conquest.

Liszt called her Mariette and cared deeply for her, and she loved him. Once, he confessed to another mistress that Marie Duplessis "was the first woman with whom I was in love." And he told his confidant and biographer, Janka Wohl, that Marie's companionship was the best he ever found in Paris. Then he elaborated: "I am not generally partial to a Marion Delorme and a Manon Lescaut. But Marie Duplessis was an exception. She had a great deal of heart, a completely ideal liveliness of spirit, and I consider her unique of her kind. Dumas understood her very well. He did not have to do very much to create her over again; she was the most absolute incarnation of womankind who has ever existed."

When Liszt prepared to depart on a tour, Marie wrote him: "I know I shan't live. I'm an odd kind of girl, and I can't hold on to this life that's the only kind I know how to lead and that I can't endure. Take me away. Take me anywhere you like. I won't worry you. I sleep all day, in the evening you let me go to the theater, and at night you can do what you want with me." He promised to take her with him to Turkey later in the year, but by then she was seriously ill. After he left on his trip, Liszt never saw her again. When it was too late, he regretted that he had not been at her bedside. "I would have tried to save her at any price," he said.

Meanwhile, Marie's old benefactor, the Viscount de Perregaux, had pressed his suit, begging her to dismiss all her other lovers. She replied, "Do you want to do me an injury? You know perfectly well that what you propose would be very damaging to my future, which you seem resolved to make miserable and sad." De Perregaux explained that what he was proposing was marriage. In a fit of self-pity, intensified by the fear that her other friends would desert her in her worsening illness, she went with de Perregaux to London. They were married at the Kensington Registry Office on February 21, 1845. But in this, her one attempt at respectability, she was thwarted by the law. Since de Perregaux feared that members of his family might intervene if they knew whom he was marrying, no banns were published. As a result, the legality of the union was not recognized in France. It was just as well. Marie was not meant for marriage, and she could not endure de Perregaux. She left him, though she retained the title of countess and displayed de Perregaux's coat of arms on her writing paper and dinner service.

Racked by coughing spells and rapidly weakening, she went to Wiesbaden for the cure. For her, there was none. She returned to Paris, and submitted her fate to two reputable physicians, one Auguste-François Chomel, who attended King Louis-Philippe of France, and the other Casimir Joseph Davaine, who was the first to discover that bacteria caused disease and who was admired by Pasteur. This pair tried to help her. One of their detailed prescriptions suggests that "Madame Duplessis" should massage her armpits with a pomade of potassium iodide, take asses' milk sweetened with syrup of fern, take a mixture of sweet and bitter milk of almonds for sleep, take syrup of Karabi to control her cough, and observe a strict diet consisting of "thin rice soup, fresh eggs lightly boiled, fish lightly grilled, poultry, light boiled vegetables, very fine bread, fruit salad, jam, chocolate with milk for lunch" and a mixture of wine and water for dinner.

Still, she was failing. A wan and feverish cameo, she appeared with her camellias at the theater for the last time. A reporter from *Le Siècle* saw her and noted: "She looked as though she had come from her tomb to reproach all the brilliant young fools and the Ninons of the day for having abandoned and forgotten her."

De Perregaux did not forget her. With death so near, she had begged his forgiveness, and now he was beside her bed as she lay staring at the image of the Virgin on her dressing table. When she recognized her viscount, she whispered, "You have come to see me. Good-bye. I am going away." A priest came, gave her the last sacraments, and left. Théophile Gautier reported the rest: "For three days, feeling herself slipping down into the gulf that awaits us all, she held tightly to the hand of her nurse as though she would never let go. But she was forced to let go in the end, when the angel of death arrived. By a last effort of youth, recoiling from destruction, she rose to her feet as though to escape; then she gave three loud cries and fell forever."

It was three o'clock in the morning of February 3, 1847. Marie Duplessis was dead at twenty-three years of age.

"Her death was a kind of event," recorded Jules Janin. "It was talked of for three days, and that is a great deal in this town of sophisticated passions and of festivals constantly coming round. . . ."

Funeral services were held in the Madeleine Church. She lay in a coffin surrounded by camellias. The old Russian count, supported by his valet as well as by Marie's sister, Delphine Paquet, was among those who saw her put to rest in the Cemetery of Montmartre. Less than two weeks later, de Perregaux, who had purchased a better burial plot and an expensive vault, had her body disinterred in the rain. He watched as the coffin holding the slight body was placed in its permanent grave, and the white marble monument with its carved camellias was set over it forever. Into the marble he had had this inscription engraved: *Here lies / Alphonsine Plessis / born on January 15th, 1824 / deceased February 3rd, 1847 / De Profundis.*

Arriving in Marseilles after a trip to Spain and Africa, young Alexandre Dumas heard of her death. He rushed back to Paris in time to attend a much-publicized auction of Marie's luxurious effects. Moving silently through his former mistress's apartment, he heard the voice of the auctioneer and realized that Marie's favorite novel was being held up for sale. As he recalled it later:

"Suddenly, I heard the shout: 'One volume, perfectly bound, gilt-edged, entitled *Manon Lescaut.* There is something written on the first page: ten francs.'

" 'Twelve,' said a voice after a fairly long silence.

" 'Fifteen,' I said. Why? I don't know. Probably because of that 'something written.'

" 'Thirty!' said the first bidder in a tone which seemed to defy anyone to go higher.

"It became a battle. 'Thirty-five!' I cried in the same tone.

" 'Forty!'

" 'Fifty!'

" 'Sixty!'

" 'A hundred!' "

Dumas's bid of one hundred francs claimed the book of his beloved.

Jules Janin observed the rest of the auction and faithfully reported it: "They sold some shoes which she had worn, and honest women fought as to who should wear Cinderella's slipper. Everything was sold, even her shabbiest shawl, which was already three years old; even her brilliant-feathered macaw, which repeated a rather sad little tune its mistress had taught it. They sold her portraits, they sold her love letters, they sold some of her hair, everything was for sale, and her family, who averted their gaze when she passed in her crested carriage, rapidly carried along by her English horses, gorged themselves triumphantly with all the gold that her relics had produced."

Eugène Sue bought her prayer book. The Duchess of Ragusa, on behalf of her nephew, de Perregaux, bought many of Marie's jewels, including some turquoise brooches. Prive, the building's concierge, bought Marie's miniature, painted in oil, for three francs. In all, the auction grossed for the estate the great sum of eighty-nine thousand francs. With this, her creditors were satisfied, and there was enough left over to enable her principal heir, her sister Delphine, to purchase an estate (perhaps the one Marie had always dreamed of owning) in Normandy.

But in the years to come, the one who received the greatest legacy from Marie Duplessis was her onetime lover, the young Dumas. For him, their old affair was not yet over. After the auction, he wrote an elegy to her. Still, that was hardly enough. The virginal face, the magnificent body, haunted his waking dreams. Five months later, he was at work on a novel, *La Dame aux camélias*.

The heroine of the novel was Marie Duplessis, renamed Marguerite Gautier. The hero—whose name, Armand Duval, had Dumas's initials—was Dumas himself. The story, basically, was their story, idealized but faithful to the facts and to Marie's background and character. The novel was written in four weeks. The first edition of twelve hundred copies, published by Cadot in 1848, was given a wide and sensational press, and it sold out at once. But it did not continue to sell. Beyond his thousand-franc advance, Dumas made little from it. He wished to find a larger audience for his story. Someone suggested a play. Dumas tried collaboration with a friend of his father's. The collaborator sought to make *La Dame aux camélias* the story of Marie and her Russian. Dumas objected. He decided to attempt the play on his own. He completed it in eight days and read it to his father, who was moved to tears. He took it to a theater. The management accepted it, but went bankrupt before the production could be presented. When this happened a second time, Dumas gave up.

On New Year's Day, 1851, walking alone in the rain, Dumas found himself outside the Cemetery of Montmartre. He entered and sat before Marie's grave. He remembered later that he wept —over his defeats, his depression, and over her. He returned to his quarters, reread the play, rewrote it, and again tried to get it produced.

The play opened in the Théâtre du Vaudeville just five years, almost to the night, after Marie's death. The audience cried and cheered, and Dumas wired his father: "Great, great success. So great that I felt I was at the *première* of one of your works." And his father replied: "My best work, my dear child, is yourself." Among the thousands who saw, and were moved by, the play was the popular Italian composer, Giuseppe Verdi, who was inspired by its theme to create his opera *La Traviata*, which had its first performance in Venice in 1853.

Dumas married twice after his affair with Marie Duplessis. In old age, he became obsessed with the wickedness of prostitution, and proposed to the government that all unmarried women be drafted and taught trades in state schools, and that all women of the streets suffer deportation to the colonies. Yet when he died in 1895 and was buried in the Cemetery of Montmartre, onlookers insisted upon snatching white camellias from his grave in order to lay them on the grave of Marie Duplessis. Despite the elderly author's tirades against the woman of pleasure, Frenchmen remembered what the younger Dumas had forgotten—that such a woman had made him famous, and had made romance flower just a moment longer in a world rapidly growing material and ever more dreary.

XI

The Damned

Bitch

> To express it delicately, I think Madame Clare
> is a damned bitch.
>
> —LORD BYRON

By 1879 Percy Bysshe Shelley, drowned near Viareggio, Italy, had been dead fifty-seven years; and Lord Byron, taken by fever in a bed at Missolonghi, Greece, had been dead fifty-five years. With them had been buried the age of the romantics.

By 1879 the world had long since entered upon the era of the industrial, the scientific, the realistic, and men whose names would stir the twentieth century were already at work. John D. Rockefeller was forty years old, Thomas Edison thirty-two, George Bernard Shaw and Sigmund Freud twenty-three, Henry Ford and William Randolph Hearst sixteen. And H. G. Wells, André Gide, and Arturo Toscanini were active youngsters.

Yet in the first part of that year, in the busy, bewildering new era, there dwelt still in Florence, Italy, obscurely, half forgotten, one of the few survivors of the misty, legendary, romantic past.

By name she was Claire Clairmont, aged eighty-one, a little English lady with white curls and black silk dress—as great an anachronism in 1879 as the thought of Lord Byron making an assignation on the newly invented telephone or Percy Shelley penning a poem supporting the railroad strikes in the United States. Yet the elderly Miss Clairmont was one of the few persons alive who had known those romantics—in fact, one of the few humans who had known them well; for she had been both friend and inspiration to Shelley, and the mother of an illegitimate child by Lord Byron.

Only a handful of the growing cult of Shelley-Byron worshipers knew that she was still alive. One of these was a retired Salem, Massachusetts, seaman named Captain Edward Augustus Silsbee. His hobby was Shelleyana. He was a fanatic about anything Shelley had written, owned, or touched. He hungered to possess every Shelley manuscript fragment, letter, or relic in existence. When he learned that a human relic still lived—a woman who had dwelt with Percy and Mary Shelley almost their entire married life—he scurried off to Italy to meet her.

It was not easy. Claire Clairmont in her last years was no longer the gregarious, aggressive hellion who had pursued Byron to his bed. She had become an ailing, querulous recluse. She shared an apartment at 43 Via Romana, in Florence, with her brother's daughter, Paula Clairmont, her somewhat plain, attentive, middle-aged companion.

In the more than half century since Claire Clairmont had last set eyes on Shelley, the spell of his persuasion and example had almost evaporated. In his presence, and for years after, she had been an atheist. Now she was a Roman Catholic convert, having written her friend Edward Trelawny eight years before: "My own firm conviction after years and years of reflection is that our Home is Beyond the Stars, not beneath them." To this Trelawny had testily replied: "Dissatisfied with this world, you have faith in another—I have not." In the old days, she had advocated free love. Now she began making notes for a book she intended to write, but which she never completed, to "illustrate from the lives of Shelley and Byron the dangers and evils resulting from erroneous opinions on the relations of the sexes."

Nevertheless, though she had finally rejected Shelley's philosophy, she still loved him dearly, loved his memory as much as she hated Byron's. Beside the crucifix that hung in her quaint bed-

room at 43 Via Romana, she kept a portrait of Shelley. She retained also two precious notebooks in which Percy and Mary
Shelley had copied his poems, more than two dozen personal letters written to her by Shelley, and a lock of Shelley's hair preserved in a small red morocco box.

These were the irresistible mementos that brought Captain Edward Augustus Silsbee from his native Massachusetts to Italy. It
was the determination to beg, buy, or steal these items, as well as
to set eyes upon the eyes that had actually seen Shelley, that made
Captain Silsbee take up the last watch in Florence. He had prepared himself for the difficult task of not only meeting the old
lady, but winning her complete confidence. This he accomplished,
finally, in a devious way. He went to the landlady at 43 Via
Romana and asked to rent rooms. There happened to be a vacancy. He promptly moved in and became Claire Clairmont's
neighbor.

Inevitably Captain Silsbee met Claire and her niece, and soon
was on intimate terms with them. Silsbee and the Clairmonts
must have made a remarkable threesome. Claire, as described by
her relatives, was "small, distinguished, very English." John Singer
Sargent, the American painter who was born in Florence, recalled that he first met her when he was thirteen. According to
Sargent's biographer Evan Charteris, Sargent was attending
dancing classes: "He told me that on one occasion the usual pianist was unable to attend, and the class was on the point of being
dissolved when it was remembered that someone who played and
might be willing to fill the vacancy lived on the floor above. Presently a handsome old lady dressed in black silk came into the
room. He noted a certain faded elegance about her as she took
her place at the piano. The lady was Jane [Claire] Clairmont."

Claire's niece Paula, who had been born in Vienna where her
father taught English to royalty, was in her fifties and a spinster
when Captain Silsbee arrived in Florence. Once there had been
prospects, apparently. Claire disclosed to a friend in 1869: "I am
troubled by circumstances. My niece during and after her Mother's sickness and death was very much assisted by an elderly Austrian retired Major—he wishes to marry her; he cannot leave Austria or he would lose his pension—if they marry I must either go
to Austria to live or live on here without one relation near me.
. . . I have told Pauline to do exactly what she thinks will be best

for her happiness. I will give no advice or take any responsibility on myself in her affairs." Here one detects the subtle tyranny of the old. For Paula, timid and unsure, docilely decided to abandon her chance for marriage, and to stay on as her aunt's companion.

Placed alongside these two retiring women, Captain Edward Augustus Silsbee was a startling figure. A veteran of the merchant marine, he looked like an uncouth pirate. He was much given to tall stories of his adventures on the China seas, and once told the youthful, wide-eyed Sargent "of a fall, when in command of a steamer, into an oil tank, and of his being left so long to struggle in that medium before he was pulled out that his hair positively refused ever to curl again."

After his retirement, Captain Silsbee's one passion was Shelley. At the drop of his idol's name, in private parlor or public hall, he would boom forth the verses of "The Cloud." Violet Paget, the English novelist who wrote under the name of Vernon Lee, remembered how Silsbee would "come and sit gloomily in an armchair, looking like some deep-sea monster on a Bernini fountain, staring at the carpet and quoting his favorite author with a trumpet-like twang quite without relevance to the conversation."

Another ardent Shelleyite, Dr. Richard Garnett, thought Captain Silsbee "a most remarkable man . . . amiable and gracious." According to Dr. Garnett: "He has traveled far and thought much. A grizzled, weather-beaten veteran of fine physique, his discourse was mainly of poetry and art, on both of which he would utter deeper sayings than are often to be found in print. He was the most enthusiastic critic of Shelley the present writer had known, but also the most acute and discriminating."

In his hunt for Shelley mementos, Captain Silsbee had shown persistence and patience. He had already tracked down the grandson of the beautiful, light-headed Jane Williams, whose common-law husband had died with Shelley, and from the grandson had obtained the very guitar Jane used to strum for the poet. Now, in Florence, he applied the same persistence and patience to winning over Claire Clairmont. He pressed her for Shelley and Byron anecdotes. She had much to recount of Shelley, but usually refused to discuss Byron.

Meanwhile, Captain Silsbee kept his eye on the Shelley treasures in Claire's rooms. As Sargent told Charteris, "It was even said that he never ventured far from the house lest the owner of the manuscripts should die during his absence." For her part, Claire liked Captain Silsbee, perhaps even saw in him one who might take care of her niece after she was gone. At any rate, she permitted him to see and read her letters from Shelley and Trelawny, and to borrow one of the Shelley notebooks. But she obviously had no intention of permanently parting with the treasures while she lived.

Captain Silsbee watched and waited. The old lady lived on. To Silsbee it must have seemed that she would live forever. Discouraged, yet secure in the knowledge that the treasures were safe, Silsbee decided to abandon his watch briefly and take a short trip to the United States.

On March 19, 1879, while Captain Silsbee was vacationing in America, Claire Clairmont finally died. The moment that Silsbee heard the news, he caught a ship and hastened back to Florence. Claire was already buried in the Catholic cemetery of Santa Maria d'Antella, in the commune or parish of Bagno a Ripoli, three miles outside Florence. But the spinster niece, Paula, was still at 43 Via Romana, surrounded by the Shelley treasures.

Captain Silsbee begged Paula to sell him her aunt's mementos. "Then arose an unfortunate complication," according to the tale Sargent told his biographer. "The niece, mature in years and gifted with few of the graces which appeal to buccaneers, had long nourished a secret flame for the Captain. She declared her passion and proposed a bargain; the manuscripts should be the Captain's, but he must take her in marriage as a term of the deal."

Undoubtedly Captain Silsbee was shocked. He had, he thought, been prepared to undergo anything to secure the Shelley treasures. He had moved to Florence, insinuated himself into Claire Clairmont's home, spent long evenings charming the two women. And, failing to get what he wanted in Claire's lifetime, he had been positive he would attain his objective after her death. Suddenly the price was too high. The last of his limited funds, yes; but marriage to the spinster, never.

After Paula's proposal, Captain Silsbee left Florence in haste. But not entirely empty-handed. He still had the 150-page notebook in which Percy and Mary had written Shelley's poems. This he presented to Harvard University eight years later. And he had a single letter Shelley had written Claire, which he quietly retained.

When the dealers who approached Paula were told that these two items were missing, they were furious with Silsbee. One accused him of having employed a disgraceful deception. Thomas J. Wise, the as yet undetected literary forger, charged that Silsbee had been loaned the precious notebook because he had promised to marry Paula, but he had not kept his word.

Four months after Claire's death and Silsbee's flight, H. Buxton Forman bought the remaining treasures from Paula—which included twenty-four letters from Shelley to Claire, sixty-five letters from Trelawny to Claire, and a miniature portrait of Allegra, Claire's child by Lord Byron. But Forman was bitter about not getting the missing notebook, which he felt Silsbee had stolen. As Forman reported later: "Of the mutilated manuscript volume, containing fair copies of many of his [Shelley's] published poems . . . there is a sad tale to tell. An American who had been residing in the same house at Florence with the Clairmonts had been bidding against me for the collection; but as his free bids turned out to be only in bills at long date, the executrix decided to accept my cash rather than his paper, in which she lacked confidence. This man, however, had 'borrowed' and not restored the precious manuscript book—which now graces the classic precincts of Harvard College."

In June 1887, a year after the Shelley Society was formed in London, Captain Silsbee lectured to a gathering of its four hundred members on the subject of Shelley, exciting them with firsthand anecdotes he had heard from Claire. In 1900, still basking in the reflected glory of having known Claire, Silsbee sat for a charcoal portrait by Sargent, which was presented to the Bodleian Library. In 1904, Captain Silsbee died. As to Paula, the spinster niece, she suffered a dizzy spell one day while mountain climbing, slipped, and plunged to her death in the river that lay below.

But if Paula and Captain Silsbee both failed to get quite what they wanted from each other while they were fencing over Claire's legacy, there was one person in Florence at that time who eventually profited greatly from the curious drama. This person was Henry James, the small, pale, shy writer, bearded and formal, who had been born in New York but had begun a self-imposed exile in England when he was thirty-three. He was living, off and on, in Florence while Claire Clairmont was still alive. He never met her. As he reflected later: "Had I happened to hear of her a

little sooner, I might have seen her in the flesh. The question of
whether I should have wished to do so was another matter. . . .
The thrill of learning that she had 'overlapped,' and by so much,
and the wonder of my having doubtless at several earlier seasons
passed again and again, all unknowing, the door of her house,
where she sat above, within call and in her habit as she lived,
these things gave me all I wanted."

Eight years after Claire's death, in January of 1887, Henry
James was again in Florence. One afternoon he went to visit at
the home of the poet Eugene Lee-Hamilton, a half brother of
Violet Paget, who had known Silsbee. During the afternoon there
were other visitors, among them the Italian Countess Gamba. Her
husband was the nephew of Teresa Guiccioli, the woman with
whom Byron had had his last affair before his death in Greece.
After the countess left, Lee-Hamilton told Henry James that the
countess possessed many letters written by Byron to Mme. Guiccioli. She felt that the letters were disgraceful, was refusing to
publish them, and had already burned one. After indignantly
relating this, Lee-Hamilton went on to tell James another story
concerning another packet of valuable letters. He told James the
story, which had been making the rounds of Florence for some
years, about Captain Silsbee's siege of the Clairmont household.

Back in his quarters, Henry James sat down to his notebook
and jotted the following:

"Florence, January 12th, 1887. Hamilton (V.L.'s brother) told
me a curious thing of Capt. Silsbee—the Boston art-critic and
Shelley-worshipper; that is of a curious adventure of his. Miss
Claremont [*sic*], Byron's ci-devant mistress (the mother of Allegra) was living, until lately, here in Florence, at a great age, 80
or thereabouts, and with her lived her niece, a younger Miss
Claremont—of about 50. Silsbee knew that they had interesting
papers—letters of Shelley's and Byron's—he had known it for a
long time and cherished the idea of getting hold of them. To this
end he laid the plan of going to lodge with the Misses Claremont
—hoping that the old lady in view of her great age and failing
condition would die while he was there, so that he might then put
his hand upon the documents, which she hugged close in life. He
carried out this scheme—and things se passerent as he had expected. The old woman *did* die—and then he approached the
younger one—the old maid of 50—on the subject of his desires.

Her answer was—'I'll give you all the letters if you will marry me!'
H. says that Silsbee court encore. Certainly there is a little subject
there: the picture of the two faded, queer, poor and discredited
old English women—living on into a strange generation, in their
musty corner of a foreign town—with these illustrious letters their
most precious possession. Then the plot of the Shelley fanatic—
his watchings and waitings—the way he couvers the treasure. The
denouement needn't be the one related of poor Silsbee; and at any
rate the general situation is in itself a subject and a picture. It
strikes me much. The interest would be in some price that the
man has to pay—that the old woman—or the survivor—sets upon
the papers. His hesitations—his struggle—for he really would give
almost anything . . ."

Six months later Henry James was at work on the story. He
finished it in Venice—it ran to a short novel, about thirty-six thousand words in length—and he mailed it off to the *Atlantic
Monthly*. This magazine published it from March through May
of 1888, under the title *The Aspern Papers*.

Henry James's fictionalization hewed close to the facts. The
hero-narrator of his tale is "a critic, a commentator, an historian"
and a "publishing scoundrel" who, with his partner, specializes
in the life and works of a long-dead American writer—the great
romantic poet, Jeffrey Aspern. Constantly on the hunt for information concerning Aspern's life, the critic is surprised to learn
that Aspern's onetime mistress, Juliana Bordereau, is living in
Venice. "The strange thing had been for me to discover in England that she was still alive: it was as if I had been told Mrs. Sid-
dons was, or Queen Caroline, or the famous Lady Hamilton, for
it seemed to me that she belonged to a generation as extinct. 'Why
she must be tremendously old—at least a hundred,' I had said."

Determined to lay his hands on some of the immortal Aspern's
extant papers and relics, the critic makes his way to Venice and
succeeds in renting a room in the "dilapidated old palace" owned
by Juliana Bordereau and her niece Tina. The critic worms his
way into the confidence of the "tremulous spinster" Tina, and
through her finally manages to set eyes on the legendary Juliana
Bordereau. "I was really face to face with the Juliana of some of
Aspern's most exquisite and most renowned lyrics. . . . She had
over her eyes a horrible green shade which served for her almost
as a mask. . . . She was very small and shrunken, bent forward

with her hands in her lap. She was dressed in black and her head was wrapped in a piece of old black lace. . . . I could see only the lower part of her bleached and shrivelled face."

Juliana, anxious to obtain money for her niece, encourages the critic to stay on and prods him to serve as Tina's escort. Once he has become friendly with Tina, the critic confesses the real purpose of his visit. Tina decides to let him have a look at the Aspern papers, but then reports that they are not in the trunk where they have always been. As the critic becomes desperate, the old lady falls ill. While she is asleep, he enters her room, determined to find the papers, but is caught red-handed.

Deeply abject, he departs the following morning on a twelve-day trip through Italy. When he returns he finds that during his absence Juliana has died. He asks Tina for the papers. She has indeed found them where they had been hidden—in her aunt's mattress. When he presses Tina for them, she hesitates. She feels that she can give them only to a "relation." With shock, the critic realizes the price Tina has set on the Aspern papers.

"What in the name of the preposterous did she mean if she didn't mean to offer me her hand? That was the price—that was the price!" The critic, horrified, rushes off to think it over. In time, he returns to Tina. "It seemed to me I *could* pay the price." But it is too late. Tina has destroyed the papers.

" 'Destroyed them?' I wailed.

" 'Yes; what was I to keep them for? I burnt them last night, one by one, in the kitchen.'

" 'One by one?' I coldly echoed it.

" 'It took a long time—there were so many.' "

When *The Aspern Papers* appeared between book covers in a 1908 New York edition, Henry James publicly, if cautiously, admitted the precise source of his inspiration in a detailed preface. Juliana Bordereau was of course Claire Clairmont. "I saw it somehow at the very first blush as romantic," wrote James, "that Jane Clairmont, the half-sister of Mary Godwin, Shelley's second wife and for a while the intimate friend of Byron and the mother of his daughter Allegra, should have been living on in Florence, where she had long lived, up to our own day." As to Tina, she was most certainly Paula Clairmont. "Legend," wrote James, "mentioned a younger female relative of the ancient woman as a person who, for a queer climax, had had to be dealt with." However, only Captain Silsbee's penchant for intrigue was apparent in the character of the narrator-critic. Speaking of Silsbee, James wrote: "I had known him a little, but there is not a reflected glint of him in *The Aspern Papers*."

Though Claire Clairmont was dead when Henry James published his novel, the other principals were still alive. This, as well as the author's inevitable use of creative license, made James change the setting of the story and the native background of his characters. As he explained in his preface, "Delicacy had demanded, I felt, that my appropriation of the Florentine legend should purge it, first of all, of references too obvious; so that, to begin with, I shifted the scene of the adventure. Juliana, as I saw her, was thinkable only in Byronic and more or less immediately post-Byronic Italy. . . . It was a question, in fine, of covering one's tracks—though with no great elaboration I am bound to admit; and I felt I couldn't cover mine more than in postulating a comparative American Byron to match an American Miss Clairmont."

Limited though he was to the small canvas of a short novel, Henry James's portrait of Juliana Bordereau followed closely the original model. In the story, Juliana is given a French ancestry, was once a governess, was in her youth "perverse and reckless," possessed a "terrible" temper, and had an inherited income from America. In actual life, Claire Clairmont was of French ancestry, served as a governess in Austria, Russia and England, admitted to Byron that she was "imprudent and vicious" though insisting she could "love gently and with affection," and was the recipient of a twelve-thousand-pound inheritance from the Shelley estate in England.

But in sketching Juliana's lover, Jeffrey Aspern, Henry James combined, into one man, both of the great poets in Claire Clairmont's life. In setting down Aspern's affairs, and his relationship to Juliana, Henry James wrote: "There had been an impression about 1825 that he had 'treated her badly,' just as there had been an impression that he had 'served,' as the London populace says, several other ladies in the same masterful way. . . . Half the women of his time, to speak liberally, had flung themselves at his head." This part of Aspern, of course, as well as "his remarkably handsome face," was Lord Byron. On the other hand, when Juliana said Aspern "liked her immensely" and that she still thought him "a god," James was drawing upon Claire Clairmont's high regard for Shelley.

Claire Clairmont lived to be eighty-one, but she was really alive only until her twenty-fourth birthday. By then she had lost both her daughter by Byron and her friend Shelley. For a few brief years, she had lived tremendously, moving among giants, and this made the long decades that followed after seem pallid and anti-climactic by comparison.

She was born Clara Mary Constantia Jane Clairmont, on April 27, 1798, the second child of a shrewish, business-minded mother and a Swiss merchant father. Her name changed as she grew, from Clara to Clare to Claire. Stubbornly, her mother persisted in calling her Jane. Three years after her father's death, her widowed mother, Mary Clairmont, moved into Skinner Street in London. Their next-door neighbor was a stocky, almost bald bookseller and publisher named William Godwin.

Godwin, a onetime preacher, had become famous less than a dozen years before for his radical work _An Enquiry Concerning Political Justice_. In 1796 he had met Mary Wollstonecraft, author of _A Vindication of the Rights of Women_. She had had an affair with an American, Gilbert Imlay, who deserted her and left her with a child that she named Fanny Imlay. Godwin and Mary Wollstonecraft lived together, without the sanction of marriage, until she became pregnant. The couple then married. Six months later Mary Godwin, the future wife of Shelley, was born, and ten days after her birth Mary Wollstonecraft died.

When the widow Clairmont moved next door, the widower Godwin was still unsuccessfully searching for a new wife to care for his adopted daughter, Fanny Imlay, and his own daughter, Mary. Setting his sights upon the widow Clairmont, he wooed and won her. Thus, in 1801 Claire Clairmont and her older brother, Charles, moved into 41 Skinner Street. To this crowded ménage was added, in 1803, a newborn son named William.

Life at the Godwins' was about as restful as the French Revolution. Amid the clatter of the brood and the comings and goings of visitors, Godwin wrote two books, quarreled with his critics, kept off his creditors. Claire's mother, in her green-tinted spectacles, constantly vocal and angry, pecked away at the nerves of all. Still, Claire found the intellectual atmosphere stimulating.

Once she hid in the octagon-shaped library to hear Samuel Taylor Coleridge recite "The Ancient Mariner."

In the early summer of 1814 occurred the event that was to be all-important to Mary Godwin—and, through Mary, it was to influence Claire's life also. Percy Bysshe Shelley appeared. He had called upon his hero Godwin two years before, accompanied by his wife Harriet. But Claire, as well as her stepsister Mary, had been out of town. Now, in London on business, Shelley dropped by almost daily for supper.

Claire was stirred by him. In a shrill voice, he held forth on Mary Wollstonecraft, revolution, poetry, vegetarianism, free love, and atheism. Claire's mother was less impressed. As she repeated it to a friend later: "I remember Mr. Godwin telling him once that he was too young to be so certain he was in the right—that he ought to have more experience before being so dogmatic and then he said some Saint, St. Cyril I think, but I know the name began with a C., had spoken most wisely that Humility was Truth. Mr. Shelley laughed and said he would listen to Socrates or Plato but not to a Saint."

Soon Shelley was directing most of his talk to Claire's stepsister, Mary Godwin. He talked less and less of books and politics, as his secret love for Mary grew. But it was she who used the word first. It happened on a Sunday evening in June of 1814, before her mother's grave in St. Pancras churchyard, with Claire standing nearby, trying not to eavesdrop. Mary's declaration sent Shelley into an ecstasy of excitement. Quickly, he confided to his friend Thomas Jefferson Hogg, "No expression can convey the remotest conception of the manner in which she dispelled my delusions. The sublime and rapturous moment when she confessed herself mine, who had so long been hers in secret, cannot be painted to mortal imagination."

There was one minor problem. Shelley already had a wife. Instead of telling her of his new love, he told Godwin. The old philosopher was furious. He denounced Shelley as a "seducer." When Shelley finally summoned his wife Harriet to London and told her about Mary, Harriet called Mary the seductress. Indignantly, Harriet wrote a friend: "Mary was determined to seduce him. She is to blame. She heated his imagination by talking of her mother, and going to her grave with him every day, till at last she told him she was dying in love for him."

When Mary realized how Harriet was reacting, she went with Claire Clairmont to call on Shelley's wife. As Claire remembered it years later, Mary "went at the end of June with me to see Harriet in Chapel Street at her father's house. I was present at the whole interview and heard Mary assure Harriet that she would not think of Shelley's love for her."

When Shelley was told of this, he raced to Skinner Street, burst into the house, elbowed past Mrs. Godwin and Claire, and confronted Mary. "They wish to separate us, my beloved, but Death shall unite us," he shouted. He handed her a bottle of laudanum, and pulled a pistol from his pocket to use on himself. Claire screamed and Mrs. Godwin ran for help. Mary burst into tears, sobbing, "I won't take this laudanum, but if you will only be reasonable and calm, I will promise to be ever faithful to you."

Shelley left, agitated but alive. His friend of two years, the satirist Thomas Love Peacock, tried to calm him, reminding him of Harriet's virtues. Shelley replied, "Everyone who knows me must know that the partner of my life should be one who can feel poetry and understand philosophy. Harriet is a noble animal, but she can do neither." Shortly after, Shelley did take poison, but recovered. Distressed, Mary and Claire met with him, and while Claire stood some distance away, Mary listened to his proposal that they elope to the Continent. Shelley argued that Harriet did not love him, was in fact having an affair with a Major Ryan whom she had met in Dublin. This convinced Mary. She consented to run off, and both she and Shelley agreed that Claire, who knew French and deserved to be liberated, must accompany them.

At four in the morning of July 28, 1814, Claire and Mary, loaded with bundles, crept down the stairs of their home and out into Skinner Street. They hurried to the spot where Shelley was restlessly waiting with chaise and horses, and united, the three started for Dover. When they reached Dover in late afternoon, the Channel boat had already left. Fearful that Godwin would overtake them, they hired two sailors who owned a sailboat, and started to cut through the swells toward Calais. A storm came up. The two-hour crossing took amost twelve hours. But they arrived safely.

That evening, while resting at Dessein's Hotel, Shelley received word that "a fat lady had arrived who claimed that he had run away with her daughter." It was Mrs. Godwin. Claire was dispatched to pacify her, and after trying to do so all through the night, finally promised that she would return to London. However, in the morning, after consulting with Shelley, Claire changed her mind again and refused to accompany her mother. Defeated, Mrs. Godwin waddled back to the dock. By accident, Shelley passed her in the street. They did not speak.

The three callow fugitives—Shelley was twenty-two years old, Mary was seventeen, and Claire only sixteen—spent six weeks in Europe. Since they had little money, they traveled through France and Switzerland on foot, on muleback, and in a two-wheeled cabriolet. They lingered six days in Paris studying Notre Dame, sitting in the Tuileries, walking through the Louvre, and visiting an old friend of Mary Wollstonecraft's.

Hiking across the war-ravaged countryside toward Switzerland, they made a curious sight—Claire and Mary in long silk dresses and Shelley in open-collar shirt and tight trousers. Claire sang a good deal, and began to keep a journal in an old notebook Shelley had given her. Mary read. Shelley told stories and wrote. They ate in open meadows, once slept in beds Napoleon and his officers had recently vacated, and were deeply impressed by the Alps. They started home by the cheapest means possible, taking a variety of dilapidated Rhine passengers boats to Rotterdam.

In London, Shelley and Mary rented quarters in Cavendish Square. Claire, learning that her mother wanted to place her in a convent, remained with the unrepentant couple. Also, Claire was briefly intrigued by Thomas Love Peacock. She thought him handsome, even if he did eat and drink too much. Peacock, in turn, was extremely impressed with Claire's vivacity, candor, and intellect. He used her as the model for Stella in *Nightmare Abbey*, and paraphrased her speech when he had Stella remark, "If I ever love, I shall do so without limit or restriction. I shall hold all difficulties light, all sacrifices cheap, all obstacles gossamer."

Soon Claire was to put her liberated attitude toward love into practice. She was becoming restless under Shelley's roof, where life was as tumultuous as it had ever been at the Godwins'. Shelley was pawning possessions daily to pay the rent and purchase their vegetarian meals. Then, hounded by Harriet's creditors and the threat of imprisonment, he fled into hiding for sixteen days. And finally, when Harriet gave birth to a child, Mary was deeply hurt by Shelley's unconcealed satisfaction. She angrily noted that he was mailing "a number of circular letters of this event, which ought to be ushered in with the ringing of bells, etc., for it is the son of *his wife.*" Mary, understandably irritated, and Claire, suffering liver trouble and ennui, began quarreling.

Claire took up temporary lodgings elsewhere, and turned her gaze upon England's greatest celebrity.

George Gordon Noël Byron, at twenty-seven, was the talk of London. Three years before, with the publication of *Childe Harold's Pilgrimage,* he had become an overnight celebrity. His incredibly attractive appearance—brown curly hair, gray-blue eyes, sensitive mouth, milky complexion, and muscular body—had attracted women by the droves. His affairs with Lady Caroline Lamb and Lady Oxford, his rumored incest with his wedded half-sister, Augusta Leigh, and his marriage to Annabella Milbanke—followed as it was by their spectacular separation the month after his daughter was born—heightened his notoriety.

It is no wonder that Claire Clairmont fell in love with him. She was alone. She envied Mary her poet. She wanted someone, and she wanted adventure. Years after, Claire explained, "I was young and vain and poor. He was famous beyond all precedent —so famous that people, and especially young people, hardly considered him as a man at all, but rather as a god. His beauty was as haunting as his fame, and he was all powerful in the direction in which my ambition turned. It seems to me almost needless to say that the attentions of a man like this, with all London at his feet, very quickly completely turned the head of a girl in my position; and when you recollect that I was brought up to consider marriage not only as a useless but absolutely sinful custom that only bigotry made necessary, you will scarcely wonder at the result."

The result was that Claire, who conveniently forgot this in her later years, set out to seduce Lord Byron. She had all of the necessary attributes. She was uninhibited, impetuous, charming. Once when she asked Shelley what he thought of her, he said there were two Claires—the bad Claire was sarcastic, irritable, gloomy, and the good Claire "the most engaging of human creatures." On another occasion, discussing her character, Claire told Lord Byron: "I may appear to you imprudent and vicious, my opinions detestable, my theories depraved, but one thing at least time shall show you, that I love gently and with affection, and that I am incapable of anything approaching to the feeling of revenge or malice." She felt that she was physically attractive. At seventeen, she was tall, shapely, vivacious, with sleek black hair, dark eyes and a Latin complexion.

In March of 1816, Claire sat down and addressed a letter to Lord Byron:

> An utter stranger takes the liberty of addressing you. . . . If a woman whose reputation has yet remained unstained, if without either guardian or husband to control her, she should throw herself on your mercy, if with a beating heart she should confess the love she has borne for you for many years, if she should secure to you secrecy and safety, if she should return your kindness with fond affection and unbounded devotion, could you betray her, or would you be silent as the grave? I am not given to many words. Either you will or you will not. Do not decide hastily, and yet I must entreat your answer without delay. . . .
>
> E. TREFUSIS.

She posted the letter. Lord Byron did not reply. Undaunted, she wrote a second letter:

> Lord Byron is requested to state whether seven o'clock this Evening will be convenient to him to receive a lady to communicate with him on business of peculiar importance. She desires to be admitted alone and with utmost privacy. If the hour she has mentioned is correct, at that hour she will come; if not, will his lordship have the goodness to make his own appointment, which shall be readily attended to though it is hoped the interview may not be postponed after this Evening. . . .
>
> G. C. B.

Claire dispatched this note by private messenger. She did not have to wait long before the messenger returned with an answer:

> Ld. B. is not aware of any "importance" which can be attached by any person to an interview with him, and more particularly by one with whom it does not appear he has the honour of being acquainted. He will however be at home at the hour mentioned.

They met that night at seven o'clock. Precisely what transpired will probably never be known. However, Claire had discovered

that Lord Byron was on the board of management of the Drury
Lane Theatre. She was seeing him, presumably, to solicit his sug-
gestions and help in furthering her acting career. She posed a
question: "Is it absolutely necessary to go through the intolerable
and disgusting drudgery of provincial theatres before commencing
on the boards of a metropolis?" In answer, he offered her a letter
of introduction to the director of Drury Lane.

Then she changed her mind. She did not want to be an actress,
after all. She wanted to be a writer. She had half of a novel completed and wished him to look at it. Soon that subterfuge was discarded, too, and she revealed plainly what she really wanted.
"Have you then any objection to the following plan?" she wrote
him. "On Thursday Evening we may go out of town together by
some stage or mail about the distance of ten or twelve miles. There
we shall be free and unknown; we can return early the following
morning. I have arranged everything here so that the slightest
suspicion may not be excited. Pray do so with your people. Will
you admit me for two moments to settle with you *where?* Indeed
I will not stay an instant after you tell me to go."

Lord Byron thought the intrigue of the coach and journey out
of town a lot of nonsense, and suggested the use of a house
nearby. Long after, Claire admitted that the house was in Albe-
marle Street and said Byron's wife saw them entering it together.

The affair progressed. Even after she had slept with him,
Claire remained in awe of the great man: "Do you know I cannot
talk to you when I see you? I am so awkward and only feel inclined to take a little stool and sit at your feet." For a short time
Byron seemed to return her love. As she told him, "Much to my
surprise, more to my happiness, you betrayed passions I had believed no longer alive in your bosom." One morning, after leaving
Byron, she burst into Shelley's home shouting, "Percy! Mary! The
great Lord Byron loves me!" Byron loved her enough, apparently,
to show jealousy toward her friend Shelley, whom he had not met.
For on one occasion she felt compelled to send him some of Shelley's letters with the note: "Pray compare them and acquit me, I
entreat you, from the list of those whom you suspect."

But Lord Byron was soon bored by her, as he was eventually
bored by most of his mistresses. He tired of her temper, her possessiveness, her indiscretions, her feminist views. He began to

break appointments, and when he did keep them, he was often rude. When Claire prepared to bring Mary Godwin to meet him, she first demanded that he show some politeness. "I say this," she wrote him, "because on Monday evening I waited nearly a quarter of an hour in your hall, which though I may overlook the disagreeableness, she is not in love and would not."

After the meeting with Byron, Mary was surprised to find that she had liked him. "How mild he is," she told Claire, "how gentle. How different from what I expected." A month later, Claire, worried that she might lose Byron to Mary, told the poet, "You will, I daresay, fall in love with her; she is very handsome and very amiable, and you will no doubt be blest in your attachment."

Claire's love for Byron persisted in spite of his growing coldness. There is evidence that her love was not primarily sexual. She told him frankly that his physical presence did not arouse her passions: "First, I have no passions; I had ten times rather be your male companion than your mistress." It would appear that she was much more excited by his fame and genius.

He was preparing to leave England, and this troubled her. He had to leave. His life was in chaos. The newspapers hammered at his questionable morals and his Francophile politics. Two facts —that his wife had left him as the rumor about his committing incest grew and that he had defended Napoleon as "Freedom's son"—turned the tide against him. When he went to the House of Lords, only one member spoke to him. When Lady Jersey gave a party for him and he arrived with his sister, the guests walked out en masse. And all the while his creditors pressed for cash.

He sailed from England on April 25, 1816, never again to return. He left with a custom-built Napoleonic coach which contained both a library and dining appurtenances, and he was attended by three servants as well as his personal physician. Claire hoped that he would take her, too. This he refused to do. He was still married and wanted no further scandal. When Claire asked whether she could visit him in Geneva, Byron was agreeable, as long as she was properly chaperoned. She persisted in declaring her love for him. "A few days ago I was eighteen," she wrote him. "People of eighteen always love truly and tenderly, and I, who was educated by Godwin, however erroneous my creed, have the highest adoration for truth. Farewell, dear kind Lord Byron. I have been reading all your poems and almost fear to think of your reading this stupid letter, but I love you."

Aware that Shelley and Mary were considering a trip to Italy, Claire pleaded with them to take her along and to include a stop-over in Geneva. After she had poured out the entire story of her involvement with Lord Byron, Shelley consented. Shelley, Mary, and Claire left England on May 3, 1816, and reached Geneva ten days later. Byron, leisurely visiting Waterloo, had not yet arrived. When he finally did, he infuriated Claire by not arranging to see her immediately, with or without Shelley. But at last, he did call upon Claire and Shelley. Dr. Newman White has described the meeting: "When he lounged into Shelley's hotel on May 25, with the slightly mortifying limp that could never be quite fully concealed, Claire Clairmont had brought about a junction of literary influences that was to have an important effect upon both men and upon English public opinion."

Although Byron and Shelley took to each other, Shelley was not exactly overwhelmed. "Lord Byron is an exceedingly interest-ing person," he wrote Peacock, "and as such is it not to be regretted that he is a slave to the vilest and most vulgar prejudices, and as mad as the winds?" When Shelley, Mary, and Claire rented a bungalow called Mont Allegre across the lake, Lord Byron leased the Villa Diodati, which was separated from them only by a vineyard.

They were neighbors slightly more than three months. The four sailed regularly on the lake, often exchanging ghost stories in the evening afterward, and during one of these sessions Mary got the idea for Dr. Frankenstein and his monster. Byron and Shelley visited Meillerie and Clarens, and they wandered across the wooded grounds where Rousseau—in his popular *La nouvelle Héloïse*—had his heroine Julie d'Étange and her lover Saint-Preux once walk; they strolled through the acacia garden where Gibbon had finished his *Decline and Fall of the Roman Empire*; they gazed upon Chillon Castle, which reminded Shelley of "cold and inhuman tyranny" and caused the inflamed Byron to exalt the "eternal spirit of the chainless mind" in his "The Prisoner of Chillon."

Claire continued to see Lord Byron and to sleep with him, all the while combating his fear that gossip might find its way back to London. Her imprudent notes and impulsive visits annoyed him, especially the latter since English tourists across the lake were observing his every movement through spyglasses. Once, leaving his villa at daybreak and hurrying through the vineyard, she lost a shoe. Vineyard workers found it and turned it over to the town mayor.

She occupied herself making copies of "The Prisoner of Chillon" and several other poems for Byron, and used this as an excuse to be with him. "I am afraid to come, dearest, for fear of meeting anyone," she said in one note. "Can you pretext the copying?" She had more and more difficulty in arranging to see Byron alone. Often his cocky, obnoxious physician, Dr. John William Polidori, was about. To get the meddlesome doctor out of the way, she demanded that Byron pack him off "to write another dictionary, or to the lady he loves."

Once when Claire was alone with Byron in his villa, a curious incident occurred. "I went up to copy out Childe Harold as was my wont," she recorded, "and he asked me whether I did not think he was a terrible person—I said No I won't believe it—and I don't. He then unlocked a cabinet and spread a number of his sister's letters upon a table; he opened some and showed them: the beginning was ordinary enough—common news of their friends, her health and then came long spaces written in cyphers which he said only he and she had the key of—and unintelligible to all other people." When he gathered up the letters, he found that one was missing. He became terribly agitated and accused Claire of stealing it. Then he found it and apologized for his suspicions.

Claire discussed the incident with Shelley. Why ciphers in letters between brother and sister? Shelley believed that they were used to disguise discussion of Byron's illegitimate children. This half satisfied Claire. But the thought always remained that the ciphers might have been used by brother and sister to discuss their love affair.

The allegation of incest hung over Byron's head throughout the last years of his life. In the more than a century since his death, the question of whether Byron committed incest has violently split his biographers into two camps. Richard Edgcumbe and John Drinkwater have denied or doubted that incest occurred; Lord Lovelace and André Maurois have been certain it was a fact. True, Byron was always touchy about the subject. A few days after his marriage, his wife had pointed at their reflection in the mirror and laughingly said, "We are as like as if we were brother and sister." Angrily, Byron grabbed her wrist and shouted, "When did you hear that?"

After the incident in Geneva, Claire apparently never gave the subject another thought. That is, not until her old age, when she told Trelawny: "There is no positive proof that the connexion between L.B. and Mrs. Leigh existed; but his verses to Augusta, by a Brother to a Sister—then his fit of hysterics at Bologna when he witnessed the performance of Myrrha [Alfieri's play depicted the love of a girl for her father]—then Manfred and Cain—all form presumptive evidence against him."

During August, Claire learned that she was pregnant. Shelley, who had to be back in London on business, insisted that Claire return with him and have the child in England. Claire agreed to this. Lord Byron wanted the baby raised by his sister. To this, Claire vehemently objected. Byron then suggested that Claire pose as the child's aunt, to avoid scandal, and that either parent could look after it until it reached the age of seven.

When Claire asked to see Byron again, he refused. His old friends—John Cam Hobhouse, Monk Lewis, and Scrope Davies— were visiting. He did not want any scenes in their presence. And he was pleased when Hobhouse, writing Lady Melbourne of life in Byron's villa, remarked: "In spite of all ridiculous rumors, none of its apartments receive any more disreputable guests than Mr. M. Lewis and myself."

Nevertheless, rumors of Byron's affair with Claire had reached London, been exaggerated into many affairs, and had provoked Augusta Leigh to write and inquire whether the rumors were true. Byron replied cheerfully: "As to all these 'mistresses,' Lord help me—I have had but one. Now don't scold; but what could I do?—a foolish girl, in spite of all I could say or do, would come after me, or rather went before—for I found her here—and I have had all the plague possible to persuade her to go back again; but at last she went. Now, dearest, I do most truly tell thee, that I could not help this, that I did all I could to prevent it, and have at last put an end to it. I was not in love, nor have any love left for any; but I could not exactly play the Stoic with a woman, who had scrambled eight hundred miles to unphilosophize me, besides I had been regaled of late with so many 'two courses and a *desert'* (Alas!) of aversion, that I was fain to take a little love (if pressed particularly) by way of novelty."

For Lord Byron, the affair was over. But Claire Clairmont would not face the truth. She wrote him a letter just before she left with Shelley and Mary for London: "When you receive this, I shall be many miles away; don't be impatient with me. I don't know why I write unless it is because it seems like speaking to you. Indeed I should have been happier if I could have seen and kissed you once before I went. . . . My dreadful fear is lest you quite forget me—I shall pine through all the wretched winter months whilst you, I hope, may never have one uneasy thought. One thing I do entreat you to remember—beware of any excess in wine . . ."

Much happened the following year in England, where Claire lived with Mary first in Bath and then in Marlow. A sensation had been caused by the appearance of Lady Caroline Lamb's novel, *Glenarvon*, in which Lord Byron was portrayed as a fictional scoundrel. The neurotic, pretty Caroline Ponsonby Lamb had been Byron's mistress for nine months before he tired of her indiscretions and dropped her. Writing *Glenarvon* was her means of revenge.

When Claire returned to London, the book was having its sensation. Teasingly, she wrote Byron: "Well, I have read it all through. You wretched creature to go about seducing and stabbing and rebelling. . . . I really am ashamed to hold communion with you. Some of the speeches are yours—I am sure they are; the very impertinent way of looking in a person's face who loves you, and telling them you are very tired and wish they'd go. But why so gentle a creature as you are should be transformed to such a fierce, mysterious monster as Glenarvon is quite inconceivable."

Lord Byron reacted to the book with disgust. According to Hobhouse: "*Glenarvon* has been read with appropriate indignation, not unmixed with contempt." Later, as the tag end of a poem he sent Hobhouse, Byron concluded:

> *I read Glenarvon, too, by Caro. Lamb,*
> *God damn.*

During Claire's stay in England, two tragedies struck close to her. Claire's foster sister, Fanny Imlay, was found in a hotel at Swansea, a suicide, with a bottle of laudanum by her bed. Shelley was sent to claim the body. Claire believed that Fanny had killed herself because she was secretly in love with Shelley. More likely, it was because she felt unwanted, and a burden to the impoverished Godwin family. Her farewell note stated: "I have long determined that the best thing I could do was to put an end to the existence of a being whose birth was unfortunate, and whose life has only been a series of pain to those persons who have hurt their health in endeavoring to promote her welfare."

This death was swiftly followed by another. On December 10, 1816, Shelley's legal wife, Harriet, was dragged out of the Serpentine in Hyde Park. She had apparently committed suicide at the age of twenty-one. Stunned, Shelley wrote Mary: "It seems that this poor woman—the most innocent of her abhorred and unnatural family—was driven from her father's house, and descended the steps of prostitution until she lived with a groom of the name of Smith, who deserting her, she killed herself." Shelley's sense of guilt made him distort Harriet's decline. There was no evidence that she had been a prostitute. For several nights Shelley, a teetotaler, drank heavily. When Peacock asked him why, Shelley answered, "I will tell you what I would not tell anyone else. I was thinking of Harriet."

Less than two weeks later Shelley legalized his union with Mary. Though he disapproved of marriage, he wanted to make Godwin (who believed in the marital state only for his daughters) happy, wanted to legitimize his own offspring by Mary, and wanted to improve his chances of getting custody of his two children by Harriet.

On January 12, 1817, Claire gave birth to a girl. The next day Mary wrote Lord Byron: "She sends her love to you and begs me to say she is in excellent spirits and as good health as can be expected." Lord Byron determined his daughter's name: "I mean to christen her Allegra, which is a Venetian name." Claire, as much as she adored the child, was determined that Byron have a hand in her upbringing. Byron's position and wealth, Claire felt, would help secure Allegra's future. The idea did not displease Byron. He wrote his sister: "They tell me she is very pretty, with blue eyes and dark hair; and though I never was attracted nor pretended attachment to the mother, still it may be as well to have something in my old age, and probably circumstances will render this poor little creature a great, and perhaps my only, comfort."

Meanwhile, Shelley had gone before the Court of Chancery to fight for his two children by Harriet. However, his heretical writings on religion and marriage weighed against him. Guardianship of the children was divided between Shelley's father and Harriet's grandfather. Disappointed by the court's ruling, and tired, also, of London, Shelley considered the idea of a trip to Italy. His doctors had been encouraging him to seek a warmer climate. What finally decided him was Claire's Allegra. He felt, as did Claire, that the little girl needed Byron's support. And Byron was in Italy.

On March 11, 1818, Claire and Allegra left England with Shelley, Mary, their two youngsters, and two nurses. Three weeks later the party arrived in Milan. Byron was not there to meet them. He wanted nothing more to do with Claire, but he had sent a messenger to pick up Allegra. Though angered by his rudeness and by the gossip about his wild new Italian mistress, Claire submitted to his demand. Allegra was shipped off to Byron with the Shelleys' Swiss nurse, Elise.

As Claire traveled through northern Italy with the Shelleys, she bombarded Byron with written inquiries about their child. "How is my Allegra?" she asked him. "Is she gay? And has she given you any knocks? I sincerely hope she has, and paid you all your unkindness to me in very innocent coin. Whenever I think of the little creature I feel myself smile. She is so funny. . . ."

Lord Byron, who genuinely liked animals, frequently said that he despised children, and once informed his sister: "I don't know what Scrope Davies meant by telling you I liked Children. I abominate the sight of them so much that I have always had the greatest respect for the character of Herod. ['Then Herod . . . was exceeding wroth, and sent forth, and slew all the children that were in Bethlehem.' Matthew 2:16.]"

Yet, Claire felt, or tried to persuade herself to feel, that Byron had a more tolerant attitude toward children than he would admit, and that he would be good to their Allegra. Writing to Byron as "My dearest Friend," she said: "I have observed one thing in you that I like. It is this: let a person depend on you, let them be utterly weak and defenceless, having no protector but yourself, and you infallibly grow fond of that person. How kind and gentle you are to children! how good-tempered and considerate toward your servants, how accommodating even to your dogs!

And all this because you are sole master and lord; because there is no disputing your power, you become merciful and just. But let someone more on a par with yourself enter the room, you begin to suspect and be cautious, and are very often cruel."

Claire's hopeful guess about Byron's feelings toward their daughter turned out to be partially correct. Byron seemed to like Allegra more than he did most children, yet not enough to resist a chance to place her in the care of friends, the British consul in Venice, Richard Belgrave Hoppner, and his Swiss wife. Hoppner thought Allegra much quieter and colder than his own boy Rizzo, and sometime later admitted: "She was not by any means an amiable child, nor were Mrs. Hoppner or I particularly fond of her, but we had taken her to live with us, not thinking Lord Byron's House . . . a very proper one for the infant."

But Byron expressed some satisfaction with his Allegra. After the child had been brought to him for a visit, he wrote his sister in England: "She is English, but speaks nothing but Venetian. 'Bon di, papa' &c &c she is very droll, and has a good deal of the Byron—can't articulate the letter *r* at all—frowns and pouts quite in our way—blue eyes—light hair growing *darker* daily—and a dimple in her chin—a scowl on her brow—white skin—sweet voice —and a particular liking of Music—and of her own way in every thing—is not that B. all over?"

As for Shelley, he adored the child. He had no reservations whatsoever:

> *A lovelier toy sweet Nature never made*
> *A serious, subtle, wild yet gentle being . . .*

Once Shelley took Claire to Venice to visit Allegra. Claire was upset by what she saw: "She is pale and has lost a good deal of her liveliness, but is as beautiful as ever." At Shelley's request, Byron permitted Allegra to remain with Claire several months at this time.

When she was forced to return Allegra to Byron, Claire decided to accompany the Shelleys on a sight-seeing tour of Rome and Naples. It was in Naples that Mary learned her Swiss maid, Elise, was pregnant by their manservant Paolo Foggi. Mary compelled the two servants to wed, then sent them off to another job. Paolo, angry with the Shelleys, determined to get even. He did so by making Elise tell the Hoppners in Venice, who in turn told Lord Byron, about a scandal that had occurred in Naples. The scandal involved an alleged affair between Shelley and Claire which, according to Elise Foggi, had resulted in the birth of a girl.

Hoppner disclosed the shocking news in a letter to Byron dated September 16, 1820. He asked Byron to keep the news secret, then went on: "I therefore proceed to divulge to you, what indeed on Allegra's account it is necessary that you should know, as it will fortify you in the good resolution you have already taken never to trust her again to her mother's care. You must know then that at the time the Shelleys were here Clara was with child by Shelley: you may remember to have heard that she was constantly unwell, and under the care of a Physician, and I am charitable enough to believe that the quantity of medicine she then took was not for the mere purpose of restoring her health. . . . This account we had from Elise, who passed here this summer. . . . She likewise told us that Clara does not scruple to tell Mrs. Shelley she wishes her dead, and to say to Shelley in her presence that she wonders how he can live with such a creature."

A year later, when Shelley visited Byron at Ravenna, Byron broke his pledge of secrecy. Whereas Byron had earlier told Hoppner, "Of the facts, however, there can be little doubt; it is just like them," he now assured Shelley that he did not believe the rumor at all. But Shelley was sufficiently disturbed to repeat the story to Mary, who promptly wrote the Hoppners a passionate denial:

"She [Elise] says Clare was Shelley's mistress . . . but I had rather die than copy anything so vilely, so wickedly false, so beyond all imagination fiendish. . . . It is all a lie—Clare is timid; she always showed respect even for me—poor dear girl! She has some faults—you know them as well as I—but her heart is good, and if ever we quarrelled, which was seldom, it was I, and not she, that was harsh, and our instantaneous reconciliations were sincere and affectionate."

Did Claire actually have a love affair with Shelley and, consequently, a child by him? The truth has never been ascertained. It is known that Claire was curiously ill in Naples. It is also a fact that Shelley arranged for a baby to be baptized in Naples, a little girl named Elena, who was later placed in an orphanage where she died of fever. And it would seem that Lord Byron, de-

spite his denials to Shelley, believed not only that Claire had had
a daughter by Shelley in Naples, but that Allegra herself might
have been Shelley's child. Once when the maid Elise was playing
with little Allegra in the nursery, Byron came in and watched.
Suddenly, indicating Allegra, he said, "She will grow up a very
pretty woman and then I will take her for my mistress." Elise
was aghast: "I suppose, my lord, you are joking, but even as a joke,
it is a very improper one." Byron insisted that he was not joking
at all. "I'll do it," he said. "I can very well do it—she is no
child of mine—she is Mr. Shelley's child."

All of this gossip made it more difficult for Claire to keep in
touch with Allegra, and rendered her helpless when Byron finally
placed their child in the austere convent of Bagnacavallo, twelve
miles outside Ravenna. Earlier, Claire had pleaded with Byron
to send the child to her in Pisa. Byron did not bother to answer—
he hated Claire's long letters, which read like "bad German
novels," he complained—but instead wrote Hoppner: "Clare writes
me the most insolent letters about Allegra; see what a man gets
by taking care of natural children! Were it not for the poor little
child's sake, I am almost tempted to send her back to her atheis-
tical mother. . . . If Clare thinks that she shall ever interfere
with the child's morals or education, she mistakes; she never shall.
The girl shall be a Christian and a married woman, if possible.
As to seeing her, she may see her—under proper restrictions; but
she is not to throw everything into confusion with her Bedlam
behavior. To express it delicately, I think Madame Clare is a
damned bitch. What think you?"

On another occasion, Byron told Hoppner he would not trust
Allegra to the Shelley household, where free love, atheism, and
vegetarianism were practiced. "The child shall not quit me again,"
he wrote, "to perish of Starvation, and green fruit, or be taught
to believe that there is no Deity." When Shelley heard the last,
he replied to Byron in the best of humor: "I smiled at your protest about what you consider my creed. On the contrary, I think
a regard to chastity is quite necessary, as things are, to a young
female—that is, to her happiness—and at any time a good habit.
As to Christianity—there I am vulnerable; though I should be as
little inclined to teach a child disbelief, as belief, as a formal
creed." Despite this disagreement, Byron had great respect for
Shelley, whom he considered—as he wrote his publisher—"with-

out exception, the *best* and least selfish man I ever knew. I never knew one who was not a beast in comparison."

When Claire first learned Allegra had been placed in a convent, she was frantic. Convents were impersonal, she felt, and Italians "unnatural mothers, licentious and ignorant." On Claire's behalf, Shelley—although busy with his own son, Percy Florence, born two years earlier, in 1819—traveled to Ravenna to plead Claire's case with Byron. But Byron was interested only in discussing his fight for Italian freedom and his latest mistress, Teresa Guiccioli, the married noblewoman. While Byron would talk about Teresa—whom Shelley thought attractive, but shallow and naïve—he would not talk about Claire. As to little Allegra, Byron had not seen her since he had placed her in the convent.

Shelley went out to the convent on his own. He found Claire's Allegra, at four and a half, thinner, taller, and extremely pale. He presented her with a little gold chain and a bag of candies. Excitedly she showed him about the convent grounds. When it was time to depart, Shelley wondered if there was any message for her mother. "I want a kiss and a beautiful dress," the little girl said. "All of silk and gold." And what did she wish from her father? "To make me a visit and bring *mammina* with him."

A short time later, when Byron had followed Teresa up to Pisa, Shelley again tried to intercede for Claire. One evening he told Byron that Claire's health was being affected by worry over her child. Byron was not interested. Women liked to make scenes, he said. His callousness infuriated Shelley, who admitted to others that it was the only time he had wanted to hit Byron. Meanwhile, a woman who was a friend of Claire's had visited the convent and reported that it was poorly run and dangerously unhealthy. Claire became extremely apprehensive. She demanded that Shelley help her kidnap Allegra. He refused on the grounds that such a scheme would not work, and if it did, it would involve him in a duel with Byron. He begged Claire to let him continue reasoning with Byron.

Impatient and frustrated, Claire vented her rage against Byron in the pages of her journal. She had an idea for a series of cartoons or caricatures that would represent the real Byron as she knew him. First, "He, sitting writing poetry, the words *Oh! faithless Woman* round the room, hearts are strewed, inscribed, *We*

died for love of you." Then, for another cartoon, "he catching a
lady by her waist, his face turned toward hers, his other hand
extended holding a club stick in the act of giving a blow to a man
who is escaping. From his mouth—The maid I love, the man I
hate/I'll kiss her lips and break his Pate." A third cartoon would
be called "Lord Byron's receipt for writing pathetic History. He
sitting drinking spirits, playing with his white mustachios. His
mistress, the Fornaria, opposite him drinking coffee. Fumes coming from her mouth, over which is written 'garlick'; these, curling,
direct themselves towards his English footman who is just then
entering the room and he is knocked backward. Lord B. is writing, he says. 'Imprimis, to be a great pathetic poet. First prepare
a small colony, then dispatch the Mother, by worrying and cruelty,
to her grave; afterwards to neglect and ill-treat the children—to
have as many and as dirty mistresses as can be found; from their
embraces to catch horrible diseases, thus a tolerable quantity of
discontent and remorse being prepared, give it vent on paper, and
to remember particularly to rail against learned women. This is
my infallible receipt by which I have made so much money.'"
As a finale, there would be a macabre cartoon: "The last his
Death. He dead extended on his bed, covered all but his heart,
which many wigged doctors are cutting open to find out (as one
may be saying) what was the extraordinary disease of which
this great man died—His heart laid bare, they find an immense
capital 'I' grown on its surface—and which had begun to pierce
the breast."

Such were Claire's angry games. Still, as she waited, hoping
that Shelley would yet persuade Byron to let her have her daughter back, there were other diversions and distractions. Many new
visitors were joining Shelley's Pisa circle, and Claire was busy
with them as well as with the Italian society of the town. She
found Shelley's cousin, Tom Medwin, attentive. Two others who
were very close to the Shelleys, Captain Edward Williams and
his common-law wife, Jane, became Claire's friends. Williams
had been an army officer in India, where he had met Jane, who
had been abandoned by her sailor husband. Then there arrived
Edward John Trelawny, a towering, dramatic figure, who had
been a pirate for six years, and would in the years to come escape
assassination in Greece, swim Niagara, and marry four wives (one
an Arab girl, another the daughter of a Greek guerrilla leader).

Trelawny fell in love with Claire, and immediately shared with her a love for Shelley and a dislike for Byron. A half century later, when someone asked Claire why Trelawny resented Byron, she replied, "Well, Byron snubbed him, you know. He said, 'Tre was an excellent fellow until he took to imitating my Childe Harold and Don Juan.' This got to Trelawny's ears, and he never forgave Byron for it."

On April 20, 1822, while Claire and Jane Williams were out hunting for a summer house near La Spezia, word reached Shelley through a personal letter from Byron that Allegra, aged five, after a week of fever, had died of typhus in her lonely convent.

"The blow was stunning and unexpected," wrote Byron. "But I have borne up against it as I best can, and so far successfully, that I can go about the usual business of life with the same appearance of composure, and even greater. . . . I do not know that I have any thing to reproach in my conduct, and certainly nothing in my feelings and intentions towards the dead. But it is a moment when we are apt to think that, if this or that had been done, such event might have been prevented,—though every day and hour shows us that they are the most natural and inevitable."

Shelley wanted to keep the news from Claire, fearing that she might attempt to murder Byron, who was living nearby. But while Shelley was discussing the child's death with Mary, Trelawny, and Williams, Claire walked in on the group. From their faces, their sudden silence, she sensed at once what had happened. "You may judge of what was her first burst of grief and despair," Mary reported. But Claire calmed quickly, and asked only to see Allegra's body, and to have a portrait of her and a lock of her hair. Byron obliged with a miniature and a lock of hair immediately, and when Claire had not the strength to view her child's body, he shipped Allegra back to England for burial. However, since she was illegitimate, Harrow Church refused to bury her inside its walls, laying her to rest outside its entrance instead.

At first Lord Byron himself seemed deeply moved. "He desired to be left alone and I was obliged to leave him," said Teresa. "I found him on the following morning tranquillized and with an expression of religious resignation on his features." When Teresa started to console him, he interrupted: "She is more fortunate than we are; besides, her position in the world would scarcely have allowed her to be happy. It is God's will—let us mention it no more." But he did mention it in a letter to London, and Thomas Moore noted in his diary: "A long letter from Lord Byron today; he has lost his little natural daughter . . . and seems to feel it a good deal. When I was at Venice, he said, in showing me this child, 'I suppose you have some notion of what they call the parental feeling, but I confess I have it not.' This, however, was evidently affected; he feels much more naturally than he will allow." Yet when a priest brought Allegra's body from Bagnacavallo to Leghorn, Byron not only would not listen to the story of Allegra's last illness, but refused to receive the clergyman at all. The priest returned to the convent "greatly mortified." And after the convent sent Byron his closing bill, he haggled over the embalming costs, insisting that the apothecary's charge was exorbitant, arguing that enough spices had been used on Allegra to embalm a full-grown adult.

When considering his overall relationship with Claire Clairmont, it is primarily his disregard for Allegra's welfare that makes Lord Byron, erratic, moody, mercurial, yet somehow most often attractive, show up badly. It is perfectly true, of course, that he did not seduce Claire. It is perfectly true, too, that he was cornered, badgered, and pestered by Claire, and that she, so to speak, asked for what she got. But the fact remains that, once he accepted her love and reciprocated it, once he had got her with child, he might well have shown a little more human understanding. This he did not have, and could not give. And his biographer Harold Nicolson possessed even less understanding when he failed to grasp the reasons for Claire's later hatred of Byron, and rudely referred to her as "that untruthful and, by then, senile wanton."

Allegra's death was followed, two and a half months later, by a greater tragedy of more far-reaching and historic consequences. Shelley and Williams had sailed in their boat, the *Don Juan*, across the Bay of Spezia to visit the newly arrived Leigh Hunt and his family. On the return trip, the pair were last seen heading into a squall before their craft disappeared from sight. Trelawny and a navy friend, Captain Dan Roberts, searched the coast for the missing men, while Mary, Claire, and Jane Williams anxiously waited. Then, after ten days, Claire intercepted a letter from Roberts to Trelawny. In it he said he had heard that two bodies had been washed ashore and he was investigating. Claire could not tell Mary. She sent for Hunt. But before he arrived,

Trelawny appeared. He had seen the bodies and his expression was enough. "He did not attempt to console me," Mary remembered later, "but he launched forth into, as it were, an overflowing and eloquent praise of my divine Shelley, till I was almost happy I was thus unhappy, to be fed by the praise of him, and to dwell on the eulogy that his loss thus drew from his friend."

While the three women—Mary, Claire, and Jane—each with her loss, remained behind—"We have one purse, and joined in misery, we are for the moment, joined in life," said Mary—Trelawny, Byron, Hunt, and several others went by carriage to cremate the bodies. It was high noon, and sweltering, when the brushwood atop Shelley's remains, which rested upon a sheet-iron box, was set blazing. Byron watched a moment. "Is that a human body?" he suddenly asked. "Why, it's more like the carcass of a sheep, or any other animal, than a man; this is a satire on our pride and folly." He started toward the water with Trelawny, exclaiming, "Let us try the strength of these waters that drowned our friends." After a brief swim, Trelawny returned to the beach. The cremation was almost over. As Trelawny recalled later, "Byron asked me to preserve the skull for him; but remembering that he had formerly used one as a drinking-cup, I was determined Shelley's should not be so profaned. . . . The only portions that were not consumed were some fragments of bones, the jaw, and the skull, but what surprised us all, was that the heart remained entire. In snatching this relic from the fiery furnace, my hand was severely burnt. . . ."

Trelawny gave Shelley's heart to Leigh Hunt, who finally surrendered it to Mary. Throughout her life she kept it in a silken shroud, and carried it along on her travels. When her son, Sir Percy, died in 1889, the heart, enclosed in a silver case, was buried with him.

After the cremation, Captain Roberts salvaged the *Don Juan*. It was never known whether the vessel had capsized in the storm, or had been rammed by Italian fishing boats whose owners hoped to find Byron aboard so they could rob and murder him. Captain Roberts auctioned off the shell of the *Don Juan* for the equivalent of two hundred dollars and distributed the personal effects he found in the hull. He presented Shelley's soggy books to Lord Byron, but turned Captain Williams's private journal over to

Leigh Hunt because it contained "many severe remarks on Lord Byron."

During the years following Shelley's drowning, as Trelawny remarked, "we all degenerated apace." In a sense, this was particularly true of Claire Clairmont. Two months after the final tragedy she set out alone, with ten pounds in her purse, to meet her older brother, Charles, who had promised to find her a job as a governess in Vienna. Yet, as she left Italy for Austria, her mind was not on the journey. "During the first part of the road," she noted, "I was too occupied with my own thoughts to attend the scenery. I remembered how hopelessly I had lingered on the Italian soil for five years, waiting ever for a favorable change, instead of which I was now leaving it, having buried there everything that I loved."

Though her brother Charles, an extrovert who taught English for his keep, was kind, Claire found Vienna impossible. The Hapsburgs and Metternich had transformed Austria into a police state, and there was no freedom of speech. When Charles spouted his opinions publicly, an anonymous letter reported this indiscretion to the police, and described his family background as well. He and Claire were given five days to leave the country. But his contacts with the Esterhazys and other members of the nobility finally enabled him to have the expulsion order set aside. Claire did not like this development any more than she liked the weather in Vienna. When an opportunity came to serve as governess for a wealthy Russian family who lived near Moscow, she decided to seize it.

Before leaving for Moscow, she had another offer. Trelawny wrote, sending her the money to return to Florence and asking her to become either his wife or his mistress, whichever she preferred. "Remember, Clare," he remonstrated, "real friendship is not nice-stomached or punctilious—we are too far apart for tedious negotiation—give me these proofs of your attachment." Trelawny was to write her regularly for fifty years. His first letters were passionate, as he tried to woo her back. "You! you! torture me, Clare —your cold, cruel, heartless letter has driven me mad—It is ungenerous under the mask of Love to enact the part of a demon. . . . In the sincerity and honesty of my affection, I wrote unhesitatingly, unreflectingly, my vaguest, wildest thoughts. . . . I am sullen, savage, suspicious and discontented. I can't help it—you have sealed me so! . . . you have made me hopelessly wretched."

Now, having learned that Claire needed money, he had borrowed fifty napoleons from a shopkeeper and sent them to her in Vienna. But she would not have him. When Mary Shelley wrote to Moscow, later, advising her to marry Trelawny, Claire replied that it could not work. "He likes a turbid and troubled life, I a quiet one; he is full of fine feelings and has no principles, I am full of fine principles but never had a feeling; he receives all his impressions through his heart, I through my head."

As the years passed, Trelawny's passion tapered off, but not the flow of letters. He wrote her from Florence: "How should I tell you, dearest, that—that—I am actually now on my road—to embark for Greece? And that I am to accompany a man whom you disesteem? Forgive me." He wrote her from Charleston, South Carolina: "The Sovereign people are working out this grand experiment—that all men are born free and equal! The only blot on their charter, slavery, will gradually disappear—it must be spunged out—or cut out, soon." He wrote her from England: "Clare hollo —do you hear? Are you alive, or transformed into a tree, girdled round by the axe—leafless, lifeless?"

After eight years of servitude, Claire claimed the female prerogative of changing her mind. Tired of contending with other people's progeny—"I never thought children could be so hideous or vicious, they never cease brawling, squabbling and fighting"— she wrote Trelawny and proposed that they live together. But Trelawny's passion had dwindled into friendship, more comfortable, less threatening. As tactfully as possible, he declined her offer.

In the summer of 1824, Claire had reached Czarist Russia. She went to work in a large house outside Moscow for a family consisting of a well-connected lawyer named Zachar Nikolaevitch, his wife Marie, and their two youngsters, John and Dunia. Claire was wide-eyed at the black-robed priests in Red Square, at the aristocratic families who possessed fifteen thousand serfs, at the acres of dark pines covering the countryside.

She had brief romances. She became enamored of a German named Harmonn, and wrote Mary: "What you felt for Shelley, I feel for him." Then there was a pianist named Genichsta. "He is a divine musician and the first that, as a man, pleased me." And finally there was an Englishman, a professor, but he was too easily shocked for her tastes. After a gossipy Miss Frewin, who had met Claire's mother in London, appeared in Moscow and revealed Claire's background to the professor, Claire wrote Jane Williams: "I can see that he is in a complete puzzle on my account. He cannot explain how I can be so extremely delightful and yet so detestable."

But mostly she vegetated. As she noted in her journal: "No talk of public affairs, no discussion of books—nothing save cards, eating, and the different manners of managing slaves." She read foreign papers when she could get them and in this way, one morning, she learned that Lord Byron had died in the pesthole of Missolonghi, Greece, on April 19, 1824.

Letters from England soon told her the rest of the story. Byron's body, preserved in a large cask filled with spirits, was returned to England by boat. Viewing the body, Hobhouse recognized the corpse as Byron's only by his so-called clubfoot. Yet, Augusta Leigh thought that his face looked "serene." His body lay in state for a week in a candle-lit, black-draped room in Great George Street. Mary Shelley went to see it. Byron's faithful valet, Fletcher, was there. Mary listened to Fletcher and then reported: "It would seem from a few words he imprudently let fall, that his Lord spoke of Clare in his last moments and of his wish to do something for her, at a time when his mind, vacillating between consciousness and delirium, would not permit him to do anything." In Russia, Claire heard of this, and heard also that Byron's last will and testament, made before Allegra's death, provided for his daughter but not for her mother.

Eventually, Claire wearied of Russia. She found herself constantly quarreling not only with her employers but with everyone around her. In her journal, she tried to explain her situation: "To a person accustomed to a quiet way of life such perpetual agitation, violence and ill humour destroys one's peace completely. You will naturally say—why do you quarrel with them. . . . But this silence which in other countries would be a sign that you are a well-educated person and would infallibly procure your respect, would here put you on the same footing as one of their slaves." When Claire's little charge, Dunia, died of complications following an ear infection, Claire could endure the household no longer. She shifted from job to job in Moscow. Continually annoyed by Russian "ill humour," resentful of gossip about her background, uncomfortable in the cold climate, she thought of going to India, but finally went to Germany with a family named Kaisaroff.

In 1828, after a decade's absence, she returned to England. For the next twenty years, except for occasional side trips to Dresden, Paris, Nice, Pisa, or Vienna, usually as a governess, she remained in London. Here she trudged from home to home, tutoring rich pupils in Italian, toiling from nine in the morning until seven at night, "condemned for life," as Trelawny put it, to "this vile servitude."

Even with advancing years, Claire wrote letters that reflected a continued liveliness. As Mrs. Julian Marshall remarked of Claire's correspondence: "We can see her with all her vivacity, versatility, and resource, her great cleverness, never at a loss for a word, an excuse or a good story—her indefatigable energy, her shifting moods and wild caprices, the bewildering activity of her restless brain and the astonishing facility with which she transferred to paper all her passing impressions. Unimpeachably correct as her conduct had been after her one miserable adventure, she had an innate affinity for anything in the shape of social gossip or scandal."

Her relationship with her stepsister, Mary Shelley, was a mixture of affection and envy. In England or out, she kept in touch with Mary, and was never shy about offering advice. "I hope you are all well," she said in closing one letter, "leave off your stays—eat no potatoes—take ginger and you will be well."

Mary, in turn, pretended to reciprocate Claire's affection, though Mary secretly resented the attraction Claire had held for Shelley. In fact, once when Claire was expected to drop in, and Mary's daughter-in-law tried to slip out to avoid the meeting, Mary exclaimed, "Don't leave me alone with her! She has been the bane of my life ever since I was three years old!"

Before Shelley's death, he had written Claire into his will for the sum of twelve thousand pounds. Mary always insisted that Shelley had intended to leave Claire only six thousand, and that through a clerical error the amount had been written in twice. The inheritance meant everything to Claire, but she could not receive it until Shelley's father, Sir Timothy, died. When Claire first left Italy, the old man, who was seventy, was given at the most five years to live. He confounded the physicians, and Claire, by remaining alive another twenty-two years. In 1844, he died at last, and Claire came into possession of her twelve thousand pounds. She lost most of it when she invested in a Lumley Opera House box, and then in a foolish Austrian speculation that her brother Charles suggested. Hoarding the little that remained, she decided to retire to Florence, where living was less dear.

She spent the last thirty years of her life secluded in Florence. Eventually she was joined by her spinster niece, Charles's daughter Paula, a plain woman who was regarded by her family as "gifted, original, high-tempered, somewhat eccentric."

Throughout the years Claire's opinions of Shelley and of Byron never changed. She felt Shelley's genius "the greatest that was ever known." For Lord Byron she retained only contempt and hatred. She never forgave him for Allegra's death. When she thought that she might die of cholera, she wrote to Mary: "You might be curious to know whether, in leaving life, my sentiments experience any change with regard to Lord Byron. Not at all; so far from it, that were the fairest Paradise offered to me upon the condition of his sharing it, I would refuse it. . . . For me there could be no happiness, there could be nothing but misery in the presence of the person who so wantonly, wilfully, destroyed my Allegra." When, after his death in the cause of Greek independence, Byron was glorified, Claire still would not relent. She told a visiting Englishman, "He simply invested a great deal of money in the Greek cause with the idea of being made a King."

When she was seventy-one, there was a final, brief flurry of excitement in her life. A rumor reached her that Allegra had not died in the convent and that Byron had made up the story of the child's death to keep Claire out of his life. Hopefully, Claire began an investigation. Learning of this, Trelawny was appalled and wrote to her uncompassionately:

"If I was in Italy I would cure you of your wild fancy regarding Allegra: I would go to the Convent—and select some plausible cranky old dried-up hanger-on of the convent about the age your child would now be, fifty-two, with a story and documents properly drawn up, and bring her to you—she should follow you about like a feminine Frankenstein—I cannot conceive a greater horror than an old man or woman that I had never seen for forty-three years claiming me as Father—do you see any of that age or indeed any age that you should like to have as son or daughter?"

Undaunted, Claire continued her search, but it turned out

that Allegra was not alive, and Claire surrendered her hopes and resumed her routine.

She did not mind old age. When she heard that Shelley's son was about to start school, she pitied him and all young people for what lay ahead of them. As she told Mary: "It is not much praise to the supreme Lord of Life what I am going to say, which is, Thank God I can never be young again. At least that suffering is spared me."

A few friends, and an occasional visitor from home, were received in her darkened old-fashioned rooms at 43 Via Romana. After her conversion to Catholicism, the parish priest dropped by to chat. Once an awed twenty-year-old English tourist, William Graham, came calling and found her "a lovely old lady; the eyes still sparkled at times with irony and fun; the complexion was as clear as at eighteen." Another time, William Michael Rossetti, brother of the Pre-Raphaelite poet, visited her and was impressed by the ailing "slender and pallid old lady . . . with dark and still expressive eyes." And finally Captain Edward Silsbee of Salem, Massachusetts, seeking romantic relics, appeared, and anxiously listened to her speak of an old passion that "lasted ten minutes, but these ten minutes have decomposed the rest of my life."

On March 19, 1879, Paula Clairmont opened her diary, took pen in hand, and made a brief entry:

"This morning my Aunt died at about 10, calmly, without agony, without consciousness—as she had predicted herself, she went out like a candle. . . . She was buried as she desired, with Shelley's little shawl at the Cemetery of the Antella."

XII

The Conversationalist

> She was a great humbug—of course with much
> talent and moral reality, or else she could have
> never been so great a humbug.
>
> —NATHANIEL HAWTHORNE

"WOULD THAT Miss Margaret Fuller might lose her tongue!" Nathaniel Hawthorne once exclaimed. The eminent author was referring to Sarah Margaret Fuller, feminist, critic, lecturer, and gadfly. But had she lost her tongue, Hawthorne would have had one heroine less. For it was Margaret Fuller who provided the stimulus that caused Hawthorne to create the energetic Zenobia of *The Blithedale Romance*.

Both Zenobia and *The Blithedale Romance* were conceived in 1841, when Nathaniel Hawthorne decided to move out of Boston and set up housekeeping in Utopia. In that year in America, Utopia was near at hand and very real. It bore the name of Brook Farm Institute of Agriculture and Education and was located on 192 acres of hard, gravel-covered land in West Roxbury, Massachusetts. This experimental community—begun, its founder stated, "to substitute brotherly cooperation for selfish competition; to prevent anxiety in men by a competent supplying in them of necessary wants"—was the pride and hope of a small band of American intellectuals, mostly transcendentalists, whose number included the loquacious Margaret Fuller.

The founders of Brook Farm were a pale, bespectacled Unitarian clergyman named George Ripley, and his wife Sophia. What he planned was not a socialist proving ground, or a free-love paradise, but rather, as he explained to Miss Fuller, a cooperative society where men might "gather and show the world how to live." Toward this end, Ripley put on sale twenty-four shares of membership stock, priced at five hundred dollars per share. The possibilities intrigued Nathaniel Hawthorne. He was almost thirty-seven years old. He had dabbled at authorship, without success, and was well into his second year of drudgery in the Boston Custom House when Brook Farm was brought to his attention. The enterprise offered him an opportunity to return to writing, with reduced overhead and increased seclusion. Here was a chance to produce that best seller which might enable him to marry the invalided Sophia Peabody, whose sister Elizabeth was the proprietor of a famous Boston bookstore. Even as he considered a change, Hawthorne lost his job at the Custom House. There was no longer any reason for him not to act. Promptly, he purchased two shares of Brook Farm stock for a thousand dollars, and on April 12, 1841, in the midst of a snowstorm, he arrived in Ripley's ideal community.

Brook Farm lasted five years. Nathaniel Hawthorne lasted one. This Utopian commune was simply too strenuous and too strange to encourage authorship. While the women, in shortened skirts, did the housework and taught in one of America's first kindergartens, the men, in smocks of flowered chintz (sewn from petticoats, it was whispered) and caps with tassels, toiled sixty hours a week in the fields. Hawthorne was awakened at four-thirty every morning. He chopped wood, milked cows, made many a "gallant attack upon a heap of manure" which he also called "the gold mine," and fell asleep at nine-thirty every evening. At first, the primitive life appealed to him. "I feel the original Adam reviving within me," he wrote his Sophia. But soon this feeling faded. His brethren, with their group singing and reform pamphlets, were too "queer." The continual physical labor left him too exhausted to put a single creative word on paper.

Emerson thought it a perfect state, but Thoreau did not. "I'd rather keep bachelor's hall in hell," said the man from Walden Pond, "than go to board in heaven if that place is heaven." After a year, Hawthorne sided with Thoreau. The cooperative life was not for him, he told Sophia, adding that their future would be determined by his "own individual strength."

When Hawthorne left Brook Farm, he did not leave with a novel under his arm, but he did have one firmly fixed in his head and in his diary. "Some day I will write a book about Brook Farm," he said, "and have super-modern inventions coming from it—a machine that makes heat from moonbeams, one that makes music from building blocks, one that makes women's dresses out of sunset clouds." And eight years after he had married Sophia, and had just published *The Scarlet Letter,* he said, "When I write another romance, I shall take the community for a subject, and give some of my experiences and observations at Brook Farm."

The most fruitful of his observations, as it turned out, were those that concerned Brook Farm's most popular visiting lecturer, Margaret Fuller, whom Emerson had called "the greatest woman of ancient or modern times." The youthful Miss Fuller, in her calico frock, was not a feminine woman. She wore her hair severely bunned. Her nose was too long, her mouth too wide, her chin too firm. She was aggressive, shocking, erudite, ambitious, but, though her nasal voice grated on the nerves, she could speak brilliantly on any cultural topic. She addressed the Utopians on the subject of Goethe and she addressed them on the subject of Impulse, the latter because there "is the great tendency here to advocate spontaneousness at the expense of reflection."

Hawthorne disliked her intensely from the first. She was, he felt, disconcertingly aggressive for a woman, overly clever, and improperly frank on the subject of sex. Also, she was better known than he. Although Miss Fuller thought that he combined "delicate tenderness" with "quiet depth and manliness," and although she gave him a bronze vase for a wedding present, he declined to be won over.

Hawthorne observed Margaret Fuller's burgeoning career and kept his private opinions in his journal. "She had not the charm of womanhood," he wrote. "She had a strong and coarse nature, which she had done her utmost to refine, with infinite pains; but of course it could be only superficially changed. . . . She was a great humbug—of course with much talent and moral reality, or else she could have never been so great a humbug. But she had stuck herself full of borrowed qualities. . . . There never was such a tragedy as her whole story—the sadder and sterner, because so much of the ridiculous was mixed up in it, and because she could bear anything easier than to be ridiculous. It was such an awful joke, that she should have resolved—in all sincerity, no doubt—to make herself the greatest, wisest, best woman of the age." This was the evaluation Hawthorne kept to himself, and which he hoarded for his future fiction against the day of Miss Fuller's death. Patiently, he merely watched and waited, as the prototype of his Zenobia lived out her short, unhappy life.

Margaret Fuller was born in May of 1810. Her father was a congressman and a lawyer. By the age of six she knew her Latin grammar, at seven she knew Vergil, at eight she knew Shakespeare, and before she was fifteen she had added French, Italian, and Greek. It is said that as a child she began her bedtime prayer with the words, "O God, if thou art Jupiter!" She entered her first school at fifteen. There she suffered from headaches, nightmares, and precociousness. When her schoolmates teased her about using rouge, she revenged herself by fabricating gossip about them and quickly turned the school into a Babel of discord. "She possessed," said Horace Mann, "the unpleasantness of forty Fullers."

After her father died, she undertook the partial support of her ten brothers and sisters by entering the profession of teaching. She was employed by Bronson Alcott to instruct classes in the Masonic Temple, where he and his fellow pedagogues conducted a school. Within three months, Margaret Fuller's students could fluently read aloud twenty pages of German. When she moved to Boston at the age of twenty-nine, she found that her reputation for erudition had preceded her. There she met the Peabody sisters and began to promote her famous "Conversations" in Elizabeth's bookshop, which had usurped the family parlor. The Conversations, actually informal lectures, were delivered in a nasal voice to thirty women who paid twenty dollars each for the series of thirteen meetings. Miss Fuller briefed her "gorgeous pedants" on Greek Mythology, Catholicism, Demonology, The Ideal, and The Fine Arts.

In 1840, having become acquainted with Ralph Waldo Emerson, she collaborated with him in the publication of a transcendentalist literary quarterly called *The Dial*. "I love your Dial," Thomas Carlyle wrote Emerson, "and yet it is with a kind of shudder. You seem to be in danger of dividing yourselves from the Fact of this present universe, in which alone, ugly as it is, can I find any anchorage, and soaring away after Ideas." *The Dial* achieved a printing of seven hundred copies—but had only three hundred subscribers—before its demise four years later.

It was in this period, shortly after she had become better acquainted with Nathaniel Hawthorne at Brook Farm, that Margaret Fuller took to visiting the author and his wife Sophia regularly at the Old Manse in Concord. At the same time that she was irritating Hawthorne with her personal visits, she was antagonizing other writers deeply through her position as book reviewer for the New York *Tribune*.

As literary oracle for the *Tribune*, she criticized Henry Wadsworth Longfellow's poetry: "We must confess a coolness towards Mr. Longfellow, in consequence of the exaggerated praises that have been bestowed upon him . . . we had supposed it so obvious that the greater part of his mental stores were derived from the work of others. He has no style of his own." She thought about as highly of James Russell Lowell: "His verse is stereotyped; his thought sounds no depth, and posterity will not remember him." In rebuttal, Longfellow labeled her review "a bilious attack," and Lowell called her a "very foolish, conceited woman." Edgar Allan Poe was one of the few who sided with Margaret Fuller. He considered her reviews "nervous, forcible, thoughtful, suggestive, brilliant, and to a certain extent scholarlike."

Her least critical, and most flowery, writings Margaret reserved for her private letters to geniuses whom she worshiped. Thus, in 1843, she gushed forth to Ludwig van Beethoven about the spiritual love she felt for him:

"Like a humble wife to the sage or poet, it is my triumph that I can understand and cherish thee; like a mistress, I arm thee for the fight; like a younger daughter, I tenderly bind thy wounds. Thou art to me beyond compare, for thou art all I want. No heavenly sweetness of saint or martyr, no many-leaved Raphael, no golden Plato, is anything to me, compared with thee. . . . Master, I have this summer envied the oriole which had even a swinging nest in the high bough. I have envied the least flower that came to seed, though the seed were thrown to the wind. But I envy none when I am with thee."

Meanwhile, in between her reviews and letters, she was writing a book of her own. It was published in 1845 under the title *Woman in the Nineteenth Century,* and it defended female foibles and advocated social and political emancipation of the weaker sex. It was an immediate success, and it gained her a reputation outside her limited New England circle. But in the end, her achievement in writing was less important than her gift for friendship. Her power over the minds of other creative people was incalculable. "In each of her friends she seemed to divine the law of his own interior growth," said Van Wyck Brooks. "She gave them to themselves, or so they felt, drew out their unsuspected faculties. Many of these friends, in later years, traced to some conversation with her the moment when they had seen their way before them, when they had formed some resolution from which their careers had sprung. It was true that she had an influence in hundreds of lives."

Despite her many friends, and the sway that she held over them, her life was empty because of her lack of a husband. She had strong lesbian tendencies—"it is so true," she wrote, "that a woman may be in love with a woman"—but, still, she wanted a man. She realized that her plain features did not attract members of the opposite sex; she did not realize that her aggressive intellectuality repelled them. "No one loves me," she once admitted. "But I love many a good deal. . . . I have no child, and the woman in me has so craved this experience that it has seemed the want of it must paralyze me."

Then suddenly, frenetically, she became involved with a number of men. It is thought that she had an affair with Samuel Ward, a well-traveled Boston broker seven years her junior, who finally married a New Orleans beauty. It is known that she fell madly in love with a New York businessman, James Nathan, and bombarded him with romantic letters. When he replied with the earthy suggestion that their love be more than platonic, she retreated in fear. The spiritual affair resumed for a short time, until Nathan, fatigued by talk and correspondence, fled to Europe.

In August 1846, Margaret Fuller followed her businessman across the Atlantic, but he was already safe in the arms of another.

She fretted briefly, and then made the best of it. She embarked upon a grand tour of the Old World's great names. In England, she met the Brownings, De Quincey, Wordsworth, and Carlyle.

The last encounter, arranged by Emerson, was not a happy meeting. Thomas Carlyle invited Margaret Fuller to a party at his home. There, before a roomful of fascinated guests, Margaret expounded on the beauties of Life. Carried away, she concluded on a high note. "I accept the Universe!" she exclaimed. To which Carlyle, feet firmly on the ground, snorted in reply, "Gad, you'd better!"

Later, Margaret made a caustic appraisal of her historian-host. "The worst of hearing Carlyle," she said, "is that you cannot interrupt him." Carlyle replied in kind. "Poor Margaret," he wrote. "Such a predetermination to eat this big universe as her oyster or her egg, and to be absolute empress of all height and glory in it that her heart could conceive, I have not before seen in any human soul." With this opinion, Jane Welsh Carlyle concurred years later: "Strong-minded, able-bodied women are my aversion, and I run out of the road of one as I would from a mad cow."

On the Continent, Chopin played for Margaret Fuller, George Sand "loved" her, and Adam Mickiewicz, a Polish poet who taught at the Collège de France, wanted to divorce his wife to marry her. Giuseppe Mazzini, the Italian liberator whom she had met in London, also wished to marry her. But she gave herself to no one until she reached Rome. There, in 1847, when she was thirty-seven years old, she met an Italian Catholic nobleman of twenty-seven, the Marchese Giovanni Angelo Ossoli, and Margaret immediately became his mistress.

Little is known of Ossoli, beyond what may be found in Hawthorne's journals, and this description may have been written in spite. "The wonder is," recorded Hawthorne, "what attraction she found in this boor, this man without the intellectual spark—she that had always shown such cruel and bitter scorn of intellectual deficiency. As from her towards him, I do not understand what feelings there could have been except it were purely sensual."

Within a year of meeting Ossoli, Margaret Fuller presented him with a son, whom they named Angelo. Friends thought that they were married, but no satisfactory evidence has ever been found to substantiate a legal union. When the French attacked

Rome, Margaret Fuller covered events as a correspondent for Horace Greeley's New York *Tribune* and worked in a hospital caring for the wounded. Finally, she retreated to Leghorn with her child and mate. "I am tired out," she wrote, "tired of thinking and hoping—tired of seeing men err and bleed. Man will still blunder and weep, as he has done for so many thousand years. Coward and footsore, gladly would I creep into some green recess."

In May 1850, Margaret, Ossoli, and Angelo sailed for New York aboard a ship weighted down with Italian marble and a statue of Calhoun. After a month at sea, the ship approached New Jersey. The following morning, rolling in stormy waters, the boat crashed into a sandbar off Fire Island. The shifting marble broke through the boat's hull and water poured in. While spectators on the shore watched with horror, passengers and crew tried to reach land by securing themselves to planks. Although Margaret Fuller had an opportunity to escape, she refused to be separated from her family, and soon the sea engulfed all three.

Young Angelo's body was washed up on the shore, but the bodies of Margaret and Ossoli were never found. Intellectual America and England grieved. Thoreau puttered about the ship's wreckage searching for keepsakes, and Emerson muttered, "I have lost in her my audience." Landor penned a hymn, and the Brownings announced their sorrow. Thomas Carlyle suggested someone write a biography—and it was Nathaniel Hawthorne who finally wrote it.

The novel about Brook Farm that he had so long wished to write, he finally began to put on paper in 1852, two years after the drowning off Fire Island. Hawthorne was also motivated by a desire to avenge an old insult. Margaret's brother-in-law, Ellery Channing, had once angrily stabbed at Sophia Hawthorne in a poem, and her husband had not forgotten it.

The Blithedale Romance was Hawthorne's third novel. It related the story of a heroine named Zenobia, a champion of women's rights, who fell in love with the blind leader of an ideal community, then lost him to her younger, prettier half-sister, and committed suicide by drowning. Even though Zenobia had the intellectual and physical characteristics of Margaret Fuller, even though Zenobia suffered the same frustrations with men, wore the same tropical flowers in her hair, and evidenced the same nervous blink of her eyes, Hawthorne would not publicly acknowledge Margaret Fuller as his real-life model. Miss Fuller's admirers castigated Hawthorne for his portrait. Thomas Wentworth Higginson, the pastor and abolitionist who wrote her biography later, attempted to deny any resemblance between Zenobia and Miss Fuller, but finally admitted, "Zenobia in Hawthorne's *Blithedale Romance* will be identified with Margaret Fuller while the literature of the English language is read."

Some few liked the book. Henry Adams praised it, and Henry James considered the heroine Hawthorne's most "complete creation of a person." But by the time Hawthorne reached London, he knew that, overall, the book was a failure. He was, therefore, amazed to find that Robert Browning had enjoyed it. Browning "spoke of his pleasure in meeting me," Hawthorne wrote, "and his appreciation of my books; and—which has not happened before—mentioned that *The Blithedale Romance* was the one he admired most. I wonder why."

Modern-day critics have never ceased wondering why. John Erskine considered *The Blithedale Romance* "the feeblest of Hawthorne's writings," and Mark Van Doren declared it "the poorest of his books" and regarded Zenobia as being "as much like Hester Prynne as waxworks are like women."

In death, that shocking and talkative female, Margaret Fuller, had lost her tongue, and Nathaniel Hawthorne had his wish— but it was to be Margaret Fuller's victory, finally. For, because of her tongue, Hawthorne had been driven to write one of the least successful of all his books. He would have been forewarned, had he known an old Japanese proverb: A woman's tongue is only three inches long, but it can kill a man six feet high.

XIII

The Sheridan

Yes, we *are* rather good-looking people.
—CAROLINE NORTON

CAROLINE NORTON, wife and mother, was implicated
in two of the major scandals that rocked England during her
lifetime. The first scandal involved a British prime minister, and
led to one of the sensational trials of the nineteenth century. The
second scandal involved *The Times* of London, an institution
almost as sacrosanct as No. 10 Downing Street, and this one inspired George Meredith to use Caroline Norton as his model when
he created the emancipated, witty Diana Warwick for his novel,
Diana of the Crossways.

Mrs. Norton was no courtesan, but she was as notorious as any
profligate woman who has ever lived, and her notoriety sprang
from her intimate relationships with titled men.

She was, it must be remembered, a Sheridan. Her grandfather
had been the tempestuous, brilliant playwright, Richard Brinsley

Sheridan, who wrote *The School for Scandal* and *The Rivals*, who championed the American Revolution and freedom of the press, who knew the insides of Parliament as a member and of debtor's prison as an inmate. It was Sheridan's first marriage that produced the son who was to become Caroline Norton's father.

She was born Caroline Elizabeth Sheridan, in 1808, the second of three daughters. Her father died early of tuberculosis, and her Scotch mother supported the family of seven by writing novels to order. When Caroline reached school age, she possessed a Grecian profile, brunette hair plaited in two long braids, dark eyes, and a low, soft voice. She had, Fanny Kemble noted, a "stately style of beauty, grandly classical." Thomas Moore, who dedicated a poem to her, first saw her on a dance floor and thought her "strikingly like old Brinsley, but very pretty." However, it was George Meredith, though he knew her only in her middle age, who described her most accurately. In his fictional portrait, he wrote of "the dark large eyes full on the brows; the proud line of a straight nose in right measure to the bow of the lips; reposeful red lips, shut, and their curve of the slumber-smile at the corners. Her forehead was broad, the chin of sufficient firmness to sustain that noble square; the brows marked by a soft thick brush to the temples; her black hair plainly drawn along her head to the knot."

She was attractive to men, and she knew it. Once, when Fanny Kemble saw Caroline with her sisters, Helen and Georgina, and with her younger brother, mother, and aunt, she remarked, "Certainly I have never seen such a bunch of beautiful creatures all growing on one stem." Caroline glanced complacently about the room at her relatives and replied, "Yes, we *are* rather good-looking people."

It was this beauty that troubled Mrs. Sheridan. She had prudently married off her daughter Helen to a naval lieutenant when the girl was only seventeen. Now she was anxious to preserve Caroline's chastity. While still at school, Caroline had fascinated the brother of Lord Grantley, a barrister named George Norton, who was a Tory member of Parliament. He had proposed marriage, but had been refused. Caroline was encouraged to accept his second offer. They were wed in July of 1827, when she was nineteen and her barrister twenty-six.

The marriage proved a dreadful mistake from the first, largely because it had joined together temperaments that were antithetical. Although Norton was impressive in appearance, from a good family, and in Parliament, he was sulky, rude, violent, opportunistic, conservative, and dull-witted. Caroline, on the other hand, was gay, bright, fiery, liberal, and clever. They fought constantly: over their families, over politics, over anything and everything. He kicked her, heaved an inkwell at her, scalded her with the contents of a teakettle. In retaliation, she savagely castrated him with words, denigrating his antecedents while boasting of her own. She had neither love nor respect for Norton, and came to regard him with the same contempt that Meredith's Diana felt for Warwick: "Husband grew to mean to me stifler, lung-contractor, iron mask, inquisitor, everything anti-natural. . . . By resisting him I made him a tyrant; and he, by insisting, made me a rebel. And he was the maddest of tyrants—a weak one."

Caroline's older sister, Helen, encouraged her to hold on, assuring her that children would make all the difference. In the next few years, Caroline was to give birth to three boys—Spencer, Brinsley, and William—but, even though she adored them, they did little to solidify her marriage. As a palliative, she escaped into authorship and social activity. At twenty, in her second year of marriage, she published her first overly romantic volume of poetry, the profits of which contributed toward the costs of delivering her first son. A year after that, her second volume of verse appeared. And then, in 1831, a melodrama that she had written, *The Gypsy King*, was presented at Covent Garden. The play was a popular, if not a critical, success. Of it, Fanny Kemble said, "What a terrible piece! What atrocious situations and ferocious circumstances, tinkering, starving, hanging, like a chapter out of the Newgate Calendar. But after all she was in the right—she has given the public what they desire." Meanwhile, the popularity of her pen, as well as her good looks and wit, won Caroline presentation at court and attracted many of England's most celebrated personalities to her drawing room. Among those who eventually came to enjoy her conversation was a famous Cabinet minister, and he brought with him—scandal.

Actually, it was Caroline Norton who first sought out William Lamb, the second Viscount Melbourne, home secretary in Lord Grey's Cabinet. In 1830, George Norton had lost his seat in Parliament. "Norton's election is lost," Caroline wrote her younger sister, "and with that mixture of sanguine hope, credulity and vanity which distinguishes him, he assures me that, although thrown out, he was the popular candidate; that the opponents are hated, and that all those who voted against him did it with tears."

An unoccupied George Norton was indeed a problem, and his wife decided that her emotional survival depended upon his having a new diversion immediately. In desperation, she dashed off a note to Lord Melbourne, since he had been a friend of the Sheridans, although she did not know him personally. She implored him to find Norton a position. Melbourne had heard of the comely Mrs. Norton. He was curious to see her. He resolved to discuss her request while making a personal visit to Storey's Gate, Westminster.

What took place when Lord Melbourne first met Caroline Norton in her drawing room has never been revealed, but the meeting produced the results she desired. Shortly afterwards, the home secretary had George Norton appointed to a judgeship in the Lambeth division of the Metropolitan Police Courts, at a salary of one thousand pounds a year. And, for the better part of the next five years, Lord Melbourne was a regular guest in Caroline's home, with the full knowledge and approval of her husband.

What were Melbourne's intentions? What exactly was his relationship with Caroline Norton? Melbourne was a gentle, moody, sensitive man. He had survived his hellish marriage to Lady Caroline Lamb, who had flaunted her affair with Lord Byron before all London. Scant months after burying his wife, Melbourne had indulged in an affair with Lady Branden, the wife of an Irish peer, their assignations occurring both in Dublin and in London. Lord Branden had brought Melbourne to court, but the suit had been dropped for lack of evidence. Now, two years later, still longing for feminine companionship, Melbourne had found a good listener and an even better talker in Caroline Norton.

He became her slave. When he was not at Storey's Gate, she was at Downing Street. Whether or not Melbourne became her lover is not known. He always denied there having been any sexual basis to their friendship. When he was accused of seducing Caroline, he wrote her: "I hope you will not take it ill if I implore you to try at least to be calm under these trials. You know that what is alleged is utterly false, and what is false can rarely be made to appear true—my only anxiety and solicitude are for you, and the situation in which you are so unjustly placed."

Most of Melbourne's fellow noblemen agreed that his relationship with Caroline was limited to conversation, which induced one peer, Lord Malmesbury, to record sadly in his diary: "Melbourne had had more opportunities than any man ever had before and had made no use of them." Yet enemies of the pair persisted in their belief that Caroline had been Melbourne's mistress, citing his need for women, her passionate nature, and the fact that they had spent years in each other's company.

For some time, Norton encouraged the friendship. It had secured him his job, and now was helping him make advantageous social contacts. Often, when Caroline visited Downing Street, Norton accompanied her as far as the entrance. He was present at Caroline's parties, where Melbourne was also in attendance. At one of these gatherings, Melbourne found himself in conversation with an odd, flamboyant young author named Benjamin Disraeli. Melbourne was curious about the fledgling author's ambitions: "What do you wish to be?" Without the least hesitation, Disraeli replied, "I want to be prime minister." It is said that Melbourne gently tried to discourage the young guest from envisaging such wild fantasies.

At any rate, it was not until 1835 that George Norton decided to sue for divorce, claiming that Lord Melbourne had alienated his wife's affections. As everyone knew, Norton had not needed outside help to alienate his wife. He had done a remarkable job of it all by himself in their eight years of marriage. The last two years had been the stormiest. They had quarreled over his parsimony. They had fought over his sister, a bloomered eccentric who came to visit them. They had battled over a lady friend of his, named Vaughan, who gave him advice about raising Caroline's children. Twice, Caroline had left him, but was induced by calmer minds to return. As for this third separation, he left her, after flinging at her the accusation that she had behaved immorally with Lord Melbourne.

There is evidence that George Norton was determined to ruin Lord Melbourne at any cost. Melbourne was by then Prime Minister of England and a Whig. Norton, a Tory, was goaded on by his fellow Tories, who hoped that a juicy scandal would cause the downfall of Melbourne's government. Furthermore, Norton, as ever, needed money, and it is thought that he anticipated a huge out-of-court settlement from Melbourne.

At first, Norton considered bringing the Duke of Devonshire and Edward Trelawny into the suit, along with the prime minister, as additional corespondents. In the end, he centered his legal wrath upon Lord Melbourne himself. In 1836, the suit was brought to trial before a jury. Norton supported his charge of infidelity with the testimony of an alcoholic coachman and several female servants, and some laconic letters Caroline had received from Melbourne. Since Melbourne's letters carried no unusually cordial or passionate greetings, Norton's barrister improvised an explanation: "It seems there may be latent love like latent heat in the midst of icy coldness."

The attorney defending Melbourne ridiculed Norton's entire case, a case which Charles Dickens later burlesqued in his Bardell-Pickwick trial in *The Pickwick Papers*. On the stand, Caroline's family, the Sheridans, pointed out that Norton had a mistress of his own, that he had treated his wife with brutality, and that he had once tried to borrow fourteen hundred pounds from Melbourne. The jury had heard enough. They returned a flat verdict of "Not proved," and thus exonerated Melbourne completely. The prime minister was cheered in the House of Commons, greeted by his king, and his reputation remained sufficiently untarnished for him to serve later as confidant and mentor to the young Queen Victoria.

For Caroline Norton, however, the acquittal was not so complete. Her good name had been sullied. While the Duchess of Sutherland took Caroline riding in an open carriage, to prove that Caroline's friends supported her, she was generally ostracized from society for some time. Although she received three hundred pounds a year from her husband as a separation settlement, she was forced to supplement this income by writing popular novels. She was prolific and her work well received, and she earned as much as fourteen hundred pounds annually from her writings. However, her most serious works were pamphlets designed to help her regain custody of the children taken from her by court decree.

The loss of her children, rather than the loss of her reputation, embittered her the most. As a friend of Caroline's commented at the time: "Her heart was wrung by her boys being torn from her; and after the verdict in her favour, when she had every right to have them with her, they were sent from place to place, and she was kept in ignorance of their well-being and all concerning them." Caroline's efforts to see her boys were pathetic. "I only saw them by stratagem," she wrote, "by getting up very early and remaining on the watch near the house till they went for their morning walk. My eldest, who is seven years old, gave me a little crumpled letter, which he said he had had in his pocket a fortnight, directed to me, but that none of the servants would put it in the post."

While neither Caroline's petitions to the government nor her pamphlets restored her sons to her, this relentless crusading contributed to the creation of the Infant Custody Act, and helped amend the Law of Divorce. As to her reputation, eventually her literary zeal, as well as her social graces, enabled her to recover her former station in society. "She discovered," Meredith wrote, "the social uses of cheap wit; she laid ambushes for anecdotes." And Lord Melbourne, as well as other celebrated figures, found their way back to her drawing room.

Five years after her separation from Norton, she met Sidney Herbert. He was an aristocratic bachelor who was serving as secretary to the admiralty. Soon she became his mistress, a relationship which lasted for four years. They often talked politics to each other and to friends, and this was the cause of their eventual breakup.

Herbert was a friend of Sir Robert Peel, who had succeeded Viscount Melbourne as prime minister, and had come into office opposing free trade and supporting the Corn Laws with their sliding scale of duties. However, the potato famine in Ireland determined Peel to go against the wishes of his Tory backers, and to advocate repeal of the Corn Laws in an effort to obtain cheap corn. He was trying to decide how to announce his radical decision when, on the morning of December 4, 1845, *The Times* of London scored a beat by prematurely announcing the prime minister's plan to repeal the Corn Laws. As a result of this sensational story, Peel's ministry was forced into resignation. His backers were curious about only one point: Who had leaked the secret to *The Times*? It was suspected that Sidney Herbert, a friend of the prime minister's, had told Caroline Norton of the decision, and that she in turn had passed it on to John T. Delane, editor of *The Times,* for money.

Actually, Peel's foreign secretary, Lord Aberdeen, had been the one to relate the secret to *The Times.* His intentions were of the best. He had hoped to win *The Times*'s support for the repeal of the Corn Laws, but the editor had released the garbled story ahead of the planned schedule. Nevertheless, despite eventual revelation of the true informant, many persisted in believing that Caroline Norton had betrayed her lover, Herbert, for personal profit. When, almost forty years after the scandal, and seven years after Caroline Norton's death, George Meredith had his fictional heroine betray her lover, there was little hope left of ever righting the calumny against Caroline's integrity.

George Meredith, a red-headed and red-bearded young writer who had once served as Dante Gabriel Rossetti's model for a head of Christ, first met Caroline Norton when she was over fifty years old. The meeting took place at Esher, the residence of Sir Alexander Duff Gordon and Lucie Gordon, longtime friends of Caroline Norton's. Caroline liked to discourse in monologue on the arts and literature, and so did young Meredith. This created an impasse which forced Caroline to remark that "she was not greatly impressed by him."

Caroline was sixty-seven when George Norton finally died. She was free at last to marry her old friend, Sir William Stirling-Maxwell, a widower whose wife had burned to death, and the pair were blissfully happy in their few months together before Caroline died in July 1877.

It was not until 1884 that George Meredith decided to publish Caroline's story. He was fifty-four and eager for one popular success. Meredith, whose many novels had gained him literary stature but no large public, had also suffered from his unhappy relationships with women. It was out of his own personal experience that he had once written: "Woman will be the last thing civilized by man." Meredith's first wife, the bright, brittle, highly sexed Mary Ellen Peacock Nicholl, daughter of Shelley's friend Thomas Love Peacock, gave him a son and a few early years of marital pleasure. Then, after nine years of marriage, she left him for a painter on Capri and returned pregnant. Meredith's second wife, a French girl named Marie Vulliamy, bore him another son and a daughter. She was polite, uninteresting, and disapproved of his experiments with vegetarianism.

Meredith, a tall, nervous, distinguished man who had worked as a publisher's reader, had encouraged Thomas Hardy to devote himself to the novel, but he had also rejected *East Lynne* and Samuel Butler's *Erewhon* and had labeled Charles Dickens "the incarnation of Cockneydom." Among Meredith's own novels, *The Ordeal of Richard Feverel* was the best known. Yet, while his works were not sold in great numbers, his literary standing was high. He pretended to be satisfied, announcing, "Thank God I have never written a word to please the public." But he did want to please the public, and when he hit upon the story of Caroline Norton, he finally succeeded.

He called the book *Diana of the Crossways,* and he called his heroine Diana Warwick. In March 1884, he wrote Robert Louis Stevenson, who was in France, that he was "finishing at a great pace a two-volume novel, to be called *Diana of the Crossways—* partly modelled upon Mrs. Norton. But this is between ourselves." And to Mrs. Leslie Stephen, wife of a mountaineer friend who was the father of Virginia Woolf, Meredith added, "I hope to finish with the delivery of the terrible woman afflicting me . . . by the end of April." The task took him until the end of August. Caroline Norton was transformed into Mrs. Warwick, "a witty Beauty"; George Norton became Augustus Warwick, whose uncle owned the Crossways; Lord Melbourne was dubbed Lord Dannisburgh, and was an admirer who helped Diana's husband find employment; Sidney Herbert became Percy Dacier, a member of Parliament who told Diana a secret which she betrayed for money; Delane of *The Times* was recognizable in Mr. Tonans; and Sir William Stirling-Maxwell was transformed into a decidedly younger Victorian suitor named Thomas Redworth, who finally married Diana.

In the latter half of 1884, twenty-six of Meredith's forty-three chapters appeared in *The Fortnightly.* The following year the complete *Diana of the Crossways* was published in a three-volume edition. It was far and away George Meredith's most widely read novel. Three printings were rushed out in three months. And though, many years after, J. B. Priestley found it "obscure and baffling," Priestley also admitted that the "critics were fascinated by Diana herself, and the faintly scandalous interest of the book attracted a wider public than that which had read and enjoyed the earlier novels." The weary and ailing Meredith was promptly signed to a seven-year contract by a London publisher, who guaranteed him one hundred pounds for each future book.

The only real challenge to *Diana of the Crossways* came from Caroline Norton's relatives. Her nephew, Lord Dufferin, Ambassador to France, published evidence that Caroline had not betrayed any Cabinet secret to *The Times*. Then Lord Dufferin, joined by the other members of the family, vigorously accused Meredith of slander. Under this intense pressure, the author retreated. The next edition of *Diana* carried an announcement on the flyleaf which read:

"A lady of high distinction for wit and beauty, the daughter of an illustrious Irish House, came under the shadow of a calumny. It has latterly been examined and exposed as baseless. The story of Diana of the Crossways is to be read as fiction."

Book Three

THE REBEL
AS A SCANDAL

XIV

The Female
Muckraker

... let all pious Generals, Colonels and Commanders of our army and navy who make war upon old women beware.

—ANNE ROYALL

BETWEEN the years 1825 and 1829 the President of the United States was John Quincy Adams, whose father had been a Chief Executive of the nation before him. Adams was a lonely introvert, learned, austere, honest, and of formal habits—except for one.

It was Adams's custom, during his single term, to rise before dawn on a mild day, usually between four o'clock and six o'clock, dress, surreptitiously leave the White House, cross the expanse of front lawn that looked out upon the Potomac River, step behind a growth of shrubbery, remove his clothes, and then, stark naked, plunge into the water for a relaxing swim. He would paddle about sometimes for an hour, then crawl up on the bank to dry himself with napkins, slowly dress again, and finally he would return to the White House fully refreshed and ready for his break-fast, his Bible, and his governmental chores.

It was impossible to tell when these presidential swims ceased to be relaxing, but everybody knew when they ceased to be private. They became a spectator sport on that early summer morning, toward the end of the President's term in office, when he emerged from the Potomac in his usual state of undress to find a rotund, unkempt, gray-haired woman casually seated on his undergarments, shirt, and breeches. Appalled, the President hastily retreated into the river, halting only when the water reached his chin.

Collecting his wits, he angrily ordered the lady to leave. Unperturbed, she informed him that she had hunted down the President so that she might interview him about the controversy surrounding the Bank of the United States, and that she intended to remain where she was until he made a statement. It must be understood that this was in an age when the President did not give interviews to reporters nor did he hold press conferences, and to grant her request John Quincy Adams would have to break historical precedent. Yet, he realized that if he did not break with precedent, he might be submerged in the Potomac for the remainder of his administration—for he knew the woman on the shore, and knew that while he might be the immovable object, she definitely was the irresistible force.

Her name was Anne Newport Royall. Raised on the Pennsylvania frontier, married to a wealthy and scholarly veteran of the American Revolution, she had been cheated out of her husband's estate and had come to Washington to obtain a government pension as a soldier's widow. Adams had first met and befriended her the year before he was elected to the Presidency, while he was still Monroe's Secretary of State. He had tolerated her obvious eccentricity, ignored her Masonic fanaticism, and promised to assist her in collecting her pension. He had also introduced her to his English-born wife, and had subscribed in advance to a book of American travel Anne Royall was planning to write. The book had since become five books, and her last three volumes, entitled *The Black Book, or a Continuation of Travels in the United States*, had shocked, irritated, and amused not only Washington but readers throughout the nation.

While other lady writers dipped their quills in treacle, Anne

Lais escaped slavery in Corinth to become a popular Greek courtesan and artist's model. She refused to spend a night with Demosthenes for any price, but gave herself to the philosopher Diogenes for nothing. This late portrait by Hans Holbein was probably done in the 16th century, and hangs in the Kunstmuseum, Basel.

Aspasia, the Greek courtesan admired by Socrates, had a child out of wedlock by Pericles, ruler of Athens.

Phryne, ancient Greece's most renowned courtesan, would make love only in the dark, yet annually bathed naked at two public festivals. Here she is

seen on trial for seducing government officials from their duties. She won acquittal only after she disrobed to prove so perfect a body could not hide an impure soul.

Cleopatra, Queen of Egypt at seventeen, may have resembled this profile of her, gracing an ancient Thebes temple relief. She was the mistress of both Julius Caesar, by whom she had a son, and Marc Antony.

In more modern times, Cleopatra's physical attractions were romanticized, as in this Victorian painting. According to Plutarch, her face was not "such as to strike those who saw her." She was said to have dyed hair and a prominent nose, yet her charm and sensuality attracted many men.

Valeria Messalina, third wife of Emperor Claudius of Rome, was notorious for her sexual excesses and public orgies. Here, through the eyes of the 19th-century Austrian artist Hans Makart, is Messalina on a rare occasion when she was alone and fully clothed.

Giulia Farnese, at the age of seventeen, was the mistress of Pope Alexander VI. Here she is the model for Guglielmo della Porta's Truth. The original sculpture, done from life, was a nude. In later and more prudish times her figure was draped in marble coverings.

HÉLOÏSE.

In the 12th century, Héloïse lost her chastity to a young Catholic clergyman of Paris, named Abélard. As a result, Abélard lost his manhood, when Héloïse's uncle had him castrated.

Ninon de Lenclos was once characterized as "a veritable Notre-Dame des Amours." In the 1660's, she founded her School of Lovemaking in France for young male aristocrats.

María Luisa was princess of Parma before she married her cousin, who was to become Carlos IV of Spain. Shortly after Laurent Pécheux painted this innocent picture of her in 1765, and following her marriage, she embarked on a life of adultery.

María Luisa as Queen of Spain. She had many affairs, the most enduring with Don Manuel de Godoy, an army private sixteen years her junior whom she rapidly elevated to prime minister. Napoleon, meeting her, saw "her past and her character written on her face." Francisco Goya's unsparing brush depicts that face and person in this painting hanging in the Palazzo Reale di Capodimonte, Naples.

Nell Gwyn, mistress of King Charles II of England, often called herself the King's "Protestant whore." In this oil, Sir Edwin Landseer, noted for his paintings of animals, restored respectability to Nell and got in his animals as well.

Lady Hamilton, born Emma Lyon, daughter of an English blacksmith, gained fame when the popular British artist George Romney fell in love with her and from 1783 onward portrayed her as Venus, Circe, Mary Magdalene, Joan of Arc and—in this picture—as herself. She won social acceptance when she married the aging Sir William Hamilton, British Ambassador to Naples.

Some time after Romney painted this portrait of her, Lady Hamilton met Lord Horatio Nelson, England's greatest naval hero, in Italy. Nelson considered her "the most beautiful woman of the age." Their love affair, which produced a daughter and a worldwide scandal, ended seven years later with his death in the Battle of Trafalgar.

Pauline Bonaparte, sister of the Emperor Napoleon, was loyal to him throughout his life but rarely heeded his advice on chastity. She was frivolous, self-indulgent, immoral. Her intense sexual activity was the despair of her gynecologist. Here, as she stands beside a bust of her brother, she is painted by Robert Lefevre in 1806.

Pauline Bonaparte posing as Venus in this work by the Italian sculptor Antonio Canova, whose chief patron was the Pope. Asked how she could pose in the nude for Canova, Pauline replied, "Why not? It was not cold. There was a fire in the studio." This reclining Pauline now rests in Rome's Villa Borghese, which she once shared with her second husband, Prince Camillo Borghese, a young millionaire to whom she was unremittingly unfaithful.

Maria Walewska, wife of an elderly Polish nobleman, submitted to Napoleon Bonaparte's advances to further the cause of Poland's independence. Later, she fell in love with Napoleon and gave him a natural son. This painting is by Robert Lefevre, who also painted Napoleon's sister Pauline.

Germaine Necker became Mme. de Staël when she married a Swedish diplomat. Known for her books, politics, salons, she was a domineering adulteress who tried to seduce Napoleon without success. This contemporary portrait is by Baron François Gérard, and is now in the Musée de Versailles.

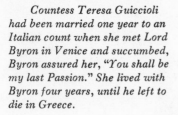

Countess Teresa Guiccioli had been married one year to an Italian count when she met Lord Byron in Venice and succumbed, Byron assured her, "You shall be my last Passion." She lived with Byron four years, until he left to die in Greece.

Claire Clairmont had an affair with Lord Byron in London and Geneva, and gave birth to his daughter Allegra. This portrait was done in Rome in 1819 by Amelia Curran, daughter of the Irish reformer.

Lady Caroline Lamb alienated her titled husband to become Lord Byron's first important mistress. In the beginning Byron thought her "the cleverest, most agreeable, absurd, amiable, perplexing, dangerous, fascinating little being that lives now." Two years later, Byron thought her "the one human being whom I do utterly detest and abhor."

Elizabeth Milbanke, later Lady Melbourne, gave birth to six children who were known to gossips as the "Miscellany" because of their uncertain paternity.

Caroline Norton, whose grandfather wrote The School for Scandal, *was an author and a reformer, and was herself involved in two major scandals. George Meredith used Caroline as the basis for his fictional heroine in* Diana of the Crossways. *This portrait is by Sir Francis Grant.*

Lady Jane Ellenborough, a glamorous nymphomaniac, had a plethora of prominent lovers, among them King Ludwig I of Bavaria, his son, King Otto of Greece, and Honoré de Balzac. This portrait, ordered by King Ludwig when Jane was twenty-four, was done by court painter Carl Stieler.

Marie Duplessis rose from peasant girl to France's most expensive and sought-after courtesan. Camellias were her trademark. Among her lovers were Alexandre Dumas fils and Franz Liszt. Dumas immortalized her in his novel and play Camille, and Giuseppe Verdi based his opera La Traviata on her life. This miniature of Marie, by an unknown artist, hangs in the Comédie Française in Paris.

Delphine Delamare was the unhappy wife of a French provincial doctor. Her adultery and tragic end inspired a neighbor, Gustave Flaubert, to create the fictional Mme. Emma Bovary. According to local tradition, Delphine is represented by the artist Court in this painting, now in the Musée de Rouen.

Léonie Léon, at twenty-four, became the common-law wife of French statesman Léon Gambetta. She agreed to be his mistress, but refused to be his legal wife.

Marguerite de Bonnemains left her army lieutenant husband to live with General Georges Boulanger, who planned to become dictator of France in 1887. She followed her lover into exile on the isle of Jersey.

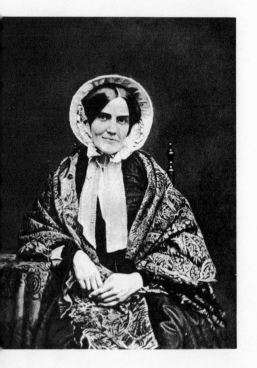

Delia Bacon, a New England schoolteacher and spinster, instigated the Shakespeare-Bacon controversy. Calling Shakespeare "that booby . . . that vulgar, illiterate . . . deerpoacher," she argued that the works attributed to him had really been written by a secret syndicate consisting of Sir Francis Bacon (no relative), Sir Walter Raleigh, Edmund Spenser and others. This daguerreotype of Delia was taken in 1853, when she was forty-two years old and days before she sailed for England in an attempt to open the grave of the Bard.

Margaret Fuller, feminist, critic, lecturer and gadfly, advocated female emancipation in an 1845 best seller and was the prototype for one of Hawthorne's fictional heroines. This daguerreotype was taken when she was thirty-five.

Anne Royall, one of America's earliest female journalists, interviewed a President of the United States while he was naked. Her weekly anti-Establishment newspaper, Paul Pry, attacked the Congress, the military, anti-Masons, Presbyterians. She was the first person in the United States ever put on trial as a common scold.

Victoria Woodhull, prostitute, spiritualist, Wall Street broker, publisher of a national newspaper, ran for President of the United States against Ulysses S. Grant and Horace Greeley in 1872. Her platform supported free love, short skirts, abolition of the death penalty, vegetarianism, excess-profit taxes, female orgasm, world government, better public housing, birth control, magnetic healing, easier divorce laws. She spent election night in jail.

Victoria Woodhull gained further notoriety by making public one of the greatest sex scandals in American history, which led to the Beecher-Tilton trial. Victoria later moved to England where she married an aristocratic British banker. She was almost ninety and almost respectable when she died in 1927.

Royall more often dipped hers in bile. She, who would meet all fourteen Presidents from Washington to Pierce, had already interviewed President Adams's eighty-nine-year-old father. "When I mentioned his son, the present President and Mrs. A, the tear glittered in his eye; he attempted to reply but was overcome by emotion. Finding the subject too tender I dropped it as quickly as possible."

She was less sentimental in reporting her encounters with other public figures. She found John Randolph of Roanoke pompous but gentlemanly: "He is said to be immensely rich but not charitable." A brigadier general, who was anti-Mason, was considered ridiculous: "He is in height not quite so tall as the Puppy-skin Parson, about five feet, I should think, and about the size of a full-grown raccoon, which he resembles in phiz." A New Haven attorney who had ejected her from his office got similar treatment: "He generally wears a blue coat, short breeches and long boots; his body is large, his legs spindling; he wears powder in his hair; his face resembles a full moon in shape, and is as red as a fiery furnace, the effect of drinking pure water, no doubt."

Anne Royall was just as frank and harsh when discussing municipalities that she visited, the sectional customs that she observed, and the national issues that she heard debated. In the pages of *The Black Book,* she made clear her distaste for the Bank of the United States. The bank, a powerful monopoly capitalized at $35,000,000, controlled the lion's share of government deposits. Its president, the socially eminent Nicholas Biddle of Philadelphia, had once remarked, "As to mere power, I have been for years in the daily exercise of more personal authority than any President." Upon meeting Anne Royall after she had castigated him in print, Biddle warned her with a smile, "Ah, Mrs. Royall, I will have you tried for your life for killing my President."

A majority of the population welcomed the prospect of the expiration of the bank's charter in 1836. However, there was a rumor that Biddle might try to force the Congress and President Adams to nullify this expiration by granting a new fifteen-year monopoly. It was to clarify this burning question for herself before finishing a forthcoming book that Mrs. Royall, tugging at her worn shawl and waving her green umbrella, had stormed the White House in an effort to see President Adams. He had refused to admit her. Indeflectable as an angry bee, Mrs. Royall investi-

gated the President's routine, learned of the morning swims, and
this particular morning had managed to secrete herself on the
White House grounds. When her prey was in the water, she had
made her way to the riverbank and planted herself upon his
clothes.

As the President impatiently immersed himself in the Potomac,
Anne Royall shrilly reiterated her demand for an interview.
Wearily, one may be sure, the President capitulated and gave
indication that he would cooperate. Mrs. Royall then asked him
several pointed questions about the Bank of the United States.
As she was a rabid Jacksonian who wanted the bank's charter re-
voked, her questions were doubtless annoying. Nevertheless, the
President answered them directly and fully. When the interview
was over, Mrs. Royall rose, graciously thanked Adams, and triumphantly hobbled away. And John Quincy Adams, having dispensed the first executive press conference in American history,
was free at last to wade out of the water and assume the dignity
that goes with full attire.

When at a later date, someone asked Adams what he made of
the remarkable Mrs. Royall, he ruefully replied, "Sir, she is like
a virago errant in enchanted armor." No man ever characterized
her better.

She was born Anne Newport near Baltimore, Maryland, on
June 11, 1769. Her father, William Newport, was a product of
the aristocratic Calvert family, but his birth was illegitimate and
an embarrassment. He was known by the name Newport instead
of Calvert, granted a small annuity, and kept at a distance from
the manor house. On reaching manhood, he married a farm girl,
and, mindful of his noble ancestry, he named the first of his two
daughters after Queen Anne of England. When the colonies
seethed with revolt, and men took sides, Newport refused to be
linked with the patriotic rabble. A dedicated Tory, he announced
himself sympathetic to the British Crown and ready to support it.
Learning of his stand, his neighbors made threats. Then the Cal-
verts fled to England and Newport's annuity disappeared with
them. Newport realized that Maryland had suddenly become a
hostile environment for him.

In 1772, when Anne was three years old, Newport took his
family for a brief stay with his wife's relatives in Virginia, and

then they joined a wagon train heading for the wilderness of western Pennsylvania. In Westmoreland County, in the vicinity of present-day Pittsburgh, he built a rough cabin, furnished it with a large bed and four crude stools, and tilled a small clearing around it. He encouraged his wife to practice herb healing on the other settlers, and he taught Anne the rudiments of reading using the phonetic method. On some unrecorded date Newport died, probably as the result of an Indian massacre. His widow and his two daughters hastily moved to the safety of the fortified settlement known as Hannastown. Anne was twelve years old when her mother, desperately in need of support, married her second husband, a man named Butler. For Anne, the products of this new union were a measure of security and a half brother named James.

The Indians, attempting to stem the tide of white settlers, were on the warpath. Life became a succession of alarms. So frequent were the hit-and-run attacks that eventually they turned into a tiresome routine. When Indians were approaching one cabin outside the fort, as Anne recalled later, the resident housewife refused to take flight until she had dusted the furniture. "I can't go off and leave such a looking house," she said. But the party of hostiles that advanced upon the thirty to forty cabins of Hannastown on July 13, 1782, was larger and more formidable than usual. Anne and her family fled to the protection of one of the three nearby forts. Meanwhile, at Miller's Station, a large crowd of wedding guests, which included the settlement's founding family, tarried too long over their celebration. The Indians fell upon them, slaughtered the men, took sixty women and children captive, put all of Hannastown to the torch, and left.

Despite the horror inspired by this attack, most of the survivors at the fort rebuilt their houses. Anne remained in Hannastown three years more. By 1785, when she was sixteen, her stepfather had died, her younger sister had married, and she, her half brother, and her mother were again destitute. Mrs. Butler decided to abandon the frontier and seek help from relations in Virginia. After arriving in Staunton, Virginia, Mrs. Butler developed blood poisoning. She was advised to visit the local health resort at Sweet Springs, situated in the valley of Monroe County, in what is now West Virginia. Though the stay at the Springs cured her, it did not replenish the family purse. Mrs. Butler would have been reduced to beggary had not the richest man in the county, Captain William Royall, heard of her lot. He immediately hired her as "his wash-woman and menial," an eccentricity frowned upon by his fellow landowners, who felt that assigning such tasks to a white woman instead of a black slave would cause general loss of face. In hiring Mrs. Butler, Captain Royall also undertook the responsibility of providing for her children. And thus it was, in the most unashamedly romantic tradition, that Anne entered the great house on the slope of Sweet Springs Mountain and first laid eyes upon her future husband.

Captain Royall had served America well during the Revolution. In 1777, at the age of twenty-seven, he had personally raised and financed Virginia's original company of militia. He claimed that Patrick Henry had served under him. He and his militia raided a ship on which the British governor, Lord Dunmore, was guarding a vast store of ammunition. He spent, Anne later stated, "a fortune in the war. He was rich and generous. He brought the troops from Virginia and North Carolina, after Gates' defeat, at his own expense to Guilford Courthouse, N. C. Entitled to ten rations a day, he never drew a dollar. He was Judge-Advocate to the Brigade, Judge-Advocate to the regiment." He was an aide to Lafayette, and belonged to the same Masonic lodge as his friend George Washington. He had left the army not with the rank of general, as Anne liked to think, but with the rank of captain, and in lieu of back salary Royall accepted the acreage at Sweet Springs Mountain.

Because he was the wealthiest landowner in the area, his eccentricities were tolerated. He freed slaves and would not buy new ones. He allowed his livestock to run wild. He would not permit "unnatural" livestock such as geldings and steers in his barns. He was obsessed with the virtues of Freemasonry. He was devoted to Thomas Paine and Voltaire, and his enormous library, filled with books by egalitarian authors and French philosophers, was generally regarded as radical. He was aristocratic and bookish, yet friendly and kind. He was disinterested in his many property holdings, and he disliked his numerous relatives. He lived the life of a puttering, retiring scholar until he became interested in Anne.

For twelve years Anne lived under the captain's vigilant eye, first as a somewhat spindly, energetic assistant who helped her

mother do household chores, than as a slender, darkly attractive
assistant who aided her employer in managing the minor affairs
of his estate, and finally, as her master's pretty and maturing protégée. After the passage of a few years Captain Royall had
learned, to his utter astonishment, that Anne possessed an intelligence beyond what might be expected in a menial. She wanted
to become as educated as he was himself. She hungered to know
everything that he knew. Only her semiliteracy held her back.
The captain's astonishment turned to delight. He made Anne
his project, determined to turn her into his Perfect Woman. After
tutoring her until she could read with ease, and teaching her to
write a legible hand, he fed her book after book from his shelves,
all of Jefferson, all of Voltaire, all of Masonic history. He drilled
his entire library into her until, as one contemporary reported,
"she became the most learned woman in all the county." For almost twelve years, he molded her to his image. Then he fell in
love with his creation.

What happened next happened with almost biblical simplicity.
It was a warm day in 1797. Anne was working in the fields. "The
dogwood was in bloom," she remembered, "and I was out sowing
seeds when the messenger came with a saddlehorse for me to go
and get married." It was proposal, betrothal, and wedding all in
one afternoon. When Anne returned to the house, the Reverend
William Martin and the captain were waiting. The marriage took
place at once. The certificate gave the date as November 18, 1797,
although Anne clearly remembered it as happening in the spring.

The marriage lasted sixteen years. Despite the disparity in their
ages—on their wedding day Royall was forty-seven years old,
Anne twenty-eight—and despite the captain's reticence about
declaring his love, their union was a happy one. Though Royall's
neighbors frowned upon this elevation of a serving wench to mistress of the manor, and though Royall's relatives were dismayed
to see their inheritance in danger of being diverted to a comparative stranger, Royall was contented with his choice of mate. By
conventional standards the marriage may have seemed bleak. It
produced no children, no gay parties, no exciting trips, and, from
all indications, no moments of high passion. But there was always,
as Anne often professed, the deeply satisfying and peaceful pleasure of intellectual affinity.

Actually Anne's relationship to the husband whom she worshiped remained that of student to mentor. Persistently he instructed her in the precepts of Voltaire and the values of Free-masonry. Month after month, Anne and her captain undertook challenging reading programs and discussed what they had read. Together, on foot and on horseback, they oversaw the estate. Occasionally, when there was a holiday, Royall permitted relaxa-tion from this routine and encouraged Anne to arrange a celebra-tion for their neighbors. At such times, he presented her with gifts of valuable property holdings. Every so often they enter-tained famous guests, among them George Washington and Thomas Jefferson. In 1813, when he was sixty-three and Anne forty-four, Captain Royall took to his bed with a mortal illness. After long weeks of suffering, he died. Interred with him was the last peace and security that Anne was ever to know.

Yet in the first days of widowhood it appeared that Anne would be independently wealthy. Her husband's last will and testament, written five years before, gave her every protection from want: "In the name of God, AMEN. I, William Royall, of Monroe County, do make and ordain this, my last Will and Testament in manner and form following viz: I give unto my wife, Ann, the use of all my Estate, both Real and Personal, (except one tract of land) during her widowhood. . . ." Aside from that one tract of land, which he left to a niece, nothing was bequeathed to Roy-all's large and indignant clan of relatives. Everything belonged to Anne as long as she did not marry again.

Immediately a number of Royall's relatives banded together to fight this unequal distribution of his wealth. Led by one of Roy-all's nephews, William R. Roane, an attorney who needed his share of the money—and was "a great fool," said Anne—they filed suit to have the will declared invalid. Their charges were three-fold: that Anne was never legally married to Royall; that Anne had influenced him to sign the will while he was senile; that Anne had entertained a succession of lovers, among them a young barrister named Matt with whom she frequently corresponded.

Without her husband to protect her, and hearing malicious slander against her from all sides, Anne decided that she wanted to get as far away from Virginia as possible. Since the court had not yet ruled on the validity of Royall's will, Anne liquidated her personal holdings to pay for her travels. She sold a house and other real property that she owned in Charlestown—all earlier gifts from her husband—and relying on the money she cleared from the sales and a small allowance granted by the court, she started south accompanied by three Negro servants and a courier.

She traveled constantly and in state for six years. Except when she was disturbed by reports of the interminable judicial wrangling at home, she found the inns and sights and people of Savannah and New Orleans, and of Charleston, West Virginia, relaxing and stimulating. "Hitherto, I have only learned mankind in theory," she wrote, "but I am now studying him in practice. One learns more in a day by mixing with mankind than he can in an age shut up in a closet." While she returned several times to Monroe County to make depositions in the legal marathon, she now leased a house in Huntsville, Alabama, and made it her home. There, early in 1823, nearly ten years after the captain's will was offered for probate, she learned that the Virginia courts had handed down their final decision. The Royall relatives had won the battle, and overnight she had become penniless.

She viewed the defeat with incredulity. She could not understand it. Actually, there was an explanation. Her failure to defend herself in court had permitted the scandal attached to her name to go unrefuted, and this had tended to weigh the final judgment against her. She was fifty-four years old and as impoverished as she had been at sixteen when first she entered Royall's household as a servant. Dazed and depressed, she was initially unable to think of the future. But, while the mentally disturbed can rarely help themselves, Anne Royall was to prove an exception. From some deep reservoir of character she soon found the strength to stir herself to action. Although her next movements may have brought her closer to her later eccentricity, they certainly helped her prevent insanity.

Her destination was Washington, D. C. Her husband had been a gallant veteran of the Revolutionary War, and as his widow, she was entitled to a pension. She would present her just claim in person. And as she journeyed toward the capital, she would gather material for a book. For, like millions of amateurs at writing before and since, Anne had long been commended for the style of her personal letters. It was encouragement enough. She told herself that the pension she was sure to get would support her, and even if she did not produce a book, writing would occupy her mind. So, in order to avoid further depressing moods, she said, "I resolved to note everything during my journey worthy of remark and commit it to writing."

She began the two-week journey on horseback, then transferred to a public stagecoach. She had money for three days' food and lodgings. When this was gone, she found her food in the garbage bins behind tavern kitchens and slept in the open. Then, remembering that her husband, a prominent Mason, had often assured her that Masons were the kindest folk on earth, she began to call upon members of the order in each community. They were indeed generous, and not one refused to provide her with enough money for necessities until she reached the next town. In Alexandria, Virginia, again reduced to pauperism, Anne called upon M. E. Clagget, a Mason who owned the City Hotel. "At ten o'clock, one cold December night, I arrived at his house without one cent in my pocket, a single change of raiment and badly dressed. I had not a friend on earth. Mr. Clagget took me in and from the 15th of December to the 6th of April following kept me—not in a style according to my appearance, but furnished me with an elegant parlor and bed-chamber and gave me a servant to wait on me the whole winter."

Refreshed, she resumed her journey toward the capital. But first she wanted to visit Richmond so that she could find evidence of her husband's war record to support her pension claim. By the time she dragged herself into Richmond, she was again destitute. Unable to ferret out Masons, she accosted ordinary citizens on the street. First she tried to borrow money and was refused. Then she begged for money and was ignored. Finally, she tried to soften the hardhearted with passages quoted from the Bible, but to no avail. In desperation she took a part-time job long enough to earn a small sum. Then, embittered by the lack of southern hospitality—and dismayed at finding that her husband's military records had been destroyed in a fire—she proceeded by boat and stage to Washington.

She arrived in the capital on the morning of July 24, 1824. Too poor to rent lodgings, she selected a house at random and told her story, simply and directly, to the occupants, who were named Dorret. They sympathized with her, gave her a room and her meals for six months "without fee or reward," and even supplied her with fresh garments. During this period Anne enlisted the support of John Quincy Adams on behalf of her pension and presented her claim to the government. But because her husband's military record had been lost, and because the legality of her marriage had once been challenged, she was faced with the double burden of proving that Royall had served his country and that their wedding had not been irregular.

For years she was to gather affidavits backing up her claims. And Adams, as Secretary of State, as President, and as congressman, faithfully would sponsor her tireless petitions. With monotonous regularity they would be rejected, and Anne Royall was not to see a dollar of her pension until almost a quarter of a century after her initial application.

Suddenly the book that she had planned to write as therapy was a financial necessity. With five-dollar subscriptions collected in advance from people as diverse as John Quincy Adams and Joseph Bonaparte, she continued her researches through New England. And all the while she wrote. In 1826, the result of this desperation and energy was issued by a press in New Haven. The book was entitled *Sketches of History, Life and Manners in the United States, by a Traveller*. Its sharp delineation of the conditions and personalities encountered in her travels caused an immediate sensation. It was widely commented upon, and it sold well. The most balanced review was published in the *Boston Commercial*:

"Sometimes she lets fall more truths than the interested reader would wish to hear, and at others overwhelms her friends with a flattery still more appalling. At any rate, hit or miss, the sentiments she gives are undoubtedly her own; nor will it be denied that she has given some very good outlines of character. Her book is more amusing than any novel we have read for years."

Anne was encouraged by this reception, and shortly thereafter she made her first—and, happily, her last—sally into fiction, a romance entitled *The Tennesseean, a Novel Founded on Facts*. It related the painful adventures of one Burlington, a Princeton student who was forced to make his own way after his wealthy father had been defrauded in business. Burlington attempted merchandising in Nashville, then sought riches in Mexico, inevitably fell into the hands of brigands and pirates, and finally escaped to freedom—monetarily poorer, but emotionally richer for having won a Spanish bride. The novel was not a success, and it might have ended Anne's creative career right there had not a dramatic political occurrence brought her unexpected literary patronage.

The setting for this dramatic political occurrence was Batavia, New York, where resided in 1826 a dissolute bricklayer and Royal Arch Mason named William Morgan. When citizens of the community decided to form a Grand Lodge, they excluded Morgan because of his reputation as a drunkard. In angry retaliation, Morgan put together a book, *Illustrations of Masonry*, which was intended to expose the secret ritual of the order. When he prevailed upon a local editor to publish it, the Masons of Batavia became worried. Somehow they contrived to charge Morgan as a debtor and a petty thief. He was arrested and transported to the Canandaigua jail. On the night of September 11, 1826, two men appeared at the jail, announced that they were Morgan's friends, and offered to bail him out. Only the jailer's wife was on hand. The offer of bail was legal, and so she complied. But a moment after Morgan was led outside, she heard him shout, "Murder!" She rushed to the door in time to see Morgan being manhandled by four abductors. Although he struggled desperately to free himself, he was shoved into a waiting carriage and spirited away. He was never seen or heard of again.

News of the incident spread across the land, and with it the rumor that Morgan had either been murdered and dumped into the Niagara River, or strapped in a canoe and sent over the falls. Even as the opponents of Freemasonry began to agitate, Governor De Witt Clinton of New York, himself a Mason of note, sought to smother the growing hysteria by offering a reward of fifteen hundred dollars for information leading to the arrest of the kidnappers. The gesture came too late. Already opportunistic politicians, led by Thaddeus Stevens, had seized upon the affair and were demonstrating to keep hatred burning. The Masonic Grand Lodge, roared Stevens, was "a chartered iniquity, within whose jaws are crushed the bones of immortal men, and whose mouth is continually reeking with human blood."

This agitation still might have died of natural causes—Morgan's widow had gone off to become one of Joseph Smith's multiple Mormon wives—had not an anti-Mason political party, dedicated to suppressing the order, come into being. The Masons, realizing that they were endangered, rallied to save their discredited order. It was then that their leaders remembered Anne Royall. She had long been one of their staunchest supporters. Her first book had proved that her pen was a rapier. And except for one girl who had become a first-degree Mason at Newmarket, Ireland, in 1713 (after having overheard the ritual in her father's house), no woman had ever been so well informed as to the purposes of the order. Why not enlist her efforts in the service of Freemasonry?

In 1827, the Masons made their bargain with Anne. They would finance an immediate tour of Pennsylvania, New York, and all of New England for her. She would be at liberty to do research for her books, and could write as she pleased—though an occasional good word for the order would not be amiss—if at the same time she would speak favorably of the Masonic cause to all she encountered. Anne was satisfied. This providential support from men whom she admired helped her visit, during the next three years, almost every section of the United States, and she produced four books published in nine volumes that would make her name a national scandal and her person a national curiosity.

While in pursuit of her research, Anne was always mindful of her benefactors. Wherever she went she crusaded for the cause of Freemasonry. Sometimes she was met with impatience. In Burlington, Vermont, where anti-Masonic sentiment was high, she cornered a shopkeeper named Hecock and chastised him for his intolerance. Hecock, a man of few words, did not bother to debate the issues. He merely reached out, lifted Anne off her feet, and heaved her down a long flight of stairs to the street below. More than her pride was injured. She suffered a fractured leg, and consequently walked with a limp for several years.

However, it was in her writings that she most fully repaid the Masons for their investment. "Was not General Washington a good man?" she asked in one of her books. "He was a Mason. Was not Dr. Franklin a good man? He was a Mason. Was not De Witt Clinton a good man? He was a Mason. These are enough. Now all of these are not only the best, but the greatest men in the world." The anti-Masons "might as well attempt to pluck the sun and moon out of the heavens, as to destroy Masonry—old as the deluge. And, to give my opinion of it in a few words,—if it were not for Masonry the world would become a herd of savages." As for the martyred Morgan, the rumors of his violent death were only "a vile speculation to make money, and not only to make money, but further designed as a political engine."

If she served the Masons well during her indefatigable travels, she served her reading public better. Despite her reiteration of personal prejudices and her lack of objectivity, the three volumes of *The Black Book*, the two volumes of *Mrs. Royall's Pennsylvania*, the three volumes of *Mrs. Royall's Southern Tour*, and the *Letters from Alabama* gave a more accurate representation of the sprawling American scene than was to be produced by the equally observant Mrs. Trollope. On foot and on horseback, by stage and by water, Anne Royall ranged the primitive land from Delaware to Missouri and from Illinois to Louisiana. She wrote precisely what she saw, which was almost everything.

In Pennsylvania she liked the smoke of Pittsburgh, but thought Philadelphia "a den of British Tories, domestic traitors, missionaries and Sunday Schoolism." In South Carolina she regarded Charleston as "the receptacle for the refuse of all nations on earth —the only reputable people there are the Jews." In Maryland she saw Baltimore as "illiterate, proud and ignorant." In Virginia she found that "the roads were as bad as its schools," and that the Germans in the southwest portion of the state "excelled in only two things: natural children and fleas." In North Carolina the ladies took snuff, and in the District of Columbia they did not know how to dress. In Louisiana there was true graciousness, but this very graciousness might lead to disaster. The southerners had lost a good deal of their initiative by depending upon slavery: "Their slaves, in the end, instead of being a benefit, has proved a very serious injury. . . . I see evident proofs of this in their deserted, worn out fields. . . . They have secured nothing to their children but poverty, whilst they have reared those children up, not to industry, but to high notions. . . . Influenced by a more than foolish pride, they neglect to encourage the useful arts; their lordly souls could not brook the indignity of teaching their sons to earn their own bread by their labor."

Anne Royall's curiosity was infinite. She tried everything once. She visited the insane in a Maine asylum. She stopped in a convent and interrogated the nuns. She smoked a peace pipe with the Cherokee Indians. She boarded a steamer in Virginia to examine the boilers. She forded a river that George Washington had once crossed. She searched for Jefferson relics at Monticello. She stayed at a female seminary in Pennsylvania, and approved, and inspected a barroom in the same state, and disapproved.

"There is too much whiskey everywhere," she decided. She never passed a college without pausing to challenge faculty members, and she enjoyed the students at Harvard who hailed her iconoclasm. And she never missed a chance to enter a bookstore, where she chastised the owner or his clerks for "pushing" British writers at the expense of struggling American authors.

Relentlessly, also, she hunted down the celebrated.

She interviewed Governor Clinton of New York, and found him corpulent and strongly silent, yet "a man of great size, great soul, great mind and a great heart." One must not forget that Governor Clinton was a Mason.

She hiked a good distance to meet Dolley Madison. In 1794, the widow Dolley Todd, who had been courted by Aaron Burr, had finally married the erudite congressman James Madison. She was younger than Madison by eighteen years, and taller than he by several inches. When he became President in 1808, Dolley Madison became America's most stylish First Lady. She wore Parisian gowns, used rouge (and snuff), and played cards. And now, in her fifties when Anne Royall came calling, Dolley Madison was legend.

"Never was I more astonished," wrote Anne of their meeting. "I expected to see a little dried up old woman. Instead, a tall, active woman stood before me . . . chiefly, she captivated by her artless, though warm, affability. Affectation and her are farther asunder than the poles. Her fine full eyes and her countenance display a majestic brilliancy found in no other face. She is a stout, tall, straight woman, muscular but not fat, and as active on her feet as a girl. Her face is large, full and oval, rather dark than fair. Her eye is dark, large and expressive. Her face is not handsome nor does it ever appear to have been so. It is suffused with a slight tinge of red and is rather wide in the middle. But her power to please—the irresistible grace of her every movement—sheds such a charm over all she says and does that it is impossible not to admire her."

Then, if Anne was not already fully won over, what happened next came near melting her completely. For, "to witness how active she was in running out to bring me a glass of water—in stooping to wipe the mud from my shoes and tie them" was almost too much for Anne. Yet, nothing ever softened Anne entirely. One last comment, which may have pleased Dolley but was hardly calculated to amuse her husband: "She appears young enough to be Mr. Madison's daughter."

It should be added that other Washington belles, especially the unmarried ones, were treated less kindly by Anne Royall's quill:

"It is painful to see handsome young females who might grace a levee, caterwauling about with a parcel of ignorant young fellows (for their singing is more like cats' mewing than anything else) every evening," noted Anne. "Here they sit, flirting their fans and suffocating with heat for hours while some cunning Missionary tells them a long story about the Lord's doings. They have the Lord's doings in the Bible better told than any Missionary tells it. Why do they not, if religiously inclined, stay at home in their father's house and read the Lord's doings? But there are no young men there. Now if these young ladies were really Christians, instead of dressing and flirting about at night with young fellows they would hunt up the destitute and afflicted and relieve their sufferings."

Anne cherished her celebrities, and would not allow her countrymen to ignore or forget them. When Samuel F. B. Morse, inventor of the telegraph, first demonstrated his invention before a congressional committee, Anne not only was present but participated. Aware that Anne was acquainted with his assistant in Baltimore, Morse asked her what message he should tap out. "Tell him Mrs. Royall is present," said Anne. The message was sent and Morse's assistant responded, "Give my respects to Mrs. Royall."

Almost two decades later, Anne Royall went to see Samuel Morse again for a newspaper article. She did not like what she found, and was enraged at the ill-treatment she fancied he had received from the government.

"We think very highly of this amiable man," she wrote, "and our opinion is that his country is unworthy of him. He has spent his life, his money and his talents in the study of Science for the benefit of mankind; the successful result, we believe, was offered to Congress but was evaded under some pretence or other. [Morse had petitioned Congress to appropriate money for an experiment, but Congress had adjourned without acting on his request.]

"When we first had the pleasure to see Professor Morse, some eighteen years since, he had just returned from Europe, where he had been to finish his studies. He was then a blooming young man and highly accomplished. He is now thin, gray and care-worn, though his manners are still fascinating. But he has lost that animation that became him so well. Thus Genius is suffered to languish and die in our country. Shame! Shame!"

Aside from Congress and anti-Masons, one other national group incurred Anne Royall's constant displeasure. She despised all Evangelicals, not only the clergymen who preached the Cal-vinistic faith, but also their fanatical followers. In her books she referred to male members of the church as Hallelujah Holdforths, and she called their women Miss Dismals. She accused their mis-sionaries of contaminating the Indians, and their lobbyists of trying to get control of the Federal Government.

In 1909, in a biography of Anne Royall published in Cedar Rapids, Iowa, Sarah Harvey Porter attempted to evaluate Anne Royall's books:

"The chief faults of Mrs. Royall's writings are: too much de-tail, especially in regard to private injuries received by the author; amateurishness; intolerance of intolerance; too free and abusive use of names, even in an age when names of persons were freely, often scandalously, published; hasty judgments based on feeling; exaggerated praise of friends.

"On the other hand, Mrs. Royall's style possesses the merits of spirit; accuracy of fact and of description; practicality; perfect clearness; a strong and telling vocabulary; humor; an underlying ethical purpose based on honest, though often mistaken, convic-tion; patriotic fervor; minute observation, and *liveness*—a genu-ine personality makes itself felt on every page."

In her own day, this genuine personality was making herself felt not only on every page but throughout the land.

Anne's books, at least her earliest books, were widely circu-lated. Her invective was admired and feared, and for a brief period she exulted in a new sense of power. But her persistent attacks on Evangelicalism brought her enemies who were deter-mined to silence her, and in 1829, when they thought they had sufficient ammunition, they struck. In the Court of the District of Columbia, a unique complaint was filed against her. According to Anne, "there were three counts in the indictment: 1. A public nuisance. 2. A common brawler. 3. A common scold. The first two charges were dismissed. The third was sustained."

The action against Anne Royall had been instigated by mem-

bers of a Presbyterian congregation that met regularly in an en-
ginehouse near her dwelling. Their peddling of tracts and their
singing of hymns exasperated Anne. When youngsters of the
congregation were encouraged to stone her residence, and when
the church's most prominent member, John Coyle, ostentatiously
prayed for her conversion under her window, she became furious.
She was especially furious, she said, because this same John Coyle
had given her black maid a bastard child. Promptly, Anne let
the congregation and the surrounding neighborhood know what
she thought of Presbyterians. She publicly berated Coyle, or Holy
Willie, as she nicknamed him, for being "a damned old bald-
headed son of a bitch." She called a friend of his Simon Sulphur,
and yet another male member of the church Love Lady, because
she vowed that he had once been observed in Capital Park trying
to convert a pretty Negro girl while both were "in a state of nature." The Presbyterians had had enough. They consulted an attorney. He consulted his legal tomes, and to his clients' delight
came up with something that they might call *her*. They called
her a Common Scold, had her arrested, and brought her to trial.

After one delay on technical grounds, Anne was arraigned before the three judges of the Court of the District of Columbia in
May 1829. There was wide interest in the trial because the charge
of being a scold, a holdover from early English law, had never
before been tried in America, and because the punishment involved tying the accused to a ducking stool and submerging her
in a body of water.

The case of the United States *v.* Royall unfolded before a
packed and noisy courtroom. The prosecution presented twelve
witnesses, among them Coyle and Henry Watterson, the Librarian of Congress (whom Anne had also insulted in one of her
books). The witnesses swore that Anne had cursed and berated
them in the streets, and in general had made a public nuisance
of herself. Anne hotly denied the charges. She was followed to the
stand by a variety of friends who vouched for her good character.
The most prominent of these was Senator John Eaton, of Tennessee. When Secretary of War, Eaton would gain notoriety by
marrying his former mistress, Peggy O'Neale Timberlake, an
innkeeper's lively daughter, whose virtue President Jackson was to
defend though it meant replacing his entire Cabinet. Now on the
stand in Anne Royall's behalf, Senator Eaton acquitted himself

gallantly. His testimony, said Anne, "was clear and unequivocal and directly opposed to that of the prosecution." Despite his defense, the judges found Anne guilty as charged.

The time came to mete out punishment, and the judges sent for an actual ducking stool that had been constructed in the Alexandria navy yard and held in readiness. But the moment it was displayed, they realized that they could not inflict so barbaric a penalty. Instead, they fined Anne ten dollars for being a scold and demanded fifty dollars as a bond against her committing the same crime again. The money was supplied by two friendly newspapermen, and Anne was free. In her way she had made history. She was the first woman ever found guilty of being a scold in America—and there would not be any others until 1947, when three sisters living in Pittsburgh were to be similarly tried and variously sentenced to from three to twenty-three months in jail.

The rigors of the trial and the humiliations suffered as a result of its outcome brought an end to Anne Royall's career as a roving author. During a final trip to the South, she realized that she was no longer strong enough to travel. Moreover, her books were being taken less seriously and their sales were on the decline. She had no choice but to make Washington her permanent home and to invest her small savings in a business. Obviously the business would have to be one in which she could make use of her only talent: the ability to observe, to describe what she saw, and to do so from an original point of view. And so, at the age of sixty-two, Anne Royall became the publisher and editor of her own weekly newspaper.

The first issue of *Paul Pry* appeared in the streets of Washington on December 3, 1831. The masthead read: "PAUL PRY/ Published every Saturday by Anne Royall/ Terms Two dollars and fifty cents per annum, one dollar to be paid in advance and the balance at the end of six months. Subscribers may discontinue their papers when they think proper, by giving notice to the publisher." Its four pages carried advertising, local news, jokes, excerpts from current novels, political comment, and a vigorous editorial from the pen of the proprietor: "The same firmness which has ever maintained our pen will be continued. To this end, let it be understood that we are of no party. We will neither oppose nor advocate any man for the Presidency. The welfare and happiness of our country is our politics. To promote this we shall oppose and expose all and every species of political evil, and religious frauds without fear, favor or affection. . . . As for those cannibals, the Anti-Masons . . . we shall meet them upon their own ground; that of extermination. For the rest, let all pious Generals, Colonels and Commanders of our army and navy who make war upon old women beware. Let all pious Postmasters who cheat the Government by franking pious tracts beware. Let all pious booksellers who take pious bribes beware. Let all pious young ladies who hawk pious tracts into young gentlemen's rooms beware, and let all old bachelors and old maids be married as soon as possible."

The headquarters for this anti-Establishment journal of opinion was a small two-story brick building behind a tumble-down house in the shadow of the Capitol dome. Anne took the Dutch oven and cast-iron spiders out of the kitchen and replaced them with a decrepit and unpredictable Ramage printing press and several fonts of worn type. Her staff consisted of a printer, two youngsters from a Catholic orphanage, a porter, and a young editorial assistant named Sarah Stack. Mrs. Stack, whom Anne called Sally, was a serious, unimaginative widow who supported five orphan children.

There was no circulation department. Anne, usually accompanied by Sally, would make the rounds of Washington, selling individual copies of the paper and soliciting subscriptions at $2.50 a year. As the two women canvassed private residences and places of business, trudged through the halls of the Senate and the House, and penetrated into the network of offices in the government buildings, they made a remarkable picture. Anne, her alert face wrinkled and toothy, her voice loud and insistent, was short and dumpy in her shabby shawl and green calico dress. She would disarm potential subscribers with jokes and gossip, and then, waving her thickly mittened hands in excitement, she would admonish them to buy her periodical. In order to escape, harried customers usually submitted to this enforced enlightenment, and would either present her with one dollar as down payment against the full subscription price or else would buy the current issue of the paper. Then Sally, lanky, thin, and somber, would emerge from the background where she had been lurking with her armful of papers.

Most of Washington officialdom—from congressmen to government clerks—was bullied into reading *Paul Pry*. Within a year, agents were soliciting subscriptions in every major American city. Those readers who ordered the paper but neglected to pay the balance of the subscription fee six months later were reminded of their delinquency in print, their names and debts being detailed in the paper under the heading "Black List."

Actually, few of those who read *Paul Pry* did not want to read it again. In its five turbulent years of existence the journal, while not the most physically attractive newspaper in America—the pulp paper was cheap, the printing an eyesore, and the casual proofing promised an adventure in myopia—was certainly one of the liveliest in the land. As in her books, Anne assailed anti-Masons, Evangelicalism, political corruption, birth control, flogging in the navy, and the Bank of the United States. She advocated free speech, open immigration, improved labor conditions, justice for the Indians, territorial expansion, nondenominational public schools, sound money, states' rights, Andrew Jackson—and her own pension.

There were items of scandal, but they were always carefully checked and edited before publication. As Anne explained in one editorial: "We have received a shocking story of abuse toward an unprotected female by a prominent man who is a Presbyterian. But we refuse to print it for several reasons: It came in too late. It is too personal. It bore no signature. It is against *a private man*. Public men are fair game." There were other diversions for the light-minded: excerpts from Charles Dickens's *The Pickwick Papers*, capsule biographies of well-known women, progress reports on Sally's erratic health, and inferior verse.

In 1836, when Anne was sixty-seven and *Paul Pry* in the last year of its life, she had a fascinating visitor in the person of the youthful Phineas T. Barnum. The gaudy entrepreneur had entered show business only one year before—by exhibiting a wizened colored woman named Joice Heth, who was, he had claimed, 161 years old and George Washington's former nurse. Joice Heth had died just recently and had been found to be only eighty years old and could not have been George Washington's former nurse. Barnum's great years with Tom Thumb, Jenny Lind, and Jumbo the Elephant were still ahead of him. Now, accused of perpetrating a hoax and faced with failure, he was grateful for the stories that Anne had published in his defense. He came to pay his respects, and departed to record in his diary a striking portrait of this "celebrated personage . . . the most garrulous old woman I ever saw."

According to Barnum, Anne mistook him for Congressman Claiborne of Mississippi. When his identity was straightened out, Anne explained that she had been expecting several members of the House of Representatives.

"All the congressmen call on me," she said with pride. "They do not dare do otherwise. Enemies and friends all alike, they have to come to me. And why should they not? I made them— every devil of them. You see how I look, ragged and poor, but thank God I am saucy and independent. The whole government is afraid of me, and well they may be. I know them all, from top to toe—I can fathom their rascality, through all its ins and outs, from the beginning to the end. By the way, Barnum, whom do you support for President and Vice-President?"

Cheerfully, Barnum replied that he thought he would vote for Martin Van Buren, the Democrat, against William Henry Harrison, the Whig. Anne turned purple. "I have seen some fearful things in my day—some awful explosions of tempestuous passion," Barnum recalled later, "but never have I witnessed such another terrible tempest of fury as burst from Mrs. Anne Royall."

Spluttering, she fell upon him. "My God! my God! is it possible? Will you support such a monkey, such a scoundrel, such a villain, such a knave, such an enemy to his country, as Martin Van Buren! Barnum, you are a spy, an electioneering fool, and I hope the next vessel you put foot on will sink with you."

Taken aback by the terrible onslaught, Barnum forced an uneasy laugh, as if to suggest that she was teasing him. But she was not teasing him.

"Oh, you villain! laugh, will you? when your country is in danger! Oh, you don't believe it, but let me tell you, the conspirators know too much to let you foolish Yankees into their secret. Remember, I was once with them, and I know all about it."

"Why, Anne," he temporized, "you must acknowledge there are some good people in our ranks."

"No, I don't. There's not one devil of you who cares a cent for his country. You would not give a farthing to save it from destruction. See how I live! see how I work to save my country! I am at work every moment—see my house—see, I have no bed to lie on—

no anything—and then *you* tell about loving your country! Oh, you deserve to be lynched, every devil of you!"

Anne had turned against the Democrats in general, and Van Buren in particular. She did not trust Van Buren, a New York attorney, governor, senator, and the Vice-President under President Jackson (whom she adored). "Mr. Van Buren is obnoxious to all parties," she had written, "because there is no dependence to be placed on the man. He is like the Irishman's flea, when you put your hand on him he is not there." Her own favorite for the Presidency was Judge Hugh White, a Tennessee Whig. But in the final election she would see Barnum's choice, Van Buren, collect 58 percent of the electoral vote against William Harrison's 25 percent and Judge White's 9 percent. She would have to wait four more years to see Van Buren crushed in a reelection attempt against Harrison. But now, she soundly castigated her visitor, Barnum, for supporting that "scoundrel" and "traitor" Van Buren.

After a half hour more of similar political harangue, through which Barnum sat benumbed, Anne finally ran out of breath and invective. Her voice reduced to a mere shout, she studied Barnum a moment, and then suddenly apologized.

"Well, Barnum," she said in a more normal tone, "you are a good fellow, and I am really glad to see you. How sorry I am that we mentioned politics, for I am so nervous. Now, I want a real good talk with you. . . . Come, Barnum, go with me into the printing office, and there we can talk and work together."

In the printing office, where a man and a boy were busy at the press, a large pile of newspapers lay in the middle of the floor. Anne commanded Barnum to sit down and help her finish the job of sorting the wrapped newspapers for the post office. "Anne then seated herself upon the dirty floor, and as there was no chair in the room, I sat down beside her, not daring even to spread my handkerchief or in any way remove the dust, lest she should construe it into an insult." As they sorted copies of her newspaper, Anne rattled on, recounting various incidents in her long and troubled life. When she finally stopped for breath, Barnum broached the idea of sponsoring her on a lecture tour through the East. She was not interested. When he left, she extracted his promise to call again. But, permanently shaken, he gave her a wide berth thereafter, and in his later years noted that he "never again met the eccentric old lady."

In November of 1836, inexplicably, *Paul Pry*—which, said *The New England Religious Weekly,* "contains all the scum, billingsgate and filth extant"—ceased publication, only to be supplanted a month later by a more dignified weekly which Anne called *The Huntress.* But this new conservatism, intended to increase circulation by toning down the muckraking, did not affect Anne's treatment of anti-Masons or Evangelicals. The smaller pages of the new paper did little to confine the editor's temper. Nor did advancing years and growing infirmity mellow her opinions. When there was protest against Catholic immigration, Anne saw that the real threat lay in the intolerant tyranny of the overpatriotic, and she cried out against this in *The Huntress:* "A Catholic foreigner discovered America, Catholic foreigners first settled it. . . . When the colonies were about to be enslaved, foreigners rescued it. . . . At present, we verily believe, that the liberty of this country is in more danger from this native combination than from foreigners."

For more than a decade, she continued to occupy herself with *The Huntress.* Circulation was small, and she barely made ends meet. Once, she wrote a three-act play, *The Cabinet: or, Large Parties in Washington,* and the father of Joseph Jefferson, the actor, agreed to produce it. On opening night, with most of the tickets already sold, the show was canceled because of pressure brought to bear by church groups and anti-Masons. Then the Masons came to her rescue, and gave the play one performance in their hall. It attracted only a small audience, and proved a financial disappointment.

All the while, Anne had persisted in her fight for a pension. When, acting on an affidavit supplied by Lafayette, Congress finally conceded that Captain Royall had served in the Revolution and that Anne had indeed been his wife, her petition was nevertheless rejected again because Anne had been married in 1797 and the law provided benefits only to widows who had been married before 1794. But in 1848 Congress liberalized this law, and Anne's excruciating, twenty-four-year struggle was capped by victory. She was offered the choice of a lifetime annuity of $480 a year or a lump-sum payment of $1,200. As she was seventy-nine years old, ill, and in debt, she took the lump sum of $1,200. It was a mistake. She was to live six years more.

When her outstanding obligations were met, and a new printing press was installed, she was left with three dollars.

In 1854, at the age of eighty-five, she was still on the job. But now when she wanted to interview the President, Franklin Pierce invited her to the White House. She may have reflected on how the times had changed. It was a quarter of a century since she had been obliged to trap an earlier President in the nude in order to obtain her story. Pierce was friendly, and her account of the visit in *The Huntress* was kind:

"He looked stout and healthy but rather pale. His countenance used to be gay and full of vivacity when he was a Senator in Congress several years ago, but now it wears a calm and dignified composure, tinctured with a pleasing melancholy. . . . We could not refrain from dropping a tear when he spoke to us of his lady, after whose health we inquired. The sad bereavement she met with in the sudden loss of her only and beloved boy has shadowed the bright walks which surround the Presidential Mansion. . . ."

It was her last major story. On Sunday morning, October 1, 1854, she died in her sleep. "To the hour of her death," noted the *Washington Evening Star*, "she preserved all the peculiarities of thought, temper, and manners, which at one time rendered her so famous throughout the land." She was laid to rest in the Congressional Cemetery. There was no money for a gravestone (although one was placed on her burial plot fifty-seven years later "by a few men of Philadelphia and Washington" in "appreciative recognition" of a "Pioneer Woman Publicist"). At her death, she still owed her landlord six dollars. With that debt absolved, her total legacy amounted to thirty-one cents. But something that transcended mere money had been left behind. Anne Royall was, in a more limited and more eccentric way, just what one biographer had claimed Zola to be—a moment in the conscience of Man.

XV

The Teacher

Who Hated

Shakespeare

Condemned to refer the origin of these works to
the vulgar, illiterate man who kept the theatre
where they were first exhibited . . . how could
any one dare to see what is really in them?

—DELIA BACON

ON APRIL 25, 1616, an entry was made in the Stratford-on-Avon parish register noting the burial of "will Shakspere
gent." He had been baptized in the Church of the Holy Trinity,
and he was laid to rest in its chancel. Across the flagstone placed
over the grave containing his wooden coffin was inscribed a verse
which, according to local tradition, had come from the pen of
the deceased:

> Good frend for Jesus sake forbeare,
> To digg the dust encloased heare:
> Blese be the man that spares thes stones,
> And curst be he that moves my bones.

Seven years after the actor-playwright had been laid to rest,
there appeared in London a volume entitled *Mr. William*

Shakespeares Comedies, Histories, & Tragedies, Published According to the True Originall Copies. This folio, edited and sponsored by Edward Blount, John Smethwicke, and William Aspley, gave credit to Blount and Isaac Jaggard as its printers, although the volume was actually printed by Isaac Jaggard and his father William. The folio contained an editors' epistle "To the great Variety of Readers," and was dedicated to the Earl of Pembroke and his brother the Earl of Montgomery. The dedication, composed by two actors who had known Shakespeare well, explained that the book had been published "without ambition either of selfe-profit, or fame; onely to keepe the memory of so worthy a Friend, & Fellow alive, as was our SHAKESPEARE. . . ."

This was the first collection of his works to be published, and it contained all but one of Shakespeare's thirty-seven plays. Eighteen had never been printed before. The other eighteen had appeared earlier as individual quartos, seventeen of them having been published—in both authorized and pirated editions—during Shakespeare's lifetime.

With the distribution of the First Folio, the playwright's genius was at last on full display to his contemporaries and to countless generations that would follow. For more than a century after Shakespeare's burial and his resurrection in the Jaggard volume, his authorship of the immortal works was accepted without question or doubt. No one disturbed Shakespeare's bones, literally or literarily, and no one directly disputed his authorship of the plays attributed to him by the First Folio. Then, gradually, the rumblings of surmise and suspicion began, instigated by scholars, critics, ordinary readers, and eccentrics who could not reconcile the brilliance and variety of Shakespeare's output with the few prosaic facts known of his middle-class life.

The first dissent was heard in 1771, when Herbert Lawrence, a surgeon and the friend of David Garrick, issued a book entitled *The Life and Adventures of Common Sense: An Historical Allegory.* Lawrence contended that Shakespeare had plagiarized much of his best writing from a certain *Commonplace Book.* The extremely "pleasant and entertaining compositions in the *Commonplace Book* had been audaciously appropriated by "a Person belonging to the Playhouse; this Man was a profligate in his Youth, and, as some say, had been a deer-stealer. . . . With these Materials, and with good Parts of his own, he commenced Play-

Writing, how he succeeded is needless to say, when I tell the
Reader that his name was Shakespear." Even though Lawrence's
effort went into two English editions, and was published in translation in France and Switzerland, his caustic remarks on the
Bard were too radical and undocumented to create any sensation.

The first half of the nineteenth century provided two mild
doubters and one vigorous dissenter. In 1811, Samuel Taylor
Coleridge delivered a series of lectures on Milton and Shakespeare
(with an admitted preference for Milton) at the Philosophical
Society in London. Discussing the plays of Shakespeare, he was
incredulous that "works of such character should have proceeded
from a man whose life was like that attributed to Shakespeare.
. . . Are we to have miracles in sport? Does God choose idiots
by whom to convey divine truths to men?" Coleridge was more
willing to accept Shakespeare as thespian than as creator: "It is
worth having died two hundred years ago to have heard Shakespeare deliver a single line. He must have been a great actor."

Twenty-six years later, a future Prime Minister of England,
Benjamin Disraeli, voiced his misgivings more indirectly. In his
eighth novel, *Venetia*, brought out the year he finally won a
Parliamentary seat, he had a fictional character remark, "And
who is Shakespeare? We know as much of him as Homer. Did
he write half the plays attributed to him? Did he ever write a
single whole play? I doubt it."

However, the liveliest assault on Shakespeare's authorship occurred in New York during 1848. A book bearing the unlikely
title of *The Romance of Yachting*, written by Joseph C. Hart, be-
labored the Bard mercilessly. Hart's narrative cheerfully recounted
his own adventures while on a sailing voyage to Spain. The sea
change apparently worked wonders on his contemplative processes. En route he thought deeply, and when he came to record
the physical highlights of his journey, he recorded also his varied
meditations on the misconceptions prevalent in civilization. One
of his meditations, to which he devoted thirty-five pages, reflected
his suspicions that Shakespeare as a playwright was an impostor.
"He was not the mate of the literary characters of the day," Hart
wrote, "and none knew it better than himself. It is a fraud upon
the world to thrust his surreptitious fame upon us. He had none
that was worthy of being transmitted. The inquiry will be, *who*

were the able literary men who wrote the dramas imputed to him?"

These isolated voices were heard by very few. But the few who heard them responded by emphasizing the crucial question: If William Shakespeare had not written the thirty-six plays in the First Folio, who had written them? Lawrence had named a little-known book as their source. Coleridge and Disraeli had credited no one. Hart had, in passing, suggested Sir Francis Bacon. But where was the proof that any specific author had written Shakespeare's plays? From 1771 to 1852 the doubters had their nagging doubts and little else. Then in 1852, with the appearance of a neurotic New England spinster named Delia Salter Bacon, the doubters suddenly had not one candidate but several for the works attributed to Shakespeare.

Miss Bacon's livelihood came from schoolteaching, and from lecturing women's groups on historical and literary subjects. For years she had been deeply immersed in the writings of the Elizabethan period, and her specialty was Shakespeare. The more she read of Shakespeare, the more she was troubled. "There was no man, dead or alive, that really on the whole gave me so much cause of offense with his contradictions," she once confessed in a letter to Nathaniel Hawthorne. "He appeared to be such a standing disgrace to genius and learning, that I had not the heart to ask anybody to study anything."

She came to think of Shakespeare, and eventually to speak of him and write of him, as "Will the Jester" and "that Player" and "that booby" and "Lord Leicester's groom." She could not reconcile the deep philosophy and daring political views she found in his plays with the "vulgar, illiterate . . . deer-poacher" who had been considered their author. With growing certainty she reasoned that Shakespeare had not written the plays credited to him, that his name had been borrowed to mask the identity of another. But what other? And why the elaborate masquerade?

She scanned the giants of the era, their activities, their writings, and suddenly, blindingly, the truth stood revealed. The plays that bore Shakespeare's name had been written in secret by a syndicate of creative men united for a single purpose. The syndicate, she decided, consisted of Sir Francis Bacon (no ancestor of hers), Sir Walter Raleigh, Edmund Spenser, and several other "high-born wits and poets." These men were idealists and potential revo-

lutionists. They possessed dangerous democratic ideas in a day
when the divine right of kings and queens went unchallenged.
Eager to promote liberty, equality, and justice, these men sought
to spread their progressive views by means of popular plays performed before the masses.

This was Miss Bacon's startling and highly imaginative proposition. She did not announce it to the world at once. The news
would be delayed four years while she reinforced her argument.
But by 1852 the theory had become a reality in her mind, and
she could not resist trying it out on her young students, her friends,
and her adult audiences.

In that crucial year she was on the genteel lecture circuit, ear-
nestly addressing groups of ladies and their daughters in the
more culture-conscious homes of New Haven, Boston, and Cambridge. The first writer to note Delia Bacon's obsession with her
new Shakespearean authorship theory was present at her Cambridge talks. A group of socially prominent ladies had purchased
tickets to attend Miss Bacon's lectures, given first in the Brattle
house and then in the parlor of the Farrar residence. Mrs. Eliza
Farrar, the wife of a professor of mathematics at Harvard and
an author of juvenile books, was responsible for Miss Bacon's
appearance, and would later recall the impression it made.

Speaking without notes, Miss Bacon began her series with a
lecture on ancient history and dramatized her account by means
of pictures and maps. "In these she brought down her history to
the time of the birth of Christ," wrote Mrs. Farrar in *Recollections
of Seventy Years*, "and I can never forget how clear she made it
to us that the world was only then made fit for the advent of Jesus.
She ended with a fine climax that was quite thrilling."

At the conclusion of one such lecture, as Mrs. Farrar was to
remember, several ladies lingered behind to have tea with Miss
Bacon and to chat informally. During the ensuing conversation
Miss Bacon mentioned a desire to visit England to search for
proofs of her "theory." Someone asked, with innocent curiosity,
what theory Miss Bacon wished to substantiate. And immediately
Miss Bacon was off on a bitter harangue against the "vulgar, illiterate" Shakespeare. Her listeners recoiled at the blasphemy, and
Mrs. Farrar did not encourage her protégée to discuss the subject
further. Nevertheless, in the days that followed, Miss Bacon
brought up her theory at every opportunity, until mention of

Shakespeare became taboo among her friends. According to Mrs. Farrar, Miss Bacon's hostess was even forced to "put her copy of his works out of sight, and never allowed her to converse with her on this, her favorite subject."

However, one person who met Delia Bacon in Cambridge and heard her discuss Shakespeare did not change the subject, but rather encouraged her and drew her out. Ralph Waldo Emerson in his forty-ninth year was actively involved in the antislavery movement and devoted a large part of his time to speaking against the Fugitive Slave Law. But only four years before, in England, he had given some lectures entitled "Shakespeare," and he could still be interested in any academic debate on the Bard. In his journal for Wednesday, May 19, 1852, he wrote:

"I saw Miss Delia Bacon, at Cambridge, at the house of Mrs. Becker, and conversed with her on the subject of Shakespeare. Miss Bacon thinks that a key will yet be found to Shakespeare's interior sense; that some key to the secret may yet be discovered at Stratford, and I fancy, thinks the famous epitaph, 'Good friend, for Jesus' sake forbear,' protects some explanation of it. Her skepticism in regard to the authorship goes beyond the skepticism of Wolf in regard to Homer, or Niebuhr to Latin history."

Apparently Emerson had shown sufficient sympathy for Miss Bacon's ideas to invite her to expound them more fully. Three weeks after their meeting, when Emerson had returned to Concord and while Miss Bacon remained in Cambridge, she sent him what she called a "voluminous note . . . on this subject." Her outline stressed Sir Francis Bacon rather than a syndicate of writers as being the real Shakespeare, and she suggested circulating her theory in print.

Emerson was impressed. On June 12, 1852, he replied at some length: "I am deeply gratified to observe the power of statement and the adequateness to the problem, which this sketch of your argument evinces. Indeed, I value these fine weapons far above any special use they may be put to. And you will have need of enchanted instruments, nay, alchemy itself, to melt into one identity these two *reputations* (shall I call them?) the poet and the statesman, both hitherto solid historical figures. If the cipher approve itself so real and consonant to you, it will to all, and is not only material but indispensable to your peace. And it would seem best that so radical a revolution should be proclaimed with great compression in the declaration, and the real grounds pretty rapidly set forth. . . ."

Emerson thought that a magazine article, followed by a book, would best place Miss Bacon's ideas before the public. He offered to assist her in securing publication. Miss Bacon was delighted and grateful, and she told Emerson: "Confirmations of my theory, which I did not expect to find on this side of the water, have turned up since my last communication to you. . . . Be assured, dear sir, there is no possibility of a doubt as to the main points of my theory. . . ."

Yet there must have been some tiny doubt. For an English trip had crystallized in Miss Bacon's mind as the necessary climax to her researches. She did not wish to set her ideas down on paper or publish them until she had visited St. Albans, where Sir Francis Bacon had once lived, or until she had examined the Shakespeare collection in the British Museum, or until she had personally lifted the flagstone off Shakespeare's grave in the Stratford-on-Avon church and rummaged through his coffin for documents that might fully substantiate her case. She told Emerson that she must go to England for a year, no more, and valiantly he rallied to her cause.

She required contacts and money. Emerson was instrumental in helping her obtain both. He supplied her with letters of introduction, notably one to his old friend Thomas Carlyle. As for financing the English expedition, Emerson wrote to Hawthorne's sister-in-law, Elizabeth Peabody, and asked that prominent educator if she could assist in obtaining magazine serialization of Miss Bacon's projected book: "I can really think of nothing that could give such éclat to a magazine as this brilliant paradox." In short order the pages of Putnam's Magazine were opened to Miss Bacon for a series of articles to be drawn from her book. This gave promise of a certain amount of income, but still it was not enough.

Emerson had one more idea. Miss Bacon would soon be in New York to deliver a series of lectures. He suggested that she call upon an old friend of his, Charles Butler, who was wealthy, well-read, and fascinated by anything bizarre. Emerson arranged the meeting, and Miss Bacon called upon Butler. Like Emerson, Butler was won over. He would be her patron. If she must go to

England, he would gladly assume the cost of her passage and support her there for half a year.

On May 14, 1853, Delia Bacon boarded the steamer *Pacific* in New York harbor, and ten days later she docked in Liverpool, ready for the showdown with "that Player" who had, so long ago, warned meddlers such as she that they would be "curst" if they moved his bones.

How well she would move those bones, even she could not know. But by the time she was forced to leave England four years later, she had initiated a heresy in literature, a controversy in academic circles, that would persist generation after generation, that persists even today after more than a century.

Delia Bacon, it is true, was not the first to doubt that Shakespeare was an author. But she was—despite the insistence of Baconians who try to trace their movement back to 1597—the first to name the names of logical contenders for Shakespeare's place frankly, and to make out a detailed case for each. Her stupendous project of challenging Shakespeare's writing ability and locating the so-called real authors of his works started a war of words that was proliferated in hundreds of volumes, and in many languages, a war that has never ceased. She pioneered a path of unique scholarship that directly, but more often indirectly, encouraged countless learned scholars as well as incredible cranks to join in the unending examination of the Bard of Avon's literary legitimacy.

When she disembarked from her steamer at Liverpool on May 24, 1853, she had little realization that the results of her visit would create such a mighty stir in future years. She knew only the gnawing immediacy of her mission: to regain for honorable and brilliant men—Bacon, Raleigh, Spenser, and their associates—the acclaim that was rightfully theirs, but which had been usurped, albeit unwittingly, by an unlettered actor who lay at rest beneath the floor of a village church, but who soon enough would rest no more.

Delia Salter Bacon's monomania was determined in the first fifteen years of her life. Her father, the Reverend David Bacon, was a descendant of an early Puritan who had once held military rank in England. He himself was made of the same sturdy stuff. Reared on a Connecticut farm, he became not only a Congregational clergyman but a fanatic. Turning his eyes westward, he saw his life's work. Accompanied by his adoring, delicate eighteen-year-old bride, Alice Parks Bacon, he headed into the wilderness and for five years preached to disinterested Indians in Detroit, Mackinac, and settlements in the back country.

His lack of success in converting Indians to Christianity brought on a crisis. Church funds were withheld, and he was left stranded. He found himself in an area that was part of Ohio's Western Reserve, and there, faced with the need to make a decision, he was divinely inspired. He realized his true mission: to establish a holy community where settlers from the East might support themselves in an atmosphere both devout and pure.

The word from on high was enough. He promptly purchased twelve thousand acres of the richest forest land in the vicinity. Having no cash, he bought on credit. As he busied himself with constructing his own log cabin and subdividing his acres into small farming tracts, he corresponded with Congregationalist families in the East who wanted to move to Ohio and dwell in piety with their beloved Reverend Bacon.

He called his religious utopia Tallmadge, and in this holy town, in the confines of the log cabin he had built, a girl whom he christened Delia Salter was born on February 2, 1811. There had been four children before her, and there would be one after her, but Delia alone would be infected with her father's fanaticism.

The burden of his growing family weighed heavily on David Bacon as he awaited the settlers who would, by purchasing farms from him, relieve his indebtedness and fulfill his dream of a heaven on earth. But in short months his dream was shattered by a congressional embargo on foreign goods which finally culminated in the War of 1812. The Connecticut parishioners who had planned to leave for Ohio changed their minds. And in the Western Reserve, David Bacon had his promised land to himself.

When he could not meet his obligations, the mortgage holder quickly repossessed the twelve thousand acres, with its phantom town of Tallmadge and Bacon's own lonely cabin. Crushed in spirit and without a livelihood, David Bacon led his large family on the weary six-hundred mile trek back to New England. Defeated, he dragged out six more years there selling Bibles, occasionally teaching, sometimes delivering sermons. He was forty-six years old at the time of his death in August 1817, when the daughter upon whom he had left the deepest impression was only six.

Penniless, and with a half-dozen mouths to feed, the widow Bacon distributed as many of her brood as she could among relatives and friends and moved to New York City to work as a milliner. Of the entire family, it was thought that six-year-old Delia fared the best. She was accepted in a Hartford home that offered her, at least materially, such comforts as she had never known before. Her guardian, Mrs. Delia Williams, was the wife of a prominent attorney and the daughter of Oliver Ellsworth, a Chief Justice of the Supreme Court.

Delia Bacon lived with the Williamses for nine years. In many respects she found them generous. For one thing, they provided her with the best education then available for a young, unemancipated American girl. In 1824, the clever Catharine Beecher, seeking an occupation after the death of her fiancé, Professor Alexander M. Fisher, established a small school for girls in Hartford. While it never attained an enrollment of more than 150 students, the institution was to become nationally respected. One of its first pupils was the founder's younger sister, Harriet, who would become world-famous after her marriage as Harriet Beecher Stowe. Another was Delia Bacon. Many years later, Catharine Beecher would remember that Delia possessed one "of the most gifted minds" that Catharine had ever encountered in male or female society, and that "she was pre-eminently one who would be pointed out as a genius. . . ."

Her three years of study under Catharine Beecher and financial support until she was old enough to go to work were the best Delia could hope for as a ward of the Williamses. She was hungry for love and companionship. These her guardians could not supply. They were well-intentioned, but they were childless, and their regime was austere. "There can be no doubt of the calm and constant kindness of patronage which the fatherless child received here," Delia's nephew, Theodore Bacon, wrote later. "But its calmness may have been somewhat stern and grim."

In 1826, Delia Bacon left the Williamses to make her own way. She was fifteen years old, without money and without connections, and her only possession was the learning imparted to her by Catharine Beecher. She had no choice but to exploit her single asset. She would emulate Miss Beecher. She would found her own academy for girls and teach others.

It took Delia four heartbreaking years to learn that she was no Catharine Beecher. Aided by an older sister, she opened an institution of learning for girls of grammar school and high school age, in Southington, Connecticut. It lasted nine months. She then tried a similar project at Perth Amboy, New Jersey. This survived less than eight months. In desperation, she established a more ambitious school at Jamaica, New York, only twelve miles from Manhattan. Larger classes were solicited, higher tuitions charged, and many of the female pupils were given board. In two years this project also became, as Delia told her oldest brother, "a tale of blasted hopes, realized fears, and unlooked-for sorrows." These failures, each of which left her more deeply in debt, had been caused by her increasingly poor health and a lack of business acumen, rather than by a lack of teaching talent. In the end, her eldest brother, Leonard Bacon, the successful Congregational pastor of the First Church of New Haven, rescued her from debt and urged her to forget about establishing her own school.

For the next decade and more, Delia Bacon did as her brother suggested. She returned to Hartford to accept a teaching position, then restlessly moved on to Penn Yan, New York, and then to West Bloomfield, New York, to toil in the same capacity. She taught with only half a mind on her work. Its better half was given over to authorship. "From her childhood," noted brother Leonard, "she has had a passion for literature, and perhaps I should say a longing, more or less distinct, for literary celebrity."

When she was twenty years old, Delia began her struggle for "literary celebrity," evidencing what Catharine Beecher had characterized in her as "the desire of human estimation, especially in the form of literary ambition." Early in 1831 the firm of A. H. Maltby in New Haven published a collection of three melodramatic, historical novelettes entitled *Tales of the Puritans*. The title page credited no writer, as the author had insisted upon maintaining anonymity. But when the imaginative if implausible stories met with no adverse criticism, Delia stepped forward to acknowledge authorship. Under her pen the Puritans unbent, and were made to indulge in protracted love scenes and dashing swordplay. The book had a brief vogue among lady readers, and

Delia was more than satisfied, admitting that it had been "written without experience, without knowledge of the subjects of which it treated, with scarcely a book to refer to beyond the works made use of in school."

Later in the same year, with less trepidation and no anonymity, Delia entered a short story, "Love's Martyr," in a competition sponsored by the *Philadelphia Saturday Courier*. Perhaps it surprised her not at all to learn that she had won the first prize of one hundred dollars. Still, it may surprise many, reading of her victory more than a century later, to know the caliber of the opposition that she bested. For among those Delia had defeated in the contest was an impoverished former West Point cadet, two years her senior, named Edgar Allan Poe. Though Delia's fiction was awarded the one-hundred-dollar prize, one of Poe's several submissions, "Metzengerstein," received the second prize which consisted of its publication during January of 1832 at space rates. With this appearance in print, Poe, who had already brought out three volumes of verse, made his debut as a writer of short stories.

Next, Delia decided to become a playwright. Her first offering, long planned, would be based on a dramatic episode that had happened during the Revolutionary War. Delia had once read of an American girl, Jane McCrea, who had fallen in love with a British officer under General Burgoyne's command. Taken captive by a party of Indians, Jane McCrea offered them a sizable reward if they would release her to the British. The proffered reward provoked a violent disagreement among the braves. Each Indian claimed he deserved the full ransom. In the heat of the argument one Indian turned upon the cause of the trouble, the captive girl. He killed her, scalped her, and made off. When the murder became public, it did much to arouse and inflame patriotic opinion against the British and their Indian allies.

Out of these tragic materials, Delia spun her romantic play. It was rejected everywhere for its verbosity, improbability, and amateurish pretensions. Undeterred, yet with some misgivings (for she warned in her foreword that her work was "*not a Play* . . . not *intended* for the stage" but was merely a "DIALOGUE"), she arranged to have her abortive theatrical effort published.

The so-called dialogue, two hundred pages of prosy blank verse, was served up to America's readers in 1839 as *The Bride of*

Fort Edward: A Dramatic Story, by Delia Bacon. "It was a failure, every way," Delia's nephew recorded. "It brought debt instead of money, and no renown; but it did the great service of ending, for a time, her attempts at literary work, and turning her back to study and instruction."

After this debacle Delia embarked upon the most profitable undertaking that she had tried to date—that of lady lecturer. It is more than likely she got the idea from observing the success of Margaret Fuller, the feminist and literary critic. In this new endeavor Delia seemed to find herself. Her knowledge of literature and history, her eloquence and wit, supplemented by a small reputation gained from her first book and by connections acquired through years of teaching and through her clergyman brother's high clerical position, helped to increase the attendance at her lectures. She might have had a long and prosperous career—and "will Shakspere gent" might have rested undisturbed through all eternity—had not scandal and shame entered her life in the malevolent shape of the Reverend Alexander MacWhorter, student of divinity and cad.

It is difficult, at best, to reconcile the stiff image evoked by her subsequent literary reputation—the studious, single-minded Delia Bacon who retreated into monomania—with the softer, shimmering vision of a warm, womanly Delia Bacon enraptured by love, sacred and profane. But as all existing evidence confirms, Delia was a woman. Beneath the prim façade of teacher and speaker, behind the protective barrier of scholarship, lay hidden the normal passions, the hungers, the longings of a woman for a man's love.

She was not, by any means, unattractive. During her lecturing phase, as Mrs. Eliza Farrar recalled, she "was tall and commanding, her finely shaped head was well set on her shoulders, her face was handsome and full of expression, and she moved with grace and dignity." A friend of Delia's, Mrs. Sarah Henshaw, remembered her as "graceful, fair, and slight. Her habitual black dress set off to advantage the radiant face, whose fair complexion was that uncommon one which can only be described as pale yet brilliant."

A daguerreotype of Delia taken in May of 1853, when she was forty-two years of age, still exists. She sits in repose, staring into the camera. She wears a bonnet, and a shawl hides the shoulders of her black satin dress. Her hair is dark and flattened down on either side of the severe part in the middle. Her brow is high, her deep-set eyes seem darker than the blue-gray described by her friends, her nose is long and classically Grecian, and her generous mouth is drawn in a tight, amused smile. If she seems more forbidding, more worn, than the woman described by her friends, it must be remembered that the portrait was taken six years after the sitter had suffered deeply at the hands of MacWhorter.

With a nice sense of respect and a poor sense of history, Theodore Bacon does not mention MacWhorter by name in his biography of his aunt. His only comment is provocatively enigmatic: "When she was mature in age, she underwent a most cruel ordeal, and suffered a grievous and humiliating disappointment."

The ordeal began in 1846 when Delia was lecturing in New Haven, where her brother Leonard had replaced his friend and mentor, Dr. Nathaniel W. Taylor, as pastor of the First Church. At the hotel where Delia boarded and roomed, she found herself often dining at the same communal table with another occupant of the hotel, a young man named Alexander MacWhorter. She learned that MacWhorter came from a wealthy New Jersey family and was a resident licentiate of Yale, studying under Dr. Nathaniel Taylor. Though there was a mutual attraction between Delia and MacWhorter, she remained briefly aloof. Perhaps it was because they had not been formally introduced. More likely, it was because Delia was then thirty-five years old, and MacWhorter twenty-three.

After a short time, Delia could no longer ignore MacWhorter's formal attentions. Nor, as it turned out, did she any longer wish to. Learning that her fellow boarder was a student under her brother's respected friend, Dr. Taylor, she felt free to respond to MacWhorter's overtures. It was her custom to give nightly receptions in her parlor. To these she invited friends and acquaintances, and to one such affair she invited MacWhorter. He attended and made it clear that his interest in his hostess was romantic as well as intellectual.

"His first visit was not his last," the *Philadelphia Times* reported rather sternly in 1886. "He was more than pleased with Delia Bacon's intellectual attainments—he was interested in her personal attractions. He called upon her frequently. He showed her marked attention. He acted as her escort in public. He professed for her a profound and lasting affection, and would not take 'no' for an answer. He even followed her to a watering-place, with no other excuse than to be near her. These two . . . were lovers. . . . Then, when he tired of the flirtation, as all men do who fall in love with women older than themselves, he turned viciously upon his uncomplaining victim and contemptuously characterized an affair, that had begun with baseness on his part, a literary intimacy."

Delia's flight to the hydropathic establishment—the "watering-place"—in Northampton, Massachusetts, had been made necessary by a bad case of nerves brought on by her family's cynicism toward young MacWhorter's motives. At first, troubled by the disparity in their ages, she had removed herself from MacWhorter's gaze by leaving the hotel and taking up residence in her brother's house. But MacWhorter insisted upon visiting her there. It was then, overwrought beyond endurance, that she sought escape elsewhere in Northampton. Again the persistent MacWhorter followed. Convinced that this was proof of true devotion, Delia gave herself to the divinity student.

Their romance became the talk of New Haven. When Delia's old teacher, Catharine Beecher, wondered if it was merely "a Platonic flirtation," Delia tartly advised her to call it whatever she wished. This was hardly enough for Miss Beecher, and it was certainly not enough for brother Leonard. Relatives and friends alike were fearful lest their beloved Delia become a fallen woman. To rescue her reputation they let the word be spread about that Delia was engaged to marry MacWhorter. When the news of his betrothal reached the philandering young licentiate, he was amazed. Abruptly his heart, so recently warm, began to chill. In a panic, he publicly denied the engagement. To make sure he was understood, he ridiculed Delia, exhibited her passionate letters of love, and insisted that though she had proposed marriage to him at least five times, he had never agreed to anything beyond friendship. Delia, immersed in a bad attack of vapors, could not believe that her beloved was acting so cruelly. Only when her most private letters were quoted back to her did the scales fall from her eyes.

Delia's camp, led by brother Leonard, called MacWhorter a practiced seducer, a brazen liar, and a disgrace to the cloth. MacWhorter's camp, led by Dr. Taylor, called Delia a temptress and likened her to the wanton women who besmirched the pages of history. At best, she was a sex-starved spinster who had attempted to entrap an artless and defenseless young Yale student. With the pastor of the First Church and its ex-pastor locked in battle, all of New England's clergy felt called to arms. Men of God chose sides and gossip ran wild.

In defense of virtue, Leonard Bacon determined to see justice done. Young MacWhorter had obtained a license to preach in the vicinity. Leonard Bacon demanded that the Congregational Ministerial Association revoke that license. His sister's seducer, he implied, was Satan incarnate. He would prove that MacWhorter was guilty of "slander, falsehood, and conduct dishonorable to the Christian ministry."

The charges came to trial before a jury of twenty-three ministers. MacWhorter put up a stout defense. His explanation, as Miss Beecher reported it, was that an older woman had ensnared "his unsophisticated affections." He swore that he "had never made a declaration of affection." In refutation Leonard Bacon revealed that he had seen "a real love letter" from MacWhorter to Delia in which the divinity student had declared, "I have loved you purely, fervently." As his sister's keeper, Leonard Bacon regarded her suitor as anything but unsophisticated (rather, as a "clerical Lothario," the press reported in clarification). MacWhorter had led Delia on and captured her affections with dishonorable intent. When he had attained his objective, he had retreated, and then had attempted to protect his reputation by maligning a simple and trusting lady. By the time Delia took the stand there was little left to say. Usually eloquent, she was tongue-tied and soon in tears.

The twenty-three jurors consulted and arrived at their verdict. Twelve ministers found MacWhorter "imprudent in his conduct" but not guilty of wrong behavior. Eleven found him guilty as charged. By a narrow margin MacWhorter had been vindicated, but he was admonished to practice what he preached in the future. Delia's admirers, and there were many, never absolved him of guilt nor did they forgive him. Catharine Beecher published a book on the scandal that was entirely sympathetic to Delia. And as recently as 1888, a disciple of Delia's, the Minnesota congressman and reformer, Ignatius Donnelly, had only contempt for "the base wretch who could thus, for the amusement of his friends, trifle with the affections of a great and noble-hearted woman."

In the years that followed, MacWhorter married Henrietta Blake, daughter of a wealthy New Haven merchant and one-time subscriber to Delia's lectures. MacWhorter, after a year's residence at the University of Troy in New York, moved into his father-in-law's house in New Haven. He produced some articles, a book entitled *Yahveh Christ, or The Memorial Name,* but no offspring. He supported Delia's ideas on Shakespeare, and lived an otherwise undistinguished life until his death from apoplexy in 1880.

After the trial, a brooding Delia went to Ohio to recover and to bury herself in the books of an earlier, and happier, age. When she returned to New England and her lectures, she was a new woman and she had a mission. For she had found in history a man whom she disliked even more than the faithless MacWhorter. This man, she would soon announce, was William Shakespeare, pretender and mountebank.

An omnivorous reader, she knew the plays credited to Shakespeare almost as well as the most eminent Elizabethan scholars of her day. Curious about the genius who had created these magnificent and varied works, she began to study Shakespeare's life. She was dismayed to find that little was known of a writer so prolific and so great.

Delia learned that there was no contemporary account of Shakespeare's schooling (or of his early life). There was evidence that his father had been a merchant and a member of the Glovers' Guild. A bond dated November 28, 1582, gave proof of Shakespeare's hasty marriage to Anne Hathaway. An assortment of documents indicated that he had performed as an actor at court, had purchased a fine house in Stratford, and had been involved in other property investments. An emended will, its rewritten sheets signed in a faltering hand about a month before his death, bequeathed his biographers information on his family, friends, and real estate. And there was the "second-best bed," which he left to his wife. This there was, and little more.

Delia found that most of the other information about Shakespeare came from secondary sources. John Aubrey, who recorded reminiscences of celebrities, had mentioned some early education, but he mentioned it sixty-five years after Shakespeare's death.

That Shakespeare had held the horses of the actors in the Earl of Leicester's company, and had later become a member of the company, was not a fact but a tradition. So was the story that he had been forced to depart from Stratford after being caught deer-poaching on the estate of Sir Thomas Lucy. The deer-poaching episode was not published until ninety-two years after Shakespeare had died.

If Shakespeare had a reputation as poet and playwright in his own lifetime, Delia could find surprisingly sparse evidence of it. In 1592, the printer and dramatist Henry Chettle mentioned Shakespeare's "facetious grace in writing." In 1598, Francis Meres listed twelve Shakespeare plays and called their author "honey-tongued." Ben Jonson made several references to Shakespeare as a writer. During the Bard's lifetime, Jonson was critical of the fact that he overwrote and did not revise enough, and once told a Scottish poet that "Shaksperr wanted arte." Beyond these principal acknowledgments, there existed also fifteen plays that bore his name while he lived, the 908-page First Folio brought out by those who admired him, and the bust in the Stratford church erected in after years by those who wished to commemorate his place as a great writer.

Delia was anything but satisfied. Question after question came to mind about Shakespeare as human being and artist. The works were there for all to see, and they were the product of a genius. But could this man have been that genius? If so, where was a record that he had ever attended school? Or owned a book? Or traveled abroad? How could he, whose parents were middle-class citizens of a bustling market town, have had so much knowledge of ancient history and of Greek and Latin classics in the original? Where could he have learned of court manners and chivalric sports? How could he have acquired so technical a background in law, medicine, and military affairs? An actor and property holder, when did he find the time to create two plays a year? And if he found the time, why did neither he nor his contemporaries ever mention or discuss his writing in personal letters? Where was one single bit of correspondence from Shakespeare to a publisher, fellow writer, critic, patron, or actor? Above all, why did no manuscript from his pen, no scrap of manuscript, even, survive his time? ("Of his less famous contemporaries," wrote Theodore Bacon in support of his aunt's suspicions, "there are autograph man-

uscripts in abundance. . . . Petrarch died two centuries and a
half, Dante three centuries, before him; yet the manuscripts of
both abound, while of him who was greater than either, and was
almost of our own time, there is nothing but the mean and sordid
will to show that he ever put pen to paper.")

As Delia questioned and questioned, and probed and researched into the Elizabethan and Jacobean past, the certainty
took hold of her that Shakespeare had not written the plays attributed to him. He had been used by someone more cultured,
more talented, or perhaps it had been several people, which would
account logically for the incredible variety of plays. But who were
the real authors and why had they used "that Player"?

Delia pored over the writings of Shakespeare's contemporaries,
searching for clues. Then she returned to the plays. In a flash, it
all came clear. She had discovered "underlying the superficial and
ostensible text" of the plays a daring and liberal "system of philosophy." Later she would explain her next step to Hawthorne,
and he would tell the world that "as she penetrated more and
more deeply into the plays, and became aware of those inner
readings, she found herself compelled to turn back to the 'Advancement of Learning' for information as to their plan and pur-
port; and Lord Bacon's Treatise failed not to give her what she
sought. . . ."

In short, Sir Francis Bacon had written the plays. To his name
she quickly added the names of two collaborators—Sir Walter
Raleigh and Edmund Spenser. And, as minor fellow conspirators
in this playwriting syndicate, she cited a "courtly company" composed of Sir Philip Sidney, Lord Buckhurst, Lord Paget, and the
Earl of Oxford.

To Delia it seemed that Sir Francis Bacon was everything that
the great plays suggested Shakespeare should have been. The
plays required in one man a knowledge of the court, politics, poetry, law, diplomacy, field sports, geography, and philosophy.
Bacon alone had such knowledge. His birth had preceded Shakespeare's by three years, and he had lived on for ten years after
Shakespeare's death. His father had been Queen Elizabeth's lord
keeper of the great seal. The younger Bacon had studied at Trinity College, Cambridge, before he was thirteen, and had prepared
for the bar at Gray's Inn. He had visited France, had served as a
member of Parliament, and had been appointed lord chancellor

by James I in 1618. He had lived extravagantly, and this, perhaps, more than anything else had forced him to accept bribes
from litigants. Once exposed, he confessed to twenty-three acts of
corruption, for which he was sentenced to be banished from the
court, fined forty thousand pounds, and committed to the Tower
of London for two days. This sentence was remitted, but he was
permanently prohibited from holding office in the future. He was
probably, as Pope remarked, "the wisest, brightest, meanest of
mankind." His philosophical ideas were far in advance of his time.
And his reputation as a writer had been secured with the publication of _The Advancement of Learning, Novum Organum, The
New Atlantis,_ and fifty-eight brilliant essays.

Yet, for all of Bacon's erudition and energy, Delia would not
credit him with the entire contents of the First Folio. Some of the
plays were attributable, she was certain, to Sir Walter Raleigh
and Edmund Spenser. Raleigh had been born a dozen years before Shakespeare and had survived him by two. The son of a gentleman, Raleigh had been to Oxford, to war, and to far-off
Virginia. From his prolific pen flowed books of travel, history, and
verse, and Jonson regarded him as the father of English literature.
One of Raleigh's closest friends was Edmund Spenser, whose
birth also predated Shakespeare's by twelve years, but who had
died a full seventeen years before "that Player." Spenser, a Cambridge graduate, was widely read, scholarly, and religious. He
had been a member of the Earl of Leicester's circle and a frequent
visitor at Elizabeth's court. His poetry showed familiarity with
Greek, Latin, and English argot. And, of course, he had written
The Faerie Queene.

These three, then, and their friends, had bestowed immortality
upon a mediocre actor named Shakespeare for their own ends. In
an era when royalty was throttling free speech, these men had
decided that the play was the thing, the only means by which they
might safely convey their inciting ideas to the masses. "It was a
vehicle of expression," said Delia, "which offered incalculable
facilities for evading these restrictions." For example, why not a
modern tirade against tyranny cloaked in the toga like those worn
by the enemies of Julius Caesar? "If a Roman Play were to be
brought out at all . . . how could one object to that which, by the
supposition, was involved in it? And what but the most boundless
freedoms and audacities, on this very question, could one look for

here? What, by the supposition, could it be but one mine of poetic treason? If Brutus and Cassius were to be allowed to come upon the stage, and discuss their views of government, deliberately and confidentially, in the presence of an English audience, certainly no one could ask to hear from their lips the political doctrine then predominant in England."

By 1852 Delia had interested Emerson in her radical theory, and a year later, with the financial backing of his New York friend, she had gone to England to complete her researches first-hand and to announce her shocking find to the literary world.

Within four weeks of her arrival in London, she had been received by Thomas Carlyle, thanks to Emerson's letter of introduction. Carlyle, at fifty-eight, was at the height of his fame as a historian. His *French Revolution*, published sixteen years before, was already a recognized classic, and he had just returned from Germany, where he had done research on a projected biography of Frederick the Great. Dyspeptic though he was, and often crabby and uncivil, this crusty idealist was astonishingly kind to Delia despite her obsession with her theory. Perhaps his affection for Emerson, whom he had met twenty years before and whose friendship he continued to cherish—or perhaps his curiosity over the fact that, as he would write, "there is an understanding manifested in the construction of Shakspere's Plays equal to that in Bacon's Novum Organum"—inspired his kindness. At any rate, he contacted Delia, saying: "Will you kindly dispense with the ceremony of being called on (by sickly people, in this hot weather), and come to us on Friday evening to tea at 7 . . . and we will deliberate what is to be done in your Shakspere affair."

Carlyle, his wife Jane, and a learned family friend were on hand in the Chelsea house to greet their strange American visitor. Carlyle liked Delia immediately because of her "modest shy dignity" and her "solid character." For her part, Delia was delighted with the historian, though startled by his booming laughter: "Once or twice I thought he would have taken the roof of the house off." The tea proceeded nicely until Carlyle asked his guest to explain her Shakespeare theory. Delia explained. When she stopped speaking, a tempest erupted amid the teacups. Carlyle may have had reservations about Shakespeare and great respect for Sir Francis Bacon, but nothing so heretical as this had he expected or, indeed, ever heard before.

"They were perfectly stunned," Delia wrote her sister. "They turned black in the face at my presumption. 'Do you mean to say,' so and so, said Mr. Carlyle, with his strong emphasis; and I said that I did; and they both looked at me with staring eyes, speechless for want of words in which to convey their sense of my audacity. At length Mr. Carlyle came down on me with such a volley . . . I told him he did not know what was in the Plays if he said that, and no one *could* know who believed that that booby wrote them. It was then that he began to shriek. You could have heard him a mile."

The argument continued well into the evening. As the discussion became more heated, Delia treated Carlyle more coolly. Perceiving her hurt, he retreated into gruff tolerance. He promised to keep an open mind and assist her in every way. He would even submit to *Fraser's Magazine* an article in which she explained her theory if she, in turn, would consent to study the primary source material available at the British Museum. "If you can find in that mass of English records," he wrote her afterward, "*any* document tending to confirm your Shakspere theory, it will be worth all the reasoning in the world, and will certainly surprise all men."

Following his meeting with Delia, Carlyle sat down to relay his impressions of her project in a letter to Emerson: "I have not in my life seen anything so tragically *quixotic* as her Shakspere enterprise; alas, alas, there can be nothing but sorrow, toil, and utter disappointment in it for her! I do cheerfully what I can,— which is far more than she *asks* of me (for I have not seen a prouder silent soul); but there is not the least possibility of truth in the notion she has taken up; and the hope of ever proving it, or finding the least document that countenances it, is equal to that of vanquishing the windmills by stroke of lance."

As the months passed, Delia utterly ignored Carlyle's plea that she test her theory against the seventeenth-century archives in the British Museum. She now wanted no proofs beyond those she already possessed as the result of using inductive reasoning, the method so beloved by her idol, Sir Francis Bacon. Also, her funds, supplied by Butler, were gradually dwindling, and she knew that she must give her great theory to the world before her money was entirely gone. She worked day and night on a detailed, booklength exposition of her hypothesis. The early chapters she expected to serialize in *Putnam's Magazine* to fulfill her commit-

ment to its editors, and the payment received from the magazine
would finance her work until its completion.

During the latter days of November 1853, Delia abruptly removed herself from London to lodgings at the nearby village of
St. Albans. There, a short walk away from Sir Francis Bacon's
old estate and his tomb, she continued to write. Her only effort
to substantiate her theory further was an attempt, with the help
of Sir Edward Bulwer-Lytton, to have Bacon's coffin opened. Her
request was refused. Feverishly—she was now suffering severe
headaches and occasional hunger pangs—she returned to her
book. Carlyle was all disapproval. "Miss Bacon has fled away to
St. Albans (the Great Bacon's place)," he reported to Emerson,
"and is there working out her Shakspere Problem, from the depths
of her own mind, disdainful apparently, or desperate and careless, of all evidence from Museums or Archives. . . . Poor Lady!
I sometimes silently wish she were safe at home again; for truly
there can be no madder enterprise. . . ."

By remaining in St. Albans, Delia had, in effect, burned her
bridges behind her. It was a dangerous decision, but there seemed
to be no choice. She had spent the money given her for suste-
nance. Only the passage money for her return to America remained. And now she began to draw on that, too. As she
explained defensively to Emerson: "I am living here as economi-
cally as I could in America; and as I think only of finishing my
work, and have no other future . . . I do not see why I should
spend so large a sum merely for the sake of being in America."

She lived meanly, totally dedicated, and driven by her holy mission. She rarely went walking, never met a native of the community except by accident, subsisted on a diet of the cheapest
staples, and scratched out her pages of manuscript while huddled
in bed for warmth. Finally, after eleven months of privation and
solitude in St. Albans, and after a month in Hatfield, she packed
her precious manuscript and fled the severe winter gripping the
countryside to seek lodgings in the more temperate climate of
London.

Armed with a list of advertisements from The Times, Delia
hired a cab. The driver, informed of her limited means, said that
he knew of reasonable lodgings in Sussex Gardens. Delia was
agreeable to anything. Thus, by good fortune, she found temporary salvation in the form of a kindly, overweight greengrocer

named Walker, and his wife. Walker had an unheated flat to let over his shop. Grateful for a haven, Delia moved in, for a time paid her fourteen shillings promptly each week, and worked steadily toward completion of her book. Soon her funds were gone. Walker, a gentleman of sensitivity and a patron of the arts, did not evict her. Instead, he permitted her to stay on for six months without payment. When Delia borrowed ten pounds and offered it to Walker, he refused it.

Mrs. Eliza Farrar, who had so admired Delia's American lectures, was visiting in London. Hearing of Delia's plight, Mrs. Farrar sent her ten pounds. Delia accepted it, and forced this windfall upon her reluctant landlord. Then she wrote Mrs. Farrar: "I would have frozen into a Niobe before I would have asked any help for myself, and would sell gingerbread and apples at the corner of a street for the rest of my days before I could stoop, for myself, to such humiliations as I have borne in behalf of my work, which was the world's work, and I knew that I had a right to demand aid for it."

Despite a letter from Carlyle recommending her "clear, elegant, ingenious and highly readable manner," portions of Delia's book were being firmly rejected by the leading British publishers. In fact, Chapman and Hall declined with a short stiff note in which they explained, according to Delia, that "as they cannot confess themselves converts to her views, they feel that it would not become them to be the instruments for opening an attack upon one of the most sacred beliefs of the nation."

Delia was filled with despair. But her black mood was of short duration. For suddenly, from New York came the first ray of hope. *Putnam's Magazine* had received a chapter of Delia's book from Emerson, and the editors liked it. They were featuring the chapter in their January issue, just six weeks off, and were prepared to pay her five dollars for every page of print. Moreover, they wanted another chapter for their February issue, and would use as many subsequent chapters as Delia desired to have serialized.

Deliriously happy, secure in the knowledge that this arrangement could support her comfortably in London until her masterwork was done, she prepared four more chapters—a total of eighty manuscript pages—and posted them. But even before her editors had received the new material, Delia's first article was in print.

The opening feature in the January 1856 number of *Putnam's Magazine* was entitled "William Shakespeare and His Plays: An Inquiry concerning Them." Delia devoted her entire first article to the task of maiming William Shakespeare. She referred to his authorship of the plays as the "great myth of the modern age." She felt "that deer-stealing and link-holding, and the name of an obscure family in Stratford" were not exactly prerequisites for erudite creativity. She stigmatized him as "the Stratford poacher" and she ridiculed him as "this Mr. Shakespeare, actor and manager, of whom no one knows anything else."

For the defenders of the Bard, who scoffed at the deer-poaching tradition, she had only the harshest words: "If he did not steal the deer, will you tell us what one mortal thing he did do? He wrote the plays. But, did the man who wrote the plays do nothing else? Are there not some foregone conclusions in them?—some intimations, and round ones, too, that he who wrote them, be he who he may, has had experiences of some sort? Do such things as these, that the plays are full of, begin in the fingers' ends? Can you find them in an ink-horn? Can you sharpen them out of a goose-quill? Has your Shakespeare wit and invention enough for that? . . . Had *he* no part of his own in time, then? Has he dealt evermore with second-hand reports, unreal shadows, and mockeries of things? Has there been no personal grapple with realities, here?" No, the "vulgar, illiterate man who kept the theatre where they were first exhibited" had not created the great plays. The very idea "has become too gross to be endured any further."

Delia did not go beyond this in her initial blast. She withheld the names of those whom she had discovered to be the real authors, merely hinting about "some friend, or friends, who could . . . explain his miracle to us."

The article was a success, and created sufficient agitation and controversy among its readers to warrant more of the same. Or so, at least, Delia was led to believe. But then, like a thunderclap, came the distressing news from New York that *Putnam's Magazine* had decided to cancel the rest of the series.

What had happened? The editors gave, as their official reason, the explanation that the four latest articles were too general and "make so little progress in the demonstration of the main proposition, that if given separately they would weaken rather than increase the interest in the subject."

Emerson agreed with the editors. While at first he had regarded Delia as a "genius, but mad" and ranked her with Walt Whitman as one of "the sole producers that America has yielded in ten years," he had now become impatient with her repetition and verbosity, and he deplored her failure to present solid, factual refutation: "The moment your proposition is stated that Shakespear was only a player, whom certain superior person or persons could use, and did use, as a mouthpiece for their poetry it is perfectly understood. It does not need to be stated twice. The proposition is immensely improbable, and against the single testimony of Ben Jonson, 'For I loved the man, and do honor his memory on this side idolatry as much as any,' cannot stand. Ben Jonson must be answered, first. Of course we instantly require your proofs. But instead of hastening to these, you expatiate on the absurdity of the accepted biography. Perfectly right to say once, but not necessary to say twice, and unpardonable after telling us that you have proof that this is not the man, and we are waiting for proof, to say it thrice . . . I am sure you cannot be aware how voluminously you have cuffed and pounded the poor pretender, and then again and still again, and no end."

If Delia found the cancellation of her series in *Putnam's Magazine* difficult to bear, she found Emerson's loss of faith in her even more crushing. All at once, in her eyes, Emerson became an unreasonable intellectual snob. He had never been interested in her, after all. He had sponsored her simply in hopes of sharing the credit for her brilliant theory. As to his challenge that she must answer Jonson's assertion that he honored Shakespeare's memory, that was typical Emersonian nonsense. Of course she could answer that challenge, if she wished. "I know all about Ben Jonson," she wrote. "He had two patrons besides 'Shakspeare.' *One* was Raleigh, *the other* was Bacon. The author of these Plays and Poems was his Patron." In short, Jonson knew that Raleigh and Bacon were really Shakespeare, so quite naturally he praised his patrons even as he praised Shakespeare.

Then, the disappearance of the four precious chapters Delia had sent to *Putnam's Magazine* added to her frenzy. Emerson had asked his brother William, in New York, to pick up the rejected chapters and return them to Concord, whence Emerson expected to forward them to Delia. William dutifully picked up the chapters and gave them to a house guest named Sophy Ripley, who was returning to Concord. "She took the sealed parcel in her hands," explained Emerson, "and came down to the Staten Island ferry with my brother in his carriage, one and a half miles, and just before reaching the boat perceived that she had not the parcel."

Miss Ripley could not find the parcel containing the chapters in the straw-covered bottom of the carriage, or along the road they had traveled, or in the ferry. Conscience-stricken, she advertised for the lost parcel, and offered a reward, but the chapters were never found. Delia blamed the magazine editors. She even blamed Emerson to some extent. But she did not blame herself for having neglected to make copies of her work. As her paranoia took stronger hold on her, she hinted darkly of a plot fostered by Shakespeare-lovers. "These are not the first of my papers that have been destroyed," she announced.

As a matter of fact, there were many who supported Delia in her view. Her friends, and later her followers, believed that reasons other than the mere redundancy of her writing had made the editors of *Putnam's Magazine* cancel her series. Elizabeth Peabody thought that Shakespeare scholars, led by Richard Grant White, had been so horrified by the heresy in the first article that they had descended upon *Putnam's* and talked them out of publishing the rest of the series. Ignatius Donnelly, on the other hand, thought that the cancellation was caused by Delia's own friends, who had begged *Putnam's* to cease encouraging her eccentricity.

At any rate, *Putnam's* could no longer be depended upon, nor could Ralph Waldo Emerson. When the eighteen pounds paid for the first article had been spent, Delia was again impoverished and at her wits' end. While she had been unable to pay her rent for six months, Delia determined not to trouble Carlyle further. However, she had a letter of introduction to the wealthy, elderly bachelor, James Buchanan, who was American Minister to Great Britain and who would in short months be elected President of the United States. Delia wrote Buchanan, asking to see him. He replied that he would call upon her. When he came, she found him formal and remote and somewhat stuffy. She could not bring herself to ask his aid.

With Buchanan's departure all hope seemed to fade. Delia searched her mind for someone in England who might come to the rescue of both her person and her completed book. Then she remembered Nathaniel Hawthorne, the brother-in-law of her friend Elizabeth Peabody. She had never met him, but she knew that his old college friend, President Franklin Pierce, had awarded him the well-paying consulship at Liverpool. If anyone could be counted upon to understand the plight of a fellow author, it was Hawthorne. He had struggled, too. Of course, he was known to have an antipathy toward women who were aggressive, erudite, talkative. He had disliked Margaret Fuller intensely, and had commented that "she had not the charm of womanhood." Would he, then, couple Delia's name with Miss Fuller's? Would he remember Delia's writings, and the lectures, and the New England scandal, and draw away from her? Delia hesitated. But only briefly. Hunger and pain and defeat gave her courage.

On May 8, 1856, she sat down and wrote:

Dear Mr. Hawthorne,

I take the liberty of addressing myself to you without an introduction, because you are the only one I know of in this hemisphere able to appreciate the position in which I find myself at this moment. . . .

Of course it is not pleasant to me to bring this subject to the attention of strangers, as I have been and still am compelled to, for it seems like a personal intrusion, and like asking a personal favor. . . .

For I want some literary counsel, and such as no Englishman of letters is able to give me. Mr. Carlyle has been a most cordial personal friend to me, but there are reasons why I could not ask this help from him, which would become apparent to you if you should look at the work at all. . . .

The work admits of publication in separate portions. What I want is to begin to publish immediately a part of it, enough to secure the discovery. . . . I would not be willing to print any part of it till some friendly eye had overlooked it, if there were no other reason for delay. It is not hard reading. Would you be willing to take a part of it, a part which you could read in an evening or so . . . ?

In Liverpool the fifty-two-year-old Hawthorne, weary of his consular job—"bothered and bored, and harassed and torn in pieces, by a thousand items of daily business," as he would write Delia—and irritated by the beer-sodden British he often had to deal with, might have been expected to possess little patience for still another American in trouble. Yet, so responsive was he to human loneliness and insecurity, and so decent and good were his instincts, that he was moved to reply to Delia. Within four days of writing him, she had her answer. He had heard of her several years before from Miss Peabody. And he had heard of her theory. He thought that he was too busy and preoccupied to criticize her work in detail, but if she wanted his general reaction, or his assistance in securing a publisher, he was ready to serve her. There was only one condition, and in this Hawthorne was firm:

"I would not be understood, my dear Miss Bacon, as professing to have faith in the correctness of your views. In fact, I know far too little of them to have any right to form an opinion: and as to the case of the 'old Player' (whom you grieve my heart by speaking of so contemptuously) you will have to rend him out of me by the roots, and by main force, if at all. But I feel that you have done a thing that ought to be reverenced, in devoting yourself so entirely to this object, whatever it be, and whether right or wrong; and that, by so doing, you have acquired some of the privileges of an inspired person and a prophetess—and that the world is bound to hear you, if for nothing else, yet because you are so sure of your own mission."

Grateful, excited, and alive again, Delia sent sections of her book to Hawthorne. And with them an apology:

"I am sorry to have hurt your feelings with my profane allusions to the Earl of Leicester's groom, a witty fellow enough in his way. But long familiarity with the facts has produced a hopeless obduracy in my mind on that point. . . . I do not, of course, expect you to adopt my views until you find yourself compelled to do so, neither do I wish you to give the faintest countenance to them till you know fully what they are and their grounds."

Soon enough, Hawthorne had opportunity to become more fully acquainted with Delia's views. After reading portions of her manuscript he wrote her that he still was not a convert to her theory and that she made too much of the parallels she had found in Bacon and Shakespeare, writers' thoughts often being similar though they "had no conscious society with one another." However, he complimented her on her knowledge of Bacon's writings and on "the depth and excellence" of her work. In voicing these opinions, he was being entirely honest with her. For, long after, when she was gone, he told the world: "Her book, as I could see by turning it over, was a very remarkable one, and worthy of being offered to the public, which, if wise enough to appreciate it, would be thankful for what was good in it and merciful to its faults. It was founded on a prodigious error, but was built up from that foundation with a good many prodigious truths."

Generously, he offered her financial assistance, and when her pride restrained her from accepting, he sent money anyway. Much as she needed his money, his literary assistance was what she sought more. And she told him so directly. "The way in which you can help me," she said, "will be to certify that you have read my book and that it is entitled to a publication." Then, in the letters that followed, Delia's requests became more demanding. Would he give her book a title? Would he write a brief foreword for it? Would he find her a publisher? The manuscript, she cried in anguish, was "perishing by inches, for want of a printer, for want of a reader. . . . If you can save it, and any good comes of it, the world will owe it to you."

Again Hawthorne understood her real need, and promised to do what he could. His own publisher in England was Routledge. This firm had sold "a hundred thousand volumes" of his books to their profit and his own, and he was certain that they would do anything he asked. But first he must meet this Delia Bacon in person and discuss the matter with her. When could he call upon her? Delia was frightened. "I am unfit to see anyone. I have given up this world entirely. . . . Still, if you are kind enough to look after me when you come . . . I will put on one of the dresses I used to wear. . . ."

On July 26, 1856, Hawthorne went from Liverpool down to London, made his way to the grocery store in Sussex Gardens, met the fat, friendly Walker and his wife, and was escorted up three flights of stairs to Delia's flat. She was still asleep, though the hour was not early. Hawthorne guessed that her hermitlike existence had made her hours erratic. While Delia was awakened, and she nervously hurried to dress, her benefactor had time to study her parlor. Naturally he was drawn to her books first. They were piled high on a table, and each in some way was related to her Shakespeare theory. There was Raleigh's *The History of the World,* Montaigne's *Essays,* Shakespeare's *Plays,* a volume of Bacon's letters, a pocket edition of the Bible, and several other works.

Hawthorne settled down with Hazlitt's translation of Montaigne, and had been reading "a good while" when suddenly Delia appeared in the doorway.

Before her entrance Hawthorne had reflected upon what her physical appearance might be. From her correspondence, from the fact that "she was a literary woman," he had conjured up an unattractive drab: "I had expected . . . to see a very homely, uncouth, elderly personage." When Delia stood before him in person, he was agreeably surprised. He saw a woman "rather uncommonly tall," with "a striking and expressive face, dark hair, dark eyes, which shone with an inward light as soon as she began to speak." Despite the fact that she was forty-five years of age, Hawthorne thought her bearing almost youthful and was sure that she had "been handsome and exceedingly attractive once."

There was no restraint. Their correspondence had made them friends, and they began to converse quickly and easily. The talk soon turned to her theory and the publication of her book. Delia admitted that she was a recluse because she had no patience with people who were not interested in her theory. She told Hawthorne that he was the fourth person to visit her apartment in all these months, and that except for a few evenings spent with Carlyle or with her friend Mrs. Farrar, who was visiting London, and business calls on the American consul, she went out to see no one. She had even become estranged from her family in New England. They disapproved of her mission, and in an effort to bring her to her senses and force her to come home, they had ceased contributing to her support. Musing over this after he had returned to Liverpool, Hawthorne decided: "If taken from England now, she would go home as a raving maniac." He would write her family and tell them so—and do everything in his power "to supply her with some small means."

She was a colorful talker. Speaking "in a low, quiet tone," she discussed "the authorship of Shakespeare's plays, and the deep political philosophy concealed beneath the surface of them." As he listened, Hawthorne was tempted to point out that the plays were so varied and so complex that a hundred conflicting philosophies and truths could be discovered in them by anyone wishing to prove anything, but he kept silent to avoid upsetting his hostess. As she went on and on, he was entranced by her presentation, but increasingly cynical about her argument. He contained his disagreement, however, because he had no wish to provoke a debate.

Next her conversation took a turn that gave Hawthorne genuine cause for dismay. The moment that her book was accepted for publication, she said, she was going to open Shakespeare's grave in Stratford. "In Lord Bacon's letters, on which she laid her finger as she spoke, she had discovered the key and clew to the whole mystery," Hawthorne recalled. "There were definite and minute instructions how to find a will and other documents relating to the conclave of Elizabethan philosophers, which were concealed (when and by whom she did not inform me) in a hollow space in the under surface of Shakespeare's gravestone. Thus the terrible prohibition to remove the stone was accounted for. . . . All that Miss Bacon now remained in England for—indeed, the object for which she had come hither, and which had kept her here for three years past—was to obtain possession of these material and unquestionable proofs of the authenticity of her theory."

Hawthorne did not attempt to dissuade her from this macabre research. He felt sure that her "sturdy common-sense" would eventually stop her from perpetrating such a sacrilege. Turning the conversation to more practical matters, Hawthorne repeated his offer to submit her book to his own publisher. She bubbled with happiness. She would deliver the full manuscript to him inside of a week. It was Providence, she said, that had brought Mr. Hawthorne into her life in this crisis.

More than an hour had passed since they had begun their conversation. Hawthorne took his leave. As he walked away from the grocery shop, he was still under the spell of Delia's eloquence and fanaticism. But after a few blocks the sanity and bustle of English life about him jarred his "temporary faith" from his head and heart. By the time he reached Paternoster Row, his meeting with Delia seemed an improbable dream. For a while, he had been transported back into the Elizabethan era by sheer witchery, and had half believed what she had been saying, but now he was again in the nineteenth century. Suddenly his promise to have her book published seemed extravagant and impossible. (Had not Elizabeth Barrett Browning, at a recent breakfast party given in his honor, been "horrified" by Miss Bacon's theory?) Nevertheless, he had given his word. He would have to do what he could and hope for the best.

In less than a week Hawthorne had received the thick manuscript. Since he had no time to read it, he turned it over to his wife. Sophia Hawthorne was impressed by its erudition. A few days later, Hawthorne took the book to London and laid it on Routledge's desk.

Hawthorne did not feel his labors in Delia's behalf were yet done. Still disturbed by what she had said about her family, he took it upon himself to address a lengthy letter to the Reverend Leonard Bacon in New Haven. He begged the clergyman not to think him impertinent for meddling in a family affair. But, he indicated, he felt it his duty to report on his relationship with Delia:

"I understand from her (and can readily suppose it to be the case) that you are very urgent that she should return to America; nor can I deny that I should give her similar advice, if her mind were differently circumstanced from what I find it. But Miss Bacon has become possessed by an idea, that there are discoveries within her reach, in reference to the authorship of Shakespeare, and that, by quitting England, she should forfeit all chance of following up these discoveries, and making them manifest to the public. . . . I will say to you in confidence, my dear Sir, that I should dread the effect, on her mind, of any compulsory measures on the part of her friends, towards a removal. If I may presume to advise, my counsel would be that you should acquiesce, for the present, in her remaining here, and do what may be in your power towards making her comfortable."

Leonard Bacon was deeply disturbed by Hawthorne's letter, and wrote his sister immediately. He tried to employ restraint and reason, but a more intemperate and irrational communication cannot be imagined. His experience having been confined to giving advice on matters spiritual, he was ill-equipped to hold forth on matters literary. He instructed Delia to concentrate on magazine articles and forget her book. He insisted that she limit her writing to criticisms of Shakespeare's plays, and stop worrying about the identity of their author. "You know perfectly well that the great world does not care a sixpence who wrote Hamlet," he pontificated, and then warned her that she had yielded "to a delusion which, if you do not resist it and escape from it as for your life, will be fatal to you." He dismissed her theory as a mere "trick of the imagination." However, if she must persist with her book, he had one good, sound Yankee suggestion that might save the day. "Your theory about the authorship of Shakespeare's plays may after all be worth something if published *as* a fiction."

Despite the fury she felt on reading her brother's advice, Delia did not bother to fight back. For by the time she heard from Leonard she was already in Stratford-on-Avon, gathering what remained of her wits to do battle with the real enemy. She had left London suddenly in late August with farewells to no one except Mrs. Eliza Farrar, and this of necessity.

Mrs. Farrar was entertaining guests one afternoon when a servant whispered to her that there was a strange lady at the door who would not leave her name. "On hearing this I went to the door," said Mrs. Farrar, "and there stood Delia Bacon, pale and sad. I took her in my arms and pressed her to my bosom; she gasped for breath and could not speak. We went into a vacant room and sat down together. She was faint, but recovered on drinking a glass of port wine, and then she told me that her book was finished and in the hands of Mr. Hawthorne, and now she was ready to go to Stratford-upon-Avon." She revealed that the purpose of her mission was to open Shakespeare's grave. Mrs. Farrar pleaded with her to abandon the scheme. Delia would not listen to words of advice. What she wanted was Mrs. Farrar's help, so that she could reach Stratford. With a heavy heart and a sense of impending tragedy, Mrs. Farrar provided Delia with money and saw her off at the railroad station.

In 1856, the market town of Stratford, in Warwickshire, was surrounded still by the "shadowy forests" and "plenteous rivers" and "wide-skirted meads" that the Bard himself had known and written about. Well-traveled country lanes led into the worn cobbled streets of the quiet, lovely old town. It was into this idyllic setting that Delia Bacon dragged her sick and exhausted body on her last English journey. She was, she felt, more dead than alive, and her mind clung to reality by tenuous threads. Even her method of finding a lodging was strange, if fortunate. She saw an attractive cottage on High Street, near Shakespeare's last residence and the church that held his grave. She rapped on the door. The maid told her that the lady of the house, a Mrs. Terrett, was out. Delia said that she would wait. She pushed her way inside and sat down, racked with illness. Presently the elderly owner of the cottage, a respectable widow who lived on her income, re-

THE NYMPHO AND OTHER MANIACS

turned. Mrs. Terrett was only mildly surprised by Delia's presence. While she had never taken in a boarder, nor intended to take one, "she remembered, she said, that Abraham had entertained angels unawares." The kindly woman sensed that her American visitor was very ill, and she knew what she must do. She made Delia lie on a sofa, covered her, and went to arrange for dinner. Later she agreed that Delia should have two front rooms, in addition to her meals, for seven shillings a week. Delia relaxed in her "little Paradise of neatness and comfort," and gazed out the window and saw "the trees that skirt the Avon, and that church and spire only a few yards from me, but so weak that I did not expect ever to go there."

It was more than a month before Delia had recovered sufficiently to leave her cottage haven and explore Stratford. She was attracted to the town at once. "I like Stratford," she wrote Hawthorne. "Shakespeare was right. It is a very nice comfortable place to stop in, much better than London for a person of a genial but retiring turn of mind." Hawthorne thought this was the only occasion on which he had ever known Delia to speak a word of praise for Shakespeare.

Although lulled by the peaceful atmosphere of the old place, she was not unmindful of her true mission. Still, as yet she lacked the strength to move Shakespeare's bones. And then, suddenly, during her sixth week in Stratford she received the thrilling news that gave her the necessary strength. Her book had at last been accepted for publication.

In an ecstasy of fulfillment, she wrote everyone. "Patience has had its perfect work," she wrote to Mrs. Farrar. "For the sake of those who have loved and trusted me, for the sake of those who have borne my burdens with me, how I rejoice!" Congratulations came back from friends and relatives and all were sincere. "Well done!" replied Carlyle. "This must be a greater joy to you than health itself, or any other blessing; and I must say that by your steadfastness you have deserved it! . . . My incredulity of your Thesis I have never hidden from you: but I willingly vote, and have voted, you should be heard on it to full length. . . ."

The printer and publisher, who had connections with *Fraser's Magazine,* was to be Parker—"you could not have a better Publisher," Carlyle assured her—and the editor of the manuscript was to be a most precise gentleman named Bennoch. In her brief de-

lirium of happiness Delia did not wonder about—nor would she
ever be told—the actual financial circumstances behind her book's
acceptance. Hawthorne had been met everywhere with resistance
to Delia's masterwork. Yet, out of his deep concern for Delia, he
had persisted in this Herculean labor. At last the respectable
Parker had agreed to publish the book if Hawthorne would lend
his name to an introduction, and take on the burden of printing
costs. Hawthorne, although it would cost him a thousand dollars,
was amenable to both conditions, and preparations for publication went ahead.

In the six months that followed, Delia proved the most difficult
of authors. She blocked Bennoch and Parker at every turn. They
wished to call the volume *The Shakespeare Problem Solved.*
Delia objected and supplied a new title with each new month.
Until the eleventh hour, there was no agreement and the book
was without a name. To the despair of her editor, she would not
delete or rewrite one sentence, let alone a chapter. "Every leaf
and line was sacred," Hawthorne deplored, "for all had been
written under so deep a conviction of truth as to assume, in her
eyes, the aspect of inspiration. A practiced book-maker, with entire control of her materials, would have shaped out a duodecimo
volume full of eloquence and ingenious dissertation. . . . There
was a great amount of rubbish, which any competent editor
would have shoveled out of the way. But Miss Bacon thrust the
whole bulk of inspiration and nonsense into the press in a
lump. . . ."

As to a preface by Hawthorne, Delia had hoped for one in the
beginning and Parker had insisted upon it, but now unexpectedly
she was determined that her book should stand alone. She had
read Hawthorne's generous foreword, and she disapproved. She
would gladly dedicate the book to him, but she would not accept
his patronage in print.

Bennoch and Parker pleaded with her. Hawthorne, exasperated, wrote: "I utterly despair of being able to satisfy you with a
preface." He wanted no dedication. The foreword was a condition of publication. The foreword was favorable in every way. He
told her that he had "merely refrained from expressing a full conviction of the truth of your theory. But the book will be in the
hands of the public. Let the public judge; as it must. Nothing
that I could say, beforehand, could influence its judgment; and I

do not agree with your opinion that I have said anything likely to prevent your cause being heard." He suggested arbitration by Carlyle. Delia turned a deaf ear to his entreaties. Even though the book was already set in type, Parker would not proceed unless Delia approved of the preface. She refused and Parker, enraged, withdrew from the project entirely.

Overnight her book was adrift again, and this brought Delia sharply to her senses. Terrified, she wrote Bennoch that she had changed her mind. Hawthorne's preface would be completely acceptable. But Parker wanted no more to do with Miss Bacon. The weary Bennoch, undoubtedly encouraged by the incredibly patient Hawthorne, turned elsewhere for a publisher. By rare good fortune, he found one in the smaller firm of Groombridge and Sons, which promptly took over the final printing and binding of the book.

Meanwhile, assured that her theory would soon be presented to the waiting world, Delia busied herself in Stratford with her last great enterprise. If she could now verify her writings with documentary evidence unearthed from Shakespeare's grave, her book would be a sensation and she would be crowned with immortality. She prepared for her "experiment" by making a preliminary visit to the Holy Trinity Church, hastily surveying Shakespeare's burial place in the chancel, and then asking a cleric of the church when the fewest visitors and tourists were about. He advised her as to the best day, and a week later she returned at eight o'clock in the morning and hovered near the grave of the Bard, awaiting a moment when she might privately examine the flagstone over the coffin more closely. But there were at least twenty visitors during the day, and Delia was at no time alone. She asked the cleric whether it was permissible to return during the evening hours. The cleric had no objection.

At seven o'clock one evening, accompanied by Mrs. Terrett, in whom she had confided her daring purpose, Delia went back to the church. The cleric was waiting with a candle. Delia and Mrs. Terrett went inside, though the elderly widow was much frightened. "I told her I was not in the least afraid," Delia related to Hawthorne. "I only wanted her to help me a little. So I groped my way to the chancel, and she waited till the light was struck. I had a dark lantern like Guy Fawkes, and some other articles which might have been considered suspicious if the police had come upon us. The cleric was getting uneasy, and I found he had followed us. . . ." The cleric was persuaded to take Mrs. Terrett outside and leave Delia in the chancel by herself. She was left alone only after she promised not to disturb the grave or do anything that might cost the cleric his job.

For the first time, Delia was able to examine the flagstone over Shakespeare's coffin. Lord Bacon had directed her to search beneath "stones." Now, she worried lest there be other stones under the top flagstone. If so, there would be room for little else beyond the wooden coffin. She was alone for three hours, poking about in the crevices around the flagstone, judging its weight, peering up at Shakespeare's bust lost in the darkness. The creak of a shoe on the floor told her that she was being watched. The worried cleric had reappeared. At last she confessed to the bewildered church officer what her real purpose was—and he, troubled, begged her to consult his vicar.

The vicar proved most considerate. He did not blench when he heard Delia's request. Solemnly he heard her out. When she was done he did not say No. "I cannot help fancying," said Hawthorne, "that her familiarity with the events of Shakespeare's life, and of his death and burial (of which she would speak as if she had been present at the edge of the grave), and all the history, literature and personalities of the Elizabethan age, together with the prevailing power of her own belief, and the eloquence with which she knew how to enforce it, had really gone some little way toward making a convert of the good clergyman." The vicar replied that he could not, under any circumstances, permit Delia to undertake the removal of the flagstone in private. However, it might possibly be permitted in his presence, if she vowed not to touch the coffin itself. At any rate, he wanted time to think about it and to consult with a Stratford lawyer who was a personal friend.

In a few days the vicar reported his decision to Delia. While he doubted that her experiment would prove anything, he saw no reason to prevent it. She could go ahead immediately, and search beneath the flagstone as he stood by, but she must guarantee to leave no "trace of harm." Whether the vicar was merely humoring her, hoping she would withdraw her request, or whether he sincerely meant to give her the chance to prove her theory, will never be known. For on the brink of discovery, at the moment of scholarly truth, she hesitated. Had Lord Bacon's cryptic message meant that she would find her confirmation in this actor's tomb—or in his own? Or had he perhaps meant that she should look in Spenser's last resting-place?

"A doubt stole into her mind whether she might not have mistaken the depository and mode of concealment of those historic treasures," Hawthorne wrote. "And after once admitting the doubt, she was afraid to hazard the shock of uplifting the stone and finding nothing. She examined the surface of the gravestone, and endeavored, without stirring it, to estimate whether it were of such thickness as to be capable of containing the archives of the Elizabethan club. She went over anew the proofs, the clues, the enigmas, the pregnant sentences, which she had discovered in Bacon's letters and elsewhere, and now was frightened to perceive that they did not point so definitely to Shakespeare's tomb as she had heretofore supposed. . . ."

She did not go to the vicar again. Instead, she began to haunt the church by night. Lantern in hand, she would make her way down the aisle to the grave and sit there staring at it. The age-worn curse leered up at her, and challenged her, but she did not accept its dare. She was afraid. And she was weary beyond all human weariness. Soon, her mind was made up. Her frail hands need not move Shakespeare's bones. Her book would accomplish the task far better.

In the first week of April 1857, the book, the product of years of privation, obsession, and hope, appeared at last. It was entitled *The Philosophy of the Plays of Shakspere Unfolded by Delia Bacon . . . with a Preface by Nathaniel Hawthorne, Author of "The Scarlet Letter," Etc.* The title page carried a quotation from a work by Lord Bacon, as well as quotations from *Love's Labour's Lost* and *The Tempest* (the last echoing Prospero's words: "Untie the spell"). One thousand copies of the huge volume—Delia devoted 100 pages to a statement of her general proposition and 582 pages to her text—were printed. Half bore the imprint of Groombridge and Sons, Paternoster Row, London, and at Hawthorne's suggestion the other half bore the imprint of Ticknor and Fields, Boston, so that his American publisher could sell the book in the United States.

The preface by Hawthorne, to which Delia had so strenuously objected, was devoted largely to quotations from Delia's earlier writings. For the rest, Hawthorne's pen treated his charge with consideration and courtliness. "My object," he wrote, "has been merely to speak a few words, which might, perhaps, serve the purpose of placing my countrywoman upon a ground of amicable understanding with the public. She has a vast preliminary difficulty to encounter. The first feeling of every reader must be one of absolute repugnance towards a person who seeks to tear out of the Anglo-Saxon heart the name which for ages it has held dearest. . . . After listening to the author's interpretation of the Plays, and seeing how wide a scope she assigns to them, how high a purpose, and what richness of inner meaning, the thoughtful reader will hardly return again—not wholly, at all events—to the common view of them and of their author. It is for the public to say whether my countrywoman has proved her theory. In the worst event, if she has failed, her failure will be more honorable than most people's triumphs; since it must fling upon the old tombstone, at Stratford-on-Avon, the noblest tributary wreath that has ever lain there."

Then followed, in almost seven hundred labored pages, the unfolding of a theory that might better have been told in one hundred pages. As Sophia Hawthorne remarked privately, "Miss Bacon cannot speak out fairly though there is neither the Tower, the scaffold, nor the pile of fagots to deter her."

The first chapter was called "The Proposition," and in its opening lines Delia grandly revealed her ultimate purpose: "This work is designed to propose to the consideration not of the learned world only, but of all ingenuous and practical minds, a new development of that system of practical philosophy from which THE SCIENTIFIC ARTS of the Modern Ages proceed. . . ." Ostensibly she was more concerned with the hidden meanings that permeated Shakespeare's plays than with identifying their true author. "The question of the authorship of the great philosophic poems which are the legacy of the Elizabethan Age to us, is an incidental question in this inquiry, and is incidentally treated here." This secret philosophy lurking beneath the surface of the so-called Shakespearean plays did not come of "unconscious spontaneity," but rather was the clever product of a "reflective, deliberative, eminently deliberative, eminently conscious, designing mind." The mind was really several minds "under whose patronage and in whose service 'Will the Jester' first showed himself."

The round table of radicals concerned with the welfare of the nation was led by Bacon and Raleigh, and included also Sir Philip Sidney, Lord Buckhurst, Lord Paget, and the Earl of Oxford. Edmund Spenser, though not highborn, was much admired by the others for *The Shepheardes Calender*, brought out in 1579, and he was invited to join the group. According to Delia, one critic of the time, unnamed, who praised Spenser as well as Sidney and Raleigh, hinted at this "courtly company" and added mysteriously: "They have writ excellently well, if their doings could be found out and made public with the rest." It was Bacon who had the idea of employing popular plays as a medium of propagandizing the masses. Delia explained his plan: "The Method of Progression, as set forth by Lord Bacon, requires that the new scientific truth shall be, not nakedly and flatly, but artistically exhibited; because, as he tells us, 'the great labour is with the people, and this people who knoweth not the law are cursed.' He will not have it exhibited in bare propositions, but translated into the people's dialect." Yes, the plays would be the medium, but their real meaning must not be too readily apparent and their authorship must not be revealed. "It was a time . . . when a *'nom de plume'* was required for other purposes than to serve as the refuge of an author's modesty, or vanity, or caprice. It was a time when puns, and charades, and enigmas, and anagrams, and monograms, and ciphers, and puzzles, were not good for sport and child's play merely. . . ." In fact, it was Delia who introduced the whole possibility of ciphers into the Bacon-Shakespeare controversy. According to Vivian C. Hopkins, in her scholarly *Prodigal Puritan*, Delia could not endure studying Lord Bacon's *Letters* because they were shallow and employed the obsequious flatteries of a sycophant. Yet, what if these letters camouflaged a cipher? Then Bacon could again be considered the genius that Delia wanted him to be.

"This idea gains some slight support," wrote Vivian C. Hopkins, "from Bacon's mention of a cipher which he invented in Paris (specifically for diplomatic correspondence), and considered a perfect device: it signified 'omnia per omnia,' and simply used five times as many letters in the cipher as in the hidden message. However dubious the honor, Delia must be credited as the originator of this notion, which sent some later Baconians into a frenzy of mathematical computations, to discover concealed secrets (especially signatures) in the Folio."

When the dangerously revolutionary plays, with their ciphers and anagrams and hidden meanings, were written, they required only some innocent to pretend to their authorship. Then it was, Delia suggested, that Ben Jonson introduced the actor and theater-manager, Shakespeare, to this "courtly company" of conspiring authors. And then it was that the "Stratford poacher," that member of the Lord Chamberlain's Men, a "dirty, doggish group of players," was pushed to the fore as the creator of the plays.

In chapter after chapter, Delia reiterated and expanded her proposition, analyzing various Shakespearean plays and exposing the secrets they hid and yet propounded. Her dissection of *King Lear* was typical: "It is all one picture of social ignorance, and misery, and *frantic* misrule. It is a faithful exhibition of the degree of personal security which a man of honourable sentiments, and humane and noble intentions, could promise himself in such a time. . . . To appreciate fully the incidental and immediate political application of the piece, however, it is necessary to observe that notwithstanding that studious exhibition of lawless and outrageous power, which it involves, it is, after all, we are given to understand, by a quiet intimation here and there, *a limited monarchy* which is put upon the stage here. . . . It is a government which professes to be one of law, under which the atrocities of this piece are sheltered. And one may even note, in passing, that that high Judicial Court, in which poor Lear undertakes to get his cause tried, appears to have, somehow, an extremely modern air. . . ." This play, and the companion plays, were part of a "great scientific enterprise," and "this enterprise was not the product of a single individual mind."

Delia's book was before the public. For even the most determined reader it was a formidable package. While its pages contained colorful writing, and wit, and sound literary criticism, the best of this was lost in a swamp of garrulous redundancy. The style was agitated and insistent. To be trapped in mid-page was like being caught in the center of an armed riot. The reader, cudgeled and bloodied by repetitive argument, staggered into long passages that led on and on but arrived nowhere. Delia's evaluation of Elizabethan literature was often profound, but her theory of joint authorship for the plays was lost in a maze of verbosity.

The theory was there in print, nevertheless, and Shakespeare scholars were outraged. Later, scholars were to dismiss the book as the product of a deranged mind, referring, of course, to its author's eventual lapse into insanity. To this, the indignant Ignatius Donnelly would reply that advocates of Shakespeare were as susceptible to lunacy as confirmed Baconians. And Donnelly would be able to cite the example of George H. Townsend, who was the first to come to Shakespeare's defense after the publication of Delia's book. Townsend, too, lost his mind, and he eventually died by his own hand.

The Philosophy of the Plays of Shakspere Unfolded had been "the world's work," and it was now before the world for judgment.

First came the reactions of the English critics, and they were, not unexpectedly, cruel. The reviewers, Bennoch wrote Delia, "are busy with it, but they seem to be bothered with it. They cannot make it out." Said *The National Review*: "She deals only in the vaguest generalities, dim hints, obscure probabilities; the slightest approach to particulars would shatter her dreams. . . . She never makes direct assertions, or draws precise deductions, but deals in hints and innuendoes, and is in mortal fear of being too plain." *The Athenaeum*, tongue in cheek, referred to Delia as a "literary Columbus." But had she offered any concrete proof to support her Baconian theory? "None!" roared *The Athenaeum*. To this, *The Leader* added: "We are a little puzzled . . . to know what was Bacon's share and what Raleigh's in the authorship of *Shakspeare*; at all events, it seems *Shakspeare* was not written by Colley Cibber."

Second, there was the reaction of the general reading public in Great Britain and in the United States. And third, there were the American critics to be heard from. It was Hawthorne who recorded the overall impact of that "ponderous octavo volume, which fell with a dead thump at the feet of the public, and has never been picked up. A few persons turned over one or two of the leaves, as it lay there, and essayed to kick the volume deeper into the mud; for they were the hack critics of the minor periodical press in London. . . . From the scholars and critics of her own country, indeed, Miss Bacon might have looked for a worthier appreciation. . . . But they are not a courageous body of men; they dare not think a truth that has an odor of absurdity, lest they should feel themselves bound to speak it out. If any American ever wrote a word in her behalf, Miss Bacon never knew it, nor did I. Our journalists at once republished some of the most brutal vituperations of the English press, thus pelting their poor countrywoman with stolen mud, without even waiting to know whether the ignominy was deserved."

The book had one distinction: It was the first of its kind. But even that celebrity was quickly challenged. In 1856, while Delia's book was still on the presses, a cheerful, forty-four-year-old Englishman named William Henry Smith offered to read to his debating society a paper espousing Bacon's authorship of Shakespeare's plays. Fellow members objected, but John Stuart Mill supported his right to be heard. Smith read his paper, which emphasized the parallel passages in Bacon and Shakespeare, and he argued that Bacon's known cultural background and creative talent made him a more likely candidate for authorship of the plays. Smith had this paper printed, and a copy was sent to Lord Ellesmere, head of England's Shakespearean Society. A year later Smith expanded his paper into a modestly priced booklet entitled *Bacon and Shakespeare: An Enquiry Touching Players, Playhouses and Play-Writers in the Days of Elizabeth.* While this publication made a convert of Lord Palmerston, it made an enemy of Delia Bacon. She screamed plagiarism. She insisted that Smith had pirated her article in *Putnam's Magazine.* Hawthorne wrote Smith on Delia's behalf. Smith proved that his advocacy of Bacon was not plagiarism but coincidence, and all hands agreed that Delia had been the first in the field.

Today, over a century later, most American reference volumes bestow upon Delia the appellation of pioneer. *American Authors* calls her the first Baconian. The *Dictionary of American Biography* says of her book: "To its author remains the credit, or discredit, of having first inaugurated the most absurd, and, in other hands, the most popular, of literary heresies." And literary historian Van Wyck Brooks refers to her as "the originator of the 'Shakespeare-Bacon' movement."

Upon its publication, however, it seemed doubtful that Delia's book would pioneer anything, for it seemed doubtful that anyone had read the entire work. "I believe that it has been the fate of this remarkable book never to have had more than a single reader," said Hawthorne. "I myself am acquainted with it only in insulated chapters and scattered pages and paragraphs. But since my return to America a young man of genius and enthusiasm has assured me that he has positively read the book from beginning to end, and is completely a convert to its doctrines."

Of course, Hawthorne was being facetious. He knew that the book had had more than "a single reader," for his own wife, Sophia, had read it through before publication. The "single reader" referred to by Hawthorne, the "young man of genius and enthusiasm" who became Delia's first convert, was William Douglas O'Connor of Boston. O'Connor was a clever and perceptive journalist who was discharged by the *Saturday Evening Post* for too staunchly defending John Brown in print. He held several government jobs, notably with the Light House Board and the Life Saving Service. He was the first to champion Walt Whitman and to call him "the good gray poet," and in 1860 he was the first to champion Delia Bacon. In his novel, *Harrington: A Story of True Love*—"a fiery and eloquent novel," Whitman called it— O'Connor's abolitionist hero believed in Delia's theory. And at the end of the book O'Connor paid tribute to Delia's brilliance. Two more books, these devoted to factual arguments in favor of the Baconian theory, followed in the next nine years.

O'Connor was not the only person of perspicacity to read Delia's book and become converted to her views. Two of the most famous converts were Ignatius Donnelly and Mark Twain. When Donnelly was preparing his 998-page *The Great Cryptogram,* he wanted to include a portrait of Delia in it. Her family refused to provide him with a picture because, said Donnelly, "They do not *want her identified with the theory that Francis Bacon wrote the Shakespeare plays!*" Yet, Donnelly added, the entire Bacon family would be remembered in future years only because of Delia's theory. Mark Twain admitted that he had read Delia's book the year after its publication while he was an apprentice pilot on the Mississippi, and he had become a believer. The pilot Twain worked under, George Ealer, worshiped Shakespeare and regarded Delia as a demon. "Did he have something to say—this Shakespeare-adoring Mississippi pilot—anent Delia Bacon's book?" asked Twain. "Yes. And he said it; said it all the time, for months—in the morning watch, the middle watch, the dog watch; and probably kept it going in his sleep."

If only a few read the book, they were enough. They read it and they argued about it, and the controversy grew and spread. One hundred years later Delia's heresy continued to intrigue, to fascinate, to excite, to anger, to amuse. It is said that James Russell Lowell once remarked that Delia "had opened a question that would never be closed." In 1946, a Northwestern University professor who was preparing a complete bibliography of publications concerning "the Shakespeare authorship and identity controversies" found that his list of titles ran to fifteen hundred manuscript pages. By 1970, there were thought to be five thousand published books and articles, in more than a dozen languages, that challenged Shakespeare's authorship of the plays and variously supported fifty-seven other Elizabethans as the true author. And of the fifty-seven candidates, Delia's nomination of Sir Francis Bacon and his syndicate was a conservative choice. The competitors included Queen Elizabeth I; John Florio, the son of an Italian refugee and secretary of Shakespeare's patron, the Earl of Southampton; Anne Whateley of Temple Gardens, who was possibly an English nun, or who was Anne Hathaway herself, whose name had been coupled with the Bard's in a 1582 Episcopal register; and a group of sixteenth-century English Jesuits who wrote the plays and used Shakespeare's name because it was similar to the name of their idol, Nicholas Breakspear, who, as Adrian IV, had been the only Englishman ever to become Pope of Rome.

Dozens of the Shakespeare dissenters who followed in Delia Bacon's footsteps—writers, scholars, lawyers, eccentrics—were oblivious of her existence. Many others knew to whom they owed their ideas, but preferred to ignore the pioneer. And when she died insane, Delia's memory became an embarrassment to the movement she had inspired. But there can be little doubt that in the decades since Delia's death almost every new theory concerning the authorship of the Shakespeare plays has owed its inception, either directly or indirectly, to her sturdy, unreadable book.

Most of those who have challenged Shakespeare since 1856 have followed Delia's lead by questioning whether the "old Player" had time for creative work. In 1879, *Appleton's Journal* would remind its readers: "Let any one try to conceive of the busy manager of a theatre, who succeeded by vigilance, exact accounting, business sagacity and prudence, in securing and saving not only a competency, but a fair fortune; in the meantime, while engaged in this engrossment of business, writing Isabel's magnificent appeal to the duke's deputy, Angelo, or Cardinal Wolsey's last soliloquy! or conceive of the man who gave the wife of his youth an old bedstead and sued a neighbor for corn delivered, penning Antony's oration before Caesar."

Thus, in 1909, Mark Twain, still under Delia's spell, would point an accusing finger at Shakespeare's will: "It was eminently and conspicuously a businessman's will, not a poet's. It mentioned *not a single book*. Books were much more precious than swords and silver-gilt bowls and second-best beds in those days, and when a departing person owned one he gave it a high place in his will. The will mentioned *not a play, not a poem, not an unfinished literary work, not a scrap of manuscript of any kind*. Many poets have died poor, but this is the only one in history that has died *this* poor. . . ." Furthermore, "When Shakespeare died in Stratford *it was not an event*. It made no more stir in England than the death of any other forgotten theatre-actor would have made. Nobody came down from London; there were no lamenting poems, no eulogies, no national tears—there was merely silence, and nothing more. A striking contrast with what happened when Ben Jonson, and Francis Bacon, and Spenser, and Raleigh and the other distinguished literary folk of Shakespeare's time passed from life!"

Thus, in 1931, Bertram G. Theobald would ask readers in *Exit Shakspere*, as Delia had asked before him, many pointed questions about the Bard. If, as most Shakespearean scholars agree, he was little educated when he arrived in London at the age of twenty-three, when did he acquire the learning needed to write the poems and plays? Why did the theater owner, Philip Henslowe, whose diary alluded to most of the great dramatists of the day, never refer to Shakespeare? Why did Richard Burbage, the great actor, never mention Shakespeare as an author? How could Shakespeare have acquired so vast a legal background? How could Shakespeare have written so knowledgeably of Italy, France, Spain, Denmark, when there is no record that he ever traveled abroad? Why has nothing been found in Shakespeare's handwriting, except six of his signatures—three on his will—and these plainly the signatures of an illiterate?

But to destroy Shakespeare was not enough, as Delia foresaw. It was necessary, by all the rules of logic, to discover the real author or authors. Only a few theorists supported her idea of group authorship. Of these, the most prominent was Gilbert Slater who, in 1931, published his *Seven Shakespeares*. This book contended that Bacon, Raleigh, Paget, Buckhurst, Marlowe, and the Countess of Pembroke, under the leadership of Edward de Vere, the Earl of Oxford, had collaborated on the plays for which Shakespeare took credit. Slater based his case on the provocative fact that the Earl of Oxford had received an annual pension of one thousand pounds from a secret fund set up by Queen Elizabeth. This sum, he speculated, was used to pay the syndicate for creating propaganda favorable to the queen—quite the reverse of Delia Bacon's contention that a similar syndicate had toiled, instead, to undermine the queen.

The great majority of theorists, however, favored one pretender —and the pretender they favored most was Sir Francis Bacon. Delia had, of course, made her strongest case for Bacon, and William Henry Smith had been right behind her. Now came the deluge. Few Baconians augmented their assaults on Shakespeare with factual deduction. One of those who did was Theobald, who in 1932 put forth Bacon as his choice on the grounds that the man was a genius who liked to call himself "a concealed poet." Furthermore, Shakespeare was dead (and Bacon very much alive) when the First Folio came out in 1623, and with its appearance, the public had six absolutely new plays and 193 lines done in faultless style added to *Richard III*. Also, Bacon's private notebook of jottings—sixteen hundred items in all—was not published until long after Shakespeare's death, though the man who was Shakespeare used many of these jottings in the plays.

Most Baconians were less restrained. They chose to arm themselves with every freakish literary weapon available. Except for her interest in the use of a secret cipher, Delia had scorned such weapons. "She never devoted herself to whims or fancies about capital letters," her nephew said, "or irregular pagination, or acrostics, or anagrams, as concealing yet expressing the great philosophy which the plays inclosed."

In 1888, just six years after publishing a novel supporting Plato's story of the sunken Atlantis, the irrepressible Ignatius Donnelly, who was to be known as the "Apostle of Protest," brought out *The Great Cryptogram*. Following a study of the First Folio, in which he found pages irregularly numbered, words unnaturally hyphenated, and abnormal columns of print, Donnelly became convinced that Bacon had been the true author of the plays. By tracking down key words like "volume" and "maske" in *The Second Part of Henry IV*, and by an ingenious method of word counting, Donnelly felt that he had proved Bacon's hidden authorship.

Six years later, a Detroit physician named Orville W. Owen carried the cipher method to an even greater extreme. After constructing a ponderous wooden deciphering machine—which consisted of two wheels mounted five feet apart, to which were attached a thousand feet of canvas bearing pages cut from Shakespeare's plays—Owen hunted out all occurrences of four guide words: *honour, fortune, reputation,* and *nature.* By examining the dialogue built around these four words, Owen discovered not only that Bacon had written Shakespeare but that he had also written the complete works of Marlowe, Spenser, Burton, and several other Elizabethan authors. Furthermore, Owen's remarkable contraption ground out titillating historic gossip: that Queen Elizabeth had secretly married Dudley, that Bacon was their son, that Bacon had murdered Shakespeare to put an end to the Bard's attempts at blackmail.

But the cipher was only one weapon employed against Shakespeare. There were many others almost as imaginative. In 1906, Edwin Reed, using coincidence as his divining rod, sought out the obvious parallels in Bacon and Shakespeare. He found, for example, that Shakespeare's plays mentioned Julius Caesar thirty-nine times, while Bacon's writings mentioned Caesar thirty-four times. He found that whereas Shakespeare had named one of his most memorable characters Falstaff, Bacon had once had an associate named Halstaff. He found that in *King Henry VI*, Shakespeare had set thirty scenes in London, three in St. Albans, twenty in France—yet, Bacon, not Shakespeare, was the one who had been born in London, raised in St. Albans, employed in France.

In 1910, Sir Edwin Durning-Lawrence, in support of his book *Bacon Is Shakespeare,* employed anagrams to defend Bacon's authorship of the Shakespeare plays. Sir Edwin pointed out that in Shakespeare's *Love's Labour's Lost* there appears the head-spinning medieval Latin word *honorificabilitudinitatibus* and that the anagram of this word spells out in Latin, "*Hi Ludi F.*

Baconis Nati Tuiti Orbi" or "These plays, offspring of F. Bacon,
are preserved for the world."

In 1922, Walter Conrad Arensberg, a wealthy Los Angeles
chess expert whose modern art collection was one of the most valuable in America, extended the use of anagrams and acrostics
even further while expounding the case for Sir Francis Bacon.
After employing these methods, Arensberg insisted that he had
located five hundred mentions of Bacon's name in the Shakespeare plays. Eight years later, he discovered a "magic ring" in a
Dürer print, and by mating the cells of this ring to chess symbols,
Arensberg was able to tell the public that Bacon was directly
descended from King Henry VI and therefore a claimant to the
British throne. Arensberg's advocacy of Bacon was so keen that,
on learning his idol's tomb might be opened, he prepared to lease
a direct wire from Los Angeles to London in order to be informed
immediately of any corroboration from the grave—but, in the
end, the tomb remained closed.

While the dazzling ingenuity of the Baconians was often much
admired and was subscribed to by a host of renowned persons—
not only Mark Twain, but also Otto von Bismarck, Walt Whitman, Henry James, Sigmund Freud—still, industrious and out-
spoken skeptics were always ready to defend Jonson's "Star of
Poets." On one occasion George Bernard Shaw took the time to
invent a cipher by which he proved to the world that *he* had written all of Shakespeare's plays. On another occasion, when Albert
Boni, the American publisher, was about to underwrite a Baconian cipher system that miraculously revealed the true authorship
of the Shakespearean plays, an office boy in the firm applied the
cipher to the *Daily Racing Form* and proved that Bacon had written that, too.

Then, in 1957, William F. and Elizebeth S. Friedman attempted
to put the cipher theorists to rout forever in their book, *The Shakespearean Ciphers Examined*. It might be added that William Friedman's credentials were of the best. As a cryptologist, he had
headed the United States government team that broke the Japanese military purple code just before Pearl Harbor. Where Ignatius Donnelly had taken a specific Shakespeare passage and
deciphered it to read that Marlowe and Shakespeare "never writ a
word of them," the Friedmans took the very same passage and
deciphered it to read, "Master Will I Am Shak'st spurre writ the

play." Where Walter Arensberg deciphered Jonson's poem, "To the Readers," in the First Folio to disclose a Bacon signature concealed within it, the Friedmans used the same method to show that Jonson's poem concealed the message, "I and onlie I, Will Shakespeare, was the author of these old plaies." In defending Shakespeare, the Friedmans concluded: "We suggest that those who wish to dispute the authorship of his plays should not in future resort to cryptographic evidence, unless they show themselves in some way competent to do so."

While the Friedmans struck a telling blow at the Baconians, Delia had offered other candidates as well, and in the century following the publication of her book, many anti-Shakespeare theorists had begun to think along her lines. However, except for the strong support thrown behind the Earl of Oxford, who had been included in Delia's syndicate, most of these theorists backed Elizabethans whom Delia had discounted or overlooked. In 1912, Professor Celestin Demblon, of Belgium, suggested Roger Manners, fifteenth Earl of Rutland, for whom Shakespeare had a shield painted in 1613. In 1919, Professor Abel Lefranc, of France, suggested William Stanley, sixth Earl of Derby, who lived for a quarter of a century after Shakespeare's death. In 1920, J. Thomas Looney, a schoolteacher—and in 1959, Charlton Ogburn, an attorney, and his wife Dorothy—suggested Edward de Vere, seventeenth Earl of Oxford. De Vere had entered Cambridge before he was nine years old, helped fight the Spanish Armada, was a lawyer, traveled to Italy, wrote comedies for the royal court, directed two groups of players, and published twenty-four lyric poems. In 1943, Alden Brooks suggested Sir Edward Dyer, who was a Rosicrucian, an alchemist, a favorite of Queen Elizabeth, and "our only Inglishe poett," according to Spenser. In 1955, Calvin Hoffman suggested (though his candidacy had been proposed before) Christopher Marlowe.

In the face of this continuing dissidence, the true believers fought back with conviction and logic. From the moment of Delia's original attack, the defenders of the Bard had rallied to preserve his name and status. Most defenders felt that Delia and her converts persisted in denying to Shakespeare one obvious asset—genius. As John Mackinnon Robertson wrote of the Baconians: "A kind of thesis which finds its motive in the assumed improbability of the possession of abnormal literary genius by an actor who had left school at 14, has accumulated through all its variants a mass of improbabilities not to be matched in speculative research on any other field."

Admitting that Shakespeare's origins were lowly, that his formal education was limited, that his background lacked nobility—were these facts enough to bar him from authorship of the plays? "This respect for the literary value of noble birth is impressive in its unanimity," remarked Marchette Chute, "but a little hard to explain logically, since the most learned of Elizabethan dramatists was a bricklayer, and the most poetic, next to Shakespeare, was the son of a cobbler." Too, had not Ben Jonson noted that Shakespeare knew at least "small Latin"? If no English university recorded his attendance, neither did it record the attendance of Jonson himself, or Henry Chettle, or Thomas Kyd. If Shakespeare had no legal training to explain the knowledge of law displayed in his plays, neither had Jonson or George Chapman, both of whom wrote plays that exhibited a far more extensive knowledge of law.

In Shakespeare's lifetime, fifteen plays appeared bearing his name. For most authors this would have been sufficient evidence of authorship. Why not for Shakespeare? During the Bard's lifetime, Francis Meres, in his book *Palladis Tamia, Wits Treasury*, and Ben Jonson, who said he "lov'd the man" and placed him in the company of Aeschylus, Euripides, and Sophocles, acknowledged his existence and praised his output. For most authors this would have been sufficient evidence of fame. Why not for Shakespeare? Robert Greene, dissolute rake and brilliant poet, playwright and pamphleteer, attacked Shakespeare in his posthumously printed pamphlet, *Groats-worth of Wit*, obliquely stating that a certain "Shakescene" had plagiarized ideas from Greene's own works. This attack, against any other playwright, would have been proof of his creativity. Why not of Shakespeare's? And when the First Folio was published some years after the Bard's death, it contained an engraving of him made by Martin Droeshout, while the parish church in Stratford erected a bust created by the brothers Johnson, a London tomb-making firm. For most authors these would have been sufficient evidences of honor and tribute paid by friends and admirers. Why not for Shakespeare?

As for the usurpers, their cases were often weaker than Shakespeare's. Unless there was a conspiracy, as Delia thought, why need any nobleman hide behind the name of Shakespeare? In the Elizabethan period, most noblemen were freely writing and publishing under their own names. If anyone had used the name of Shakespeare as a disguise, how (in that tight, gossipy little world of the London theater) could that secret have been kept from all men at all times? And what about the candidates themselves? Were their qualifications perfect? If Bacon knew more about the nobility and law than Shakespeare, he knew less about country life, glove-making, and architecture, three subjects which are to be found in the plays. If the Earl of Rutland had written the plays, then he had started writing them at the age of fourteen, and if Sir Edward Dyer had written them, he had begun at the age of forty-six. As to the Earl of Oxford, whose surviving work shows no humor, whose life exhibited only arrogance and extravagance, and whose experience was for the most part confined to the narrow court circle, he had expired seven years before many of Shakespeare's greatest plays were presented.

Frank Ernest Hill has summarized the pro-Shakespeare position admirably in *To Meet Will Shakespeare*: "The Shakespeare case is supported by many facts and specific comments. The evidence for it is direct, and it is great both in volume and in variety. In contrast, all other cases are 'if' cases. . . . Not one clear statement from a seventeenth-century writer or other person in a position to know says 'Oxford (or Bacon or Derby or Rutland) wrote the works supposed to be William Shakespeare's.' "

But in April 1857, the forty-six-year-old Delia Bacon could not begin to imagine the literary stir her volume would one day provoke. In fact, she knew little of the reception it was accorded in the British press, or how poorly it was selling in her own time. Ill, exhausted, inert, she dwelt now with a friendly shoemaker and his family in Stratford, paying them seven shillings a week and trying them sorely with her recurring hallucinations. To her brother Leonard, with whom she had become reconciled, she wrote: "Having fulfilled my work as I thought . . . I have not cared to know the result. Since the day I heard it was published I have made no inquiry on the subject. . . . I am calm and happy. I do not want to come back to America."

Two months after the publication of the book, Hawthorne received a short letter, directed to him in Liverpool, from David Rice, a physician who was also mayor of Stratford. Rice wrote that he was attending Miss Bacon and was much concerned: "She is in a very excited and unsatisfactory state, especially mentally, and I think there is much reason to fear that she will become decidedly insane."

Hawthorne had not been in touch with Delia since the disagreement over the preface—in almost her last letter to him she had said that he was "unworthy to meddle with her work." Nevertheless, he immediately assumed responsibility for her welfare. He asked Rice to provide for her and charge all expenses to him. He wrote to the Reverend Leonard Bacon, informing him of her condition and asking his advice. Bacon replied: "The crisis at which my sister's case has arrived, requires me to say, plainly, that in my opinion her mind has been 'verging on insanity' for the last six years. . . . My fear has been, all along, that whenever and wherever her book might be published, the disappointment of that long and confident expectation would be disastrous if not fatal to her." He agreed that Delia must be returned to her family in America.

While Dr. Rice saw to it that she had adequate care for the moment, Hawthorne went ahead with preparations for her transportation home. But it was too late. Delia's condition had worsened. She could no longer travel alone. And unfortunately, Hawthorne soon would be unable to assist her. His consulship at Liverpool, which he had come to detest, was being ended at his own request, and he had arranged to spend a year and a half in the "poetic fairy precinct" of Italy. By December Delia's insanity had become sufficiently acute to necessitate her removal to a private insane asylum at Henley in Arden, eight miles outside Stratford. There, in the forest of Arden, she remained confined for over three months.

In March 1857, twenty-one-year-old George Bacon, a son of the Reverend Leonard Bacon, arrived in England on an American frigate after two years spent in and about China. He was hurrying back to America, but he remembered that he had an ailing aunt in Stratford and went to call upon her. When he learned that she had been removed to an insane asylum in Henley, he was shocked. Without consulting his elders, he determined to take Delia home where she belonged. He delayed his passage one week, secured his aunt's release from the asylum, packed her onto a vessel, and, on April 13, 1858, led her down the gangplank in New York.

Her family placed her in a sanitarium called The Retreat, which was located in Hartford, Connecticut. Her brothers and sisters and their children were in constant attendance upon her. She sank deeper and deeper into the distorted regions of unreality. But in a few last lucid moments she recognized the members of her family and spoke to them happily and warmly. She asked to be shown a picture of her beloved father. Not once did she mention William Shakespeare.

On September 2, 1859, the Reverend Leonard Bacon wrote that at the age of forty-eight "she died, clearly and calmly trusting in Christ, and thankful to escape from tribulation and enter into rest." She was buried in the old cemetery at New Haven, and over her grave was placed a brown cross inscribed with the words "So He bringeth them to their desired haven." This was decent, and it was kind, but it was not enough. There was one more thing to be said, and four years later, in his autobiographical volume *Our Old Home,* Nathaniel Hawthorne said it:

"No author had ever hoped so confidently as she; none ever failed more utterly. A superstitious fancy might suggest that the anathema on Shakespeare's tombstone had fallen heavily on her head, in requital of even the unaccomplished purpose of disturbing the dust beneath, and that the 'old Player' had kept so quietly in his grave, on the night of her vigil, because he foresaw how soon and terribly he would be avenged. But if that benign spirit takes any care or cognizance of such things now, he has surely requited the injustice that she sought to do him—the high justice that she really did—by a tenderness of love and pity of which only he could be capable. What matters it though she called him by some other name? He had wrought a greater miracle on her than all the world besides. This bewildered enthusiast had recognized a depth in the man whom she decried, which scholars, critics, and learned societies devoted to the elucidation of his unrivalled scenes, had never imagined to exist there. She had paid him the loftiest honor that all these ages of renown have been able to accumulate upon his memory. And when, not many months after the outward failure of her lifelong object, she passed into the better world, I know not why we should hesitate to believe that the immortal poet may have met her on the threshold and led her in, reassuring her with friendly and comfortable words, and thanking her (yet with a smile of gentle humor in his eyes at the thought of certain mistaken speculations) for having interpreted him to mankind so well."

XVI

The Prostitute
Who Ran
for President

I am a Free Lover. I have an inalienable, constitutional, and natural right to love whom I may, to love as long or as short a period as I can, to change that love every day if I please! And with that right neither you nor any law you can frame have any right to interfere.

—VICTORIA WOODHULL

WHEN that greatest of Athenian orators, Demosthenes, after failing to lead his fellow Greeks in a successful revolt against the Macedonians, fled to a temple on the isle of Calauria and there took his life by biting off a portion of a poisoned pen, he could hardly have imagined how soon and for what purpose he would return to the earth he had so reluctantly left. Yet, more than two thousand years later, in the summer of 1868, in the unlikely city of Pittsburgh, Pennsylvania, this same Demosthenes returned to inspire another orator to undertake a revolt against puritanical convention, a revolt which would rock America for a decade and more.

The hostess to Demosthenes' resurrection and visitation was an attractive, aggressive, outrageous young lady named Victoria

Claflin Woodhull. For some years previous to this, Mrs. Woodhull, who had been reared on mesmerism and had been much addicted to trances, had consorted with an anonymous apparition clad in a Greek toga. In Ohio, California, Kansas, and Illinois, this friendly spirit-creature had materialized frequently, and each time he had promised Mrs. Woodhull future wealth and power. He answered all her questions except one. He would not reveal his identity.

But in Pittsburgh, where Mrs. Woodhull, her zestful sister, and her zany family were now earning a meager livelihood out of spiritualism, magnetic healing, cancer cures, and prostitution, the apparition in the Greek toga appeared once more and this time he revealed his identity. He traced his name, so Mrs. Woodhull later related, on a marble parlor-table, and the eerie brightness of the letters illuminated the entire gloomy room. His name was Demosthenes. And, having gone through this long-postponed formality, the old Attic orator imparted to Mrs. Woodhull a crucial instruction that was to change her life. He ordered her to proceed to a house at 17 Great Jones Street, New York City, and enter it, and occupy it, and know that thereafter only good and great events would befall her.

Not unexpectedly, Demosthenes was sufficiently persuasive to send Mrs. Woodhull scurrying to the house on Great Jones Street, near Broadway, in New York City. She found it was to let "furnished," entered it, and explored it. In the library all was in order except for one book lying open on a table. Curious, she picked up the book, glanced at the title, and what she saw, she admitted, was "blood-chilling." The book was entitled *Orations of Demosthenes*. Mrs. Woodhull promptly rented the house, sent for her relatives, and prepared to make her mark in the world.

Whether or not her next step was stimulated by a follow-up visitation from the ether world is not known. More likely, Mrs. Woodhull took her immediate future into her own hands. Her Greek vision had promised her wealth and power. She was hardheaded enough to know that these she might obtain only through use of her natural advantages, which included sex appeal, psychic experience, and unlimited audacity.

At the age of thirty, Victoria Woodhull was a handsome, clever, brash woman, who looked chic and exciting in shirtwaists and in fitted checked dresses cut daringly short (to the calves). Samuel Gompers, first president of the American Federation of Labor, remembered her as "a slight, sparkling little creature, with expressive brown eyes and short brown hair." Her sister, twenty-two-year-old Tennessee Celeste Claflin, a gay, somewhat hoydenish girl, was even more beautiful, but less intelligent, and totally uninhibited. In her own person, and in that of her younger sister, Victoria Woodhull saw sufficient combined assets for the founding of a fortune and a national reputation. The question was: Where to begin? The answer came to her immediately: Begin at the top.

In New York in 1868 the one person at the top was "Commodore" Cornelius Vanderbilt, the richest man in the United States, whose principal interests in his seventy-fourth year were females with sex appeal who were not too swift of foot, and anyone with psychic experience who would give him assurances of health and longevity. To reach him required only unlimited audacity. Undoubtedly, the idea of meeting the bluff, bewhiskered old Commodore originated in Mrs. Woodhull's fertile brain. She decided to effect the introduction through her male parent, Buckman Claflin, who, though a disreputable, one-eyed monster, was still her father and would lend to the entire enterprise an air of respectability. Thus, Mrs. Woodhull and her sister were chastely escorted to the Vanderbilt mansion in Washington Place and announced as famous miracle-healers from the Midwest.

It is not surprising that they were promptly admitted. Commodore Vanderbilt was an ailing man who had become impatient with conventional medicine and was now employing the services of a Staten Island seer and an electrical wizard to give him hope and comfort. He was ready to listen to almost any miracle worker. Mrs. Woodhull quickly explained that she was a successful medium, and that her sister Tennie was a magnetic healer who gave patients strength through physical contact. This last, as well as the provocative appearance of his fair guests, convinced the blasphemous old Commodore that he could do worse than put himself in their hands.

However, it should be remarked that Commodore Vanderbilt was neither an easy nor a pliable patient. He was tough, he was ruthless, and he was nobody's fool. He had pyramided possession of a single sailboat, purchased when he was sixteen, into a shipping company that deployed one hundred steamers along the East Coast, and parlayed that into control of the New York Central Railroad. Through instigating price wars, indulging in stock-market trickery, and bribing courts and legislatures, he had accumulated $100,000,000 in his prime, and he would increase the sum before his death. "Law?" he once bellowed. "What do I care about law? Hain't I got the power?"

As Victoria, and so many of her contemporaries knew, Commodore Vanderbilt had used this power mercilessly. When the freebooter William Walker gave him trouble in Nicaragua, the Commodore armed three Central American republics to crush Walker. When financier Daniel Drew stood in the Commodore's path, he obliterated Drew. When Jay Gould and James Fisk took advantage of him, he brought them to their knees. Once, when the Commodore was in Europe on a vacation, his bankers craftily stole control of his Accessory Transit Company. The Commodore wrote his bankers a short letter. It read, in its entirety:

Gentlemen:
You have undertaken to cheat me. I will not sue you because the law takes too long. I will ruin you.
                                    Sincerely yours.

And ruin them he most certainly did. He was as ruthless in his personal relationships. When his first wife annoyed him with her depressed moods, he tucked her into a Flushing insane asylum for two years over the protests of his family.

Obviously such a man would not be easy to please. Yet, by some alchemy of understanding, Victoria Woodhull transformed this blustering giant into an intimate friend and patron. When she realized his need for sex—indeed, few housemaids escaped his lust—she fed him the willing and vigorous Tennessee. The magnetic treatments, whereby Tennessee laid her hands on the Commodore's hands and passed electrical energy from her body into his, proceeded magnificently. Tennessee was soon installed in his bed as his mistress. He called her his "little sparrow" and she called him "old boy."

A year and a half of Tennessee's special brand of magnetic healing softened up the Commodore for Victoria Woodhull's machinations. The idea of how she might best use the Commodore came to Mrs. Woodhull from her lover of four years, a bemused Civil War veteran and fellow spiritualist named Colonel James H. Blood. It was the astute Blood who had realized that the Commodore might aid his protégées in that art at which he was past master—the art of making money by speculation. The Commodore possessed huge stock holdings, manipulated shares by the thousands, dominated Wall Street as no other man did. Might not his greatest value be as the silent sponsor of a brokerage firm?

The very idea of lady stockbrokers, in an era when women were only child bearers and men retired to the library alone, was farfetched. Yet, it appealed to Mrs. Woodhull, and in her next séance with the Commodore she made the earthly suggestion. The Commodore was enthusiastic from the first. He gave Mrs. Woodhull $7,500 with which to open a business account, he gave her funds to rent offices, and he gave her free use of his mighty name. Eventually, he gave her the most valued asset of all—inside stock-market advice. On January 20, 1870, the *New York Herald* announced, incredulously, the opening of a new brokerage house—Woodhull, Claflin and Company—operated solely by two pretty and fashionably dressed lady partners. Their headquarters, the newspaper continued, was to be found in parlors 25 and 26 of the Hoffman House. Parlor 25 was furnished with reception-room chairs, piano, and oil paintings, and beside a photograph of Commodore Cornelius Vanderbilt hung a framed inscription reading, significantly: SIMPLY TO THY CROSS I CLING. To its description the *Herald* added a comment: "The notion prevails among the lame ducks and old foxes of Wall Street that Vanderbilt, the oldest fox of them all, is at the bottom of the experiment."

If this announcement created a furor among the newspaper's readers, it was as nothing compared to the excitement generated among investors and members of the exchange when Victoria Woodhull and her sister invaded Wall Street itself. Before long Hoffman House proved too confining, and the ladies then opened new business quarters at 44 Broad Street. Seven thousand visitors, fascinated by the oddity of a brokerage house run by women and by the silent partnership of Vanderbilt, flocked to their offices in the first week. When the traffic did not abate, the proprietors were obliged to post a notice in their vestibule reading: ALL GENTLEMEN WILL STATE THEIR BUSINESS AND THEN RETIRE AT ONCE.

Gentlemen were admitted by a uniformed doorman to a front office which was furnished with leather sofas and walnut desks, and this was separated by a glass-and-wood partition from a rear cubicle reserved for female customers.

Mrs. Woodhull and her sister, fresh roses in their hair and gold pens cocked jauntily behind their ears, were cordial to legitimate customers, but evasive with the press. They were in business for themselves, they said. They would not discuss their patron. "Commodore Vanderbilt is my friend," said Tennessee, "but I will not say anything more concerning that matter." The press was, for the most part, generous in its praise, and headlines referred to the sisters as the "Lady Brokers," the "Queens of Finance," the "Bewitching Brokers," the "Vanderbilt Protégées." Banks and financial firms respectfully came calling, and were impressed, and the new business boomed.

In three years, by Victoria Woodhull's public estimate, the new brokerage house "made seven hundred thousand dollars." Where did these huge profits come from? One historian has been unkind enough to remark that "it is to be suspected they sold much more than railroad shares." But even those renowned whorehouse madams, the Everleigh sisters of Chicago, more expert than the Claflins at handling fleshly commodities, had never been able thus to make almost three quarters of a million dollars' profit in three years. It may be said with some certainty that the greatest share of the profits earned by Woodhull, Claflin and Company came from employing not sex but brains. And the brains belonged to Commodore Vanderbilt. For during those exciting financial years, he constantly provided the eager sisters with inside market information. In 1857, having disposed of his steamships, the Commodore became a director—and later president—of the New York and Harlem Railroad, which ran a line from central Manhattan to Albany. The Commodore purchased stock in this line at $9 a share. By bribing the City Council to extend the Harlem's track and then by outwitting Daniel Drew, who was selling short, the Commodore sent the company's stock rocketing up to $179 a share. Mrs. Woodhull, lady broker, was his spiritual solace during this coup, and her own profits in the Harlem Railroad came to almost $500,000.

When the Commodore determined to acquire control of the Erie Railroad, which ran from New York to Chicago and competed with his own New York Central, he took Mrs. Woodhull along for the ride. It was a rocky road, and for once the Commodore failed to achieve his purpose. Jay Gould and James Fisk reached the other directors of the Erie first, had them issue $10,-000,000 worth of bonds, had these converted into fifty thousand shares of stock, and dumped the lot on the market. The Commodore bought and bought, while Fisk joyfully chortled, "We'll give the old hog all he can hold if this printing press holds out." When the Commodore learned how he had been tricked, he salvaged his pride—and his investment—by forcing Gould and Fisk to make good the stock they had issued and to buy back $5,000,000 worth of it.

Finally, on that September day in 1869 known as Black Friday, Mrs. Woodhull was again able to profit with the Commodore's assistance. Gould, after encouraging President Grant to keep the nation's large gold reserve locked up in Treasury vaults, bought $47,000,000 worth of free gold and drove its greenback price up from $132 for $100 in gold, to $150 and finally to $162.50. The exchange was in a panic. Angrily, Grant released $4,000,000 in government gold, and Wall Street had its Black Friday as the price of gold plummeted to $135. On that terrible day, the Commodore handed out loans adding up to $1,000,000 to help stabilize the market. Due to his advice, Mrs. Woodhull had sold at $160, and at an enormous profit, before the real panic set in.

As time passed, the Commodore was subtly, gently removed from the influence of Victoria Woodhull by his second wife, Frank C. Crawford, a tall, dignified, religious Alabama girl whose unique given name had not seemed to hamper her. She barred entrance to all spiritualists, and surrounded her sickly husband with orthodox physicians and a Baptist pastor. Mrs. Woodhull was unperturbed. She already had what she wanted from the Commodore. She had wealth. Now she went after that which she desired even more—power.

On April 2, 1870, in the pages of the *New York Herald*, she made a proclamation that amazed the metropolis and was destined to make her a national figure. "While others argued the equality of woman with man," she declared, "I proved it by successfully engaging in business. . . . I therefore claim the right to speak for the unenfranchised women of the country, and believing as I do that the prejudices which still exist in the popular mind against women in public life will soon disappear, I now announce myself as candidate for the Presidency."

It is unlikely that there ever existed, before the advent of Victoria Claflin Woodhull, a presidential candidate with a background so unstable, chaotic, and sexually scandalous. She was born September 23, 1838, in the squalor of the frontier town of Homer, Ohio. She was the seventh of ten children, and she was named Victoria in honor of Great Britain's new queen. Her father, Reuben Buckman Claflin, was an uncouth conniver who earned a poor living as a surveyor and a postmaster. Her mother, Roxanna, was a strange, martial creature, probably of German-Jewish descent, probably fathered out of wedlock by a governor of Pennsylvania. Long years later, Victoria told the *Philadelphia Press* that she was raised "in a picturesque cottage, white painted and high peaked, with a porch running round it and a flower garden in front." In fact, she was raised in a broken-down shack on an unkempt hill, and every room of the shack from basement to parlor was filled with beds for the squalling Claflin children and visiting relatives.

Victoria's mother, who believed in fortune-telling and the spirit world, treated her unruly household according to the precepts of that Austrian mystic, Friedrich Mesmer, who preached that human cures could be accomplished by occult force. Mrs. Claflin preferred Mesmer to the local physician, and three of her children died in their infancy. According to Victoria, when she was three years old, a housekeeper also died. Victoria saw her lofted on high by several muscular angels, and promptly swooned. Thereafter, Victoria was in constant touch with supernatural beings. Angels were her only friends, except for the visions of two sisters who had died in childhood and with whom she continued to play. "She would talk to them," a friend reported, "as a girl tattles to her dolls." By her eleventh year she had had only three years of formal education, but her teachers had found her uncommonly intelligent. She was prevented from continuing her education when a painful episode forced her to leave school and Homer, Ohio, abruptly.

One auspicious day in 1849, Buckman Claflin, a man who ordinarily had little interest in his possessions, suddenly had a change of heart. He took out insurance on his wooden gristmill. As he had barely enough funds to feed his family, and since the mill lay rotting from disuse, the precaution seemed unusually extravagant. One week later, while he was on a business trip ten miles away, the gristmill went up in flames. Claflin returned to collect his insurance. He was met not by an agent bearing the recompense guaranteed by his premium, but by a vigilante committee of leading citizens. He found himself accused of arson and fraud. He was given a summary choice of the hemp or decamping. Within the hour he departed for Pennsylvania. In the week following, the town raised enough money to send the rest of the family after him.

Thus, necessity forced Roxanna Claflin, and Victoria, and the rest of the hungry clan, to call upon their powers of invention. They formed a medicine show and sold a vegetable juice concoction—"Life Elixir for Beautifying the Complexion"—affixing a woodcut of Tennessee to each container, which sold for two dollars a bottle. In the community of Mount Gilead, Ohio, where they were evicted from their first boardinghouse because Victoria evoked spirit music, they prospered briefly. And there, in 1853, when she was fifteen years of age, Victoria married Dr. Canning Woodhull.

She had met him two years earlier, at a Fourth of July picnic, and had seen him more or less steadily thereafter. He has been referred to as a "young dandy" and a "gay rake" and a "brilliant fop" who treated Victoria "abominably." Most latter-day judgments have been derived from a biased biography of Victoria written by Theodore Tilton after he had become her lover. Tilton declared that Victoria had been forced into the marriage with Woodhull by her mother. "Her captor, once possessed of his treasure, ceased to value it. On the third night after taking his child wife to his lodgings, he broke her heart by remaining away all night at a house of ill-repute. Then for the first time, she learned to her dismay that he was habitually unchaste, and given to long fits of intoxication."

As a matter of fact, Dr. Woodhull was anything but the cloven-footed devil depicted by the prejudiced Tilton. Woodhull, who had received his medical training in Boston, came from a respectable Rochester, New York, family. He had hoped to acquire great riches by joining the gold rush in California, but he had fallen ill in Ohio. There he had remained, and once he was well enough, he resumed his practice of medicine. When the Claflins rode into Mount Gilead, he was a bachelor who dreamed of a peaceful home and a large family. He thought that Victoria

would help him fulfill that dream, but he miscalculated the character of his mate, and the mistake ruined his life. The problem
that plagued Dr. Woodhull's eleven discordant years of marriage—
and may have driven him to drink—was that he had bargained
for a wife and had got a self-absorbed St. Joan. Victoria, like the
Maid herself, heard voices and had a destiny (inspired by excessive devotion to the writings of George Sand) higher than that
of the kitchen. Nevertheless, the energetic and ambitious Victoria
spent sufficient time with Dr. Woodhull to bear him two children
—in 1854 a boy, Byron, who suffered brain damage and became
a "near-idiot" after he stumbled out of a second-story window, and
in 1861 a girl, Zulu Maud, who was to be the comfort of Victoria's later years.

Soon after her marriage, Victoria decided that Ohio inhib-
ited her natural abilities. She induced her befuddled husband
to abandon his practice and take her to California. There,
through the recommendation of an actress named Anna Cogswell,
she obtained a small role in a stage comedy entitled *New York by
Gas Light*. This play led to others. But Victoria's progress was
slow, and in time she realized that her future lay in a different
form of entertainment. For in the East, another pair of sisters,
Margaret and Katherine Fox, of Hydesville, New York, had
achieved a meteoric success in the performing arts without ever
appearing in greasepaint.

The Fox sisters had heard weird rappings at night "as though
someone was knocking on the floor and moving chairs." When
these mysterious sounds persisted, the elder Foxes brought in
neighbors and relatives to hear them. Soon the young Fox sisters,
certain that the rappings were communications from the spirit
world, began interpreting the sounds with their own decoding
alphabet. And soon their visitors were asking questions of the
spirits and the sisters were translating the ghostly replies.

An older married Fox sister, seeing the commercial value of the
girls' amazing "psychic power," took them on a tour of the nation.
Addressing overflow audiences that included such reputable personages as Horace Greeley, James Fenimore Cooper, and William Cullen Bryant, the sisters continued to describe the rappings
they produced as communications from the spirit world. Even
though a conclave of conservative medical men in Buffalo announced that the so-called spirit rappings were created when the

sisters cracked their knee and ankle joints, their eager audiences refused to be so easily disillusioned. Séances became the rage, and accomplished mediums were much in demand. In California, word of this need finally reached the ears of Victoria Woodhull, who had long before communed with the spirits for mere pleasure, but who now determined to forgo her amateur standing for an opportunity to share in the large sums being paid to talented spiritualists.

Victoria, trailed by her sodden husband, caught up with the rest of her family in Cincinnati, where they were treating the gullible with a new cancer cure. When Victoria explained her plan, the entire family was in agreement. A house was rented. A sign was posted, reading: TENNESSEE CLAFLIN, AND VICTORIA WOODHULL, CLAIRVOYANTS. The sisters gave noisy séances, at a dollar a head, and even attracted as a client Jesse R. Grant, the father of Ulysses S. Grant. To the conjuring up of good spirits, the ladies added fortune-telling and magnetic healing. Their youth and attractiveness brought in a preponderance of male customers, who were prepared to pay well for closer communion with their mediums. Apparently Victoria and Tennessee were not above practicing prostitution. Victoria once remarked that the illegal status of the oldest profession worked a hardship on its practitioners. To prevent arrest, a prostitute had to pay bribes, giving "the patrolman $3.00 to $10.00 a week and the privilege of visiting her gratis," while police captains and sergeants came to "$20.00 to $30.00 when these officers need money." The combination of soothsayer and whore might have enriched Victoria enormously had not Tennessee crudely spoiled the game. When Tennessee began to utilize information she had gained as seer and strumpet for the purpose of blackmail, she was sued.

The Woodhulls and the Claflins left Cincinnati in haste, and embarked on a spiritual tour of Illinois, Kansas, and Missouri. In St. Louis, Victoria found true love. She had been invited to appear before the local Spiritualist Society to defend her doctrines against the attack of a clergyman. Since spiritualism, which already had from three to four million followers in the United States, had somehow attracted persons interested in free love, feminine emancipation, and social reform, it was not surprising that Colonel James Harvey Blood was also in the audience. Although ostensibly Blood was covering the debate for the *St. Louis*

Times, his real motive for attending was his interest in socialism and other advanced economic theories. Blood, a personable veteran of the Civil War who had been wounded five times and who served as city auditor of St. Louis after the war, was married and the father of two children. Disenchanted by his wife's materialism, by his job, and by the avaricious men he was brought in contact with, he sought comfort in a private vision of utopia. When from the debate platform, Victoria Woodhull spoke of the same utopia, Blood was impressed. And when she spoke of the slavery of matrimony, when she announced that there was no such thing as sin, he knew that he must meet her.

To meet her, Blood pretended to be a patient in need of advice. His delicacy was not necessary. According to Tilton, it was Victoria who promptly saw a soul mate in Blood and seduced him forthwith: "Col. James H. Blood . . . called one day on Mrs. Woodhull to consult her as a Spiritualistic physician (having never met her before), and was startled to see her pass into a trance, during which she announced, unconsciously to herself, that his future destiny was to be linked with hers in marriage. Thus, to their mutual amazement, but to their subsequent happiness, they were betrothed on the spot by 'the powers of the air.'"

After that impromptu betrothal, Victoria and Blood lived together as lovers. Blood abandoned St. Louis and his family so that he could travel with Victoria to Chicago. Victoria also permitted the cuckolded, unprotesting Dr. Woodhull to accompany her, assigning him the task of looking after their children. In Chicago, with some legal difficulty, Victoria divorced Dr. Woodhull on the charge of adultery, and Blood obtained a divorce from his wife after he had promised her a substantial settlement. Victoria and Tennessee rented a house on Harrison Street and performed as oracles. When neighbors suspected that they were also performing as women of easy virtue, the police were summoned. There being no proof of prostitution, the law accused them of "fraudulent fortune-telling." Once again the ménage was on the road. Then, in Pittsburgh, Victoria saw the name *Demosthenes* spelled out on the glowing marble table—and this vision led her to Commodore Vanderbilt.

Having acquired, through Vanderbilt's friendship and advice, a profit of $700,000 by stock speculation (though she complained that her business and family expenses amounted to $300,000 a year) and assured of a net income of $50,000 annually from her thriving brokerage firm (which recommended investments in subway projects and silver mines), Victoria turned her full attention to promoting her candidacy for the office of President of the United States. Probably no one, not even Victoria, could properly define her real purpose in competing for the nation's highest office. In an age when women in America did not even have the vote (except in Wyoming Territory), her candidacy was regarded as a pure chimera. Her motivations undoubtedly were a mixture of her need for publicity and attention, and an honest desire to dramatize the rising clamor among feminists for equal rights and a single moral standard.

However, Victoria's candidacy would have died stillborn had it not been for the astute direction of two men who cleverly plotted her every action. One was, of course, Colonel Blood, who saw in his mistress a mouthpiece for his own ideas on fiat money, female emancipation, and labor reform. The other, a newcomer to Victoria's growing circle of intimates, was the aged, bearded Stephen Pearl Andrews, a brilliant and renowned scholar, philosopher, and anarchist.

Andrews, the son of a Baptist minister, had college degrees in both law and medicine. He had taught in a ladies' seminary in New Orleans, had narrowly escaped lynching in Houston for expressing his abolitionist views, and had become an advocate of Isaac Pitman's system of shorthand, which he introduced into the United States. An extraordinary linguist, he knew thirty-two languages, including Chinese, for which he published a textbook in 1854. When he had had enough of learning languages, he invented one of his own which he called Alwato. A forerunner of Esperanto, it assigned new written symbols to the basic phonic sounds. As he grew older, Andrews became more deeply interested in sociology. He conceived an anarchistic perfect state that he called Pantarchy. According to the dictates of Pantarchy, the governing body took care of one's children and one's property, leaving the individual free to live as he wished. Quite naturally, as the government "had no more right to interfere with morals than with religion," Andrews's utopia advocated free and natural love.

As spiritualism was also an expression of revolt against convention, hundreds of spiritualists soon subscribed to Andrews's

Pantarchy. But Andrews, a sweet, sincere radical, wanted not hundreds but thousands to support his views. While he had debated, in the press, with Henry James and Horace Greeley on the subjects of love and marriage, unfortunately he was inept at promoting his grand idea. In Victoria Woodhull, with her daring and originality, he saw a useful ally. If she would be President, she must have a platform. Why should not her platform embody the tenets of Pantarchy? Andrews managed to meet her and to enthrall her (she thought him the corporeal representation of her beloved Demosthenes). Soon Andrews joined Blood in laying out a campaign that would promote her name—and their own ideas.

To open Victoria's campaign, a series of articles appeared in the *New York Herald*. Advocating a universal government and a universal language, these articles—which were published as a book in 1871 under the title *Origin, Tendencies, and Principles of Government*—were signed by Victoria Woodhull, but they had been written by Andrews and Blood. When the last *Herald* article reached the public, it occurred to Victoria that she could not depend upon the New York press to continue to publicize her radical views. If she was to gain speedy prominence, and successfully promote her theories, she must have her own newspaper. She had the necessary capital and she had the staff. Consequently, on May 14, 1870, the first number of a sixteen-page, slick-paper journal called *Woodhull & Claflin's Weekly* made its debut. Beneath its name, the five-cent newspaper bore the legend: PROGRESS! FREE THOUGHT! UNTRAMMELED LIVES! And then, in smaller print, the promise: BREAKING THE WAY FOR FUTURE GENERATIONS.

Squeezed in among the financial advertisements that crowded the first issue was a statement of policy. The *Weekly* would refrain from "scurrility in journalism." And it would be "devoted to the vital interests of the people." Above all, it would "support Victoria C. Woodhull for president with its whole strength" and would "advocate Suffrage without distinction of sex." The articles in the first issue, as well as in the issues that followed in the next four months, were tame, restrained, ladylike—this, because two male idealists with little sense of showmanship were writing the copy. There were stories praising Commodore Vanderbilt ("who stands alone in his sphere, the envy of little minds"), deploring women's "voluptuous" fashions, and supporting business training for young ladies. There was a novel by George Sand offered in serial form.

This editorial gentility did little to draw the public's attention to Victoria, and it was costing a fortune. In September 1870, Victoria herself decided to take a more active part in publishing the newspaper—and, at once, her newspaper was itself front-page news. Starting then, and for two years thereafter, the *Weekly* gave its faithful readers their five cents' worth and more. Article after article appeared supporting free love, abolition of the death penalty, short skirts, vegetarianism, excess-profit taxes, spiritualism, world government, better public housing, birth control, magnetic healing, and easier divorce laws. Fearlessly, Victoria advocated legalized prostitution, exposure of Wall Street's financial swindlers, and compulsory classes in physiology for women. At her insistence, the *Weekly* featured the *Communist Manifesto*, published for the first time in its entirety in English, self-help articles on the subject of abortion, Thomas Carlyle's views on labor—and every letter that backed Victoria for President. Once circulation became national, the paper sold up to twenty thousand copies every week.

It was not enough for Victoria to plead her progressive ideas in print. She insisted upon practicing them, too. It was an era when women did not patronize public restaurants unescorted after dark. Victoria, accompanied only by Tennessee, brazenly seated herself in Delmonico's at seven o'clock one evening and demanded service. Charles Delmonico refused to serve her. "I can't let you eat here without some man," he said. Whereupon Victoria sent Tennessee outside to locate a cabdriver and bring him to their table. They were served.

In an era when women did not participate in rude labor movements, Victoria joined Section 12 of the International Workingmen's Association, which had been organized in 1864 by Karl Marx. What happened after Victoria and her followers became active members filled Samuel Gompers with alarm. "Section 12 of the American group was dominated by a brilliant group of faddists, reformers and sensation-loving spirits," observed Gompers. "They were not working people and treated their relationship to the labor movement as a means to a 'career.' They did not realize that labor issues were tied up with the lives of men, women and children—issues not to be risked lightly." When Victoria had Section 12 issue "a circular in which they made the International responsible for free love, anarchy, and every extreme doctrine," Gompers was appalled. Victoria, he concluded, added "no luster to the movement."

Finally, it was an era when women talked and agitated about equal rights, but did nothing more about them. Victoria was the first woman to take direct action in Washington. Her motives in planning to storm the nation's capital may not have been entirely altruistic. She was beginning to realize that her newspaper was not influential enough to promote her person or her theories properly. To acquire a larger audience, she knew that she must air her views in the nation's capital. Diligently, she studied the records and personalities of congressional leaders, seeking one man who stood above the rest. When this man visited New York, Victoria went to meet him. He was General Benjamin Franklin Butler, the pudgy, cross-eyed representative from Massachusetts. As military governor of New Orleans after the Civil War, he had been called by such epithets as Beast Butler and the Bluebeard of New Orleans for his uncavalier attitude toward southern womanhood. While his management of the city had been above reproach, his brusque handling of its female population left much to be desired. When the southern belles of New Orleans insulted northern soldiers, Butler retaliated by declaring that each female offender would "be treated as a woman of the town plying her avocation." Even though this put a prompt end to all obvious gestures of contempt, the southern ladies still turned their backs on Butler when they saw him, which provoked his memorable remark, "These women know which end of them looks best." Yet, as a congressman the general proved more considerate than his colleagues toward American women in peacetime. He believed not only in justice for black citizens, and in fiat money issued on the basis of faith in the United States government, but also in equal rights for women. It was this last that gave Victoria Woodhull hope.

Victoria apparently had no difficulty in convincing Butler that he should support her plan. She wished to present a memorial on behalf of woman suffrage to the Senate and the House of Representatives. Butler thought this a splendid idea. It is said that he wrote the memorial himself and then had the House

Judiciary Committee invite Victoria to appear in person and read it to them.

Victoria, attired in an attractive Alpine hat, blue necktie, and dark dress, arrived in Washington prepared to address the august representatives on the morning of January 11, 1871. It was a decisive appearance for her, and the timing (surely her own suggestion) had behind it a Machiavellian purpose. For, as Victoria well knew, on that very morning the influential National Woman Suffrage Association, led by Susan B. Anthony, Isabella Beecher Hooker, Elizabeth Cady Stanton, and Paulina Wright Davis, was about to begin its third annual convention. Victoria sensed that, by her dramatic and highly publicized appearance, she might accomplish what no member of the suffrage movement had yet accomplished. Furthermore, if her memorial did impress the committee of men, it might also impress the association of women. And thus, with one stroke, Victoria could overcome female resistance to her radicalism and eccentricity and at the same time claim the suffragette following as her very own. Certainly her instinct was correct. For, when members of the House committee assembled behind their long table in the crowded room, Susan B. Anthony, Isabella Beecher Hooker, and Paulina Wright Davis were on hand, too, eagerly watching and waiting.

When Victoria was introduced, she rose gracefully, respectfully, and in a clear, musical voice began to read aloud her brief memorial. After stating that she had been born in Ohio, that she had been a resident of New York for three years, and that she was a citizen of the United States, she went on:

"The right to vote is denied to women citizens of the United States, by the operation of Election Laws in the several States and Territories . . . the continuance of the enforcement of said local election laws, denying and abridging the right of citizens to vote on account of sex, is a grievance to your memorialist and to various other persons, citizens of the United States, being women—

"Therefore, your memorialist would most respectfully petition your Honorable Bodies to make such laws as in the wisdom of Congress shall be necessary and proper for carrying into execution the right vested by the Constitution in the Citizens of the United States to vote, without regard to sex."

It was an impressive reading. Victoria's simplicity, modesty, and femininity won the hearts of the members of the committee, but not their heads. Later, with only two dissents, they voted against the memorial as being outside the province of congressional action. The two dissents were made by Loughridge of Iowa, and, of course, General Butler of Massachusetts, whose minority report to the House vigorously backed Victoria's demand for equal rights. But if Victoria failed to win over the Judiciary Committee, she won another victory almost as important that morning. For the suffragette leaders, who had seen her and heard her for themselves, saw and heard not a strident harlot but a restrained and dignified lady who voiced their deepest yearnings more effectively than any of their members had yet done. Immediately, without hesitation, they congratulated Victoria and invited her to attend the Suffrage Association convention that afternoon so that she could address the delegates.

The association convened at Lincoln Hall in Washington, D. C. Victoria was seated on the platform with Susan B. Anthony and the other renowned feminists. When she was introduced by Isabella Beecher Hooker, who cautioned the audience that it was to be Mrs. Woodhull's first public address, Victoria appeared faint and needed assistance to come forward. She reread the contents of her memorial and spoke briefly of the impression it had made upon members of the Judiciary Committee. The suffragettes applauded her and welcomed her as their newest heroine.

For the remainder of the convention, Victoria merely listened as others praised her memorial. Inspired by the memorial, the suffragettes agreed to a program of direct action. In the coming election they would insist upon registering and voting, and if they were barred, they would sue. Victoria suppressed her elation, and a reporter for the Philadelphia *Press* noted: "Mrs. Woodhull sat sphinxlike during the convention. Gen. Grant himself might learn a lesson of silence from the pale, sad face of this unflinching woman. No chance to send an arrow through the opening seams of her mail. . . . She reminds one of the forces in nature behind the storm, or of a small splinter of the indestructible, and if her veins were opened they would be found to contain ice."

In the days immediately following the convention, the acceptance of Victoria Woodhull as a legitimate suffragette hung briefly in the balance. From every corner of the country, members of the movement protested. But the new friends Victoria had made in Washington remained staunch. When several persons called Victoria an infamous woman, Susan B. Anthony snapped back that "she would welcome all the infamous women in New York if they would make speeches for freedom."

Among those who worried about Victoria's lurid past was Lucretia Mott, who voiced her concern to Elizabeth Cady Stanton. After some reflection, Mrs. Stanton replied: "I have thought much of Mrs. Woodhull and of all the gossip about her past, and have come to the conclusion that it is great impertinence in any of us to pry into her private affairs. To me there is a sacredness in individual experience which it seems like profanation to search into or expose. This woman stands before us today as an able speaker and writer. Her face, manners and conversation, all indicate the triumph of the moral, intellectual and spiritual. The processes and localities of her education are little to us, but the result should be everything."

When male members of the movement objected to Victoria because she had practiced prostitution, Mrs. Stanton gave a vehement rebuttal from a public platform: "In regard to the gossip about Mrs. Woodhull, I have one answer to give all my gentlemen friends: When the men who make the laws for us in Washington can stand forth and declare themselves pure and unspotted from all sins mentioned in the Decalogue, then we will demand that every woman who makes a constitutional argument on our platform shall be as chaste as Diana. . . . Women have crucified the Mary Wollstonecrafts, the Fanny Wrights, the George Sands, the Fanny Kembles of all ages; and now men mock us with the fact, and say we are ever cruel to each other. Let us end this ignoble record and henceforth stand by womanhood. If Victoria Woodhull must be crucified, let men drive the spikes and plait the crown of thorns."

Back in New York, Victoria tried to consolidate her new power and sudden respectability. She made a mild defense of woman suffrage at the Cooper Union and followed this up with several windy lectures on labor reform. However, her main effort was directed toward gaining the support of the many still-reluctant suffrage leaders, among them Mrs. Lillie Devereux Blake, president of the New York State Association. Victoria asked Mrs. Blake to call. Mrs. Blake called, accompanied by her husband, Grinfill Blake, and was met by both Victoria and the as ever uninhibited Tennessee. Mrs. Blake recorded the experience in her diary: "In the evening went to Woodhull and Claflin's, where we had a curious time." The curious time was elaborated upon, later, in a memoir written by Mrs. Blake's daughter, Katherine D. Blake:

"I remember vividly that the next morning she [Mrs. Blake] said at the breakfast table, 'Grinfill! You know you behaved disgracefully last night!'

"His reply was, 'Well, Lillie, my dear, if you will take me to a house where there are not chairs enough to sit on, so that a pretty plump young lady [Tennessee] with nothing on but a Mother Hubbard comes and sits on the arm of my chair and leans over me, you must expect me to put my arm around her.'"

Thereafter, Mrs. Blake was an implacable enemy. She kept her distance, and kept her husband distant, from Victoria. She also withheld as much suffragette support from Victoria as she could. Presently she began to receive anonymous letters threatening her life. "One morning," recalled her daughter, "she received by mail a printed slip headed, 'Tit for Tat' in which the leading suffragists were assailed by name with scurrilous accusations, charges as baseless as vile. She herself was threatened with exposure of her 'divorce,' showing that whoever penned the stuff was ignorant of the events of her life. Accompanying the printed slip was an anonymous note saying that unless she paid $500 her misdeeds would be 'shown up' in Woodhull and Claflin's scurrilous paper, which by then had a wide distribution. I remember clearly the scene in our parlor, my mother walking up and down, wringing her hands, while I tried to comfort her, protesting, 'But, Mama, you never have been divorced, so it won't matter if they do print that.'

"During her girlhood she had had one personal experience with unfounded scandal, so she cried, 'Yes, it will matter! The truth never catches up with a lie! The lie runs too fast.'

"When Mr. Blake came home she threw herself into his arms, crying, 'Grinfill, what shall I do? What shall I do?'"

In the end, she did nothing. The threatened slander never appeared in print. Regardless, Mrs. Blake laid the blame for the attempted blackmail squarely on Victoria's shoulders, accusing her of having "had similar letters written to many other people." Some of those other people, too, accused Victoria of resorting to blackmail to bludgeon antagonistic suffragettes into compliance, though Victoria always vehemently denied the charges. At any rate, by this time she realized that there would always be some resistance to her candidacy. Since she would have to be satisfied with the support of the liberal element within the feminist movement, she decided to move quickly to exploit this support.

The anniversary of the launching of the suffrage movement was scheduled to be celebrated in Apollo Hall, New York City, on May 11, 1871. Victoria Woodhull was announced as one of the principal speakers. The moment the announcement was made, many right-wing suffragettes withdrew their promise to attend the convention. On the night of the anniversary, Elizabeth Cady Stanton and Lucretia Mott arranged to seat Victoria on the platform between them. "To give her respectability," said Mrs. Stanton defiantly.

Victoria, who had by now found her stage presence, made a ringing, emotional bid for followers and front-page attention. "If the very next Congress refuses women all the legitimate results of citizenship," she cried, "we shall proceed to call another convention expressly to frame a new constitution and to erect a new government. . . . We mean treason; we mean secession, and on a thousand times grander scale than was that of the South. We are plotting revolution; we will overthrow this bogus Republic and plant a government of righteousness in its stead."

The good effects of this speech were nullified five days later, when a public scandal was fomented by Victoria's mother. Some months earlier, Dr. Canning Woodhull had appeared at the three-story house at 15 East Thirty-eighth Street which Victoria maintained for herself and her relatives. Since the divorce Dr. Woodhull had lost himself in alcoholism. He was impoverished and he was ill, and he begged Victoria for help. She took him in to care for their two children. She did not think it unusual that her lover, Colonel Blood, remained under the same roof. But Roxanna Claflin thought it unusual, and she thought that she saw her chance to get rid of Colonel Blood. She hated him. She felt that he had filled her daughter's head with high-flown ideas, that he had taken her away from the happier life of the medicine show and spiritualism, and that he was after Victoria's money, which might be put to better use by the Claflins. Moreover, Blood had little respect for Mrs. Claflin and had often threatened her.

In a fine frenzy, Mrs. Claflin went to the police. At the Essex Street station she swore out a complaint against Colonel Blood for assault and battery. "My daughters were good daughters and affectionate children," she told the law, "till they got in with this man Blood. He has threatened my life several times and one night last November he came into the house on Thirty-eighth Street and said he would not go to bed until he had washed his hands in my blood. I'll tell you what that man Blood is. *He* is one of those who have no bottom in their pockets. . . . I say here and I call Heaven to witness that there was the worst gang of free lovers in that house in Thirty-eighth Street that ever lived. Stephen Pearl Andrews and Dr. Woodhull and lots more of such trash."

The case went to court. Called to testify, Colonel Blood said that he had never laid a hand on Mrs. Claflin. Once he had threatened to "turn her over my knee and spank her," but that was the extent of his actions. He insisted that he was Victoria's husband, despite the fact that there was no proof of it. When asked whether he and Dr. Woodhull both shared a bedroom with Victoria, he would not reply. Victoria appeared in defense of her lover: "Colonel Blood never treated my mother otherwise than kind. . . . Sometimes she would come down to the table and sit on Mr. Blood's lap and say he was the best son-in-law she had. Then again she would abuse him like a thief." Tennessee testified that Colonel Blood had rescued her from the evil influence of her mother and family. "Since I was fourteen years old, I have kept thirty or thirty-five deadheads. . . . I have humbugged people, I know. But if I did it, it was to make money to keep these dead-heads." Dr. Woodhull wobbled up to the stand to state that, contrary to Mrs. Claflin's charges, it was actually she who was threatening poor Blood. In the end, the judge threw the case out of court—and into the lap of the press.

The press, less interested in mother love than in free love, was fascinated by the fact that a presidential candidate, female, was keeping two lovers, male, to share her bedroom at her bidding. In faraway Ohio, the Cleveland *Leader* branded Victoria "a vain, immodest, unsexed woman" and a "brazen snaky adventuress." And in New York, where all who knew her could read it, Horace Greeley wrote in the *Tribune*: "Let her be the one who has two husbands after a sort, and lives in the same house with them both, sharing the couch of one, but bearing the name of the other (to indicate her impartiality perhaps) and cause and candidate will be so fitly mated . . . that there will be no occasion even under the most liberal and progressive enlightened regime to sue for their divorce."

In her *Weekly*, Victoria lashed out, first at Greeley, then at those who mocked and criticized her. "Mr. Greeley's home has always been a sort of domestic hell. I do not mean that Mr. Greeley has proved an unfaithful husband. . . . On the contrary, he has been held up . . . as a model husband in that particular, and for that reason the fault and opprobrium of domestic discord has been heaped on Mrs. Greeley. . . . Whenever a scold, a nervous, an unreasonable, or even a devilish tendency is developed in a wife, it is well to scrutinize closely the qualities of the husband."

As for the rest of them, let them cower in their glass houses. "At this very moment, awful and herculean efforts are being made to suppress the most terrific scandal in a neighboring city which has ever astounded and convulsed any community. . . . We have the inventory of discarded husbands and wives and lovers, with dates, circumstances and establishments."

Still Victoria was not finished. Her blood boiled at the injustice of being severely and universally condemned and censured. She must let more than just the readers of her *Weekly* know her true feelings. She must be vindicated in everyone's eyes. Thus, on May 20, 1871, she addressed a letter, or "card" as such communications were then called, to the editor of the *New York World*, with a duplicate copy written out and sent to *The New York Times*. Two days after its receipt, her letter was published prominently in the *World*. It was not just another angry protest. For in its contents was an elaboration on that "most terrific scandal in a neighboring city" which she had previously mentioned in her *Weekly*. Here was a scandal that not only would rock America, but would bring an idol crashing down from his high pedestal. Victoria's memorable revelation began:

"Sir: Because I am a woman, and because I conscientiously hold opinions somewhat different from the self-elected orthodoxy which men find their profit in supporting, and because I think it my bounden duty and my absolute right to put forward my opinions and to advocate them with my whole strength, self-

orthodoxy assails me, vilifies me, and endeavors to cover my life with ridicule and dishonor.

"This has been particularly the case in reference to certain law proceedings into which I was recently drawn by the weakness of one very near relative and the profligate selfishness of other relatives."

Victoria went on to admit candidly that she did, indeed, dwell "in the same house with my former husband . . . and my present husband." She could not, she said, do otherwise, for Dr. Woodhull was ill and needed her support. Despite this charity, "various editors have stigmatized me as a living example of immorality and unchastity." Victoria said that she was always prepared for criticism, but on this occasion her enemies had gone too far.

"I know that many of my self-appointed judges and critics are deeply tainted with the vices they condemn. . . . I advocate Free Love in its highest, purest sense, as the only cure for the immorality, the deep damnation by which men corrupt and disfigure God's most holy institution of sexual relation. My judges preach against free love openly, practice it secretly; their outward seeming is fair, inwardly they are full of 'dead men's bones and all manner of uncleanliness.' For example, I know of one man, a public teacher of eminence, who lives in concubinage with the wife of another public teacher, of almost equal eminence. All three concur in denouncing offenses against morality. 'Hypocrisy is the tribute paid by vice to virtue.' So be it. But I decline to stand up as the 'frightful example.'"

Several hours after the publication of this letter, Victoria sent a message to Theodore Tilton, a "public teacher" who was also the editor of the *Golden Age* magazine. She asked him to call upon her, at once, at her office. He appeared, at once, wary and puzzled. Victoria handed him the morning edition of the *World*, folded open to her letter.

Victoria indicated the letter. "I wish you would read it aloud."

He read it aloud. He read every word of it, including the part about "a public teacher of eminence, who lives in concubinage with the wife of another public teacher, of almost equal eminence." He finished his reading lamely, and looked up.

"Do you know, sir, to whom I refer in that card?" asked Victoria.

"How can I tell to whom you refer in a blind card like this?"

"I refer, sir, to the Reverend Henry Ward Beecher and your wife."

Tilton showed his surprise. Not at the knowledge of his wife's infidelity, about which he already knew, but at the realization that such knowledge was public property.

Victoria watched him. "I read by the expression on your face that my charge is true."

Tilton did not deny that it was true. When Victoria went on to outline the affair in detail, he was forced to agree that her account, although "extravagant and violent," was substantially accurate. Tilton had to face an ugly fact: His pious wife's adultery, begun three years before but made known to him only eleven months before, could no longer be kept secret.

The scandal had had its beginnings on that day in 1855 when the Reverend Henry Ward Beecher, pastor of the wealthy Plymouth Church in Brooklyn, officiated at the wedding of a worshipful member of his flock, the darkly attractive, charming Elizabeth Richards, who had chosen a handsome, twenty-year-old journalist named Theodore Tilton to be her husband.

In the fifteen years following the wedding, the short, stocky, dynamic Beecher became the highest-paid preacher in America. He received $20,000 a year from the grateful Plymouth Church. He collected an additional $15,000 annually from speaking tours and his writings. Not only had his colorful sermons made him a god to the three thousand Congregationalists who packed his church every week, but he was also an opinion maker of national prominence. Even though Beecher frowned upon the free-love theories held by Victoria Woodhull and her followers, he considered himself liberal and open-minded. He permitted the celebrated atheist Robert Ingersoll to address his congregation. He defended his Jewish brethren against the anti-Semitism of Judge Henry Hilton during the notorious Grand Union Hotel ostracization of Joseph Seligman in Saratoga. He staged the mock auction of a slave woman from his pulpit to publicize his sister's book, *Uncle Tom's Cabin*. Because of his magnetic personality, his followers were fanatically devoted to him. Yet, for all of his success and acclaim, he was a lonely and restless individual. An early marriage had bound him to a thin-lipped, disapproving, forever unamused New England woman named Eunice Ballard. She gave him nine children and little else. Her conversation,

Beecher admitted, was "vapid" and "juiceless." Eventually, Beecher turned from his unhappy wife to the company of more admiring women. And finally, as an outlet for his passions and desires, he settled upon the wife of his protégé and closest friend.

Elizabeth Richards had, in a sense, been a product of Beecher's sermons and of his religious fervor. She had gone to school with one of his daughters, and she had been a member of his church for fifteen years before she met young Tilton and brought him into the church. Tilton was the eternal juvenile. Greeley dubbed him "Boy Theodore." The son of a carpenter, Tilton had been educated at New York City College. Upon leaving school he became a reporter on the *New York Observer*. Tall and strong, he was virile in appearance, yet there was something feminine about his manner. He was brilliant, he was idealistic, and he was weak.

The year after his marriage Tilton fell completely under Beecher's influence as the result of the pastor's patronage. Through Beecher's intervention, Tilton became editor, and then part owner, of the *Independent*, his salary climbing from $700 to $15,000 a year. Tilton and Beecher became close companions, and the lonely pastor was constantly in the Tilton home.

Beecher had always been aware of Elizabeth Tilton, first when she was an awed member of his congregation, then as the wife of his best friend. But soon enough he began to consider the warm, slight brunette as something more than a friend. And Elizabeth Tilton, now "Lib" to her pastor, found herself drawn closer to Beecher because of problems that had arisen with her husband. Tilton had become a zealous abolitionist and had abandoned religion for free thought. Too, it was rumored that he was neglecting his wife and spending his time in the company of other women. One of these other women was a mere girl—pretty, sixteen-year-old Bessie Turner, who had been employed to help care for his five children. Tilton was strongly attracted by this girl, and on a night in 1867 he entered her bedroom lightly clad and slid into bed beside her. Tilton made it clear, according to Miss Turner, "that if I would allow him to caress me and to love me as he wanted to that no harm should come to me, and that a physical expression of love was just the same as a kiss or a caress."

In August 1868, Elizabeth Tilton lost a son to cholera. If ever she needed consolation, this was the time. But her husband was off on a lecture tour. In her grief, she went to see Beecher at his home. She said that she needed him. As it turned out, he needed her equally as much. And that night, in her diary, Elizabeth wrote: "October 10, 1868. A Day Memorable." A more detailed account of the illicit affair was later made public by Tilton himself:

"She then said to me . . . that this sexual intimacy had begun shortly after the death of her son Paul . . . that she had received much consolation during that shadow on her house, from her pastor; that she had made a visit to his house while she was still suffering from that sorrow, and that there, on the 10th of October, 1868, she had surrendered her body to him in sexual embrace; that she had repeated such an act on the following Saturday evening at her own residence . . . that she had consequent upon those two occasions repeated such acts at various times, at his residence and at hers, and at other places—such acts of sexual intercourse continuing from the Fall of 1868 to the Spring of 1870 . . . that after her final surrender, in October, 1868, he had then many times solicited her when she had refused; that the occasions of her yielding her body to him had not been numerous, but that his solicitations had been frequent and urgent, and sometimes almost violent. . . ."

Tilton was able to reveal these details because he had heard them from his wife's lips on the evening of July 3, 1870. Conscience-stricken, she had belatedly broken away from Beecher and decided to confess all to her husband. She told him that her fall had been precipitated not by "vulgar thoughts," but by gratefulness to Beecher for his sympathy and kind attentions in her bereavement, and by his authoritative insistence that the act was not sinful. Throughout the year-and-a-half affair, she said, she had been in a "trance." She asked her husband to vow that he would keep his knowledge secret. And he agreed.

But *secret*, as they were to discover, is probably the most elastic word in the English language. Tilton, his reaction varying between hurt and happy martyrdom, unburdened himself to his close friend, Martha Bradshaw, a deaconess of Beecher's church. He then repeated the same story to Henry Bowen, his publisher, whose own wife had earlier been seduced by Beecher. As for Elizabeth, she sought to expiate her sin further by disclosing it to her overly emotional and talkative mother, Mrs. Nathan B. Morse, who in turn babbled about it to her intimate friends.

When Victoria Woodhull revealed to Tilton her own full knowledge of the scandal, he concluded that she had heard it from Mrs. Morse. He was wrong. Victoria had heard the story on May 3, 1871, from her fellow suffragette, Elizabeth Cady Stanton, during a private chat they had had on marriage and free love. Not long before, Mrs. Stanton had been told about the Beecher affair by a friend who had also witnessed some discord at the Tiltons'. And Mrs. Stanton repeated what she had heard to Victoria.

It appeared that Tilton had dined with Mrs. Stanton and a Mrs. Bullard at the latter's home. They planned to discuss the policy of *The Revolution*, a suffragette newspaper, which Tilton was helping them edit. But Tilton had no mind for journalism that evening. When the talk turned to marriage reform, Tilton exploded with a tirade against the influence of Beecher. He said that he despised "the damned lecherous scoundrel." And he told the startled ladies why.

Having got the story off his chest, Tilton returned to his home after dinner, where he found that Susan B. Anthony was spending the evening with his wife. Either because he came home late, or because he had failed to take her to the dinner at Mrs. Bullard's, Tilton was soon involved in a violent argument with his wife. Embarrassed, Miss Anthony tried to escape to the guest room. Elizabeth fled after her, and Tilton pursued both of the women. Elizabeth locked the door of Miss Anthony's room in her husband's face. When Tilton hammered at the door, Miss Anthony shouted, "If you enter this room, it will be over my dead body!" Elizabeth spent the rest of the sleepless night in Miss Anthony's comforting arms, weeping out the miserable tale of her adultery. The following day, Miss Anthony repeated the entire story to Mrs. Stanton, who informed her that she had already heard about Elizabeth's affair with Beecher from Tilton himself.

This was the morsel of gossip which Mrs. Stanton passed along to Victoria Woodhull. Had Mrs. Stanton held her tongue, it is possible that there would never have been a Beecher-Tilton case in American history.

When Theodore Tilton left Victoria Woodhull's presence that late morning of May 22, 1871, he realized that he was faced with a single but difficult duty. He must preserve his wife's reputation and his own by convincing Victoria that the scandal should be given no further publicity. To this end, employing the principal figures involved, the services of his pen, and even his own sexual prowess, Tilton sought for more than a year to divert Victoria from any indulgence in sensationalism.

Despite Elizabeth's protests, Tilton brought Victoria to meet her, to prove to Victoria that his wife was really decent and did not deserve further punishment. When Victoria entered the house, he introduced her to his wife, adding, "Elizabeth, Mrs. Woodhull knows all." Elizabeth was troubled. "Everything?" she asked. Tilton nodded. The rest of the meeting went smoothly. As Elizabeth sewed, she voiced her opinion on many subjects, and even presented her guest with a favorite volume of verse before she left.

Next, Tilton went to Henry Ward Beecher and advised him to receive Victoria and "treat her with kindness." Apparently the pastor was agreeable to the suggestion, for Tilton was able to write Victoria: "My dear Victoria . . . you shall see Mr. Beecher at my house on Friday night. He will attend a meeting of the church at ten o'clock and will give you the rest of the evening as late as you desire."

Victoria was waiting in the Tilton parlor when Beecher arrived. She greeted him warmly, arms extended. They discussed the subject of marriage, and Beecher agreed that it was "the grave of love." Victoria chided him for not preaching what he believed, and he replied, uncomfortably, "If I were to do so, I should preach to empty seats and it would be the ruin of my church." Now she came to the topic foremost in her mind. She wanted his public endorsement. She had written him the day before, telling him that she was scheduled to speak at Steinway Hall and "what I say or shall not say will depend largely upon the result of the interview." Bluntly she asked him to appear on the platform with her and introduce her.

Beecher recoiled at Victoria's request. She was going to discuss free love, and he would have no part of it. Victoria called him "a moral coward." It is possible that she threatened him. At any rate, as she remembered it, he immediately climbed "upon the sofa on his knees beside me, and taking my face between his hands, while the tears streamed down his cheeks, he begged me to let him off." When Victoria remained unmoved and repeated that she might yet expose his infamy, he exclaimed, "Oh! if it must come, let me know of it twenty-four hours in advance, that I may take my own life." Years after, Victoria confessed to one of her associates that "she herself had had sexual relations . . . with Beecher."

When Victoria finally appeared at Steinway Hall on the evening of November 20, 1871, it was not Beecher but Tilton who introduced her. This pacified her sufficiently to make her omit, in her talk on social freedom, any mention of the scandal. Even without further revelation, her speech proved inflammatory enough. She called marriage laws "despotic, remnants of the barbaric age in which they were originated." She predicted that free love would be the religion of the next generation. There was sporadic heckling from the vast, unruly audience, and at one point during the evening a voice bellowed, "Are you a free lover?" Victoria abandoned her text to shout back, "Yes! I am a free lover!" Half the audience cheered, the other half booed. Angrily, speaking extemporaneously, Victoria went on:

"I have an inalienable, constitutional, and natural right to love whom I may, to love as long or as short a period as I can, to change that love every day if I please! And with that right neither you nor any law you can frame have any right to interfere. . . ."

In the ensuing months, Tilton continued to conciliate Victoria in every way. He wrote lectures for her. He wrote, and rewrote, from notes supplied by Colonel Blood, a nauseatingly saccharine biography of her entitled "An Account of Mrs. Woodhull," which was printed as a special issue of *Golden Age* magazine. Finally, after swimming with her at Coney Island and spending long evenings conversing with her, Tilton became Victoria's lover. Whether this consummation of their affair was a studied effort on Tilton's part to placate her, or was the natural result of his being in the proximity of her seductive person, will never be known. But the affair occurred, and Victoria acknowledged it publicly several years later, much to Tilton's embarrassment and his wife's distress. A reporter on the *Chicago Times* asked her for an opinion of Theodore Tilton.

"I ought to know Mr. Tilton," Victoria replied frankly. "He was my devoted lover for more than half a year, and I admit that during that time he was my accepted lover. A woman who could not love Theodore Tilton, especially in reciprocation of a generous, overwhelming affection such as he was capable of bestowing, must be indeed dead to all the sweeter impulses of our nature. I could not resist his inspiring fascinations."

"Do I understand, my dear madame," asked the incredulous reporter, "that the fascination was mutual and irresistible?"

"You will think so," said Victoria, "when I tell you that so enamored and infatuated with each other were we that for three months we were hardly out of each other's sight day or night. He slept every night for three months, in my arms. Of course we were lovers—devoted, true and faithful lovers."

However, Victoria disengaged herself from Tilton's embraces long enough during those months to set in motion a new scheme that might enhance her chances of becoming President of the United States. She mentioned to Mrs. Stanton, Mrs. Hooker, and other gullible feminists that the Woman Suffrage Association would be wise to create its own political party and sponsor its own candidates for public office. The suffragettes, thrilled by the idea, summoned delegates to a convention at Steinway Hall in New York City on May 9 and 10, 1872. Their printed invitation stated: "We believe that the time has come for the formation of a new political party whose principles shall meet the issues of the hour and represent equal rights for all." To these announcements, at Victoria's suggestion, Mrs. Stanton appended the commanding name of Susan B. Anthony.

Miss Anthony was lecturing in Illinois when she picked up the latest issue of the *Woodhull & Claflin's Weekly* and discovered that she was sponsoring a new political party. Instantly, she perceived Victoria's ulterior purpose. Victoria was making a daring bid to reorganize the suffragette movement so that she might take it over. Miss Anthony acted with firmness and dispatch. She telegraphed the association to remove her name from the list of sponsors. She told them that she was returning to New York on the first train to protect their interests. She wrote them: "Mrs. Woodhull has the advantage of us because she has her paper, but she persistently means to run our craft into her port and none other."

Once in New York, Miss Anthony made it known that none of Victoria's vast and varied following, which had been organized as the Victoria League, would be eligible to attend the suffragette convention. Mrs. Stanton thought Miss Anthony unreasonable, but Miss Anthony could not be moved from her stand. If there was to be a woman-suffrage convention, it would be for legitimate suffragettes only.

The convention began on schedule in Steinway Hall, with Miss Anthony firmly in the chair and Mrs. Stanton delivering the keynote address. Victoria was nowhere to be seen. The business meeting continued on into the night, and as it neared adjournment, there was a sudden commotion backstage. Dramatically Victoria Woodhull materialized, determined to challenge Miss Anthony before the great assembly.

As Miss Anthony rushed to block her way, Victoria faced the audience and made a motion that the convention adjourn and reconvene the following day in Apollo Hall, which she had rented for her supporters. From the floor, an anonymous voice seconded the motion. Hastily Victoria called for a vote, and was answered by a scattering of ayes. But Miss Anthony was equal to the crisis. She spoke rapidly and forthrightly. There could be no vote, for there had been no motion by a legitimate member of the Suffrage Association. "Nothing that this person has said will be recorded in the minutes," she cried. "The convention will now adjourn to meet tomorrow at eleven o'clock *in this hall.*" Victoria tried to be heard again, but Miss Anthony overrode her, shouting to the janitor to turn down the gaslights. In a matter of minutes the hall was darkened, emptied of delegates, and Victoria was alone. Defeated at her own game, she had lost the support of the woman-suffrage movement forever.

The following morning, cleansed and chastened, the Suffrage Association met again and it unanimously elected Susan B. Anthony as its leader. Elsewhere, a determined Victoria Woodhull and her aides were busily herding 660 followers—defected suffragettes, spiritualists, socialists, members of Section 12 of the International, free lovers, and free-lance cranks—into Apollo Hall for the purpose of creating a new radical political party.

Judge Reymart, of New York, presided. He introduced Stephen Pearl Andrews, who moved that the members of the new convention call themselves the Equal Rights Party. His motion was carried. Then other orators followed him. There was a speech in favor of a minimum wage. There was a poem that deplored bribery and corruption. And, by evening, at last there was Victoria.

To thunderous applause she spoke against the corporations, against the Astors, against the two-party system, against the republic of men. With evangelical fervor she reached the climax of her address:

"From this convention will go forth a tide of revolution that shall sweep over the whole world. What does freedom mean? The inalienable right to life, liberty and the pursuit of happiness. What is equality? It is that every person shall have the same opportunities to exercise the inalienable rights belonging to the individual. And what is justice? That the alienable rights belonging to individuals shall be jealously guarded against encroachment. Shall we be slaves to escape revolution? Away with such weak stupidity! A revolution shall sweep with resistless force, if not fury, over the whole country, to purge it of political trickery, despotic assumption, and all industrial injustice. Who will dare to attempt to unlock the luminous portals of the future with the rusty key of the past!"

The moment had come. Judge Carter, of Ohio, leaped to the edge of the platform. "I nominate Victoria C. Woodhull for President of the United States!" he shouted. "All in favor of the nomination say aye!" Apollo Hall trembled under the roar of ayes. Hundreds were on their feet screaming, cheering, waving hats and handkerchiefs, as Tennessee Claflin—herself a candidate for Congress—led four hundred Negro soldiers and a band up the frenzied, crowded aisles.

When the tumult had been stilled and order restored, Victoria made a short, modest speech of acceptance and thanks. The chair then opened nominations for Vice-President. A man in the audience introduced the name of a prominent American Indian, Chief Spotted Tail. An emancipated woman shouted that Colonel Blood rightly belonged on the ticket alongside Victoria. Moses Hull, of Kentucky, nominated Frederick Douglass, a onetime fugitive slave who had acquired an international reputation as a reformer, author, and lecturer. "We have had the oppressed sex represented by Woodhull," stated Hull. "We must have the oppressed race represented by Douglass!" The candidates were put to a vote, and it was Douglass for Vice-President by an overwhelming majority.

Later, after ratification of the ticket took place, the thirty-four-year-old Victoria Woodhull made another speech of acceptance to the delegates, concluding that "I have stood by you so long, sometimes meriting your applause, and sometimes encountering your rebuffs, but I have been always faithful to my principles and without saying more, I again thank you for the great honor you have shown me."

As delegates shrieked their delight and waved their banners, Tennessee's band played again. The tune was "Comin' thro' the Rye." But the words of the opening stanza, boomed forth by hundreds of hoarse voices, were new and exciting:

> *If you nominate a woman*
> *In the month of May*
> *Dare you face what Mrs. Grundy*
> *And her set will say?*
> *How they'll jeer and frown and slander*
> *Chattering night and day:*
> *Oh, did you dream of Mrs. Grundy*
> *In the month of May.*

The singing continued, louder and louder, and concluded on a high note of anticipation:

> *Yes! Victoria we've selected*
> *For our chosen head;*
> *With Fred Douglass on the ticket*
> *We will raise the dead.*
> *Then around them let us rally*
> *Without fear or dread,*
> *And next March, we'll put the Grundys*
> *In their little bed.*

The flush of recognition was only briefly enjoyed by Victoria. While a Kentucky congressman soberly announced that female agitation might give Mrs. Woodhull his state by twenty thousand votes, the Suffrage Association made it clear that their female members and their members' husbands were going to boycott the Equal Rights Party. Though Colonel Blood estimated that the shrewd nomination of Douglass might give Victoria the lion's share of the four million Negro votes, Douglass himself quickly shattered that dream. According to Mrs. Blake's diary: "Douglass knew nothing of the performance until, horrified, he read about it in the morning papers." Hastily, Douglass wrote an open letter to the press declining the nomination. The New York papers, as one, ridiculed Victoria in cartoon and print. Horace Greeley's comment was in verse: "Gibbery, gibbery, gab, the women had a confab, and demanded the rights to wear the tights, gibbery, gibbery, gab." Politicians were even less tolerant. The governor of Massachusetts made it clear that he would not permit Mrs. Woodhull to campaign in Boston: "You might as well have the undressed women of North Street on the stage there."

It was immediately apparent that by formalizing her candidacy for President, Victoria had weakened her position. Before the nomination, she had been regarded as a progressive, if somewhat bold, eccentric. With the nomination, and a following that did not include the more stable suffragettes, she was regarded as a potentially dangerous radical. The yearly rent on her brokerage house was raised $1,000, and this meant it had to be shut down. *Woodhull & Claflin's Weekly*, neglected and already in debt, lost the support of Commodore Vanderbilt. Finance firms withdrew their advertising, and the periodical was temporarily suspended. The landlord of the house on Thirty-eighth Street, hinting at outside pressure, asked Victoria and her family to vacate the premises. No hotel or boardinghouse would take her in, and for at least one night she and her family were forced to camp in the street. Eventually, friends located a residence, but Victoria's troubles continued to mount.

By now Theodore Tilton had had enough of pacifying and loving the presidential candidate, and he was through. He told relatives that he broke with Victoria because he resented her public remarks against suffragettes who were his old friends. Victoria countered that it was she who had broken with Tilton because he preferred to support Horace Greeley, rather than her, for the Presidency. Meanwhile, two of Beecher's most respected sisters savagely fought Victoria in print. Earlier Catharine Beecher, resentful of Victoria's hints at scandal, had warned her, "Remember, Victoria Woodhull, that I shall strike you dead." She struck through her more famous sister, Harriet Beecher Stowe, who had become wealthy and world-renowned twenty years before with the publication of *Uncle Tom's Cabin*. The puritanical Mrs. Stowe, who had only recently raised a storm of controversy in England by charging Lord Byron with incest (in explanation of the separation demanded by Lady Byron, who was her friend), now set her sights on Victoria. She wrote a series of sharply worded articles denouncing Victoria for the *Christian Union*, and she published a novel in which a thinly disguised Victoria was portrayed in anything but a flattering light. Victoria was deeply stung. Angered by the renewed persecution and aware of her impending defeat, she determined to punish her enemies and regain her position of national prominence on the eve of the presidential election.

It was September 11, 1872, and Victoria, despite the governor's threatened ban, was in Boston to address the American Association of Spiritualists. Though she was president of the organization, she wished to speak about something more earthly than spiritualism. Naming names for the first time, she revealed the adulterous affair between Beecher and Elizabeth Tilton. "Henry Ward Beecher suffered severely," reported the *Memphis Appeal,* in covering her speech. "She said . . . he preached every Sunday to his mistresses, members of his church, sitting in their pews, robed in silks and satins and high respectability!" Boston and New York papers also covered her speech, yet only one dared mention her Beecher-Tilton revelation in print. The *Boston Journal* reported that a "prominent New York clergyman was personally accused of the most hideous crimes."

Met by this relative conspiracy of silence, Victoria took matters into her own hands. If the popular press would not be honest, then she would "ventilate the scandal" in her own periodical. With the assistance of Blood and Tennessee, she revived *Woodhull & Claflin's Weekly,* and on the morning of October 28, 1872, she launched her national sensation. She headlined the entire issue—which was dated five days later—THE BEECHER-TILTON SCANDAL CASE. THE DETAILED STATEMENT OF THE WHOLE MATTER BY MRS. WOODHULL.

She wrote: "I intend that this article shall burst like a bombshell into the ranks of the moralistic social camp." She pretended that her story had originally been released to a Boston paper, which had suppressed it. She repeated everything that she had heard from Mrs. Stanton and from Tilton. She made it plain that she did not disapprove of Beecher's affair with Elizabeth—after all, she was an advocate of free love. And she was understanding about Beecher's passion. "With his demanding physical nature, and with the terrible restrictions upon a clergyman's life," she could not see fit to condemn him severely. She even went so far as to praise "the immense physical potency of Mr. Beecher. . . .

Passional starvation, enforced on such a nature, so richly endowed . . . is a horrid cruelty. . . . Every great man of Mr. Beecher's type, has had in the past, and will ever have, the need for and the right to, the loving manifestations of many women."

But, continued Victoria, Beecher had given grave offense to Tilton. When Tilton first learned of his wife's unfaithfulness, he had been impelled to tear the wedding ring off her finger, and he had smashed Beecher's framed picture. Beecher, Victoria concluded eleven columns later, was undeniably "a poltroon, a coward and a sneak" for not owning up to his clandestine affair, and what she objected to most vehemently was his sanctimonious airs.

The uproar that followed was tremendous. Newsboys hawked the weekly throughout the city, and over one hundred thousand copies were sold. As copies became scarce, single issues began to sell for ten dollars each, and finally for forty. Beecher was confronted with the scandal. A friend wanted reassurance that the whole thing was untrue. "Entirely!" said Beecher. His attitude made it clear that he was above the battle. "In passing along the way, anyone is liable to have a bucket of slops thrown upon him," he remarked. But if he pretended to ignore the exposé, Anthony Comstock did not. This part-time guardian of the nation's morals read the story after midnight and felt it to be a "most abominable and unjust charge against one of the purest and best citizens of the United States." When Beecher refused to sue for libel, or for anything else, Comstock himself instigated criminal action against Victoria. The morning after the publication of her exposé, he sought out the district attorney, who was also a member of Beecher's congregation, and demanded that Victoria and her sister be arrested for sending obscene printed matter through the mails. The district attorney was reluctant to press charges. Comstock then went to the Federal Commissioner, demanding action, and the Commissioner proved more cooperative. He promptly assigned two deputy marshals to serve warrants.

The deputy marshals found Victoria and Tennessee in a carriage on Broad Street with five hundred freshly printed copies of their weekly beside them, waiting to be arrested. A prohibitive bail of $8,000 was placed on each sister, and they were hustled into a cramped cell at the Ludlow Street Jail. After a month had passed without their being brought to trial, they were released on bail, then rearrested on another charge and again released on bail, and

finally they were arrested yet a third time when Comstock discovered that they were continuing to send reprints of their
scandalous edition through the mails. After six months of inter-
mittent confinement, Victoria and Tennessee faced a jury trial.
Their savior proved to be none other than Congressman Butler,
the man who had first brought Victoria into public prominence
in Washington. Fortunately, he had helped write the law against
sending obscene material through the mails and now explained
that this law was meant to cover only "lithographs, prints, en-
gravings, licentious books." In court Victoria's attorney pointed
out that the offending weekly was none of these. The jury concurred and found the sisters "Not guilty."

However, in the eyes of the editorial writers of *The New York
Times*, Victoria was still guilty. In attacking Beecher so unfairly
she had "disgraced and degraded . . . the female name." It was
not until three years later that Victoria found herself partially
vindicated. After Beecher's backers, who accused Tilton of slandering their leader, had drummed Tilton out of the Plymouth
Church by a vote of 210 to 13, and after an examining committee
composed of church members had completely exonerated their
beloved pastor, Tilton was moved to act. He filed suit against
Beecher for $100,000 for alienation of his wife's affections, and
on January 11, 1875, in Brooklyn, the details of the great scandal
belatedly became common knowledge as the result of a court trial.
Tilton testified that Beecher had seduced his wife, and for a
year and a half had "maintained criminal intercourse" with her.
He presented letters to prove that the good pastor had told his
wife that she was not properly appreciated by her husband and
had suggested that they find other ways to express their love beyond "the shake of the hand or the kiss of the lips."

Beecher, for his part, admitted only platonic affection, denied
adultery, and, after 112 days of wrangling and 3,000 pages of testimony, got a hung jury (with a vote of 9 to 3 against Tilton
after 52 ballots). Beecher's followers gave him a hero's welcome.
But the *Louisville Courier-Journal*, reflecting the sentiment of
the press, branded Beecher "a dunghill covered with flowers."
Beecher had once hoped to become President of the United States.
Now, with the scandal, his hopes of holding public office were
ended. Yet, not only had he held onto his vast following, but his
lecture audiences increased, and this enabled him to charge as

much as $1,000 for a single speech. As the accused, he had survived nicely.

As his accuser, Victoria Woodhull fared not half so well. The scandal she had brought to light had done little to aid her in her bid for the Presidency. She was behind bars in the Ludlow Street Jail on November 5, 1872, when General Ulysses S. Grant soundly defeated Horace Greeley to win reelection to the Presidency. Victoria received no electoral votes and but "few scattered popular ones." At first she blamed her crushing rejection on the corruption of the Grant machine. Later sensing that her theories and reforms were too advanced for the general public, she told a San Francisco audience, "If Jesus Christ had been running against this man, he'd have been defeated."

For a while, although suffering illness and exhaustion, she persisted in giving her lectures on free love. Every so often, a speech she delivered caught fire, as on the occasion when she addressed the National Association of Spiritualists in Chicago.

"This sexual intercourse business may as well be discussed now," she said in one portion of her speech, "and discussed until you are so familiar with your sexual organs that a reference to them will no longer make the blush mount to your face any more than a reference to any other part of your body. . . . I'll tell you what I'm after. I am seeking the truth about sexual intercourse, and I will follow it if it lead me either to heaven or hell."

And the truth, she persisted, was that sexual intercourse carried on without mutual release was destructive to the female. Every man must learn, she said with emphasis, that every woman has the right to experience orgasm. Her listeners were as impressed as ever, and despite some earlier lobbying against her, they reelected Victoria to the presidency of the American Association of Spiritualists. But most of her public lectures, while still well attended, no longer generated the old excitement.

As always, Victoria continued to live her personal life without regard for public opinion. She had several love affairs, and when she was thirty-five she had one with a nineteen-year-old college boy whom she had hired to help manage her lectures. The youth's name was Benjamin R. Tucker, and in 1926 (while Victoria was still alive in England) he revealed the extent of his involvement with her to Emanie Sachs, who published it in *The Terrible Siren*. Young Tucker had been shy when he first went to work for Victoria, yet he professed to believe in her doctrines, and tried not to appear surprised when she kissed him or sat on his lap. One Sunday morning, he entered her parlor to find her stretched out on a lounge. According to Tucker, "After some conversation, she said: 'Do you know, I should dearly love to sleep with you?' Thereupon any man a thousandth part less stupid than myself would have thrown his arms around her neck and smothered her with kisses. But I simply remarked that were her desire to be gratified, it would be my first experience in that line. She looked at me with amazement. 'How can that be?' she asked." The arrival of Colonel Blood interrupted any further discussion. Tucker left, and when he returned that afternoon, Victoria was waiting to seduce him. "Mrs. Woodhull was still obliged to make all the advances; I, as before, was slow and hesitating. . . . But, despite all obstacles, within an hour my 'ruin' was complete, and I, nevertheless, a proud and happy youth."

Victoria, apparently, was insatiable, for young Tucker was required to return for the same purpose not only that night but frequently in the days and months that followed. Tucker, whom Victoria called "boy lover" and whom Tennessee called "Bennie," accompanied his mistress on a trip to Utah and California, and then, in the summer of 1874, he traveled with her to France and continued to share her bed while they were in Paris.

The affair lasted ten months, and toward the end young Tucker began to cool. When Victoria wanted to make their liaison a family affair, Tucker revolted for the first time. "One afternoon, when I was walking up town with Victoria from the office, she said to me suddenly, 'Tennie is going to love you this afternoon.' I looked at her wonderingly. 'But,' I said, 'I don't care to have her.' 'Oh, don't say that,' she answered; 'nobody can love me who doesn't love Tennie.'" Free love or no, Tucker refused to comply. Finally, in Paris, Tucker decided that he had had enough. "Slowly, I came to the realization that however worthy the ends that the Claflin sisters claimed to be pursuing, the means to which they resorted were unjustifiable and even disgraceful; and in consequence, I resolved to break away."

Break away from her he did, and seven years later, when he was the exchange editor of the Boston *Globe* and he heard that Victoria had arrived to protest to the managing editor about a recent article, Tucker prudently stayed out of sight to avoid his onetime mistress.

Although Victoria expected tolerance toward her own affairs, she demanded complete faithfulness on the part of her lovers. In 1876, when she heard that Colonel Blood had been overly attentive to several young females, she was wild with rage. She told him that she was tired of supporting him and demanded that he leave. Ignoring the fact that they had never been married, Victoria formally divorced Blood on the complaint that he had consorted with a prostitute. Except for one occasion, years later, when she silently passed by him on the street, she never saw him again. Sometime after, she learned that Blood had married an elderly widow in Maine, and then had sailed for the Gold Coast of Africa with a Captain Jackson (whose wife had been Blood's mistress) to make his fortune working a gold mine located inland from the port of Accra. There, in December 1885, having contracted "African fever," Colonel Blood died—far from the utopian world of free love and fiat money that he had so long adored.

At about the time of Blood's eviction from her home, Victoria began to lose interest in radicalism and reform. Such ideals now seemed as tired and passé as was Victoria herself. Her existence seemed to have lost all point and purpose. Once the noble Demosthenes had guided her onto the path that led to wealth and power. She had tasted both and found them bitter. Now her deepest yearning was to find peace, normality, and refuge in some placid orthodoxy. And so, in her thirty-eighth year, she abandoned Demosthenes for Jesus Christ.

The startling conversion first became apparent on the editorial page of the *Weekly*, which was again appearing, although erratically. The standard quotation from John Stuart Mill on "the diseases of society" was abruptly replaced by more soothing words from St. Paul. Also, a series of interpretative articles on the Book of Revelation crowded out shrill arguments for equal rights. Gradually, Victoria replaced her popular lectures on the prostitution of marriage with lectures, well punctuated by biblical references, on her discovery that the Garden of Eden was in the body of every married woman.

Before this vague and confused exploration into religion could go any further, an event occurred that completely changed Victoria's life. On the morning of January 4, 1877, after shouting for his wife to sing him some hymns, the mighty Commodore Vanderbilt expired. In death, even as in life, he rescued Victoria from need and oblivion. The Commodore's will left over $100,000,000 to his heirs. Of this total, $95,000,000 went to his eldest son, William, and the paltry sum of $5,000,000 was left his other son, Cornelius, and to his eight daughters. The indignant minority sued on the grounds that the deceased had been mentally incompetent at the time that the will was written. Though son Cornelius settled for $1,000,000 out of court, the eight Vanderbilt daughters fought on. To prove their father's incompetence, they consulted, among many others, Victoria Woodhull, who had once been his medium.

In the clash over the Commodore's will, Victoria saw a golden opportunity to recoup her fortune. The Commodore had left her nothing, although he had left Tennessee an oil painting and had entrusted to them both "certain large sums" to be used in advancing the cause of spiritualism. Victoria made it known that the Commodore owed her more than $100,000, the residue of an old, unresolved business deal. While there exists no documentation on what happened next, it seems obvious that William Vanderbilt, as main heir and defendant, took the hint. Rather than have Victoria aid his sisters' case by testifying to the Commodore's mental lapses, William paid off.

In 1876, Victoria had turned to Christ for salvation, but in 1877, it was the Commodore who saved her. No one knows the precise sum she extracted from Vanderbilt's son. Figures ranging between $50,000 and $500,000 have been mentioned. But a condition of William's settlement on Victoria apparently was that Victoria and Tennessee remove themselves from American soil and stay away for the duration of the contest over the will. And so, late in 1877, with new wardrobes, new servants, and six first-class staterooms to accommodate their entourage, Victoria and Tennessee sailed for England.

Arriving in London, Victoria leased a fashionable suburban home and decided to make herself known by resuming her career on the lecture platform. She had posters printed which announced the forthcoming personal appearance of "the great American orator." On an evening in December 1877, she addressed a large audience at St. James's Hall. Her subject was "The Human Body, the Temple of God," and while her lecture concerned various problems of motherhood and heredity, there was at least one male member of the assemblage who listened with rapt attention. This was John Biddulph Martin, the rich and aristocratic son of a rich and aristocratic father. Both Victoria's appearance and her personality moved him deeply. "I was charmed with her high intellect and fascinated by her manner," Martin recalled later, "and I left the lecture hall that night with the determination that, if Mrs. Woodhull would marry me, I would certainly make her my wife."

Before long, Martin succeeded in meeting the astonishing American "orator." It was not surprising that Victoria found him agreeable, and that she would reciprocate his affection. She wanted security, acceptance, love, and all of these John Biddulph Martin could give her in abundance. At thirty-six—Victoria was then thirty-nine—Martin was a full partner in the prosperous Martin's Bank at 68 Lombard Street, London, a firm that traced its origin back to 1579. Beyond this financial attraction, Martin possessed several others. He had been an athlete at Oxford, and despite his sedate garb and full beard, he still presented the trim appearance of an athlete. He was a quiet man, devoted to culture and scholarship, and Victoria was his first real love.

If Victoria hoped for a quick, happy ending to a tumultuous career, it was not to be that simple. Martin's parents, who resided at Overbury Court, were appalled by his choice for a wife. When they wished to investigate Victoria, they had to look no further than their daily newspapers. The press, if restrained, made it clear that Mrs. Woodhull's past had been a checkered one. She had been twice married and twice divorced, the elder Martins were incorrectly informed. She had crusaded—horror of horrors—for free love. She had been the inmate of an American jail. And her name had been linked with such public scandals as the Beecher-Tilton trial and the Vanderbilt will case. Were these the qualifications for an English banker's wife? Decidedly not. The elder Martins made their disapproval heard. Their son was desolate, their future daughter-in-law indignant.

Like the ancient Chinese emperor who burned all preexisting books and records so that recorded history might date from his dynasty, Victoria Woodhull now desperately and grimly set out to obliterate her past. She had been, she insisted, the editor of *Woodhull & Claflin's Weekly* in name only. Colonel Blood had written those reprehensible articles on free love, and Stephen Pearl Andrews had exposed the Beecher-Tilton scandal, both acting without her knowledge. While she did, indeed, believe in the emancipation of women, everything else attributed to her pen and tongue was deliberate misrepresentation. Her own life, from birth, had been one of morality and conformity.

She went so far as to place an advertisement, which Martin might then show to his parents, in *The Times* of London. It read:

"Mrs. Victoria C. Woodhull, being again compelled to commence libel suits against Americans who are constantly circulating malicious slanders, offers a REWARD OF FIFTY POUNDS for every letter that contains enough libel to enable her to proceed criminally and civilly, and Five Pounds will be given to any and every person who will give information that can be proceeded with legally against persons who are circulating foul stories by word of mouth."

It took six years to convince the elder Martins. Then, no doubt worn down by Victoria's persistent chatter about her purity and by their son's endless romantic pleadings, they withdrew their threats of disinheritance and gave their consent. On October 31, 1883, at the age of forty-five, Victoria Claflin Woodhull became Mrs. John Biddulph Martin, London lady and legal mistress of a stately, gray residence at 17 Hyde Park Gate.

But for Victoria, in the eighteen years of contented marriage that followed, the fight to suppress or revise her shocking and eccentric past was never done. When some of the wives of Martin's friends cut her dead, Victoria offered 1,000 pounds' reward for a list of those in "conspiracy to defame" her. Just as book publishers print excerpts from favorable reviews of their outstanding authors, Victoria printed and circulated broadsides containing good character references taken from carefully screened American sources. One pamphlet that she and Tennessee prepared contained a detailed genealogical chart which revealed that Victoria, on her father's side, was a descendant of "King Robert III of Scotland, King James of England from whom are descended The Dukes of Hamilton, to whom was related Alexander Hamilton the friend of Washington." And by some alchemy the product of this superabundance of royalty was Reuben Claflin who, in turn, sired Victoria Claflin Woodhull.

On one occasion, a researcher employed by Victoria found two unfavorable booklets concerning the Beecher-Tilton scandal, with ample references to the part played in it by Victoria Woodhull, on the shelves of the British Museum. The researcher reported his find to Victoria, and she begged her husband to act.

On February 24, 1894, Martin brought suit against the trustees of the British Museum for libel. The trial, such as it was, lasted five days. Defended by a peer of the realm, Victoria was described as a victim of constant persecution—married by force to "an inebriate" at an early age, unjustly incarcerated merely because she had defended Tilton and taken "a strong view" against the Reverend Mr. Beecher's adultery, maligned because she had bravely sought to elevate the status of her sex. The British Museum, which had never before been brought to court for libel, was represented by a renowned barrister who was also one of its trustees. His cross-examination of Victoria was relentless and thorough. However, her answers were so discursive and obscure as to make the usually attentive London *Times* confess to its readers that it could not grasp her testimony. In the end, the jury agreed that while libel had been committed, there had been no intent at injury, and they awarded Victoria twenty shillings in damages.

Ever vigilant, Victoria continued to compel her husband to defend her good name even when foul aspersions were cast from great distances. Time and again, Victoria took Martin from his coin collection and from the history he was writing of his family's bank, and induced him to accompany her to America to have justice done. When the *Brooklyn Eagle* featured a series of popular articles by the stern and exacting Thomas Byrnes, a celebrated police inspector, on infamous female intriguers, and when one of these intriguers turned out to be Victoria Woodhull, she hastened to New York with Martin for a showdown with Byrnes. Despite her protests of "a great injustice," despite Martin's demands for retraction, Byrnes would not budge. Facts were facts, and he had published plain facts. Martin was dismayed. "I'm very sorry you will do nothing," he said. Byrnes was obdurate. "I am sorry, too, but I am a public official and any statement I make I may be held responsible for. And you have the courts to which you can have recourse at once." Whereupon Victoria and Martin retreated to finish their side of the battle in the press. They told reporters that Byrnes had been cordial and apologetic. Byrnes

heard this with "no little surprise," and announced that he had
been neither cordial nor apologetic.

On another occasion, the *Chicago Mail* published an unflatter-
ing article entitled "Tennie and her Vicky." Victoria, with Martin
in tow, sailed from Southampton directly, and was soon in
Chicago prepared to sue the *Mail* for $100,000 on the charge of
criminal libel. Rallying its entire investigative corps to its defense,
the *Mail* sent its staff scurrying after the full story. From the day
the Claflins were forced to flee Homer, Ohio, until the time when
Victoria and Tennessee were expelled from Cincinnati for prostitution, the painful history of Mrs. Martin was recounted in the
pages of the ungallant *Mail*. The Martins did not press further
for their $100,000.

Happily, not all of the Martins' married life was spent com-
muting to America in Victoria's defense. There were calmer
times in the English years, and during those Victoria sponsored
brilliant dinners and evening affairs at Hyde Park Gate for her
growing number of London friends and followers. Yet, she could
never resist a chance to be before the public. In 1892, she returned
with Martin to the United States to meet with fifty prominent
women in Washington, D. C., whose purpose was to nominate
her as a presidential candidate once again. She was so nominated,
and a series of Victoria Leagues was organized to drum up votes,
and back Victoria's demand for female equality and her campaign
to "drive anarchy, crime, insanity and drunkenness from our
midst by our humanitarian efforts." Victoria hoped her supporters
would "put me in the White House," but she did not expect to
"carry any of the doubtful states." In 1892, Grover Cleveland
carried twenty-three states, Benjamin Harrison carried sixteen
states, Populist James Weaver carried four states, and Victoria
Woodhull Martin carried not even one state.

When residing in London, Victoria also occupied herself by
publishing a sedate monthly periodical called *The Humanitarian*,
to which she assigned her conservative twenty-eight-year-old
daughter, Zulu Maud, as editor. The magazine was pleasant,
bland, and its most radical crusade was in behalf of birth control.

During 1895, Victoria started to write an autobiography. "Sitting here today," she began, "in this north room of 17 Hyde Park
Gate, London—dreary, smoky, foggy, insulated as you are in the
customs and prejudices of centuries—I am thinking with all the

bitterness of my woman's nature how my life has been warped and twisted out of shape by this environment, until, as I catch a glimpse of my haggard face in the mirror opposite, I wonder whether I shall be able to pen the history of this stormy existence."

She found that she was not able to relive the entire history of her stormy existence. After a single chapter, which she eventually issued in a brochure, she decided to evoke the past no further but to enjoy the peaceful days of her marriage and turn her attention to tamer projects. John Martin basked in the contentment reflected by her activity, stirring himself only to fulfill his obligations as head of the Royal Statistical Society.

In his fifty-sixth year Martin fell ill. After a partial recovery he was advised to recuperate at Las Palmas, in the Canary Islands, off Africa. There, in his weakened condition, he contracted pneumonia, and on March 20, 1897, he died. Victoria's daughter, Zulu Maud, wrote his obituary for *The Humanitarian*. "Theirs was a perfect union," she concluded, "marred only by persecution."

Four years later, Victoria, now in possession of an inheritance valued at over $800,000, sold her home at Hyde Park Gate and moved to her late husband's country manor at Bredon's Norton, Worcestershire. Her venerable residence, thickly peopled with servants, was set in a sprawling estate that looked out upon the River Avon. In this manor house, on the eve of his becoming King Edward VII, the Prince of Wales dined with her. But such honors, and the retired life, were not enough. Without her husband's restraining influence, Victoria quickly reverted to form. While he was alive, she had in her monthly publication denounced socialism and similar advanced political theories. Now, at sixty-three, insisting that a "charming woman has no age," she plunged into a whirl of reform activities.

Victoria gave over a portion of her estate to a project called Bredon's Norton College, in which young amazons were invited to study agriculture. She flayed the English school system as outmoded and opened her own progressive kindergartens for village youngsters in the vicinity. She again embraced spiritualism and presided over a salon attended by those who believed as she believed. In 1912, she offered a piece of antique silver as a trophy and $5,000 to the first person who would successfully fly the

Atlantic Ocean. In 1914, she contributed $5,000 toward the purchase of Sulgrave Manor, the home George Washington's English ancestors had built in 1531, and this edifice was presented to the Anglo-American Association. In 1915, with World War I under way, she worked for the Red Cross and appeared at fundraising campaigns for the Belgian and Armenian refugees, and sent Woodrow Wilson a stiff cable reading: WHY IS OLD GLORY ABSENT FROM SHOP WINDOWS IN ENGLAND TODAY WHEN OTHER FLAGS ARE FLYING?

At the war's end she was very old and lived in seclusion. Her daughter was ever beside her, but Tennessee remained her most understanding companion. Tennessee, brash and amoral as ever, had fared well in the English climate. In 1885, during a séance with a wealthy, elderly English widower named Francis Cook, she disclosed that the late Mrs. Cook was urging her husband to marry his medium. The wedding took place with dispatch. Cook, who had amassed his money importing shawls from India after Queen Victoria made them fashionable, maintained an expensive establishment near the Thames and another in Portugal. When he was knighted and Tennessee became Lady Cook, the title did not inhibit her. Upon her husband's death in 1901 she was left a fortune of approximately 465,000 pounds, the equivalent of about $2,000,000, and she dispensed it with reckless philanthropy. She traveled regularly to the United States, scolding Theodore Roosevelt in person for not doing something about woman suffrage, attempting to establish a chain of homes for reformed prostitutes in the South, trying to build a "school for fathers" on Long Island, and endeavoring to raise a female army of 150,000 in 1915. She died in January of 1923, and though she left a tearful Victoria $500,000 richer, she deprived her elder sister of the last link to the past.

Victoria knew that her own time was near. Yet, she would not accept the fact. She felt most alive during afternoons when, seated in her white sports car, she urged her nervous chauffeur to drive at recklessly high speeds. In her manor house, she tried to ward off death through innumerable eccentricities. She refused to shake hands with visitors for fear that their germs might contaminate her. At night she avoided her bed as she would a coffin, preferring to fall asleep in a rocking chair.

But on the morning of June 9, 1927, while Englishwomen were

awakening and American women were going to sleep, all fully possessed of the equal rights for which she had so long fought, death came to Victoria Claflin Woodhull Martin as she napped in her rocking chair. In another three months she would have been ninety years old.

Her last will and testament left her sizable estate to her daughter Zulu Maud, who would, in turn, pass the fortune on after her own death in 1940 to the Royal Institution of Great Britain for future research in eugenics.

Victoria's memorial, then, was not only the emancipated woman but the continuing work done in that science concerned with improving the race of man by controlling such hereditary qualities as intelligence and physical structure.

Her obituary in *The New York Times* on June 11, 1927, was kind, and gave no more than a hint of the turbulent past. She was a "suffragist," yes, and a "nominee for the United States presidency in 1872," yes, but finally, she was the "Mrs. Martin, who has been known chiefly as one of the donors of Sulgrave Manor, home of Washington's ancestors in England."

However, the handful of persons surviving her who knew her true story would have agreed that her epitaph had been prepared long years before, by a grudgingly admiring editor in Troy, New York. He had carved history's verdict in a sentence:

"She ought to be hanged, and then have a monument erected to her memory at the foot of the gallows."

In life, Victoria Woodhull stood as a composite symbol embodying every type of outrageous, liberated, nonconforming, scandalous woman who had preceded her in history. During her hectic time on earth, Victoria was as defiant about her right to enjoy sexual freedom as had been Teresa Guiccioli and Jane Ellenborough; Victoria was as determined to achieve a career in a man's world as had been Margaret Fuller and Delia Bacon; Victoria was as vigorous in her fight for female emancipation and social and economic equality as had been Mme. de Staël and Anne Royall.

Yet, precisely what did she symbolize in the end? Simply this—she was every woman in times before, every woman who had heard a different drummer than that heard by the more subservient and compliant members of her own sex, and so she represented something more than merely the eccentric, the crackpot, the adventuress. Victoria and her predecessors became scandalous ladies because they had refused to adopt the traditionally passive female role. Whether by plan or by accident, wittingly or unwittingly, these rebels refused to accept any simplistic biological definition of the female as a mere child bearer and the second best of the sexes. Constantly, by their various expressions of revolt, by abandoning their Doll Houses and implying society's mores be damned, these women challenged and modified the role of the female in the age in which each lived.

The gains accomplished by these scandalous ladies were not always long-lasting, let alone permanent. Societies of men rose to impede and set back the cause of female fulfillment. But from each step forward, from each small gain, from each new effort at wresting equality from their male peers, something survived so that, because of these women, all women reached the middle of the twentieth century standing not behind man, not in man's shadow, but nearly abreast of him—nearly, but not completely.

Yet, were the accomplishments of these women, their redefinitions of woman's role through the changing pages of history, merely illusory?

Consider the matter of The Other Woman in the first half of the twentieth century. At first glance, it would seem that the grand courtesan, the brilliant kept woman, had become as extinct by then as the dodo. Neither an Aspasia nor a Ninon, it appeared, could thrive in style in the age of the telephone, the high-rise apartment, the clinical Dr. Freud. Still, upon a closer look, there have been kept women aplenty, defying the conventions and morals of a hypocritical Western society. And so, even with the decline of the mistress as a power, the interest in her and the gossip about her did not abate.

The modern roll call of immorals is too long to recount. But in the first half of the twentieth century there were mistresses such as Apollinaire's Marie Laurencin, John Murry's Katherine Mansfield, Amedeo Modigliani's Jeanne Hebuterne, President Warren Harding's Nan Britton, King Carol's Mme. Lupescu, William Randolph Hearst's Marion Davies, Benito Mussolini's Clara Petacchi, Adolf Hitler's Eva Braun, James Joyce's Nora Barnacle.

Still, despite the existence of these daring and colorful ladies, one might say they represented a small and unimpressive battalion.

Not quite so.

For as they passed into history, as upon Victoria Woodhull's passing, the torch for female freedom—sexually and otherwise—was lit anew, and the march toward female emancipation became more resolute than ever. In the 1960's, and with mounting intensity in the 1970's, a coalition of seemingly countless militant female groups—the Women's Liberation Movement—set out to end their repression in a world dominated by males.

In one of their journals, a spokeswoman for the movement stated: "When applied to women's oppression, liberation is the struggle *against* the limitations of our reproductive function which minimizes our personal potential, against the concepts which make us solely responsible for raising children, against the rigid social mores which limit our contribution to the world. . . . A woman cannot fulfill herself through her children or through her husband; she must do it alone. Identity comes only through making choices and liberation is the process of obtaining ever-wider choices for people."

Among the leaders of the new Women's Liberation Movement few personalities as widely known or individually notorious as those of the past can be singled out. Certainly, there are no Victoria Woodhulls or Anne Royalls or Caroline Nortons or Claire Clairmonts or Lady Melbournes. But the reason for this may be a change in society—for the isolated iconoclastic individual of the past, who acted without inhibition, has now become a massive horde of women, a vast army of women demanding their rights as human beings. These contemporary women are the children of the scandalous ladies described in the preceding pages, the products of women who were once ridiculed, jeered, ostracized, condemned. They are the heiresses of the feminist pioneers.

Once, there was a young woman who, having been bartered off to an elderly man, defied this role to cohabit openly with Great Britain's greatest naval hero. Once, there was another woman who conducted a school to teach young men how to make love. Once, there was one who turned her back on convention to live as freely as men lived, with many members of the opposite sex, and who found peace after marriage to a male of a different race and in an alien land. And another who committed the heresy of not believing in the genius of literature's greatest playwright, and another who used a pen to stab at men's most sacred institutions, and still another who demanded the right to enter into man's business world and his politics, to challenge his sexual double standard, and to end his monopoly on the orgasm.

Today, perhaps because of the actions of these females of the past, their descendants number millions—millions of women who insist upon the right to equality in politics and to a career, the right to sexual freedom and legal abortion, the right to dress (or undress) as they wish and to speak out as they wish. These millions are demanding a new world—the end of a man's world— the beginning of a man's *and* a woman's world, one shared and enjoyed mutually.

With the advent of the second half of the twentieth century, with the old order giving way to the new, a vision of a just world for both sexes could be seen. For a majority of men and a minority of women, this just world may have seemed threatening, uncomfortable, drearied. But for a majority of women and a minority of men, it seemed that woman's new role gave promise of a utopia in human relationships.

Certainly, the mistress as a scandal has become a creature almost extinct. The new feminism with its sexual freedom due to the Pill, its permissiveness, the easier divorce, and economic equality are changing the landscape of scandalous sex.

In the bustling world of urban renewal, there is no place left for Back Street.

And in the radical world of no bra, women's demonstrations, communal child-raising, co-ed dormitories, myth-breaking (Eve did *not* cause the fall of man), female jockeys (and physicians, professors, senators), there is no room for either the dependent wife or the servile single girl. There is room only for the Human Being.

Perhaps this, and this alone, is what the Victoria Woodhulls of the past finally wrought. And it is enough.

Bibliography

ABOUT, EDMOND, *La Grèce Contemporaine*. Paris, L. Hachette, 1858.

ANON., *The Great and Eccentric Characters of the World*. New York, Hurst, [188–].

APPONYI, ALBERT GROF, *Vingt-cinq Ans à Paris (1826–1850)*. Paris, Plon-Nourrit, 1913–14. 3v.

ARENSBERG, WALTER CONRAD, *The Cryptography of Shakespeare*. Los Angeles, Howard Bowen, 1922.

——, *The Magic Ring of Francis Bacon*, Pittsburgh, Pa., n.p., 1930.

ARETZ, GERTRUDE (KUNTZE-DOLTON), *The Elegant Woman from the Rococo Period to Modern Times*. New York, Harcourt, Brace, 1932.

BACON, DELIA SALTER, *The Philosophy of the Plays of Shakspere Unfolded*. London, Groombridge and Sons, 1857.

BACON, MARTHA SHERMAN, *Puritan Promenade*. Boston, Houghton-Mifflin, 1964.

BACON, THEODORE, *Delia Bacon*. Boston, Houghton-Mifflin, 1888.

BALZAC, HONORÉ DE, *The Correspondence of . . .* Translated by C.
    Lamb Kenney. London, Richard Bentley & Son, 1878.

——, *Le Lys dans la Vallée*. Paris, n.p., 1836.

——, *The Lily of the Valley*. London, Caxton, 1897. (Vol. 5 of *The
    Human Comedy*.)

——, *The Unpublished Correspondence of Honoré de Balzac and
    Madame Zulma Carraud, 1829–1850*. Translated by J. Lewis
    May. London, John Lane, 1937.

——, *The Works of . . .* Introduction by George Saintsbury. New
    York, National Library Co., n.d. (Vol. IX).

BARNUM, PHINEAS TAYLOR, *Struggles and Triumphs*. Edited by
    George S. Bryan. New York, Knopf, 1927. 2v.

BECKER, BERIL, *Whirlwind in Petticoats*. New York, Doubleday,
    1947.

BEECHER, CATHARINE, *Truth Stranger than Fiction*. Boston, Samp-
    son, 1850.

[BENJAMIN, LEWIS SAUL], *Nell Gwyn* by Lewis Melville [pseud.].
    New York, George H. Doran, 1924.

BENJAMIN, RENE, *Balzac*. London, William Heinemann, 1929.

BERGER, ADOLF FRANZ, *Felix Fürst zu Schwarzenberg, k.k. minister-
    präsident etc. Ein biographisches denkmal*. Leipzig, O. Spamer,
    1853.

BLAKE, KATHERINE DEVEREUX, *Champion of Women, the Life of
    Lillie Devereux Blake*. New York, Revell, 1943.

BLESSINGTON, MARGUERITE (POWER) FARMER GARDINER, COUNTESS
    OF, *The Idler in France*. London, H. Cobern, 1842.

BLIGH, E. W., *Sir Kenelm Digby and His Venetia*. London, S. Low,
    Marston, 1932.

BLOCH, IWAN, *A History of English Sexual Morals*. Translated by
    William H. Forstern. London, F. Aldor, [1936].

BLUNT, LADY ANNE ISABELLA NOEL (KING NOEL), *Bedouin Tribes
    of the Euphrates*. London, John Murray, 1879. 2v.

——, *Pilgrimage to Nejd, the Cradle of the Arab Race*. London,
    John Murray, 1881.

BOPP, LEON, *Commentaire sur Madame Bovary*. Neuchâtel, À la
    Baconnière, 1951.

BROOKS, VAN WYCK, *The Flowering of New England*. New York,
    E. P. Dutton, 1936.

——, *Life of Emerson*. New York, Literary Guild, 1932.

——, *New England: Indian Summer*. New York, E. P. Dutton,
    1940.

BROUN, HEYWOOD CAMPBELL, and LEECH, MARGARET, *Anthony Comstock, Roundsman of the Lord.* New York, A. & C. Boni, 1927.

BROWN, IVOR, *This Shakespeare Industry.* New York, Harper, 1939.

BUCHON, JEAN ALEXANDRE, *Voyage dans l'Eubée, les îles Ioniennes et les Cyclades en 1841* . . . Paris, É. Paul, 1911.

BURTON, JEAN, *Sir Richard Burton's Wife.* New York, Knopf, 1941.

BURY, LADY CHARLOTTE (CAMPBELL), *The Divorced.* London, H. Cobern, 1837.

——, *The Exclusives.* London, H. Cobern, 1830. 3v.

BYRON, GEORGE GORDON NOËL BYRON, *His Very Self and Voice; Collected Conversations of Lord Byron.* Edited with an introduction and notes by Ernest J. Lovell, Jr. New York, Macmillan, 1954.

——, *Byron, a Self-portrait; Letters and Diaries.* Edited by Peter Quennell. London, John Murray, 1950. 2v.

CALVERTON, VICTOR FRANCIS, *Where Angels Dared to Tread.* Indianapolis, Bobbs-Merrill, 1941.

CAMPBELL, OSCAR JAMES, ed., *The Reader's Encyclopedia of Shakespeare.* New York, Thomas Y. Crowell, 1966.

CANTWELL, ROBERT EMMETT, *Nathaniel Hawthorne, the American Years.* New York, Rinehart, 1948.

CHANNON, HENRY, *The Ludwigs of Bavaria.* London, Methuen, 1934.

CHAPMAN, GUY, *Beckford.* New York, Scribner's, 1937.

CHARTERIS, HON. EVAN EDWARD, *John Sargent.* New York, Scribner's, 1927.

CHUTE, MARCHETTE GAYLORD, *Shakespeare of London.* New York, E. P. Dutton, 1949.

CLARKE, HELEN ARCHIBALD, *Hawthorne's Country.* New York, Baker and Taylor, 1910.

[CLEMENS, SAMUEL LANGHORNE], *Is Shakespeare Dead?* by Mark Twain [pseud.]. New York, Harper, 1909.

CONNELY, WILLARD, *Brawny Wycherley, First Master in English Modern Comedy.* New York, Scribner's, 1930.

CONWAY, MONCURE DANIEL, *Life of Hawthorne.* New York, n.p., n.d. (Robertson's Great Writers).

CORYN, MARJORIE, *Enchanters of Men.* London, Naldrett Press, 1954.

CREEVY, THOMAS, *The Creevy Papers.* London, John Murray, 1904.

DARGAN, EDWIN PRESTON, *Honoré de Balzac.* Chicago, University of Chicago Press, 1932.

DARK, SIDNEY, *Twelve Royal Ladies.* New York, Thomas Y. Crowell, [c1929]

D'AUVERGNE, EDMUND BASIL FRANCIS, *Lola Montez*. London, T. Werner Laurie, 1909.

DAVIS, PAULINA W., *A History of the National Woman's Rights Movement*. New York, Journeymen Printers' Co-operative Association, 1871.

DAY, LILLIAN, *Ninon, a Courtesan of Quality*. Garden City, N. Y., Doubleday, 1957.

DEARDEN, SETON, *The Arabian Knight; A Study of Sir Richard Burton*. London, Arthur Barker, 1953.

Debrett's Peerage, Baronetage, Knightage and Companionage. London, Odhams Press; Dean & Co., 1713–1967.

DE FORD, MIRIAM ALLEN, *Love-Children*. New York, L. MacVeagh, The Dial Press, 1931.

DELDERFIELD, RONALD FREDERICK, *Napoleon in Love*. London, Hodder and Stoughton, 1959.

DELL, ERNEST F., ed., *Love Letters of Famous Men and Women*. New York, Dodd, Mead, 1941.

DELPECH, JEANINE, *The Life and Times of the Duchess of Portsmouth*. New York, Roy Publishers, 1953.

Dictionary of American Biography. New York, Scribner's, 1946.

Dictionary of National Biography. London, Oxford University Press, 1937–8.

DIGBY, SIR KENELM, *Private Memoirs . . .* London, Saunders and Otley, 1827.

DONNELLY, IGNATIUS, *The Great Cryptogram*. Chicago, R. S. Peale, 1888.

DORR, RHETA LOUISE (CHILDE), *Susan B. Anthony*. New York, Frederick A. Stokes, 1928.

DRINKWATER, JOHN, *Mr. Charles, King of England*. New York, George H. Doran, [c1926]

DUMAS, ALEXANDRE, *Camille*. New York, Modern Library, n.d.

DUMESNIL, RENE, *Flaubert et Madame Bovary*. Paris, Socièté les belles lettres, 1944.

DURNING-LAWRENCE, EDWIN, *Bacon Is Shakespeare*. London, Gay & Hancock, 1910.

ELLENBOROUGH, EDWARD LAW, EARL OF, *A Political Diary*. London, Richard Bentley and Son, 1881.

EMERSON, RALPH WALDO, *Journals of . . .* Boston, Houghton-Mifflin, 1909–14.

Encyclopaedia Britannica. Chicago, Encyclopaedia Britannica, 1949.

ENFIELD, D. E., *A Lady of the Salons: The Story of Louise Colet*. New York, Scribner's, 1923.

FAGUET, ÉMILE, *Flaubert*. Boston, Houghton-Mifflin, 1914.

FARRAR, ELIZA WARE (ROTCH), *Recollections of Seventy Years*. Boston, Ticknor and Fields, 1866.

FLAUBERT, GUSTAVE, *Letters; selected, with an introduction by Richard Rumbold*. Translated by J. M. Cohen. London, Weidenfeld, 1950.

——, *Madame Bovary*. New York, International Collectors Library, 1949.

——, *Madame Bovary*. Zurich, Limited Editions Club, 1938.

——, *Madame Bovary: Ébauches et Fragments Inédits . . .* Edited by Gabrielle LeLeu. Paris, Louis Conard, 1936.

——, *Madame Bovary: Moeurs de Province*. Montreal, B. D. Simpson, 1857.

——, *Madame Bovary: Nouvelle Version Precedée des Scenarios Inédits*. Edited by Jean Pommier and Gabrielle LeLeu. Paris, Librairie Jose Corti, 1949.

——, *Selected Letters of . . .* Edited by Francis Steegmuller. New York, Farrar, Straus and Young, [c1953]

FLOYD, JUANITA HELM, *Women in the Life of Honoré de Balzac*. New York, Henry Holt, 1921.

FOSS, KENELM, *Unwedded Bliss . . .* Kingswood, Surrey, The World's Work, 1949.

FRIEDMAN, WILLIAM F., and FRIEDMAN, ELIZEBETH S., *The Shakespeare Ciphers Examined*. Cambridge [Eng.] University Press, 1957.

GIBSON, H. N., *The Shakespeare Claimants*. London, Methuen, [1962].

GODWIN, MARY (WOLLSTONECRAFT), *The Love Letters of Mary Wollstonecraft to Gilbert Imlay*. Philadelphia, J. B. Lippincott, 1908.

GOMPERS, SAMUEL, *Seventy Years of Life and Labor*. New York, E. P. Dutton, 1925.

GORDON, ARMISTEAD CHURCHILL, *Allegra, the Story of Byron and Miss Clairmont*. New York, Minton, Balch, 1926.

GORMAN, HERBERT SHERMAN, *The Incredible Marquis, Alexandre Dumas*. New York, Farrar and Rinehart, 1929.

GRANVILLE, HARRIET ELIZABETH (CAVENDISH) LEVESON-GOWER, COUNTESS, *Letters of Harriet, Countess Granville 1810–1845*. Edited by the Hon. F. Leveson-Gower. London, Longmans, Green, 1894.

[GREENWOOD, WILLIAM DE REDMAN], *Romances of the Peerage* by Thornton Hall [pseud.]. London, Holden and Hardingham, 1914.

GRIBBLE, FRANCIS HENRY, *Balzac*. New York, E. P. Dutton, [1930].

——, *Dumas, Father and Son.* New York, E. P. Dutton, 1930.

GRYLLS, ROSALIE GLYNN, *Claire Clairmont, Mother of Byron's Allegra.* London, John Murray, 1939.

HAWTHORNE, JULIAN, *Hawthorne and His Circle.* New York, Harper,
1903.

HAWTHORNE, NATHANIEL, *Our Old Home.* Boston, Houghton-Mifflin,
1907.

HIBBEN, PAXTON, *Henry Ward Beecher: An American Portrait.* New
York, Press of the Readers Club, 1942.

HILL, FRANK ERNEST, *To Meet Will Shakespeare.* New York, Dodd,
Mead, 1949.

HOPKINS, VIVIAN CONSTANCE, *Prodigal Puritan: A Life of Delia Bacon.* Belknap Press, Cambridge [Mass.], Harvard University
Press, 1959.

IRWIN, INEZ (HAYNES), *Angels and Amazons.* Garden City, N. Y.,
Doubleday, Doran, 1933.

JACKSON, GEORGE STUYVESANT, *Uncommon Scold, the Story of Anne
Royall.* Boston, Bruce Humphries, 1937.

JAMES, HENRY, *The Art of the Novel, Critical Prefaces by* . . . New
York, Scribner's, 1937.

——, *Henry James Selected Fiction.* Edited by Leon Edel. New
York, E. P. Dutton, 1953.

——, *The Notebooks of* . . . Edited by F. O. Matthiessen and Ken-
neth B. Murdock. New York, Oxford University Press, 1947.

JAMES, HENRY ROSHER, *Mary Wollstonecraft.* London, Oxford University Press, 1932.

JEKYLL, JOSEPH, *Correspondence of Mr. Joseph Jekyll with His
Sister-in-Law, Lady Gertrude Sloane Stanley.* London, John
Murray, 1894.

KAUN, ALEXANDER SAMUEL, *Maxim Gorky and His Russia.* New
York, Jonathan Cape and Harrison Smith, 1931.

KEEN, ALAN, *The Annotator; the Pursuit of an Elizabethan Reader
of Halle's chronicle, Involving Some Surmises about the Early
Life of William Shakespeare.* London, Putnam, 1954.

KINGSTON, CHARLES, *Rogues and Adventuresses.* London, John Lane,
[1928].

KUNITZ, STANLEY J., ed., *British Authors of the Nineteenth Century.*
New York, H. W. Wilson, 1936.

LANE, WHEATON JOSHUA, *Commodore Vanderbilt.* New York, Knopf,
1942.

LANGTRY, LILY (LADY DE BATHE), *The Days I Knew.* New York,
George H. Doran, 1925.

LATHROP, GEORGE PARSONS, *Memories of Hawthorne*. Boston, Houghton-Mifflin, 1876.

LAWTON, FREDERICK, *Balzac*. London, Grant Richards, 1910.

LUTZ, ALMA, *Created Equal, a Biography of Elizabeth Cady Stanton*. New York, John Day, 1940.

MACQUEEN-POPE, W., *Ladies First*. London, W. H. Allen, 1952.

MARCHAND, LESLIE ALEXIS, *Byron*. New York, Knopf, 1957. 3v.

[MARRECO, ANNE (ACLAND-TROYTE)], *Caroline Norton* by Alice Acland [pseud.]. London, Constable, 1948.

MARTIN, BENJAMIN ELLIS, and MARTIN, CHARLOTTE M., *The Stones of Paris in History and Letters*. London, Smith, Elder, 1909.

MARTIN, VICTORIA (CLAFLIN) WOODHULL, *Humanitarian Money. The Unsolved Riddle*. London, n.p., 1892.

MAUGHAM, WILLIAM SOMERSET, *Great Novelists and Their Novels*. Philadelphia, John C. Winston, 1948.

MAUROIS, ANDRÉ, *Lelia, the Life of George Sand*. Translated by Gerald Hopkins. New York, Harper, 1953.

———, *Seven Faces of Love*. Translated by Haakon M. Chevalier. New York, Didier, 1944.

MELSOME, WILLIAM STANLEY, *The Bacon-Shakespeare Anatomy*. New York, Russell F. Moore, n.d.

MOORE, DORIS (LANGLEY-LEVY), *The Late Lord Byron*. London, John Murray, 1961.

MORRIS, LLOYD R., *The Rebellious Puritan: Portrait of Mr. Hawthorne*. New York, Harcourt, Brace, 1927.

NAPOLEON I, *Napoleon Self-Revealed in Three Hundred Selected Letters*. Translated and edited by J. M. Thompson. Boston, Houghton-Mifflin, 1934.

NICOLSON, HON. HAROLD GEORGE, *Byron, the Last Journey April 1823–April 1824*. London, Constable, 1924.

[O'DONOGHUE, ELINOR MARY], *Portrait of Ianthe* by E. M. Oddie [pseud.]. London, Jonathan Cape, 1935.

ORIGO, IRIS (CUTTING), MARCHESA, *The Last Attachment; the Story of Byron and Teresa Guiccioli as Told in Their Unpublished Letters and Other Family Papers*. New York, Scribner's, 1949.

ORR, LYNDON, *Famous Affinities of History*. New York, McClure, [c.1912]. 4v.

OSSOLI, [SARAH] MARGARET (FULLER), MARCHESA D', *Memoirs of* . . . Boston, Phillips, Sampson, 1852. 2v.

OWEN, ORVILLE WARD, *Sir Francis Bacon's Cipher Story*. Detroit, Howard Publishing, 1894–95.

PAUL, CHARLES KEGAN, *William Godwin: His Friends and Contemporaries*. London, Henry S. King, 1876.

PEARS, SIR EDWIN, *Forty Years in Constantinople*. London, Herbert Jenkins, 1916.

PORTER, SARAH HARVEY, *The Life and Times of Anne Royall*. Cedar Rapids, Iowa, The Torch Press Book Shop, 1909.

PRASTEAU, JEAN, *The Lady of the Camellias*. Translated by Stella Rodway. London, Hutchinson, 1965.

QUENNELL, PETER, *The Singular Preference*. London, Collins, 1952.

QUINT, HOWARD H., *The Forging of American Socialism*. Columbia, S. C., University of South Carolina Press, 1953.

REDESDALE, ALGERNON BERTRAM FREEMAN-MITFORD, BARON, *Memories* . . . New York, E. P. Dutton, [1916]. 2v.

REED, EDWIN, *Coincidences, Bacon and Shakespeare*. Boston, Coburn, 1906.

RICHARDSON, JOANNA, *The Courtesans*. Cleveland, World Publishing, 1967.

ROGERS, CAMERON, *Gallant Ladies*. New York, Harcourt, Brace, 1928.

ROGET, JOHN LEWIS, *A History of the 'Old Water-colour' Society, Now the Royal Society of Painters in Water Colours* . . . London, Longmans, Green, 1891.

ROSS, ISHBEL, *Ladies of the Press*. New York, Harper, 1936.

ROYALL, ANNE, *Letters from Alabama 1817–1822*. University, Ala., University of Alabama Press, [c1969]

RUBIN, ISADORE, *Sexual Life After Sixty*. New York, Basic Books, 1965.

RUSK, RALPH LESLIE, *The Life of Ralph Waldo Emerson*. New York, Scribner's, 1949.

SACHS, EMANIE LOUISE (NAHM), *The Terrible Siren, Victoria Woodhull*. New York, Harper, 1928.

SADLEIR, MICHAEL, *The Strange Life of Lady Blessington*. New York, Farrar, Straus, 1947.

SANDARS, MARY FRANCES, *Honoré de Balzac, His Life and Writings*. London, Stanley Paul, [1914].

SAUNDERS, EDITH, *The Prodigal Father*. London, Longmans, Green, 1951.

SEITZ, DON CARLOS, *The Dreadful Decade*. Indianapolis, Bobbs-Merrill, 1926.

SMITH, ROBERT METCALF, et al., *The Shelley Legend*. New York, Scribner's, 1945.

SPENCER, PHILIP, *Flaubert*. London, Faber and Faber, 1952.

STACTON, DAVID, *The Bonapartes*. New York, Simon and Schuster, 1966.

STANHOPE, MARIANNE, *Almack's, a Novel*. London, Saunders and Otley, 1826. 3v.

STARKIE, ENID, *Flaubert: The Making of the Master*. London, Weidenfeld, and Nicolson, 1967.

STEARNS, FRANK PRESTON, *The Life and Genius of Nathaniel Hawthorne*. Boston, Richard G. Badger, 1906.

STEEGMULLER, FRANCIS, *Flaubert and Madame Bovary; A Double Portrait*. London, Collins, 1947.

STERN, ROBERT, *Love Affairs That Have Made History*. New York, The New Home Library, 1942.

STEWART, RANDALL, *Nathaniel Hawthorne*. New Haven, Conn., Yale University Press, 1948.

STIRLING, ANNA MARIA DIANA WILHELMINA (PICKERING), *Coke of Norfolk and His Friends*. London, J. Lane, 1912.

SYMES, LILLIAN, *Rebel America*. New York, Harper, 1934.

[SYMONDS, EMILY MORSE], "To Lord Byron," *Feminine Profiles Based Upon Unpublished Letters, 1807–1824* by George Paston [pseud.] and Peter Quennell. New York, Scribner's, 1939.

TARVER, JOHN CHARLES, *Gustave Flaubert*. New York, D. Appleton, 1895.

TAYLOR, GEORGE ROBERT STIRLING, *Mary Wollstonecraft*. New York, John Lane, 1911.

TAYLOR, GORDON RATTRAY, *Sex in History*. London, Thames and Hudson, [c1953].

TERHUNE, ALBERT PAYSON, *Superwomen*. New York, Moffatt, Yard, 1916.

THEOBALD, BERTRAM GORDON, *Enter Francis Bacon*. London, Cecil Palmer, 1932.

——, *Exit Shakspere*. London, Cecil Palmer, 1931.

THIBAUDET, ALBERT, *Gustave Flaubert*. Paris, Gallimard, 1935.

THOMPSON, JAMES MATTHEW, *Napoleon Bonaparte*. New York, Oxford University Press, 1952.

THOUVENEL, ÉDOUARD ANTOINE, *La Grèce du Roi Othon; Correspondance de M. Thouvenal avec Sa Famille . . .* Paris, Calmann Lévy, 1890.

WADE, MASON, *Margaret Fuller*. New York, Viking, 1940.

WALLACE, EDGAR, et al., *Great Stories of Real Life Retold by Edgar Wallace, William Le Queux . . . and Others*. New York, Jonathan Cape and Harrison Smith, 1930.

WATSON, PAUL BARRON, *Some Women of France*. New York, Coward-McCann, 1936.

WHITE, NEWMAN IVEY, *Portrait of Shelley*. New York, Knopf, 1945.

WHITTON, MARY ORMSBEE, *These Were the Women*. New York, Hastings House, 1954.

WILENSKI, REGINALD HOWARD, *An Outline of English Painting from the Middle Ages to the Period of the Pre-Raphaelites*. London, Faber and Faber, 1933.

WILLIAMS, FRAYNE, *Mr. Shakespeare of the Globe*. New York, E. P. Dutton, 1941.

WOODWARD, HELEN BEAL, *The Bold Women*. New York, Farrar, Straus and Young, 1953.

WRIGHT, RICHARDSON, *Forgotten Ladies*. Philadelphia, J. B. Lippincott, 1928.

WRIGHT, WILLIAM, *An Account of Palmyra and Zenobia*. New York, Thomas Nelson, 1895.

WYNDHAM, HORACE, *Feminine Frailty*. London, E. Benn, 1929.

——, *Judicial Dramas*. London, T. Fisher Unwin, 1927.

ZWEIG, STEFAN, *Balzac*. Translated by William and Dorothy Rose. New York, Viking, 1946.

PERIODICALS

CARGILL, O., "Nemesis and Nathaniel Hawthorne." (In: *PMLA*, September 1937.)

"Fresh Troops Join the Battle of the Bard." (In: *Life*, September 7, 1962, p. 4.)

HAMBLIN, D. J., "History's Biggest Literary Whodunit." (In: *Life*, April 24, 1964, p. 69–70.)

"The Other Shakespeares." (In: *Newsweek*, April 27, 1959, p. 112.)

RANDEL, W. P., "Hawthorne, Channing, and Margaret Fuller." (Reply to O. Cargill. In: *American Literature*, January 1939.)

La Revue Britannique, Paris. March and April, 1873.

ROBERTSON, LORRAINE, "The Journal and Notebooks of Claire Clairmont—Unpublished Passages." (In: *Keats-Shelley Memorial Bulletin*, No. IV, London, 1952.)

STEEGMULLER, FRANCIS, " 'Madame Bovary' on Trial." (In: *The Saturday Review of Literature*, January 21, 1939.)

WARREN, A., "Hawthorne, Margaret Fuller and Nemesis." (Reply to O. Cargill. In: *PMLA*, June 1939.)

"Victoria Claflin Woodhull" (obit). (In: *New York Times*, June 11, 1927.)

Index

p